CAMBRIDGE GREEK AND LATIN CLASSICS

GENERAL EDITORS

E. J. KENNEY
Emeritus Kennedy Professor of Latin, University of Cambridge
AND
P. E. EASTERLING
Regius Professor of Greek, University of Cambridge

JUVENAL
SATIRES
BOOK I

EDITED BY

SUSANNA MORTON BRAUND

Professor of Latin, Royal Holloway,
University of London

CAMBRIDGE
UNIVERSITY PRESS

PUBLISHED BY THE PRESS SYNDICATE OF THE UNIVERSITY OF CAMBRIDGE
The Pitt Building, Trumpington Street, Cambridge, United Kingdom

CAMBRIDGE UNIVERSITY PRESS
The Edinburgh Building, Cambridge CB2 2RU, UK
40 West 20th Street, New York, NY 10011–4211, USA
477 Williamstown Road, Port Melbourne, VIC 3207, Australia
Ruiz de Alarcón 13, 28014, Madrid, Spain
Dock House, The Waterfront, Cape Town 8001, South Africa

http://www.cambridge.org

First published 1996

Reprinted 1999, 2002

A catalogue record for this book is available from the British Library

Library of Congress cataloguing in publication data

Juvenal.
[Saturae. Liber 1]
Satires / Juvenal; Susanna Morton Braund.
p. cm. – (Cambridge Greek and Latin classics)
Text in Latin with pref., introd., and commentary in English.
Includes bibliographical references and index.
ISBN 0 521 35566 4 (hardback) ISBN 0 521 35667 9 (paperback)
1. Verse satire, Latin. 2. Rome–Poetry.
I. Braund, Susanna Morton. II Title. III. Series.
PA6446.A61 1996
871'.01–dc20 95-11014 CIP

ISBN 0 521 35566 4 hardback
ISBN 0 521 35667 9 paperback

Transferred to digital printing 2003

CE

CONTENTS

CONTENTS

PREFACE

'Satire is a sort of glass, wherein beholders do generally discover everybody's face but their own.' Thus Swift, in his Preface to *The Battle of the Books*. The Preface to a commentary such as this is conventionally the place for self-justification and explanation of the approach adopted. In true satiric spirit, then, I subvert the generic conventions and start with speculation. It is indeed hard to discover oneself in satire; yet, I suppose that anyone who has worked on Juvenal for a decade or more must be rather odd. Whether this is cause or effect, I cannot say. But it seems to me that immersion in *indignatio* is not necessarily good for the soul, even if it sharpens the tongue . . .

Of course, I was delighted to be offered the opportunity of writing a new commentary on the Satires of Juvenal, especially when the Press agreed to the inclusion of Satire 2, since this meant I could present an integrated reading of Book I as an organic structure. But during the ten years or so it has taken to bring this project to fruition, there were times when I despaired of completing it, not least because of the government's obsession with accountability, which has surely doubled the administrative workload on university lecturers during this period. I therefore wish to express profound gratitude to the numerous friends and colleagues who offered multifarious encouragement: to David Braund, Duncan Cloud, Charles Martindale, Adam Morton, Patricia Moyer, Jonathan Walters, John Wilkins, Peter Wiseman. Thanks to Barbara Gordon for her scrupulous proof-reading. To Ted Kenney is due the highest accolade for scrutinising the entire typescript more than once; as always, I have benefited enormously from his advice (even if I have not always taken it).

My thanks also go to the classes of students at the University of Exeter in the 1980s who responded so helpfully to my Juvenal lectures, especially Julia Mobsby and Jack Marriott; the desire to introduce new generations of undergraduates to Juvenal has provided inspiration for the undertaking and parameters for the book. Throughout, therefore, I have tried to be aware of the needs of those who will use this volume. Happily, the text of Juvenal has received a good deal of attention during the last hundred years and the decision to base my text upon Clausen's OCT, with only a few departures, was straightforward. In the Commentary I have aimed to include explication of Roman thought and culture and of literary, linguistic and stylistic matters. It seemed appropriate to illuminate these by indicating analogies from three specific areas: from Juvenal's work, from other authors in the genre of Roman satire and from post-Augustan literature. Juvenal's exploitation of the 'grand style' is demonstrated by exemplifying his revitalisation of 'classic' texts of Latin literature. The result is, inevitably, a *farrago*. The reader must select what she or he finds helpful and neglect the rest. My hope is that this volume is not judged to be *crambe repetita*. So, in Byron's words (*English Bards and Scottish Reviewers* 5), themselves inspired by the opening of Juvenal's first Satire: 'I'll publish, right or wrong: | Fools are my theme, let satire be my song.'

NOTE TO THE SECOND IMPRESSION

I take the opportunity offered by a second impression to point out that my use of the word 'homosexual' in the commentary to *Satire* 2 is inappropriate. The term 'effeminate', which minimises the anachronism, is preferable.

INTRODUCTION

1. JUVENAL AND SATIRE

Juvenal, perhaps more than anyone else, is responsible for the modern concept of satire. Satire was a genre of poetry invented and developed by the Romans. When it came into Juvenal's hands, he stamped his mark upon it: indignation. Not all of Juvenal's Satires are indignant; but that is what he is remembered for. His angry voice had an overwhelming influence upon later satirists and persists into modern manifestations of satire, although what we mean by 'satire' is different: for the Romans and for English satirists of Elizabethan and Jacobean times, 'satire' denoted a particular form of discourse, a genre of poetry with 'rules', whereas for us 'satire' tends to imply an attitude and a tone of voice. In this Introduction we shall briefly examine the origins of the genre of Roman satire and discuss Juvenal's predecessors in the genre, Lucilius, Horace and Persius. The evidence for Juvenal's life will be considered, then the characteristics of his satire, including his style and metre, will be discussed. There follows an integrated reading of Book I; discussions of the five individual poems of Book I will be found after the commentary on each poem. The Introduction is concluded by an overview of Juvenal's influence from antiquity to the present and a discussion of the text and its transmission.

2. THE GENRE OF ROMAN VERSE SATIRE

For a full understanding of Roman verse satire, two possibly unfamiliar concepts must be grasped. The first is that the Roman writers of satire, like all authors of Greco-Roman literature, were working within a particular literary genre which had its unwritten 'laws'. In the case of Roman verse satire, these 'laws' prescribed the choice of metre and form, material, presentation and language. The metre was the dactylic hexameter (the metre of epic poetry such as Virgil's *Aeneid*) and the form required compositions of short to middle length, usually in the range of 50–250 lines. The material included matters of morality, education and literature. The type of presentation was the auto-biographical monologue with occasional extensions into dialogue, epistle or narrative. The language was permitted to range from the extravagances of mock-epic grandeur, through the everyday discourse of polite gentlemen, to explicit crudity. This set of 'laws' was established by Lucilius, the founder of the genre, writing in the second century BC, who is discussed below. Although only fragments of Lucilius' thirty books of satires survive, it is clear from these and from the tributes offered by later satirists that his role in the genre was central. His successors followed his example in a blend of imitation and innovation. Imitation – for Roman poets the highest form of compliment – established the chosen genre and indicated the poet's acknowledgement of his debt to his predecessor(s). Innovation avoided stagnation and permitted the gradual development of the genre.

The second fundamental idea is one which rescues us from trying to read the satires as self-revelation. Roman verse satire uses the autobiographical monologue as the chief mode of presentation. This does not mean that the satirists are (necessarily) using their satires to convey their personal feelings to the world. Far from it. Authors in all genres of Roman literature, including Roman verse satire, were accustomed to creating characters. In some genres this is more obvious than in others, for example in drama and in epic, where these characters are given names. But in the personal genres of poetry – love elegy, lyric poetry, epigram and satire – the character (or *persona*, 'mask') is frequently presented as a first-person voice.[1]

Authors and their audiences were accustomed to this convention thanks to their experience of the education in rhetoric enjoyed by members of the Roman élite. This training developed the ability to adopt with conviction a (temporary) mood of, say, anger or sorrow. It guaranteed a relationship between speaker and audience, providing a sense of immediacy and demanding a response from the listener, who is implied if not implicated in the text. The analogy between rhetoric and poetry is reinforced by the fact that most Greek and Latin

---

[1] On the *persona* in satire see Kernan (1959) 14–30 and in Roman satire see Anderson (1982) 3–10 and Dessen (1968) 6–9. The *persona* theory is not without problems: it runs the risk of containing and thus making safe the potentially explosive and anarchic character created, by positing a mature and sophisticated authorial figure. But it offers a useful counterweight to earlier, naïve readings of satire.

literature, including poetry, was written for oral delivery by the author or another voice to a live audience. In the light of this, the identification of the views of the characters in satire with those of the authors becomes unnecessary and crude. To read the poems as autobiographical self-revelations from which 'facts' about the poet's life may be deduced (the 'biographical fallacy' propounded by, notably, Highet (1954)) is to neglect other, more rewarding, questions.

So when we read these poems, we profit from regarding them as dramatic monologues and from examining the character or characters presented in them for their strengths and weaknesses, just as we examine a dramatist's skills in characterisation. To make clearer the distinction between poet and *persona*, the *persona* is referred to as 'the speaker'; J. will be mentioned only in his capacity as poet, as creator of this character.

3. THE ORIGINS OF ROMAN SATIRE

For the Romans, there were two types of satire, one in prose and one in verse. The two share many characteristics, yet in their discussions of the genre the Romans privilege the verse form. This is perhaps because the prose type, often called Menippean satire, had its roots in Greek culture, specifically in the diatribe, which was a kind of sermon associated with the Hellenistic philosophical schools such as Cynicism.[2] In contrast, the verse form was claimed as Roman.

The origins of the genre of satire and the significance of its name *satura* have been much debated in antiquity and since.[3] Probably the most famous Roman statement about the origins of the genre is Quintilian's: 'Satire is entirely our own' (*Institutio Oratoria* 10.1.93 *satura quidem tota nostra est*). What he meant by that is open to debate; we will return to it shortly. Apart from Quintilian's comments, theory about the genre of *satura* appears incidentally in the historian Livy's discussion of the history of Roman drama and directly in the writings of Diomedes, a fourth-century grammarian. Livy presents an elaborate theory of the development of Roman drama, including a dramatic

[2] On Menippean satire see Relihan (1993).
[3] For modern discussions see van Rooy (1965) 1–29, Knoche (1975) 3–16, Coffey (1989) 3–23, Gowers (1993) 109–26.

satura, which is unconvincing since it appears that he is attempting to find a similar pattern of development in Roman drama to that attested for Greek drama. But one significant aspect of his theory is that he regards *satura* as an early dramatic form. This helps explain the links drawn by the satirists between satire and Greek Old Comedy (Hor. *Sat.* 1.4.1–5, 1.10.16, Pers. 1.123–4).

The only directly theoretical discussion of the genre of *satura* is that of Diomedes, a fourth-century grammarian who may have derived this material from the antiquarian scholar Varro, who was writing in the late Republic. Diomedes offers four possible explanations of the word *satura* (Diomedes, *GLK* 1 485):

> *satura* takes its name either from satyrs, because in this form of poetry laughable and disgraceful things are said in the same way as if produced and performed by satyrs; or from a full dish which, stuffed with many varied first-fruits, was offered to the gods in religious ritual among the ancients and was called *satura* from the abundance and fullness of the material; ... or from a certain type of sausage which, stuffed with many ingredients, Varro says was called *satura*. ... Others think that its name came from the *lex satura* [lit. 'full law'] which combines together many provisions in a single bill, because in the poetry form *satura* many poems are combined together.

Of these derivations, the first, which connects *satura* with Satyrs (*Satyri*), seems tenuous (although Petronius clearly plays on it in his *Satyrica*): Roman satire does not share the ribald and obscene nature of Greek satyr drama. The second, deriving *satura* from the *lanx satura*, 'mixed dish', a plate filled with many different offerings which was presented to the gods at religious festivals, makes *satura* a metaphor which evokes abundance and variety. The third explanation is similar to the second: that *satura* designates a kind of stuffing or sausage made from many ingredients. This presents another metaphor of fullness and variety, but of a more mundane nature than the second. Diomedes' fourth suggestion derives *satura* from the *lex per saturam*, a law with mixed provisions of Republican times. This explanation, like the second and third, again hinges upon the notion of mixture and variety.

It is impossible to make a firm choice between Diomedes' four explanations, although the first is doubtful on linguistic grounds.[4] But what is significant is that explanations two, three and four all present satire as a genre of abundance and variety. As Gowers says,[5] 'foraging in the sewers and filth of Rome, he makes his *saturae* grow fat on vice'. The genre is perhaps the poet's offering of a 'mixed dish' to the inspiring deity; or the poet is like a moral legislator on a variety of topics. But it is perhaps most appealing to view the satirist as a cook, serving up to his audience a sausage stuffed full of varied ingredients – including, incidentally, a substantial quantity of feasting and food. This explanation at least gives a piquant taste to Juvenal's description of his work as a *farrago* (1.86): by styling his poetry as 'mixed cattle fodder' he may very well be demonstrating his awareness of learned speculation on the origin of the word *satura* and at the same time debunking that theorising.

Theories of the origin of the word *satura* must remain guess-work, although they are suggestive about the origin of the genre. But Diomedes' introductory comments on the nature of the genre and its practitioners are most helpful (*GLK* 1 485):

> Satire is the name of the Roman form of poetry that is nowadays abusive and composed to criticise the vices of men in the manner of Old Comedy, such as was written by Lucilius and Horace and Persius; but formerly satire was the name given to the form of poetry made up of a variety of poems, such as was written by Pacuvius and Ennius.

Immediately striking is the link with Greek Old Comedy. Equally striking is his division of the genre historically into, on the one hand, the form written by Lucilius, Horace and Persius and, on the other hand, the older form written by Pacuvius and Ennius. Quintilian, writing before Juvenal, similarly names Lucilius, Horace and Persius as the chief exponents of the genre:

> The first to win renown in *satura* was Lucilius who has some devotees who are so dedicated to him that they without hesitation prefer him not just to other authors in the same genre but

---

[4] See van Rooy (1965) 1–29 and Coffey (1989) 11–18 for a fuller discussion of Diomedes' account of *satura*.

[5] Gowers (1993) 219.

to all poets. I disagree with them as much as with Horace, who thinks that Lucilius is a muddy river with a lot of stuff that you could remove. His learning is remarkable, as is his freedom of speech and the sharpness and abundant wit which derives from it. Horace is much terser and purer and, unless I lapse because of my affection for him, the best. Persius has won a considerable and legitimate reputation, although he wrote only one book. There are eminent satirists today who will be celebrated in the future.   (*Institutio Oratoria* 10.1.93–4)

Lucilius, it is clear, was regarded both by theorists and by the satirists themselves as the founder of the genre; most memorably Horace calls him its 'inventor' at *Satires* 1.10.48.

But where does this leave Ennius and his nephew Pacuvius, mentioned by Diomedes? And what does Quintilian mean by claiming that 'Satire is entirely our own'? Nothing is known of Pacuvius' works. Quintus Ennius (239–169 BC), his uncle, was from Calabria in the south of Italy and hence was influenced by the cultures of Greece, Italy and Rome. This multi-culturalism manifested itself in the literary innovations made by Ennius. Of prime importance is his establishment of the form and discourse of Latin epic poetry in hexameters in his *Annals*. The nature of his Satires, *Saturae*, is difficult to judge because only 31 lines survive from the four books he wrote. But it appears that Ennius' *Saturae* were a real miscellany written in a variety of metres and sometimes using autobiographical presentation.[6] They include a multiple word-play,[7] a debate between Life and Death,[8] a fable of Aesop,[9] with the tone sometimes critical,[10] sometimes humorous.[11] This is not much to go on. We have to accept the judgement of the ancients in pronouncing Lucilius and not Ennius the inventor of the genre of satire.

Finally, we return to the significance of Quintilian's comment about satire. This has been interpreted in two different ways. Firstly, to mean

[6] 21W [= Warmington].
[7] 28–31W.
[8] Quint. *I.O.* 9.2.36.
[9] Preserved by Aulus Gellius 2.29.
[10] 23W.
[11] 21W.

that there is no original Greek form which the Roman satirists are imitating, a view apparently supported by the line of Horace where he calls satire 'verse never handled by the Greeks' (*Sat.* 1.10.66 *Graecis intacti carminis*) and by the fact that this is the only genre discussed by Quintilian which is identified by a Latin name. Secondly, to mean that the Roman satirists are so completely superior to Greek satirists that they win hands down and do not permit Quintilian even to mention any Greek satirists by name.[12] In assessing these interpretations, it is crucial to bear in mind the context of Quintilian's comments. In this part of his *Institutio Oratoria* he is prescribing the ideal components of the school syllabus, with a view to selecting the very best elements of Greek and Latin literature for a Roman school-child to read and study. He divides up his material into Greek authors and Roman authors and proceeds through a genre-by-genre evaluation of the relative merits of different authors. When he reaches satire, he mentions no Greek original of Roman verse satire. Of course, there are satirical passages (in the general sense in which we use the term) in Greek authors writing in other genres, but there was no Greek satire in the form used by Lucilius, Horace and Persius. Thus it seems that the first interpretation of Quintilian's statement is correct: Quintilian is indeed claiming originality – and, therefore, superiority – for the Romans in the genre of Roman satire.

4. JUVENAL'S SATIRIC PREDECESSORS

The young satirist Persius, writing under the emperor Nero, gives this thumbnail sketch of earlier exponents of the genre of satire (1.114–18):

> Lucilius crunched
> the city – Lupus and Mucius and all – and smashed his molar.
> While his friend is laughing, that rascal Horace lays his finger
> on all his faults; gaining admission, he plays on the conscience –
> so clever at holding the public up on that well-blown nose.

This provides a useful starting-point for a brief survey of Juvenal's predecessors.

---

[12] See Gratwick (1982) 160–2 for a succinct summary of the debate and van Rooy (1965) 117–23 for a fuller discussion.

(a) Lucilius

The 'inventor' (Hor. *Sat.* 1.10.48) of the genre was Gaius Lucilius (180 BC or 168/7 BC to 102/1 BC), who was a wealthy member of the Latin aristocracy (an *eques*) in Campania, and was closely connected with the intellectual and political élite in Rome through his association with Scipio Aemilianus, a general, politician and patron of the arts. This gave him a powerful position from which to write his satires, which are highly engaged politically.[13] Lucilius was writing his *Satires* from about 130 BC onwards, to a total of thirty books of which only 1300 lines survive; unfortunately these cannot be considered representative, since most were preserved by later grammarians for their linguistic interest, but they do afford a glimpse of the content and tone which influenced his successors so profoundly.[14]

Lucilius initially experimented with the metrical form of satire before establishing the hexameter as the metre of the genre. It is perhaps surprising that the metre of epic poetry – the highest genre of poetry, which recorded the inspiring exploits of heroes, kings and generals – was hijacked for a genre of starkly contrasting mundane content and critical tone (although Ennius had perhaps shown the range of potential uses to which the hexameter could be put). The inherent conflict between form and content must have been striking to the Roman ear. Although it is hard to reconstruct the content of the books of Lucilius' *Satires*, some evidently contained a medley of several short poems, while others consisted of a single, longer poem. It is clear that he used a variety of forms in his poems, including monologue, dialogue and the letter, with the monologue the most prevalent. All three forms appear in subsequent Roman satire.

In terms of content, too, Lucilius established the repertoire of the genre. Most striking is Lucilius' criticism of individuals. He attacks both eminent men and the more lowly for a variety of faults ranging

---

[13] Raschke (1987) 318 rightly describes Lucilius' poetry as 'highly partisan satirical verse'; this is epitomised graphically in Horace's portrayal of Lucilius at *Sat.* 2.1.62–74.

[14] The fragments of Lucilius are most easily accessible in Warmington's *Remains of Old Latin* volume III (Loeb Classical Library (1979)); references here are given to Warmington's edition (W) and to the edition of Marx (M). For a survey of Lucilius see Braund (1992a) 10–15 and bibliography cited there.

from incompetence to arrogance. This was the essence of his reputation. That is why his successors in the genre portray him as raging
against or even physically attacking his victims (as well as the Persius
passage quoted above cf. Hor. *Sat.* 1.10.3–4, 2.1.62–70; Juv. 1.19–20
and 165–6). Criticisms of elements of what may loosely be termed
'everyday life' feature prominently: the hustle and bustle of city life;[15]
feasting and drinking;[16] morality, philosophy and religion;[17] literary
issues;[18] matters of spelling.[19]

But what is most notable about Lucilius, apart from his fierce
invective, is the distinctive autobiographical presentation of the
Satires,[20] frequently with a marked element of criticism and irony at his
own expense,[21] a characteristic to which Horace draws attention at
Sat. 2.1.30–34 (cf. 2.1.71–4):

> In the past he would confide his secrets to his books, which he
>   trusted
> like friends; and whether things went well or badly he'd always
> turn to them; in consequence, the whole of the old man's life
> is laid before us, as if it were painted on a votive tablet.

Lucilius' autobiographical presentation and in particular his self-irony
were especially significant influences upon later satirists. Of course,
like the later satirists, he presents a multi-faceted *persona*, at times the
humble poet, at others the cynic preacher or the buffoon.

To match this mundane subject-matter and humble stance, Lucilius
adopts an informal, unelevated style of diction. His language can be
explicit and even obscene,[22] particularly in his descriptions of women
and sex.[23] A conversational flavour, highly suited to these *sermones*

[15] 1145–51W = 1228–34M.
[16] 1022–3W = 1073–4M, 601–3 W = 1174–6M.
[17] E.g. the longest surviving fragment, the so-called *Virtus* fragment, 1196–
1208W = 1326–38M; 1189–90W = 1225–6M; 805–11W = 784–90M; 524–9W =
484–9M.
[18] 1085W = 1015M, 1079–80W = 1022–3M; 401–10W = 338–47M.
[19] 394–5W = 375–6M and 384–7W = 358–61M.
[20] E.g. 650–1W = 671–2M.
[21] E.g. 1183W = 1248M, 635W = 592–3M, 1039W = 1039M, 1131W =
1279M.
[22] E.g. 354–5W = 331–2M, 1081W = 1018M, 1183W = 1248M.
[23] On Lucilius on women see Richlin (1983) 164–74, Henderson (1989)
99–102.

('chats') is generated by a repetitiveness and looseness of structure.[24] Particularly distinctive is his use of Greek words and quotations, for a variety of effects.[25]

Lucilius was an educated man writing for an educated audience and as such he is very much a product of his time and place. He reflects the interests, ideals and aspirations of the men with whom he consorted, in particular Scipio Aemilianus, more often by exposing failure to attain these ideals than by overt articulation of positive principles. He blends a profound knowledge of Greek culture with Roman ideology and is aptly described by Cicero as 'an educated and highly civilised man'.[26] The striking vigour, bluntness and aggression of Lucilius' *Satires* are not incompatible with Cicero's words of praise: Cicero approves of his forceful assertion of Roman ideology.

(b) Horace

The next exponent of satire after Lucilius was Horace, writing one century later at the end of the Roman Republic (65–8 BC).[27] He covered the same broad range of subjects as Lucilius but adopted a more limited and refined range of vocabulary and a more modest tone and *persona* in his four books of satirical works, *Satires* I and II, *Epistles* I and II, which span his poetic career. His first book of *Satires* was his earliest publication (35–34 BC) and the second book followed the battle of Actium, in 30–29 BC. *Epistles* I appeared in 20–19 BC and *Epistles* II.2 a year later. *Epistles* II.1 and the so-called *Ars poetica* are hard to date.[28] Each of the books differs in approach. They are best examined in sequence: in this way Horace's development of the genre emerges most clearly.

Lucilius is ever-present in the background, but, significantly, Horace chooses to establish a new character at the start of his satirical

---

[24] Cf. Horace's criticisms of his lack of stylistic polish and his looseness of composition (e.g. *Sat.* 1.4.9–13, 1.10.50–64), tempered by his concession that for his time Lucilius exhibits a high level of sophistication (*Sat.* 1.10.64–71).

[25] 1048W = 1058M; 267–8W = 231–2M.

[26] *De orat.* 3.171: *homo doctus et perurbanus.*

[27] For an overview of Horace see Braund (1992a) 16–32 and bibliography cited there.

[28] See Brink (1963) 239–43.

writings before he engages directly with the issue of his relationship with the founder of the genre. The first three poems of Book 1 present Horace as the type of philosopher delivering his strident lectures on popular morality on the street corner (*Sat.* 1.1–3), probably a lowlier pose than that assumed by Lucilius in his aggressively political poetry. Characteristics of the Greek diatribe (sermon) abound, e.g. proverbs, animal fables and analogies, anecdotes and mythological examples, personification, quotation and parody; the language is generally elegant in an understated way without the verbal extravagance and exuberance of Lucilius. Only in *Sat.* 1.4 does Horace situate himself within the genre: he is following Lucilius' practice of criticising people's faults, but not his style, which he condemns for its verbosity. He goes on to attribute his frankness to the upbringing he received from his father. In this way he marries his literary with his moral credentials. This manifesto of his worth is portrayed as bringing the desired result: acceptance into the coterie surrounding Maecenas (*Sat.* 1.4–6). He immediately adopts the values of his new friends and proceeds to act as the defender of those values in social and literary matters (*Sat.* 1.7–10). In the last poem of the Book he refines his earlier assessment of Lucilius and offers his own poetic manifesto: he values terseness, linguistic purity, humour and, perhaps above all, appropriateness (*decorum*).

In short, he presents himself as the new Lucilius, in literary terms and politically too, since he too is engaged in articulating the ideology of his circle. He has taken the autobiographical mode of Lucilius and used it to present, in a series of monologues, a narrative sequence in which he explores issues of friendship, freedom and power and their relation to and expression in literature.[29] Horace's first Book is a highly complex book of poetry, with subtle patterning and multiple levels of interpretation; it was doubtless influenced profoundly by the recent publication of Virgil's book of *Eclogues*. Horace's modest claim that this is not poetry is not to be believed. He has taken the genre as he inherited it from Lucilius and turned it into something which reflects the sophistication and self-consciousness of his era and which reveals the exclusive standards and exclusivity of his clique.

The second book of Satires offers a different type of experiment.

[29] On Horace *Satires* 1 see Zetzel (1980), DuQuesnay (1984).

Here Horace takes the dialogue form from Lucilius and develops it in a sophisticated way which places the onus of interpretation upon the audience. In this series of dialogues Horace takes a passive and minor role while the 'wisdom' of others is exposed in sermons, lectures and conversations. He can rightly be labelled 'the Roman Socrates'[30] since he resembles Plato's portrayal of the great philosopher in allowing his interlocutors to pursue their ideas and theories to the point of folly or impossibility, on the topics of literature, philosophy and morality. Friendship, freedom and power remain important concerns, but in this book they are frequently manifested in negative forms. The dominance of food, which features in four of the eight poems, displays Horace reworking and adapting a prominent theme of Lucilius. In portraying himself as the victim of the 'advice' or aggression of many of his interlocutors he maintains the element of self-irony which he established in Book I.

When he returns to satire after writing *Odes* 1–3 Horace further exploits the flexibility of the genre.[31] In *Epistles* I he adopts the letter form, with which Lucilius appears to have experimented briefly, to produce an artfully arranged assemblage of twenty 'letters'. He uses this as a vehicle to present the character of a mature and worldly adviser sharing his wisdom on matters of education, philosophy, literature, friendship, leisure and etiquette with a variety of addressees mostly junior to him in years or status, but also including his friend and patron Maecenas. Although frequent reference is made, explicitly or implicitly, to various philosophical doctrines, the chief positive ideals which emerge belong to no single philosophical school: these are tolerance, tranquillity and independence.[32] Again, in themes, self-ironic presentation and stylistic level, *Epistles* I closely resembles the earlier *Satires*. What is new is the choice of form: the book of letters allows him to explore different ways of living: the collection is a reflection of the variety and complexity of life.

Epistles II broadly continues the same stance but with a shift towards a more teacherly pose by Horace, chiefly because the poems are significantly longer. The three poems, *Epistles* 2.1 addressed to

[30] Anderson's phrase: see (1982) 41–9.

[31] For a brief overview of the evidence and debate about the genre of the letters, see Braund (1992a) 25–8 and notes.

[32] On *Epistles* I see McGann (1969), Kilpatrick (1986) and Mayer's edition.

Augustus himself, *Epistles* 2.2 addressed to Florus (a young man of Tiberius' circle of friends) and the so-called *Ars poetica* addressed to members of the Piso family aspiring to be poets,[33] feature themes familiar from *Satires* I and II and *Epistles* I: morality, education, literature and philosophy, friendship and right conduct. It is possible to read *Epistles* II as a celebration of the Augustan ideal. At the same time, these poems continue the earlier unelevated, conversational tone, incorporating illustrations from many varied activities together with the autobiographical mode of presentation which includes a strong element of self-irony.

Horace has taken the genre he inherited from Lucilius and refined it to be an instrument of contemporary ideology. Above all, in Horace's hands satire is an articulation of the standards of the powerful élite group at Rome with which he is associated. The aggression of Lucilius lies well beneath the surface in Horace, covered with a veneer of humility which has persuaded or seduced many readers into acquiescence with his perspective and his standards. It is Horace's subtlety and indirection which Persius characterises so adeptly and accurately, in contrast with Lucilius' full-frontal assault, in the lines quoted above.

(c) *Persius*

After Horace, the next exponent of satire whose work survives is the Neronian satirist Persius. Aules Persius Flaccus (AD 34–62) was born in Etruria into an important family of high status and educated at Rome as a pupil of Cornutus the Stoic. He seems to have moved in elevated circles and was acquainted with the poet Lucan, who greatly admired his single book of *Satires*. This brief book, which may or may not be complete, consists of six *Satires* preceded by a prologue in the choliambic metre. They are packed with literary echoes and allusions, showing in particular an intimate familiarity with the satirical works of Lucilius and Horace. Yet at the same time they are fresh and original, thanks to Persius' creation of the *persona* of the angry and alienated young man.[34]

---

[33] On the debate whether the *Ars poetica* belongs to *Epistles* II or not, see Rudd (1989) 19–37.
[34] For a survey of Persius and bibliography see Braund (1992a) 33–9.

He presents a stance of scornful isolation immediately, in the prologue, where he describes himself as 'a semi-clansman' (*semipaganus*, a word invented by Persius), that is, not a full member of the group of bards: he rejects their poetic imagery of inspiration. Even his choice of a metre other than the hexameter for the prologue marks out his rebellious stance. This stance is confirmed by the opening lines of *Satire* 1, where he appears content with a small or non-existent audience, and maintained by his wholesale rejection of contemporary poetry on the grounds that it is too smooth, weak and artificial. This attack spreads to become a broader attack on the moral spinelessness of contemporary society.

The rejection of society and its standards is maintained throughout the book. Frequently the ideal of independence and self-reliance is expressed in the uncompromising terms of extreme Stoicism, which is Persius' idiom.[35] The intolerance of contemporary literature and morality expressed in *Satire* 1 is followed by an intolerant condemnation of the hypocrisy and foolishness of people's prayers in *Satire* 2. In the third *Satire* we meet an angry young student who appears to have lapsed and who receives a lecture on the madness of people who will not allow philosophy to help them. *Satire* 4 uses Socrates as the voice of self-knowledge in conversation with the young politician Alcibiades whose superficiality and lack of knowledge and expertise are attacked. The central message of the poem is a graphic version of the ancient Delphic maxim 'Know thyself'. *Satire* 5 is the longest in the book. It begins in a strongly autobiographical mode with a personal tribute to Cornutus, Persius' instructor in Stoicism, closely modelled in literary terms upon Horace's presentation of his relationship with his father (*Satires* 1.4 and 1.6), and incorporates a substantial sermon on the theme of freedom (treated in Horace *Satires* 2.7) delivered by a Stoic extremist. The sixth *Satire* is presented as an epistle (following the tradition of Lucilius and Horace) in which withdrawal from Rome to the coast is the logical consequence and physical realisation of the isolation proclaimed throughout in the book, a violent, symbolic expression of independence and detachment from society and its obligations. The harsh, aggressive attitude adopted in the poem towards his heir continues this theme to the end of the book.

Persius' *Satires* are marked by their dense literary texture and the

[35] See Reckford (1962) 490–8.

very startling and at times humorous juxtaposition of images. The compressed language and startling images frequently overturn or rejuvenate literary and philosophical clichés and commonplaces (e.g. the prologue and the opening of *Satire* 5 satirise the conventional language of poetic inspiration through an over-literal interpretation). Some of the images arouse ridicule of their victims by puncturing pretentiousness and unveiling the hypocrisy of people's behaviour and aspirations. Another function is to provide a source of unity to individual poems. The theme of *Satire* 1 – Style is the Man (literary style is an indicator of morality) – is conveyed through images drawn from disease, clothing, food and drink, homosexuality and effeminacy;[36] similar sexual imagery equates the politician with the male prostitute in *Satire* 4.[37] The dominant metaphor of *Satire* 3 is that of disease, spiritual and physical, while in *Satire* 5 the central theme of freedom and slavery occurs with imagery drawn from shadow and substance, food, astrology and particularly numbers. In *Satire* 2 the theme of bribery of the gods is associated physically with food and *Satire* 6 again uses food imagery, including the banquet of life, together with the image of land and sea. Throughout, the imagery is an important element of Persius' rejection of society: his subjects are deglamourised by the startling, shocking metaphors. Persius' angry young man and his graphic language are undoubtedly his most important and original contribution to the genre. In particular, the development of English satire in the sixteenth and seventeenth centuries owed a great deal to Persius.

5. JUVENAL'S LIFE

Virtually nothing is known of the life and circumstances of Juvenal. It is not even certain that the name we give him, Decimus Iunius Iuuenalis, is correct. The ancient biographies seem worthless and even the best of these, attributed by Valla in his 1486 edition to 'Probus',[38] offers the same kind of reconstruction from details in the Satires as presented by some recent scholars, a method which fails to take account of the generic convention of using first-person presentation.

[36] See Bramble (1974) esp. 26–59.
[37] Reckford (1962) 484–7, Dessen (1968) 58–70, Richlin (1983) 187–9.
[38] See Anderson (1965).

There is no convincing evidence for his alleged exile by Domitian, and his hostility towards Domitian is explicable on grounds other than personal animosity, connected with the prevailing ideology in the late Trajanic/early Hadrianic years.[39] Nor is the inscription from Aquinum which was believed to depict Juvenal as commander of a Dalmatian cohort reliable evidence, leaving aside the fact that it disappeared long ago; moreover, the date it suggested is earlier than other indicators. As Syme says, there is a 'scarcity of facts' in this field, although that has not prevented its being 'infested with credulity and romance'. His own assessment of the little evidence afforded by Juvenal's name and the poems leads him to suggest, tentatively, an African origin.[40]

Juvenal is the addressee of three epigrams of Martial (7.24, 7.91, 12.18) written in AD 92 and AD 101-2. Martial refers to Juvenal's oratorical skill (7.91.1 *facundo*) and depicts him living a hectic life in Rome (12.18.1-6). This is appropriate, since his Satires reflect the rhetorical training received by members of the Roman élite. The fact that the Satires are not dedicated to any patron may indicate that he was of relatively high social status, like Lucilius and Persius. The few dateable references confirm Syme's assessment that the five Books were written during the second and third decades of the 2nd century AD (or later), at about the same time as Tacitus was writing his *Annals*, which seem strikingly similar in their biting tone.[41] There is no reason to doubt that the Satires were written and published in Books. It seems likely that the first two books (Book I comprising Satires 1-5 and Book II Satire 6 alone) were written in the second decade of the second century AD, towards the end of Trajan's reign or, possibly, soon after Hadrian's accession in AD 117. The third book (Satires 7-9) appears to have been written early in Hadrian's reign and the fifth book (Satires 13-16, the last unfinished) dates from after AD 127.[42]

[39] Cf. Braund (1993) esp. 67; explored in depth by Ramage (1989).

[40] Syme (1984) 1120-34, urging avoidance of speculation based upon this inscription 1120-2, quotations from 1133-4.

[41] Syme (1984) 1135-57, esp. 1156-7 and 1143: 'There is no sign, let alone proof, that Juvenal published or even wrote anything before 115, or indeed before 117.'

[42] For a survey of Juvenal's five Books with bibliography see Braund (1992a) 40-55.

6. THE CHARACTERISTICS OF JUVENAL'S SATIRE: INDIGNATION, RHETORIC AND EPIC

The chief characteristics of Juvenal's satire are immediately evident in the opening lines of Satire 1. An indignant barrage of rhetorical effects (1–6) assails our ears. Sarcastic mythological allusions (7–11) are followed by a statement of familiarity with the education in declamation given to young men of the Roman élite (15–17[43]) and the implication that Lucilius, the founder of the genre of satire, is an epic warrior manoeuvring his chariot across the battlefield (19–20). Indignation, rhetoric and epic are the keys to understanding the early Satires of Juvenal. In later poems he will experiment with more indirect modes of satire, including irony, but for the first two books (Satires 1–6), the patterns of thought, the diction and the tone are provided by epic, declamatory rhetoric and indignation. All of these features are succinctly evoked in the phrase used by Scott in her 1927 study of the Satires: Juvenal writes in 'the grand style'. His adoption of the grand style – which is continually punctured or debased – seems to be an innovation within the genre and it is one of lasting impact.

(a) Indignation

The first and lasting (though perhaps not last) impression of Juvenal is of indignation. From antiquity to the present day the satirist has been regarded as an angry champion of morality, as 'the scourge of villainie'.[44] But only recently has the nature of Juvenal's *indignatio* been analysed more closely. Thanks to the work of Anderson, above all, we can now appreciate the broader rhetorical and moral context of Juvenal's choice of an angry voice for his early Satires.[45] The intellectual milieu of the early empire was a culture which acknowledged the moral ambiguity of anger: it had the potential to be a noble emotion or a serious fault. Anger might be used in a rhetorical context, of forensic or epideictic oratory, to arouse the emotions of the listeners;

---

[43] For discussion see 1.16n.

[44] To use the title given by the Elizabethan poet John Marston to his collection of satires, which are heavily influenced by Juvenal.

[45] Anderson (1982) 197–486; of prime importance is the essay 'Anger in Juvenal and Seneca', 293–361; cf. Braund (1988) esp. 1–23, 178–98.

yet an excess of anger might alienate them. At the same time, the stance of *indignatio* itself may have had a political dimension, since it could be a sign of true praise (*laudatio*) as opposed to the false flattery (*adulatio*) of the Domitianic era and therefore appropriate for the denigration of the past which is such a recurrent trope in Juvenal.[46]

For the Romans, anger was not simply a tone of voice. It imbued content, presentation and style. Anger dictates the kinds of material chosen for the satirist's spotlight and the arrangement of that material as well as the tone of voice adopted. So Juvenal's choice of anger as his mode in the early Satires is closely bound up with rhetoric and epic: he exploits the resources of rhetoric and the expansiveness of epic to produce angry rantings which often seem spontaneous, incoherent and rampaging catalogues of wickedness. To identify the linguistic signs of anger – such as rhetorical questions and exclamations, rapid changes of addressee, repetition, anaphora, apostrophe, diminutives, bathos and hyperbole along with vocabulary conveying the 'blaze' of anger and the impossibility of 'enduring' the outrages all around[47] – is only the beginning.

(b) Rhetoric

Rhetoric is not something grafted onto Juvenal; it is his idiom. In Kenney's words: 'The Satires are pervaded through and through by the influence, not merely of formal rhetorical training, but specifically of the schools of declamation.'[48] This holds good for much of Roman literature, of course; what is remarkable about Juvenal is that he obtrudes the tropes and figures which he uses in order to draw attention to his own rhetoricality. This was well understood by De Decker, whose monograph *Juvenalis declamans* of 1913 quantifies in detail the presence of rhetoric under the headings of *inuentio* (broadly speaking, subject-matter), composition and expression. More recently, Cairns includes several of Juvenal's Satires in his investigation of *Generic composition in Greek and Roman poetry* (1972). These detailed analyses assist progression beyond generalisations (often dismissive) about Juvenal's penchant for rhetorical expression.

---

[46] See Ramage (1989) esp. 705–7 on the political dimension of *indignatio*.
[47] See Anderson (1982) 278, 427.
[48] Kenney (1963) 707.

On the largest scale the influence of declamation is evident in the choice of subject and framing of ideas. Satire 6, for example, gains from being read as a *progymnasma*, more specifically, an exaggerated example of the *thesis* 'Ought a man to marry?', a theme which was a standard exercise given to Roman schoolboys.[49] Similarly, Satire 12 is a satiric version of the *prosphonetikon*, the speech of welcome.[50] Of the poems contained in this edition, Satire 3 is illuminated by being read as a (satiric) version of the *syntaktikon*, the farewell speech of the departing traveller.[51] Satire 5 can be seen as a dissuasion from the life of a parasite, with its opening and closing addresses to the servile client Trebius. Satires 1 and 2 perhaps have more in common with forensic than declamatory oratory, in their presentation respectively as the self-defence of the satirist and invective on the theme of deviant sexuality (which featured prominently in legal speeches[52]), but these poems nonetheless exhibit many of the hallmarks of declamation. The fact that Juvenal's audience of élite men had all shared in experience of the declamation schools makes it likely that they would have understood immediately Juvenal's rhetorical framework and would have appreciated the divergences from that framework introduced for satirical purposes.

One of the most prominent features of the declamatory education was the presentation of material in terms of exemplarity. Conduct was frequently described in terms of role models, *exempla*, both positive and negative, for protreptic and apotreptic purposes. Quintilian discusses the use of *exempla*, which he regards as a kind of proof, at *I.O.* 5.11 and a handbook of such *exempla* survives from antiquity in the *Facta et Dicta Memorabilia* ('Deeds and Sayings Worthy of Record') of Valerius Maximus, writing under Tiberius, a collection of 967 stories about named individuals taken from various authors and organised into categories to illustrate various characteristics, e.g. 3.4 and 3.5 on the rise from humble origins and decadence of the nobility (cf. Juvenal Satire 8), 5.4–6 on *pietas* and 9.3 on anger. The difference between oratory and satire is, not surprisingly, the predominance in the latter of apotreptic *exempla*: the extremes of bad conduct. Juvenal's Satires are

---

[49] Thus Cairns (1972) 75; discussed in detail in Braund (1992b).
[50] See Cairns (1972) 17–31.
[51] Cairns (1972) 47–8.
[52] Richlin (1983) 96–104.

teeming with negative *exempla*; the fewer positive *exempla* function as a foil, for example, towards the close of Satire 2 where Juvenal uses characters from the Republican era as *exempla* of pristine virtue (*Curius, Scipiadae, Fabricius, Camilli, Cremerae legio* and *Cannis consumpta iuuentus*, 2.153–5). Satire 1 is a striking case of the phenomenon of exemplarity on a larger scale: the catalogue of the wicked people who populate Rome presents an inversion of a parade of the finest and most glorious *exempla*, such as the parade of Aeneas' descendants in Virgil, *Aeneid* 6.756–853.

Another element of the training in declamation was the use of *loci communes*, literally 'commonplaces', stock themes which might usefully be inserted in a variety of contexts. The elder Seneca lists four chief types of *loci* as *de fortuna, de crudelitate, de saeculo, de diuitiis* (*Contr.* 1 pref. 23), that is, changes in luck, human cruelty and pity, contemporary decadence and praise of former times, and the advantages and inconveniences of wealth. To these can be added the *loci philosophumeni* (Sen. *Contr.* 1.7.17) on conscience, remorse, true nobility and similar ideas. All of these *loci* are present in Juvenal's satirical output, as shown by De Decker's detailed examination. Two manifestations of the *locus de saeculo* in the form of signs of luxury and decadence will suffice by way of illustration: the topic of over-ambitious building which occurs at 3.190–6 and that of gluttony which occurs at 1.135–41 and 5.93–6.

More specifically, certain *loci* were considered especially appropriate for the arousal of *indignatio*, which is the mode of presentation which Juvenal chooses for his early Satires. The list of such topics provided by Cicero at *De inuentione* 1.100–5 illuminates Juvenal's choice of presentation in his Satires.[53] They include, for example, reference to outrage of the gods or ancestors; demonstration that the deed was cruel or tyrannical and unknown among barbarians; comparison with other crimes to enhance the horror of the deed; detailing of the circumstances to make the crime as vivid as possible; and requests to the audience to identify with the speaker. These and numerous other similarities indicate the influence of rhetorical theory and practice upon Juvenal.

Many devices of articulation and of style too which were inculcated through the training in declamation feature in Juvenal's Satires. These

---

[53] For fuller discussion see Braund (1988) 3–5.

include dramatic features such as the fictitious adversary or interlocutor (e.g. the dialogue at 1.150–71 which begins *dices hic forsitan*)
and the incorporation of snatches of direct speech (listed below in the
section on Juvenal's style). They also include statements of intent
(*propositiones*: 1.19–21 is a classic case), progression by degree (e.g. the
use of Gracchus as the climax of shamelessness at 2.143–8) and progression by antithesis (e.g. between *nos* and *uos* at 2.51–7, between the
country and Rome frequently in Satire 3, between host and guest
throughout Satire 5). Features of the 'grand style' assumed at times in
oratory are found in abundance in Juvenal's Satires, for example,
rhetorical questions and exclamations, hyperbole, repetition, apostrophe, prosopopoeia and *sententiae*: examples of these will be found in the
discussion of Juvenal's style, below.

(c) *Epic*

From early in the history of the genre satire had a close relationship
with epic. After experimentation with a variety of metres by Ennius
and Lucilius in his earlier works, Lucilius definitively appropriated the
metre of epic, the dactylic hexameter, for his acknowledgedly humble
genre (starting with Book 30 and continuing with Books 1–21). Choice
of the hexameter must have seemed especially right for parody of epic
scenes such as that in Book 1, where he models a scene of the council of
the gods on Book 1 of Ennius' *Annales*.[54] The effect to the Roman ear
was perhaps one of counterpoint: the audience is invited to sense the
gap between the lofty tones of epic and the bathos of satire. Lucretius,
writing maybe fifty years or more later, exploits precisely this tension
in his *De Rerum Natura* in which he combines the high emotional style
with the subliterary tradition of the diatribe.[55] Horace's 'refinement'
of the genre of satire for the Augustan 'gentleman' represented a shift
away from Lucilius' relationship with epic a century earlier: the
implicit counterpoint is rarely acknowledged, although it is not
entirely absent. For example, Horace incorporates a mock-epic invocation of the muse before his description of the verbal duel of the jesters
at *Sat.* 1.5.51–69, alludes to Homer in the closing words of *Sat.* 1.9 and

[54] Discussed briefly by Gratwick (1982) 169–70.
[55] On the two styles in Lucretius see Kenney's edition of Book III, 14–20.

casts *Sat.* 2.5 as a parody of Odysseus' consultation of Tiresias in the Underworld in Odyssey Book 11. But for the most part, Horace eschews the 'grand style' and prefers to create an impression of elegant and witty conversation. Persius explicitly reiterates Horace's stylistic principles at *Sat.* 5.1–18. In his revival of the vehemence associated with Lucilius he includes epic words and phrases, but his novel style is so dense – almost constipated with ideas jostling for expression – that it lacks the expansiveness of epic. Among the extant satirists, then, it remained for Juvenal to explore and exploit the relationship between satire and epic most thoroughly.[56]

Epic makes its first appearances early and often in Juvenal's first Satire. The speaker refers to trite and predictable rehashings of mythological themes in epic at lines 7–11 and 52–4. The searing boredom inspired by these and their irrelevance to his vision of contemporary Rome as seething with vice are, he claims, his motivation for satirical attack. This stark contrast between epic and satire bills satire as a phenomenon that will shock the sensibilities with penetrating and highly topical revelations. That is, the antithesis between epic and satire is an important element in the generic justification. Satire in Juvenal's hands is very confident and assertive: it can replace epic.

Accordingly, satire accepts the epic frame of reference, but only to appropriate it for its own purposes. Perhaps the most striking example of this is where the satirist is portrayed as an epic hero. In Satire 1 Juvenal depicts Lucilius racing in his chariot across the plain (19–20) and raging with his sword against wrong-doers (165–6). The epic imagery casts the satirist in the role of avenging warrior or destroyer of monsters. He is a modern-day Hercules or Diomedes or Theseus (1.52–4) fighting against crime and vice, such as the corruption of traditional morality and the inversion of social status by selfishness and greed. The speaker's attitude is one of moral righteousness, as befits the tone of *indignatio*. He accordingly assumes the agreement of his audience and launches his initial attacks upon various enemies:[57] in Satire 1 those who disregard the unwritten rules of Roman society, whether

---

[56] Scott (1927) gathers many useful examples of the grand style in Juvenal, although her division into 'humorous effect' and 'serious imitation' is hard to sustain.

[57] Called 'out-groups' by Richlin: (1984) 67.

they are social climbers who are millionaires or impoverished nobles jostling for tiny financial handouts, and in Satire 2 those who deviate from active masculine sexuality. Umbricius in Satire 3 renews the attack upon social climbers and unleashes a virulent attack on foreigners. Then in Satires 4 and 5 the speaker turns his attack upon the powerful, the patrons who humiliate their inferiors, and upon those inferiors who tolerate this degrading treatment. Here too he is assuming the agreement of his audience: the conduct he describes of both patrons and clients is presented as a deviation from traditional Roman morality.

By presenting himself as a new-style epic hero, savaging the modern-day 'monsters' which ravage Rome, Juvenal legitimises the use of anger. Moreover, this stance permits him to re-present epic topoi and tropes in a new satiric guise. Epic imagery redefines the enterprise of satire onto a grand scale, for example when the speaker urges himself to action at 1.149–50 with the words *utere uelis, totos pande sinus* and when he depicts Roman wives as creatures swept along by the power of their emotions with an epic-style simile (6.649–50).[58] Epic allusions mark the gap between the satiric 'reality' and the escapist world of epic. For example, Virgil's description of the Underworld in *Aeneid* 6 reappears at 2.150–1 as the backdrop for the ultimate humiliation of the warriors of the Republic by the arrival of a pathic (i.e. passive homosexual) ghost and at 3.265–6 as the destination of a man annihilated in a traffic accident. Similarly, Achilles' sleepless grief over the death of his friend Patroclus in *Iliad* 24 is reworked in the scene of the drunken thug itching for a fight at 3.278–80. In Satire 5 the allusions to epic draw attention to the selfish luxury of Virro, the host, for example at 5.44–5 where his cup is associated with Aeneas and at 138–9 where Dido's words are reworked into a reference to the sordid practice of legacy-hunting. Finally, the vocabulary of epic is taken over for satiric use when it underlines how much what is described falls short of its epic name, for example when the old nobility are called *Troiugenae* (1.100) and when Domitian is called *induperator* (4.29) and his advisers *proceres* (4.73, 133).[59]

---

[58] Particularly in Satire 6, Juvenal presents his relationship with the heroic in terms of tragedy too; cf. Smith (1989).

[59] See discussion of Juvenal's style below for further examples.

Epic also provides narrative tropes and frames which are appropriated for satiric purposes, inevitably through an antithesis of elevation and bathos. This is evident on a small scale in Satire 1 where the speaker initiates the second half of the poem by adopting the grand style to tell the story of the flood and mankind's recreation by Deucalion and Pyrrha (1.81–4; narrated at length by Ovid at *Metamorphoses* 1.253–416). The elevated tone creates a stark contrast with the preceding self-deprecation (1.79–80) and, inevitably, the epic tone is quickly deflated.[60] The same technique is evident in Satire 4, on a larger scale. This is a rare case of extended narrative, which is not a prominent feature within the monologue form adopted for Roman verse satire. The larger part of the poem is presented as a mock-epic narrative, heralded by a mock-epic invocation of the muses (4.34–6). Throughout, the alternation of epic stylistics and satiric mundanities (for a full discussion see Essay on Satire 4) is a reminder of the genre and functions to shed an un-heroic light on the characters and events described. Both in this case of epic parody – the target appears to be a panegyrical epic by Statius – and more generally, Juvenal revives the counterpoint effect between the genres which is evident in the founder of the genre, Lucilius.

Finally, Juvenal's new-style epic hero for the modern world tackles his task in epic-sized chunks. When the poems of Book I are taken as an organic whole (as argued below: see §9), they amount to a sustained denunciation of public life at Rome on an epic scale: approximately a thousand lines, the size of a book of an epic poem. Likewise Book II: a single, massive poem of seven hundred lines denouncing Roman marriage. Together Books I and II present a huge indictment of Roman life broader in scope than anything attempted by Horace or Persius: in Juvenal's hands, satire can indeed claim to replace epic.

7. JUVENAL'S STYLE

There follows a brief overview of the chief characteristics of Juvenal's style. To avoid disrupting the exposition, examples of the features mentioned will be found listed at the end of this section.

---

[60] See 1.84n.

The range of Juvenal's vocabulary is very wide, from elevated to lowly, drawn from many different types of discourse. This is one of several factors which make him a difficult author. Unlike Horace, Juvenal includes elements of the grand style appropriate to the heights of epic or rhetorical display [A]. The grand style is intermingled with lowly vocabulary relating to the mundane and the coarse and with constructions from everyday speech (ἀπὸ κοινοῦ) [B], yet avoiding the blatant obscenity present in Horace on occasion[61] through indirection (e.g. through metaphor or synecdoche, the substitution of part for whole) [C]. This mixture makes possible Juvenal's characteristic surprise technique (παρὰ προσδοκίαν), when he juxtaposes two words from different registers, usually with the purpose of deflating an elevated word, line or sentence with something incongruous or bathetic. Often the shocking word is positioned powerfully at the end of the line [D] or enjambed into the next line for maximum impact [E]. Juvenal often exploits Greek words [F] (which were condemned by Horace, *Sat.* 1.10.20–35) and diminutives [G] for the same kind of effect. Similar effects are often achieved by epic quotation, allusion or parody [H], another prominent element in his style. Another manifestation of the clash between different elements is his use of the so-called 'golden line', the balanced line consisting of two adjectives and two nouns in agreement flanking a verb, ideally in the arrangement abVAB (i.e. adj. 1, adj. 2, verb, noun 1, noun 2), but with various other permutations possible [I]. Emotional effects abound: rhetorical questions [J], exclamations [K], apostrophe [L], repetition often with anaphora [M], prosopopoeia [N] and hyperbole [O]. He presents great variety in sentence length and structure. Extensive lists [P] or lengthy complex sentences [Q], with varied run-on effects into the next line [R], with defining periphrasis [S] or with the pithy future participle [T], are intermingled with brief sentences [U], compressed expressions and occasionally with snatches of conversation in direct speech [V]. His use of ellipse [W] often conveys the passion of anger or the vividness of real speech. Quintessential is his use of *sententiae* (pithy maxims) [X] and of paradox and oxymoron [Y]: both highly compressed forms of expression, the latter delivering two conflicting ideas in a single phrase.

---

[61] Adams (1982) 221–2.

These lists are not intended to be exhaustive or definitive; examples are drawn only from Satires 1–5. The particular effect in its context is often discussed in the note in the commentary.

A Grand style

1.19–20 *decurrere campo* | *per quem magnus equos Aurunca flexit alumnus*, 1.52–3, 1.81–4, 1.89–92, 1.100 *ipsos Troiugenas*, 1.149–50 *utere uelis*, | *totos pande sinus*, 1.165 *ense uelut stricto*, 1.168–9, 2.121, 3.213, 4.73, 4.133 *proceres*, 2.154 *Scipiadae*, 4.29 *induperator*, 4.34–6 *incipe, Calliope ... narrate, puellae Pierides*, 4.37 *semianimum laceraret*, 4.39–40, 4.56 *letifero*, 4.58 *stridebat deformis hiems*, 4.65 *itur ad Atriden*, 4.81 *Crispi iucunda senectus*, 4.107, 4.133 *Prometheus*, 4.140 *tempestate*, 4.146 *dux magnus*, 5.49 *uinoque ciboque*, 5.78–9, 5.93 *Tauromenitanae rupes*, 5.100 *gurgite de Siculo*

B Lowly tone

1.36 *summissa*, 1.143 *crudum*, 2.32 *uuluam*, 2.33 *offas*, 3.118 *caballi*, 3.265 *nouicius*, 3.288 *rixae*, 4.5 *iumenta*, 4.28 *gluttisse*, 4.31 *ructarit scurra*, 4.67 *stomachum, sagina*; ἀπὸ κοινοῦ 3.11, 3.69–70, 3.98–9, 3.274, 4.145–9

C Avoidance of explicit obscenity through metaphor, synecdoche

1.39 *uesica*, 1.41 *inguinis*, 1.131 *non tantum meiere fas est*, 2.10 *fossa*, 2.13 *mariscae*, 3.112 *resupinat*, 3.134 *palpitet*, 4.9 *iacebat*, 4.105 *offensae ueteris ... atque tacendae*

D Surprise or deflation at end of the line

1.28 *aurum*, 1.116 *salutato ... nido*, 1.146 *plaudendum*, 2.10 *inter Socraticos notissima fossa cinaedos*, 2.106 *Bebriaci ... Palati*, 2.129 *uir*, 2.165 *tribuno*, 3.9 *poetas*, 3.207 *mures*, 3.229 *Pythagoreis*, 3.231 *lacertae*, 4.31 *purpureus magni ructarit scurra Palati*, 4.33 *siluros*, 4.106 *cinaedo*, 5.106 *Suburae*

E Enjambment

1.101 *nobiscum*, 2.59 *liberto*, 4.101 *uenator*, 4.121 *belua*, 5.59 *friuola*, 5.79 *Iuppiter*, 5.88 *lanternam*, 5.122 *cultello*

F Greek words

1.53 *labyrinthi*, 1.65 *cathedra*, 2.10 *cinaedos*, 2.41 *opobalsama*, 2.46 *phalanges*, 2.92, 2.141 *pyxide Lyde*, 3.61–70, 3.76–7, 3.103 *endromidem*, 3.288 *prohoemia*, 3.296 *proseucha*, 5.38–9, 5.72 *artoptae*, 5.121 *chironomunta*

G   Diminutives

1.11 *pelliculae*, 3.78 *Graeculus*, 3.97 *uentriculum*, 3.102 *igniculum*, 3.149 *sordidula*, 3.204 *paruulus*, 3.226 *hortulus*, 3.253 *seruulus*, 4.98 *fraterculus*, 5.73 *improbulum*, 5.85 *patella*, 5.105 *uernula*, 5.138 *paruulus*

H   Epic quotation, parody, allusion

1.7–11, 1.61 *puer Automedon*, 1.162–4, 2.77, 2.99–100, 2.150–1, 3.199 *Vcalegon*, 3.265–7, 3.279–80, 4.34–149 *passim* (see nn.), 5.45, 5.100–2, 5.115, 5.125, 5.138–9, 5.151–2

I   'Golden line'

2.74 *montanum positis audiret uulgus aratris*, 2.91 *talia secreta coluerunt orgia taeda*, 3.207 *et diuina opici rodebant carmina mures*, 4.31 *purpureus magni ructarit scurra Palati*, 4.118 *blandaque deuexae iactaret basia raedae*, 4.149 *anxia praecipiti uenisset epistula pinna*, 5.17 *tertia ne uacuo cessaret culcita lecto*; cf. 4.64 *exclusi spectant admissa obsonia patres*; 5.29 *pugna Saguntina feruet commissa lagona*, 5.85 *ponitur exigua feralis cena patella*

J   Rhetorical questions

1.1–6, 1.77–8, 2.8–10, 2.24–8, 2.126–8, 3.81–91, 4.23–5, 4.101–3, 5.8–11, 5.62–3, 5.127–30

K   Exclamations

1.91–2, 1.140–1, 5.24, 5.132–4

L   Apostrophe

1.50 *prouincia*, 2.37, 2.67, 2.78, 2.121 *o proceres*, 2.126 *o pater Vrbis*, 2.128, 3.60 *Quirites*, 4.23–4, 4.103, 4.124 *Bellona*, Satire 5 *passim* e.g. 5.71, 5.119 *o Libye*, 5.136 *o nummi*

M   Repetition, often with anaphora

1.15 *et nos*, 1.51–2 *haec ego non*, 1.56–7 *doctus*, 1.77–8 *quem*, 1.88–9 *quando*, 1.94 *quis*, 1.150–1 *unde*, 2.53 *paucae*, 2.110–11 *hic*, 2.127 *unde*, 2.135–6 *fient*, 3.6 *tam*, 3.26–7 *dum*, 3.51 *nil*, 3.107–8 *si*, 3.110–11 *non*, 3.166–7 *magno*, 3.197–9 *nulla . . . nulli, iam . . . iam . . . iam*, 3.211 *nemo*, 3.216–20 *hic, haec*, 3.245 *ferit*, 3.309 *qua*, 3.312 *felices . . . felicia*, 4.56–7 *iam*, 5.14–15 *imputat*, 5.100–1 *dum*, 5.108–9 *quae*, 5.112–13 *esto*, 5.114 *anseris . . . anseribus*, 5.129 *quis*, 5.133–4 *quantus*, 5.136–7 *uobis . . . uos*

N   Prosopopoeia
1.12, 1.88 *auaritia*, 1.113 *Pecunia*, 3.15–16, 3.275 *fenestrae*, 4.60–1,
4.149 *epistula*, 5.6 *uentre*, 5.95–6, 5.100 *Auster*, 5.158 *plorante gula*

O   Hyperbole
1.12–13, 1.34 *nobilitate comesa*, 3.310–11, 4.25–6, 4.48–9 *algae* |
inquisitores, 4.69 *ipse capi uoluit*

P   Lists, catalogues
1.75–6, 1.85–6, 1.115–16, 2.24–8, 2.124, 2.145–6, 2.153–5, 2.169,
3.7–9, 3.31–3, 3.41–8, 3.76–7, 4.72–118, 4.121–2, 5.109

Q   Lengthy complex sentences
1.30–9, 1.52–61, 1.109–16, 3.21–8, 4.37–44

R   Run-on effects
1.26–7 *uerna Canopi* | *Crispinus*, 1.32–3 *lectica Mathonis* | *plena ipso*,
1.34–5 *de nobilitate comesa* | *quod superest*, 1.37–8 *qui testamenta merentur*
| *noctibus*, 1.49–50 *fruitur dis* | *iratis*, 1.61–2 *nam lora tenebat* | *ipse*,
2.20–1 *de uirtute locuti* | *clunem agitant*, 2.117–18 *quadringenta dedit*
Gracchus sestertia dotem | *cornicini*, 3.17–18 *speluncas* | *dissimiles ueris*,
3.182–3 *hic uiuimus ambitiosa* | *paupertate omnes*, 4.47–8 *cum plena et*
litora multo | *delatore forent*, 5.20–1, 5.111–12, 5.129–30 *quis* | *perditus*

S   Defining periphrasis
3.118 *ad quam Gorgonei delapsa est pinna caballi*, 3.138–9, 4.42–4, 5.45
zelotypo iuuenis praelatus Iarbae, 5.154–5

T   Future participle
1.34 *rapturus*, 1.44 *dicturus*, 1.70 *porrectura*, 4.10 *subitura*, 4.50
dubitaturi, 4.88 *locuturi*, 4.148 *dicturus*, 5.32 *missurus*

U   Brief sentences
1.87–9, 1.168 *inde ira et lacrimae*, 2.131–6, 3.29 *cedamus patria*,
3.60–1, 3.78 *in caelum iusseris ibit*, 3.100 *natio comoeda est*, 3.100–3,
3.182–4, 3.198–200, 3.259–60, 3.290–2, 4.22, 4.136, 5.18–19,
5.111–13, 5.156–8, 5.170–1

V   Direct speech
1.102–9, 1.125–6, 2.21–2, 2.37, 2.70–1, 2.89–90, 2.132–5,
3.141–2, 3.153–8, 3.187–8, 3.292–6, 4.65–9, 4.76, 4.124–8,
4.130–5, 5.18, 5.74–9, 5.118–19, 5.135–6, 5.166–8

W   Ellipse
1.1, 1.52–4, 1.87–9, 1.130–1, 1.158–9, 2.4, 2.14–15, 2.65, 2.119,
3.21–2, 3.73–4, 3.78, 3.93, 3.100–1, 3.140, 3.212–13, 3.250, 4.11,
4.23–5, 5.8–10, 5.14, 5.18, 5.24–5, 5.30, 5.56, 5.135–6

X   Sententiae

1.74 *probitas laudatur et alget,* 2.8 *frontis nulla fides,* 2.47 *magna inter molles concordia,* 2.60 *diues erit magno quae dormit tertia lecto,* 3.152–3 *nil habet infelix paupertas durius in se* | *quam quod ridiculos homines facit,* 4.97 *prodigio par est in nobilitate senectus*

Y   Paradox and oxymoron

1.50 *tu uictrix, prouincia, ploras,* 1.57 *uigilanti stertere naso,* 1.78 *praetextatus adulter,* 1.140 *luxuriae sordes,* 2.3 *Curios simulant et Bacchanalia uiuunt,* 2.103 *speculum ciuilis sarcina belli,* 2.134 *nubit amicus,* 3.61 *Graecam Vrbem,* 4.106 *saturam scribente cinaedo,* 5.25 *de conuiua Corybanta,* 5.59 *Gaetulum Ganymedem,* 5.72 *artoptae reuerentia*

8. JUVENAL'S METRE

Juvenal's metrical practice coheres closely with his stylistic practice, as outlined above. In contrast with the informal metrical style adopted by Horace for his satirical writings, which is designed to evoke the leisure of elegant conversation, Juvenal's metre is dominated by features characteristic of declamation and epic. In his avoidance of repetition of metrical patterns and penchant for variety he is atypical of so-called 'Silver Age' poets and resembles Virgil and possibly Lucilius.[62] The phenomenon of the 'golden line', a feature associated with elevated and highly-wrought poetry and alien to satire, not strictly a metrical phenomenon, is discussed above (§7, I). Similarly Juvenal uses hiatus (absence of elision between two words with final and initial vowel), a feature absent from Horace and Persius but found in Virgil [A]. Spondaic lines (i.e. where a spondee replaces the normal dactyl in the fifth foot) are another feature of elevated poetry avoided by Horace and Persius but present in abundance in Juvenal (34 instances in all) [B]. Alongside such metrical features of the grand style are other incongruous or bathetic metrical effects which conflict with and deflate the grand pretensions and emphasise that this is satire. Most prominent is Juvenal's frequent use of a single final monosyllable (a pair of monosyllables at the end of the line seldom have the same effect), which disrupts the coincidence of word accent and metrical beat (ictus) usually found in the last two feet of the hexameter [C]:

[62] See Duckworth (1967) 109–17.

Juvenal obtains a variety of effects from this device. Although it is often hard to gauge the precise effect of other unusual features it seems likely that polysyllabic endings [D], multiple elision [E], unusual pauses [F] and caesurae [G] along with unusual prosody [H] are designed to clash with the declamatory flow as a generic marker, since these features find analogues in Horace. For a fuller discussion of Juvenal's metrical practice see Eskuche's article in the Introduction to Friedländer's edition, 57–80, and Courtney 49–55.

A Hiatus: 1.151, 2.16, 3.70, 5.158

B Spondaic lines: 1.52, 3.120, 5.38 (Greek word or name); 2.145, 4.53, (Roman name); 3.17, 3.273, 4.87

C Final monosyllable: 1.31, 1.49, 1.97, 1.108, 1.159, 2.22, 2.115, 2.129, 3.191, 3.203, 3.305, 5.8, 5.15, 5.20, 5.129, 5.132, 5.137, 5.141; cf. 5.1, 5.14

D Polysyllabic line-ending: 1.112 *sanctissima diuitiarum*, 3.70 *Alabandis*, 3.182 *ambitiosa*

E Unusual elision: 2.34, 4.150: three elisions in a single line; 3.70: only strong caesura elided

F Unusual pause: 1.62, 3.25, 3.66, 3.246, 3.248: after first trochee; 3.119: after first syllable of fifth foot; 5.129: before last syllable of line

G Unusual caesura: 4.70–1

H Unusual prosody: 1.3 and 3.104 *ergŏ*, 3.2 *laudŏ*, 3.59 *properabŏ*, 3.232 *uigilandŏ* (the short final -o occurs also in Seneca's tragedies), 3.317 *muliŏ*; 3.76 *gĕōmētrēs*; 3.174 *redĭt*

9. AN OVERVIEW OF BOOK 1

Not so long ago, it was conventional to prescribe Satires 1, 3, 4 and 10 as a Juvenal set book. The desire to include Satire 10, the poem which was the inspiration for Johnson's *The Vanity of Human Wishes*, was clearly one important factor in this. So too was the bowdlerisation of the supposedly scurrilous and corrupting content of the second Satire. Times have changed and, happily, it is now possible to study the first Book of the Satires as a whole, as they were probably published originally. There exist many good reasons for studying this as a single piece of artistry;[63] similarly, the later Books benefit from being read as

---

[63] See Cloud and Braund (1982) on external and internal reasons for reading the book as a single organic unit.

artistic entities.[64] The persistence and development of important
themes through Book I will be sketched below, with an indication of
how Satire I anticipates the contents of the book.

(a) Rome

The city of Rome provides both setting and subject for Book I. The
speaker is on the streets of Rome from the start. This is evident
throughout the opening of Satire I, e.g. 32 *cum ueniat lectica*, and
becomes most explicit at 63–4, *medio ... quadriuio*, and 69 *occurrit
matrona potens*. The only time he ventures out of Rome in his imagin-
ation is for the evasion with which he closes, after being warned of the
dangers of satire,[65] when he states his intent to attack those buried
alongside the *via Flaminia* and *via Latina*, roads leading from the city.
He remains in Rome throughout Satire 2 (e.g. *quis enim non uicus abundat
| tristibus obscenis?* 2.8–9), despite his opening wish to run away (2.1–2),
moving with the crowds to the gladiatorial arena towards the end of
the poem (2.143–8). Satire 3 begins with him strolling with Umbricius
down into the grove of Egeria (3.1–20) where he listens to Umbricius'
condemnation of Rome, a complaint full of specific locations in the
metropolis (e.g. 71 Esquiline and Viminal hills, 85 Aventine hill, 93–9
and 153–9 the theatre, 212 the *Asturici ... domus*). The grove is near the
gate through which the *via Appia* led south to the Bay of Naples where
Umbricius plans to make a new home for himself. Satire 4 maintains
the city setting in its opening attack upon Crispinus, who is described
as *scurra Palati* (4. 31), the resident jester in Domitian's imperial
residence on the Palatine Hill. But then, as if to indicate that nowhere
is free from corruption, the setting for the mock-epic attack on Domitian shifts to Alba, which is, appropriately after Satire 3, on the *via
Appia*. The setting returns to Rome for Satire 5, a shift engineered by
mention of the jesters (*scurrae*) of Augustus (5.3–4) and confirmed by
details such as mention of the tombs lining the *Via Latina* (5.55
monumenta Latinae), the client's complaint that he has to race up the
Esquiline (5.77–8) and the provenance of the fish, caught from the
Tiber at the heart of Rome, near the great sewer and the Subura
(5.103–6).

---

[64] See Braund (1988) 178–98 on Books III, IV and V.
[65] See Essay on Satire I.

Rome, then, is the setting. Not only is it the centre of political power but also the (by ancient standards) enormous metropolis, teeming with people and objects from all parts of the known world and offering countless opportunities for satire. And, as well as providing the setting, Rome is also the subject throughout the Book, most obviously in Satire 3. One of the first exclamations uttered by the speaker makes this clear: *quis iniquae | tam patiens Vrbis, tam ferreus, ut teneat se, | ... cum ...* (1.30–2): the Book is a catalogue of Rome's vices. Perhaps satire could only develop fully once there were large enough conurbations to provide the setting and material: satire is, indeed, 'an urban art', as Juvenal demonstrates.[66]

(b) Patrons and clients

The speaker's criticisms centre upon the degradation of the patron-client relationship (*amicitia*) which was the backbone of Roman society. In essence, this was a code for regulating social relationships, a code based upon reciprocity between unequals. The code prescribed what goods and services should pass between people, whatever their status. For example, a client was expected to visit his patron when he arose from bed (the 'greeting', *salutatio*) and to accompany him on his daily round to the law-courts in the forum and then to the baths (see 1.127–34n.). In return for this, the client might then be invited to dinner. The emperor is the patron par excellence, surrounded by clients who are themselves powerful men who in turn have crowds of clients of their own. The picture of Roman society as a pyramid is useful here in indicating how any individual may be both patron and client simultaneously.[67]

Juvenal's first Book of Satires portrays in extraordinarily vivid terms the perversion and dysfunction of this code.[68] (There is, of course, no necessity to take this portrayal exactly at face value: satire, like all

---

[66] Hodgart (1969) 129; cf. 135–7; cf. Kernan (1959) 7–14, Braund (1989a) 23–6.

[67] Cf. 1.95n.; see Cloud (1989).

[68] See LaFleur (1979). In stark contrast is Horace, *Epistles* 1, which constitutes a demonstration of the code in action, presented in positive terms: see Mayer's Introduction.

other forms of discourse, selects and distorts its material.) Again and again, the speaker attacks patrons and clients for their selfish greed which he depicts as the cause of the degradation of social relationships. This emerges strongly from the part of Satire 1 devoted to the patron–client relationship (lines 95–146) especially in the central panel of his depiction of the *sportula* (the money given as a reward for a client's attendance upon his patron: 1.95n.) where he asserts the supremacy of money, despite the fact that there is no temple to *Pecunia* – yet (1.109–16, *nondum* 114). Umbricius in Satire 3 develops this topic in his long lament about the displacement of impoverished clients like himself (see Essay on Satire 3). Clients like him are, he alleges, displaced by shameless criminals (3.21–57), by Greeks and other foreigners (3.58–125) and by the greedy rich (3.126–314), because money is all-powerful. Satire 5 sees a humble client receiving as his 'reward' for his services to the patron an invitation to dinner (*cena*). But the overwhelming motive of greed by both parties renders this *cena* an inversion of the ideal patron–client relationship: the client's greed to maximise his reward and the patron's disinclination to spend money on his humble clients.

The speaker's attitude towards patrons remains static throughout Book I. Not so his attitude towards clients. He moves from expressions of identification and sympathy in Satire 1 through the slight distancing by having the character Umbricius deliver the poor client's lament in Satire 3 to overt scorn in Satire 5.[69] This increasing hostility towards clients is connected with the ideas about the abuse of power which emerge most strongly in Satires 4 and 5. These poems portray graphically the kind of degradation which a patron (in Satire 4 the supreme patron, the emperor Domitian) can inflict upon his clients. In both cases, the clients are satirised for enduring humiliations with supine servility, in Satire 5 in passages prominent at the opening and close of the poem (5.1–23 and 156–73). Book I when read as a continuous whole presents a progressively harsher and starker view of the dysfunction and perversion of the patron–client relationship caused by greed and selfishness.

[69] See Cloud and Braund (1982) 83 and Braund (1988) 31–3 with 137–42 and 178–80 on the further development of the patron–client theme in Book III, specifically Satires 7 and 9.

(c) A day in the life?

This is reflected in the chronological movement from morning in
Satire 1 to evening in Satire 5. In Satire 1 the focus is upon the
beginning of the client's day with a glance at the *cena* with which it
should end (135–46); Satire 5 presents a nightmare version of the *cena*
with a glance back to the morning *salutatio* which has 'earned' the poor
client the 'honour' of the dinner (19–23). Within this chronological
framework we have been treated to Umbricius' appalling picture,
placed symmetrically at the centre of the book, of the set-backs faced
by a poor Roman client. Part of this is, appropriately, presented as a
twenty-four hour catalogue of horrors, starting with insomnia and the
duties of the morning and finishing with the dangers of the evening
and the night (232–314: see Braund (1989a) 34).

(d) Corruption at the core

Satires 2 and 4 present a counterpoint to the emphasis upon patrons
and clients in Satires 1, 3 and 5. They focus upon the corruption of the
aristocracy, crystallised at length in Satire 4 in its worst instance in the
person of the emperor Domitian: the rot at the core of Roman society.
The condemnation of the aristocracy in Satire 2 uses sexual behaviour,
namely the adoption of a passive sexuality combined with a desire to
parade it, as an index of the degradation of society. The central image
in the poem is that of corruption spreading outwards from the rotten
core (2.78–81, in Rudd's translation):

> This plague of yours has been caught through contact,
> and will spread to others, as in the country a single pig
> with scab or mange can cause the collapse of the total herd,
> and as one grape can develop mould at the sight of another.

Satire 2 features Domitian in passing, as a paradigmatic case of
hypocrisy in his committing incest while holding the title of censor
(2.29–33), and obliquely, in the background of the legislation mentioned: he is supposed to have revived the *lex Iulia* and *lex Scantinia*
which feature in the poem.[70] His role in Satire 4 is much more

---

[70] See 2.29–33n., 2.37n., and 2.43–4n.

dominant. The effect of his looming over his cabinet of ministers is achieved by devoting a minimal amount of description to him. The catalogue of the terrified and servile ministers – all members of the élite – provides a reflection of their master. And Domitian's abuse of his power to humiliate his advisers by compelling them to attend a meeting to decide what to do with an enormous fish, as if the issue were of great military importance, portrays graphically the perversion of traditional values and the degradation of the aristocracy. Satires 2 and 4, then, depict the self-degradation of the aristocracy and form a complement to the focus upon patrons and clients in Satires 1, 3 and 5.

(e) Running away from the city

The broad pattern of alternation of theme within Book 1 is complemented by links between adjacent poems. The first of these is escape from Rome. Satires 2 and 3 both open with this idea. In Satire 2 the speaker expresses a desire to run away (2.1–3) to the far north from the sexual hypocrisy and degradation which makes Rome un-Roman (2.162–3). In Satire 3 Umbricius actually departs from the un-Roman Rome (3.61) to a Greek establishment in the south (3.24–5) which is, ironically, more accommodating to the true Roman Umbricius considers himself to be. The difference is that in Satire 2 escape seems impossible, because Rome has infected the world with sexual corruption, whereas for the misfit Umbricius in Satire 3 retreat is the only answer.

(f) Immigrants take over

Umbricius' hostility towards foreigners in Satire 3, which amounts to extreme racism, provides a subtle but important prelude to Satire 4. Umbricius alleges that the impoverished native Roman clients like himself are displaced by foreigners from the east, especially Greeks (3.58–125). That is one of his reasons for leaving the metropolis. And the moment he leaves for voluntary exile his place is taken by the successful Egyptian immigrant Crispinus, who is introduced in the opening words of Satire 4, *ecce iterum Crispinus*. Juvenal has created a clever link between the two poems by suggesting that Umbricius' complaint is proved true.

(g) *The power of food*

As Satires 2 and 3 both feature the motif of escape and Satires 3 and 4
cohere on the topic of immigrants, so Satires 4 and 5 share the topic of
food. In Satire 4 the food features in the form of fish: the expensive fish
which Crispinus purchases for his personal consumption and the
gigantic turbot presented to Domitian, which provokes his abuse of
power. In Satire 5 the food features in the form of the parallel menus:
the menu of the finest food for the host Virro and his peers and the
menu of revolting or non-existent fare served up to the humble clients
like Trebius.

(h) *Satire 1 as programme poem of Book 1*

Satire 1 fulfils its function as a programme poem by providing a
foretaste of all these features of Book 1.[71] From its opening words, Satire
1 clearly sets the scene as the bustling metropolis of Rome (*a*) and
initiates the focus upon the relationship between patrons and clients
and upon the degradations of the aristocracy (*b*) and (*d*): the first four
cases in the catalogue of vice illustrate the perversion of sexual roles
and the inversion of social status through the power of wealth. The
chronological sequence of the day (*c*) is anticipated at 127. Escape (*e*)
is perhaps implicit in the speaker's indignant exclamations such as
1.30–1; the successful immigrant (*f*) features at 1.26–9; and food (*g*) is
depicted as an index of selfishness and the abuse of power at 1.132–46.

These points of correspondence, together with verbal links between
the poems,[72] suggest that Juvenal wrote Book 1 as an organic whole.
The power of Juvenal's satire is substantially enhanced by reading the
book like this.

10. JUVENAL AND HIS INFLUENCE FROM ANTIQUITY TO THE PRESENT

From the re-emergence of his Satires in the fourth century onwards,
Juvenal provided a huge fount of quotations for moralists and inspired

---

[71] See Essay on Satire 1 for full discussion of the term 'programme poem'.
[72] E.g. *rex* and *parasitus* in Satires 1 and 5; *monstrum, adulter, proceres* and *dux* in
Satires 2 and 4: see Cloud and Braund (1982) 81.

many imitations by poets. In the late fourth to early fifth century Jerome and Augustine present moralising quotations, although not attributed to him by name, and the poet Claudian imitated him in his satirical epic *In Eutropium*; Boethius in his *Consolation of Philosophy* (early sixth century) adapts a line from Satire 10. Clearly, Juvenal's Satires contained much that appealed to the Christian mind, much that could be assimilated to a Christian point of view, perhaps more than any other pagan text. This phenomenon continued in the medieval period. Juvenal's poems were imitated and echoed by poets, e.g. by Joseph of Exeter (late twelfth century), and were used as a source of epigrams and examples by writers of prose, e.g. by William of Malmesbury and Geoffrey of Monmouth. Juvenal was also widely used in anthologies and was a standard feature of the student curriculum.[73] Thus Chaucer (?1340–1400) presents him as a sage and Erasmus (?1466–1536) culls numerous epigrams from him.

From the start of the Renaissance onwards Juvenal is a source of inspiration for all kinds of poets. In Italy, Petrarch (1304–74) owned a manuscript of Juvenal and knew the Satires well and Boccaccio (1313–75) imitated the sixth Satire. In England John Skelton (c. 1460–1529) playfully attributes his attack on Cardinal Wolsey to Juvenal; in France the blunt satires of Régnier (1573–1613) include numerous adaptations from Juvenal; and in Spain Quevedo (1580–1645) writes *Moral Sonnets* which include close adaptations of passages from the Satires. In the late sixteenth–early seventeenth centuries a group of English satirists reworked their classical models, Horace, Persius and Juvenal, and produced a blend of vigour and violence reminiscent of the indignation of Juvenal's early Satires in particular. These included John Marston (1575–1634), Joseph Hall (1574–1656), the author of the anonymous *Whipper Pamphlets* (1601) and John Donne (1573–1631). Juvenal was also a source of inspiration to dramatists, notably Ben Jonson (1573–1637), Molière (1622–73) and Corneille (1606–84).

But it was during the seventeenth and eighteenth centuries that Juvenal reached his zenith of influence. The first English translation of the Satires, that of Stapylton, appeared in 1647; that of Holyday was published in 1673; and Dryden's famous version in 1693. Satires 1, 3,

---

[73] On Juvenal in medieval culture see Highet (1954) 197–203.

6, 7, 8, 13, 14 and above all 10 were especially admired and imitated. In his early satires Boileau (1636–1711) followed Juvenal's biting style in his condemnation of life in Paris. Dryden (1631–1700) reflects the vigour of Juvenal in his original satires as well as his translations. Alexander Pope (1688–1744), despite his explicit debts to Horace, reworks Juvenal's indignation. And Samuel Johnson's (1709–84) versions of Satires 3 and 10, entitled respectively *London* and *The Vanity of Human Wishes*, are well known in their own right.

In the eighteenth century Juvenal was enlisted in various causes by poets and writers who identified with his attacks upon the corruption of the nobility. Most notable is Byron (1788–1824), who opens his *English Bards and Scotch Reviewers* with the indignant questions of the opening of Juvenal's first Satire. In the nineteenth century, Flaubert (1821–80), Baudelaire (1821–67) and Hugo (1802–85) all admired and imitated Juvenal's grand, angry style. Juvenal has found few direct imitators in the twentieth century, chiefly because there are so many other outlets for satire that verse satire is unfashionable; yet the poems of Roy Campbell are indirect descendants. But it is in the form of brief, pithy quotations, lifted from their original contexts, that Juvenal survives, as he has for centuries. Words and phrases drawn originally from Juvenal which are still used in public discourse include *farrago* (1.86), *panem et circenses* (10.81), *crambe repetita* (7.154), *quis custodiet ipsos custodes?* (6.347–8) and, most famous and most frequently cited, *mens sana in corpore sano* (10.356). Of course, he is appropriated for different purposes by different writers, speakers and thinkers, who are usually oblivious of the original context. But, more than most classical authors, Juvenal still lives.

11. TEXT AND MANUSCRIPTS

Martial is the only one of his contemporaries to mention Juvenal. Whether or not this implies that his Satires were badly received is difficult to say. From then he virtually disappears until the fourth century, when Lactantius (*c.* AD 240–320) quotes him by name (*Div. Inst.* 3.29 = *PL* VI 443B). He is cited more than seventy times in Servius' commentaries on Virgil and at some time between 352 and 399 the Satires were edited and published with a commentary. By the end of the fourth century he was very popular, as indicated by the imitations by Ausonius (d. *c.* AD 395) and others. The historian Ammianus reports that at the end of the fourth century he was read by people who read no other poetry (Amm. Marc. 28.4.14).[74] Thereafter his survival was not in jeopardy.[75] The Satires were present in the library of Charlemagne which was established during the ninth century and, together with the Satires of Persius, MSS circulated widely. More than five hundred MSS of Juvenal survive. The first printed edition appeared in the late 1460s in Rome and in 1486 Valla's transcription of the commentary of 'Probus grammaticus' was published in Venice. Many more editions of the Satires followed during the next hundred years but it was not until 1585 that Pithou published the text based on the superior Pithoeanus MS (P below).

As early as the fourth century, a number of spurious lines were present in the text and therefore persisted in the later MSS which form the majority in the transmission of Juvenal (Φ). Those MSS cannot easily be organised into a stemma (family tree) because of the amount of cross-copying (contamination) that has occurred over the centuries. A much smaller group of MSS and fragments are freer from interpolation, though corrupt in many other ways. Of these the most important is P (Montpellier medical school 125), written at Lorsch in the ninth century. Between them these sources provide a broad basis for establishing the text.

After Pithou's publication of P in the sixteenth century, the next landmarks were Ruperti's commentary of 1801 and Jahn's 1851 text, based upon the rediscovered P. Two events called the authority of P into doubt. In 1859 Ribbeck labelled about one-third of the transmitted text as spurious, thus provoking closer scrutiny. In 1899 an Oxford undergraduate discovered thirty-four lines of Satire 6 in a MS of the eleventh century in the Bodleian Library which do not survive in any other existing MS. But most scholars, including Bücheler (1886, 1893) and Friedländer (1895), continued to accept the transmitted text and to accept the authority of P implicitly. In response to this, Housman in the Preface to his magisterial edition (1905, second

---

[74] Amm. Marc. 28.4.14 *quidam detestantes ut uenena doctrinas, Iuuenalem et Marium Maximum curatiore studio legunt, nulla uolumina praeter haec in profundo otio contrectantes.*

[75] See Highet (1954) 180–90 on Juvenal in the late empire and dark ages.

edition 1931) explicated the issues facing editors of Juvenal (and of other Latin texts) in typically trenchant form. The central decision is the balance between P and Φ: the reading of P may be corrupt but that of Φ may be an interpolation. Another issue is the identification of spurious lines, some of which are present even in the P-class of MSS. It may be rash to say that a consensus seems to have arisen since Housman's edition; but Knoche's text (1950), based on his full collation of all the important MSS, the Oxford Classical Text of W.V. Clausen (1959, revised 1992) and the recent editions of E. Courtney (Edizioni dell'Ateneo, Rome 1984) and J.R.C. Martyn (Hakkert, Amsterdam 1987) show few significant differences except in matters of punctuation. Accordingly, in this edition, the text of Clausen's OCT is reproduced, by permission of Oxford University Press, with the differences noted below. For fuller accounts of texts and transmission see the article 'Juvenal' by R.J. Tarrant in *Texts and transmission*, ed. L.D. Reynolds (Oxford, 1983), 200–3, and the relevant sections of Clausen's OCT, Courtney's commentary and Martyn's edition.

Departures from Clausen's OCT

Clausen	This edition
Satire 1	
14	*bracket line*
29	*bracket line*
31 urbis	Vrbis
111 urbem	Vrbem
147 *new paragraph*	*no break*
149 *no break*	*new paragraph after* stetit
153–3 ... simplicitas? "cuius	... simplicitas?' cuius
... an non?" pone ...	... an non? 'pone ...
	lacuna between 156 and 157 (thus Housman)
Satire 2	
17 inputo	imputo
45 uiros; faciunt peiora,	uiros; faciunt peiora:
53 luctantur,	luctantur
64 *new paragraph*	*no break*
65 *no break*	*paragraph after* Laronia?
82 *no break*	*new paragraph*

105–6	*bracket* summi ... campis
111 Cybeles et fracta	Cybeles est fracta
117 *no break*	*new paragraph*
126 urbis	Vrbis
162 urbe	Vrbe
163–5 et tamen ... tribuno.	'et tamen ... tribuno.'
167 urbem	Vrbem
168 indulsit	induerit (*Nisbet*)
168–9 amator. ... flagellum:	amator, ... flagellum.

Satire 3

4	*add to OCT apparatus* limen (*Nisbet*)
9 urbis	Vrbis
	lacuna between 9 and 10
12–16 *follow line 17*	*12–16 follow 20*
amicae (nunc ... Camenis),	amicae, nunc ... Camenis.
22 urbe	Vrbe
38 foricas, et cur non omnia?)	foricas – et cur non omnia? –
44 possum;	possum: (*Braund (1990) 504*)
52 honesti.	honesti:
61 urbem	Vrbem
93 melior	melior,
102	*add to OCT apparatus* ac dolet (*Schäublin*)
106 manus	manus,
109	*add to OCT apparatus* nil restat ab (*Martyn*)
116–18 Baream delator amicum	Baream, delator amicum,
164 *no break*	*new paragraph*
193 urbem	Vrbem
205	*add to OCT apparatus* sub eodem e marmore (*Matthias, Housman*); sub eo de marmore (*Valesius*)
214 urbis	Vrbis
217–18 Polycliti, haec	Polycliti aera, (*Housman*)
231	*add to OCT apparatus* lacernae *GU*, lacerti *Heinsius*, latebrae

235 urbe	Vrbe
236 morbi. raedarum	morbi: raedarum
241–3 dormiet intus; namque	dormiet intus (namque
. . . fenestra. ante tamen	. . . fenestra), ante tamen
260 uolgi	uulgo (*Eremita*)
285 lampas.	lampas:
305 rem:	rem,
307 pinus,	pinus:
321	*add to OCT apparatus* conpelle (*Bücheler*)

Satire 4

7–8 aedes [nemo malus . . . et idem]	aedes? nemo malus felix,
10 sacerdos?	sacerdos.
23–5 hoc tu succinctus . . . papyro? hoc pretio squamae?	hoc tu, . . . papyro, hoc pretio squamas? (*Dorleans*)
34 *no break*	*new paragraph*
37 *new paragraph*	*no break*
77 urbi	Vrbi
78–81 anne aliud tum praefecti? quorum . . . iustitia	(anne aliud tum praefecti, quorum . . . iustitia?)
79 quamquam	quippe (*Housman*)
106 inprobior	improbior
116	bracket
150 *no break*	*new paragraph*
151 urbi	Vrbi

Satire 5

14 inputat	imputat
15 inputat	imputat
66 [maxima . . . superbis.]	maxima . . . superbis:
82 asparagis	asparagis,
104 †glacie aspersus†	†glacie†
110–11 namque . . . gloria.	(namque . . . gloria).
138 tunc	tum
140 [iucundum . . . amicum.]	iucundum . . . amicum.

D. IVNII IVVENALIS
SATVRARVM LIBER PRIMVS

D. IVNII IVVENALIS
LIBER PRIMVS

SATVRA I

Semper ego auditor tantum? numquamne reponam
uexatus totiens rauci Theseide Cordi?
inpune ergo mihi recitauerit ille togatas,
hic elegos? inpune diem consumpserit ingens
Telephus aut summi plena iam margine libri   5
scriptus et in tergo necdum finitus Orestes?
nota magis nulli domus est sua quam mihi lucus
Martis et Aeoliis uicinum rupibus antrum
Vulcani; quid agant uenti, quas torqueat umbras
Aeacus, unde alius furtiuae deuehat aurum   10
pelliculae, quantas iaculetur Monychus ornos,
Frontonis platani conuolsaque marmora clamant
semper et adsiduo ruptae lectore columnae.
[expectes eadem a summo minimoque poeta.]
et nos ergo manum ferulae subduximus, et nos   15
consilium dedimus Sullae, priuatus ut altum
dormiret. stulta est clementia, cum tot ubique
uatibus occurras, periturae parcere chartae.
cur tamen hoc potius libeat decurrere campo,
per quem magnus equos Auruncae flexit alumnus,   20
si uacat ac placidi rationem admittitis, edam.
    cum tener uxorem ducat spado, Meuia Tuscum
figat aprum et nuda teneat uenabula mamma,
patricios omnis opibus cum prouocet unus
quo tondente grauis iuueni mihi barba sonabat,   25
cum pars Niliacae plebis, cum uerna Canopi
Crispinus Tyrias umero reuocante lacernas
uentilet aestiuum digitis sudantibus aurum
[nec sufferre queat maioris pondera gemmae,]

difficile est saturam non scribere. nam quis iniquae   30
tam patiens Vrbis, tam ferreus, ut teneat se,
causidici noua cum ueniat lectica Mathonis
plena ipso, post hunc magni delator amici
et cito rapturus de nobilitate comesa
quod superest, quem Massa timet, quem munere palpat   35
Carus et a trepido Thymele summissa Latino;
cum te summoueant qui testamenta merentur
noctibus, in caelum quos euehit optima summi
nunc uia processus, uetulae uesica beatae?
unciolam Proculeius habet, sed Gillo deuncem,   40
partes quisque suas ad mensuram inguinis heres.
accipiat sane mercedem sanguinis et sic
palleat ut nudis pressit qui calcibus anguem
aut Lugudunensem rhetor dicturus ad aram.
quid referam quanta siccum iecur ardeat ira,   45
cum populum gregibus comitum premit hic spoliator
pupilli prostantis et hic damnatus inani
iudicio? quid enim saluis infamia nummis?
exul ab octaua Marius bibit et fruitur dis
iratis, at tu uictrix, prouincia, ploras.   50
haec ego non credam Venusina digna lucerna?
haec ego non agitem? sed quid magis? Heracleas
aut Diomedeas aut mugitum labyrinthi
et mare percussum puero fabrumque uolantem,
cum leno accipiat moechi bona, si capiendi   55
ius nullum uxori, doctus spectare lacunar,
doctus et ad calicem uigilanti stertere naso;
cum fas esse putet curam sperare cohortis
qui bona donauit praesepibus et caret omni
maiorum censu, dum peruolat axe citato   60
Flaminiam puer Automedon? nam lora tenebat
ipse, lacernatae cum se iactaret amicae.
nonne libet medio ceras inplere capaces
quadriuio, cum iam sexta ceruice feratur

hinc atque inde patens ac nuda paene cathedra   65
et multum referens de Maecenate supino
signator falsi, qui se lautum atque beatum
exiguis tabulis et gemma fecerit uda?
occurrit matrona potens, quae molle Calenum
porrectura uiro miscet sitiente rubetam   70
instituitque rudes melior Lucusta propinquas
per famam et populum nigros efferre maritos.
aude aliquid breuibus Gyaris et carcere dignum,
si uis esse aliquid. probitas laudatur et alget;
criminibus debent hortos, praetoria, mensas,   75
argentum uetus et stantem extra pocula caprum.
quem patitur dormire nurus corruptor auarae,
quem sponsae turpes et praetextatus adulter?
si natura negat, facit indignatio uersum
qualemcumque potest, quales ego uel Cluuienus.   80
    ex quo Deucalion nimbis tollentibus aequor
nauigio montem ascendit sortesque poposcit
paulatimque anima caluerunt mollia saxa
et maribus nudas ostendit Pyrrha puellas,
quidquid agunt homines, uotum, timor, ira, uoluptas,   85
gaudia, discursus, nostri farrago libelli est.
et quando uberior uitiorum copia? quando
maior auaritiae patuit sinus? alea quando
hos animos? neque enim loculis comitantibus itur
ad casum tabulae, posita sed luditur arca.   90
proelia quanta illic dispensatore uidebis
armigero! simplexne furor sestertia centum
perdere et horrenti tunicam non reddere seruo?
quis totidem erexit uillas, quis fercula septem
secreto cenauit auus? nunc sportula primo   95
limine parua sedet turbae rapienda togatae.
ille tamen faciem prius inspicit et trepidat ne
suppositus uenias ac falso nomine poscas:
agnitus accipies. iubet a praecone uocari

ipsos Troiugenas, nam uexant limen et ipsi   100
nobiscum. 'da praetori, da deinde tribuno.'
sed libertinus prior est. 'prior' inquit 'ego adsum.
cur timeam dubitemue locum defendere, quamuis
natus ad Euphraten, molles quod in aure fenestrae
arguerint, licet ipse negem? sed quinque tabernae   105
quadringenta parant. quid confert purpura maior
optandum, si Laurenti custodit in agro
conductas Coruinus ouis, ego possideo plus
Pallante et Licinis?' expectent ergo tribuni,
uincant diuitiae, sacro ne cedat honori   110
nuper in hanc Vrbem pedibus qui uenerat albis,
quandoquidem inter nos sanctissima diuitiarum
maiestas, etsi funesta Pecunia templo
nondum habitat, nullas nummorum ereximus aras,
ut colitur Pax atque Fides, Victoria, Virtus   115
quaeque salutato crepitat Concordia nido.
sed cum summus honor finito conputet anno,
sportula quid referat, quantum rationibus addat,
quid facient comites quibus hinc toga, calceus hinc est
et panis fumusque domi? densissima centum   120
quadrantes lectica petit, sequiturque maritum
languida uel praegnas et circumducitur uxor.
hic petit absenti nota iam callidus arte
ostendens uacuam et clausam pro coniuge sellam.
'Galla mea est' inquit, 'citius dimitte. moraris?   125
profer, Galla, caput. noli uexare, quiescet.'
    ipse dies pulchro distinguitur ordine rerum:
sportula, deinde forum iurisque peritus Apollo
atque triumphales, inter quas ausus habere
nescio quis titulos Aegyptius atque Arabarches,   130
cuius ad effigiem non tantum meiere fas est.
uestibulis abeunt ueteres lassique clientes
uotaque deponunt, quamquam longissima cenae
spes homini; caulis miseris atque ignis emendus.

optima siluarum interea pelagique uorabit   135
rex horum uacuisque toris tantum ipse iacebit.
nam de tot pulchris et latis orbibus et tam
antiquis una comedunt patrimonia mensa.
nullus iam parasitus erit. sed quis ferat istas
luxuriae sordes? quanta est gula quae sibi totos   140
ponit apros, animal propter conuiuia natum!
poena tamen praesens, cum tu deponis amictus
turgidus et crudum pauonem in balnea portas.
hinc subitae mortes atque intestata senectus.
it noua nec tristis per cunctas fabula cenas;   145
ducitur iratis plaudendum funus amicis.
nil erit ulterius quod nostris moribus addat
posteritas, eadem facient cupientque minores,
omne in praecipiti uitium stetit.
                                        utere uelis,
totos pande sinus. dices hic forsitan 'unde   150
ingenium par materiae? unde illa priorum
scribendi quodcumque animo flagrante liberet
simplicitas?' cuius non audeo dicere nomen?
quid refert dictis ignoscat Mucius an non?
'pone Tigillinum, taeda lucebis in illa   155
qua stantes ardent qui fixo gutture fumant,

                  *   *   *

et latum media sulcum deducit harena.'
qui dedit ergo tribus patruis aconita, uehatur
pensilibus plumis atque illinc despiciat nos?
'cum ueniet contra, digito compesce labellum: 160
accusator erit qui uerbum dixerit "hic est."
securus licet Aenean Rutulumque ferocem
committas, nulli grauis est percussus Achilles
aut multum quaesitus Hylas urnamque secutus:
ense uelut stricto quotiens Lucilius ardens   165
infremuit, rubet auditor cui frigida mens est
criminibus, tacita sudant praecordia culpa.

inde ira et lacrimae. tecum prius ergo uoluta
haec animo ante tubas: galeatum sero duelli
paenitet.' experiar quid concedatur in illos   170
quorum Flaminia tegitur cinis atque Latina.

SATVRA II

Vltra Sauromatas fugere hinc libet et glacialem
Oceanum, quotiens aliquid de moribus audent
qui Curios simulant et Bacchanalia uiuunt.
indocti primum, quamquam plena omnia gypso
Chrysippi inuenias; nam perfectissimus horum,   5
si quis Aristotelen similem uel Pittacon emit
et iubet archetypos pluteum seruare Cleanthas.
frontis nulla fides; quis enim non uicus abundat
tristibus obscenis? castigas turpia, cum sis
inter Socraticos notissima fossa cinaedos?   10
hispida membra quidem et durae per bracchia saetae
promittunt atrocem animum, sed podice leui
caeduntur tumidae medico ridente mariscae.
rarus sermo illis et magna libido tacendi
atque supercilio breuior coma. uerius ergo   15
et magis ingenue Peribomius; hunc ego fatis
imputo, qui uultu morbum incessuque fatetur.
horum simplicitas miserabilis, his furor ipse
dat ueniam; sed peiiores, qui talia uerbis
Herculis inuadunt et de uirtute locuti   20
clunem agitant. 'ego te ceuentem, Sexte, uerebor?'
infamis Varillus ait, 'quo deterior te?'
loripedem rectus derideat, Aethiopem albus.
quis tulerit Gracchos de seditione querentes?
quis caelum terris non misceat et mare caelo   25
si fur displiceat Verri, homicida Miloni,
Clodius accuset moechos, Catilina Cethegum,
in tabulam Sullae si dicant discipuli tres?

qualis erat nuper tragico pollutus adulter
concubitu, qui tunc leges reuocabat amaras   30
omnibus atque ipsis Veneri Martique timendas,
cum tot abortiuis fecundam Iulia uuluam
solueret et patruo similes effunderet offas.
nonne igitur iure ac merito uitia ultima fictos
contemnunt Scauros et castigata remordent?   35
    non tulit ex illis toruum Laronia quendam
clamantem totiens 'ubi nunc, lex Iulia, dormis?'
atque ita subridens: 'felicia tempora, quae te
moribus opponunt. habeat iam Roma pudorem:
tertius e caelo cecidit Cato. sed tamen unde   40
haec emis, hirsuto spirant opobalsama collo
quae tibi? ne pudeat dominum monstrare tabernae.
quod si uexantur leges ac iura, citari
ante omnes debet Scantinia. respice primum
et scrutare uiros; faciunt peiora: sed illos   45
defendit numerus iunctaeque umbone phalanges.
magna inter molles concordia. non erit ullum
exemplum in nostro tam detestabile sexu.
Tedia non lambit Cluuiam nec Flora Catullam:
Hispo subit iuuenes et morbo pallet utroque.   50
numquid nos agimus causas, ciuilia iura
nouimus aut ullo strepitu fora uestra mouemus?
luctantur paucae, comedunt colyphia paucae.
uos lanam trahitis calathisque peracta refertis
uellera, uos tenui praegnantem stamine fusum   55
Penelope melius, leuius torquetis Arachne,
horrida quale facit residens in codice paelex.
notum est cur solo tabulas inpleuerit Hister
liberto, dederit uiuus cur multa puellae.
diues erit magno quae dormit tertia lecto.   60
tu nube atque tace: donant arcana cylindros.
de nobis post haec tristis sententia fertur?
dat ueniam coruis, uexat censura columbas.'

fugerunt trepidi uera ac manifesta canentem
Stoicidae; quid enim falsi Laronia?

                       sed quid   65
non facient alii, cum tu multicia sumas,
Cretice, et hanc uestem populo mirante perores
in Proculas et Pollittas? est moecha Fabulla;
damnetur, si uis, etiam Carfinia: talem
non sumet damnata togam. 'sed Iulius ardet,   70
aestuo.' nudus agas: minus est insania turpis.
en habitum quo te leges ac iura ferentem
uulneribus crudis populus modo uictor et illud
montanum positis audiret uulgus aratris.
quid non proclames, in corpore iudicis ista   75
si uideas? quaero an deceant multicia testem.
acer et indomitus libertatisque magister,
Cretice, perluces. dedit hanc contagio labem
et dabit in plures, sicut grex totus in agris
unius scabie cadit et porrigine porci   80
uuaque conspecta liuorem ducit ab uua.
    foedius hoc aliquid quandoque audebis amictu;
nemo repente fuit turpissimus. accipient te
paulatim qui longa domi redimicula sumunt
frontibus et toto posuere monilia collo   85
atque bonam tenerae placant abdomine porcae
et magno cratere deam. sed more sinistro
exagitata procul non intrat femina limen:
solis ara deae maribus patet. 'ite, profanae,'
clamatur, 'nullo gemit hic tibicina cornu.'   90
talia secreta coluerunt orgia taeda
Cecropiam soliti Baptae lassare Cotyton.
ille supercilium madida fuligine tinctum
obliqua producit acu pingitque trementes
attollens oculos; uitreo bibit ille priapo   95
reticulumque comis auratum ingentibus implet
caerulea indutus scutulata aut galbina rasa

et per Iunonem domini iurante ministro;
ille tenet speculum, pathici gestamen Othonis,
Actoris Aurunci spolium, quo se ille uidebat   100
armatum, cum iam tolli uexilla iuberet.
res memoranda nouis annalibus atque recenti
historia, speculum ciuilis sarcina belli.
nimirum summi ducis est occidere Galbam
et curare cutem, [summi constantia ciuis   105
Bebriaci campis] solium adfectare Palati
et pressum in faciem digitis extendere panem,
quod nec in Assyrio pharetrata Sameramis orbe
maesta nec Actiaca fecit Cleopatra carina.
hic nullus uerbis pudor aut reuerentia mensae,   110
hic turpis Cybeles est fracta uoce loquendi
libertas et crine senex fanaticus albo
sacrorum antistes, rarum ac memorabile magni
gutturis exemplum conducendusque magister.
quid tamen expectant, Phrygio quos tempus erat iam   115
more superuacuam cultris abrumpere carnem?
   quadringenta dedit Gracchus sestertia dotem
cornicini, siue hic recto cantauerat aere;
signatae tabulae, dictum 'feliciter,' ingens
cena sedet, gremio iacuit noua nupta mariti.   120
o proceres, censore opus est an haruspice nobis?
scilicet horreres maioraque monstra putares,
si mulier uitulum uel si bos ederet agnum?
segmenta et longos habitus et flammea sumit
arcano qui sacra ferens nutantia loro   125
sudauit clipeis ancilibus. o pater Vrbis,
unde nefas tantum Latiis pastoribus? unde
haec tetigit, Gradiue, tuos urtica nepotes?
traditur ecce uiro clarus genere atque opibus uir,
nec galeam quassas nec terram cuspide pulsas   130
nec quereris patri. uade ergo et cede seueri
iugeribus campi, quem neglegis. 'officium cras

primo sole mihi peragendum in ualle Quirini.'
quae causa officii? 'quid quaeris? nubit amicus
nec multos adhibet.' liceat modo uiuere, fient,   135
fient ista palam, cupient et in acta referri.
interea tormentum ingens nubentibus haeret
quod nequeant parere et partu retinere maritos.
sed melius, quod nil animis in corpora iuris
natura indulget: steriles moriuntur, et illis   140
turgida non prodest condita pyxide Lyde,
nec prodest agili palmas praebere luperco.
uicit et hoc monstrum tunicati fuscina Gracchi,
lustrauitque fuga mediam gladiator harenam
et Capitolinis generosior et Marcellis   145
et Catuli Paulique minoribus et Fabiis et
omnibus ad podium spectantibus, his licet ipsum
admoueas cuius tunc munere retia misit.

    esse aliquos manes et subterranea regna,
Cocytum et Stygio ranas in gurgite nigras,   150
atque una transire uadum tot milia cumba
nec pueri credunt, nisi qui nondum aere lauantur.
sed tu uera puta: Curius quid sentit et ambo
Scipiadae, quid Fabricius manesque Camilli,
quid Cremerae legio et Cannis consumpta iuuentus,   155
tot bellorum animae, quotiens hinc talis ad illos
umbra uenit? cuperent lustrari, si qua darentur
sulpura cum taedis et si foret umida laurus.
illic heu miseri traducimur. arma quidem ultra
litora Iuuernae promouimus et modo captas   160
Orcadas ac minima contentos nocte Britannos,
sed quae nunc populi fiunt uictoris in Vrbe
non faciunt illi quos uicimus. 'et tamen unus
Armenius Zalaces cunctis narratur ephebis
mollior ardenti sese indulsisse tribuno.'   165
aspice quid faciant commercia: uenerat obses,
hic fiunt homines. nam si mora longior Vrbem

induerit pueris, non umquam derit amator,
mittentur bracae, cultelli, frena, flagellum.
sic praetextatos referunt Artaxata mores.   170

SATVRA III

Quamuis digressu ueteris confusus amici
laudo tamen, uacuis quod sedem figere Cumis
destinet atque unum ciuem donare Sibyllae.
ianua Baiarum est et gratum litus amoeni
secessus. ego uel Prochytam praepono Suburae;   5
nam quid tam miserum, tam solum uidimus, ut non
deterius credas horrere incendia, lapsus
tectorum adsiduos ac mille pericula saeuae
Vrbis et Augusto recitantes mense poetas?
           *   *   *
sed dum tota domus raeda componitur una,   10
substitit ad ueteres arcus madidamque Capenam.   11
in uallem Egeriae descendimus et speluncas   17
dissimiles ueris. quanto praesentius esset
numen aquis, uiridi si margine cluderet undas
herba nec ingenuum uiolarent marmora tofum.   20
hic, ubi nocturnae Numa constituebat amicae,   12
nunc sacri fontis nemus et delubra locantur
Iudaeis, quorum cophinus fenumque supellex;
omnis enim populo mercedem pendere iussa est   15
arbor et eiectis mendicat silua Camenis.   16
    hic tunc Vmbricius 'quando artibus' inquit 'honestis   21
nullus in Vrbe locus, nulla emolumenta laborum,
res hodie minor et here quam fuit atque eadem cras
deteret exiguis aliquid, proponimus illuc
ire, fatigatas ubi Daedalus exuit alas,   25
dum noua canities, dum prima et recta senectus,
dum superest Lachesi quod torqueat et pedibus me
porto meis nullo dextram subeunte bacillo.

cedamus patria. uiuant Artorius istic
et Catulus, maneant qui nigrum in candida uertunt,   30
quis facile est aedem conducere, flumina, portus,
siccandam eluuiem, portandum ad busta cadauer,
et praebere caput domina uenale sub hasta.
quondam hi cornicines et municipalis harenae
perpetui comites notaeque per oppida buccae   35
munera nunc edunt et, uerso pollice uulgus
cum iubet, occidunt populariter; inde reuersi
conducunt foricas – et cur non omnia? – cum sint
quales ex humili magna ad fastigia rerum
extollit quotiens uoluit Fortuna iocari.   40
quid Romae faciam? mentiri nescio; librum,
si malus est, nequeo laudare et poscere; motus
astrorum ignoro; funus promittere patris
nec uolo nec possum: ranarum uiscera numquam
inspexi; ferre ad nuptam quae mittit adulter,   45
quae mandat, norunt alii; me nemo ministro
fur erit, atque ideo nulli comes exeo tamquam
mancus et extinctae corpus non utile dextrae.
quis nunc diligitur nisi conscius et cui feruens
aestuat occultis animus semperque tacendis?   50
nil tibi se debere putat, nil conferet umquam,
participem qui te secreti fecit honesti:
carus erit Verri qui Verrem tempore quo uult
accusare potest. tanti tibi non sit opaci
omnis harena Tagi quodque in mare uoluitur aurum,   55
ut somno careas ponendaque praemia sumas
tristis et a magno semper timearis amico.
   quae nunc diuitibus gens acceptissima nostris
et quos praecipue fugiam, properabo fateri,
nec pudor obstabit. non possum ferre, Quirites,   60
Graecam Vrbem. quamuis quota portio faecis Achaei?
iam pridem Syrus in Tiberim defluxit Orontes
et linguam et mores et cum tibicine chordas

obliquas nec non gentilia tympana secum
uexit et ad circum iussas prostare puellas.   65
ite, quibus grata est picta lupa barbara mitra.
rusticus ille tuus sumit trechedipna, Quirine,
et ceromatico fert niceteria collo.
hic alta Sicyone, ast hic Amydone relicta,
hic Andro, ille Samo, hic Trallibus aut Alabandis,   70
Esquilias dictumque petunt a uimine collem,
uiscera magnarum domuum dominique futuri.
ingenium uelox, audacia perdita, sermo
promptus et Isaeo torrentior. ede quid illum
esse putes. quemuis hominem secum attulit ad nos: 75
grammaticus, rhetor, geometres, pictor, aliptes,
augur, schoenobates, medicus, magus, omnia nouit
Graeculus esuriens: in caelum iusseris ibit.
in summa non Maurus erat neque Sarmata nec Thrax
qui sumpsit pinnas, mediis sed natus Athenis.   80
horum ego non fugiam conchylia? me prior ille
signabit fultusque toro meliore recumbet,
aduectus Romam quo pruna et cottana uento?
usque adeo nihil est quod nostra infantia caelum
hausit Auentini baca nutrita Sabina?   85
quid quod adulandi gens prudentissima laudat
sermonem indocti, faciem deformis amici,
et longum inualidi collum ceruicibus aequat
Herculis Antaeum procul a tellure tenentis,
miratur uocem angustam, qua deterius nec   90
ille sonat quo mordetur gallina marito?
haec eadem licet et nobis laudare, sed illis
creditur. an melior, cum Thaida sustinet aut cum
uxorem comoedus agit uel Dorida nullo
cultam palliolo? mulier nempe ipsa uidetur,   95
non persona, loqui: uacua et plana omnia dicas
infra uentriculum et tenui distantia rima.
nec tamen Antiochus nec erit mirabilis illic

aut Stratocles aut cum molli Demetrius Haemo:
natio comoeda est. rides, maiore cachinno   100
concutitur; flet, si lacrimas conspexit amici,
nec dolet; igniculum brumae si tempore poscas,
accipit endromidem; si dixeris "aestuo," sudat.
non sumus ergo pares: melior, qui semper et omni
nocte dieque potest aliena sumere uultum   105
a facie, iactare manus, laudare paratus,
si bene ructauit, si rectum minxit amicus,
si trulla inuerso crepitum dedit aurea fundo.
praeterea sanctum nihil †aut† ab inguine tutum,
non matrona laris, non filia uirgo, nec ipse   110
sponsus leuis adhuc, non filius ante pudicus.
horum si nihil est, auiam resupinat amici.
[scire uolunt secreta domus atque inde timeri.]
et quoniam coepit Graecorum mentio, transi
gymnasia atque audi facinus maioris abollae.   115
Stoicus occidit Baream, delator amicum,
discipulumque senex ripa nutritus in illa
ad quam Gorgonei delapsa est pinna caballi.
non est Romano cuiquam locus hic, ubi regnat
Protogenes aliquis uel Diphilus aut Hermarchus   120
qui gentis uitio numquam partitur amicum,
solus habet. nam cum facilem stillauit in aurem
exiguum de naturae patriaeque ueneno,
limine summoueor, perierunt tempora longi
seruitii; nusquam minor est iactura clientis.   125
   quod porro officium, ne nobis blandiar, aut quod
pauperis hic meritum, si curet nocte togatus
currere, cum praetor lictorem inpellat et ire
praecipitem iubeat dudum uigilantibus orbis,
ne prior Albinam et Modiam collega salutet?   130
diuitis hic seruo cludit latus ingenuorum
filius; alter enim quantum in legione tribuni
accipiunt donat Caluinae uel Catienae,

ut semel aut iterum super illam palpitet; at tu,
cum tibi uestiti facies scorti placet, haeres   135
et dubitas alta Chionen deducere sella.
da testem Romae tam sanctum quam fuit hospes
numinis Idaei, procedat uel Numa uel qui
seruauit trepidam flagranti ex aede Mineruam:
protinus ad censum, de moribus ultima fiet   140
quaestio. "quot pascit seruos? quot possidet agri
iugera? quam multa magnaque paropside cenat?"
quantum quisque sua nummorum seruat in arca,
tantum habet et fidei. iures licet et Samothracum
et nostrorum aras, contemnere fulmina pauper   145
creditur atque deos dis ignoscentibus ipsis.
quid quod materiam praebet causasque iocorum
omnibus hic idem, si foeda et scissa lacerna,
si toga sordidula est et rupta calceus alter
pelle patet, uel si consuto uolnere crassum   150
atque recens linum ostendit non una cicatrix?
nil habet infelix paupertas durius in se
quam quod ridiculos homines facit. "exeat" inquit,
"si pudor est, et de puluino surgat equestri,
cuius res legi non sufficit, et sedeant hic   155
lenonum pueri quocumque ex fornice nati,
hic plaudat nitidus praeconis filius inter
pinnirapi cultos iuuenes iuuenesque lanistae."
sic libitum uano, qui nos distinxit, Othoni.
quis gener hic placuit censu minor atque puellae   160
sarcinulis inpar? quis pauper scribitur heres?
quando in consilio est aedilibus? agmine facto
debuerant olim tenues migrasse Quirites.
    haut facile emergunt quorum uirtutibus obstat
res angusta domi, sed Romae durior illis   165
conatus: magno hospitium miserabile, magno
seruorum uentres, et frugi cenula magno.
fictilibus cenare pudet, quod turpe negabis

translatus subito ad Marsos mensamque Sabellam
contentusque illic veneto duroque cucullo.   170
pars magna Italiae est, si uerum admittimus, in qua
nemo togam sumit nisi mortuus. ipsa dierum
festorum herboso colitur si quando theatro
maiestas tandemque redit ad pulpita notum
exodiurn, cum personae pallentis hiatum   175
in gremio matris formidat rusticus infans,
aequales habitus illic similesque uidebis
orchestram et populum; clari uelamen honoris
sufficiunt tunicae summis aedilibus albae.
hic ultra uires habitus nitor, hic aliquid plus   180
quam satis est interdum aliena sumitur arca.
commune id uitium est: hic uiuimus ambitiosa
paupertate omnes. quid te moror? omnia Romae
cum pretio. quid das, ut Cossum aliquando salutes,
ut te respiciat clauso Veiiento labello?   185
ille metit barbam, crinem hic deponit amati;
plena domus libis uenalibus: accipe et istud
fermentum tibi habe. praestare tributa clientes
cogimur et cultis augere peculia seruis.
    quis timet aut timuit gelida Praeneste ruinam   190
aut positis nemorosa inter iuga Volsiniis aut
simplicibus Gabiis aut proni Tiburis arce?
nos Vrbem colimus tenui tibicine fultam
magna parte sui; nam sic labentibus obstat
uilicus et, ueteris rimae cum texit hiatum,   195
securos pendente iubet dormire ruina.
uiuendum est illic, ubi nulla incendia, nulli
nocte metus. iam poscit aquam, iam friuola transfert
Vcalegon, tabulata tibi iam tertia fumant:
tu nescis; nam si gradibus trepidatur ab imis,   200
ultimus ardebit quem tegula sola tuetur
a pluuia, molles ubi reddunt oua columbae.
lectus erat Cordo Procula minor. urceoli sex

ornamentum abaci, nec non et paruulus infra
cantharus et recubans sub eodem marmore Chiron,   205
iamque uetus Graecos seruabat cista libellos
et diuina opici rodebant carmina mures.
nil habuit Cordus, quis enim negat? et tamen illud
perdidit infelix totum nihil. ultimus autem
aerumnae cumulus, quod nudum et frusta rogantem   210
nemo cibo, nemo hospitio tectoque iuuabit.
si magna Asturici cecidit domus, horrida mater,
pullati proceres, differt uadimonia praetor.
tum gemimus casus Vrbis, tunc odimus ignem.
ardet adhuc, et iam accurrit qui marmora donet,   215
conferat inpensas; hic nuda et candida signa,
hic aliquid praeclarum Euphranoris et Polycliti
aera, Asianorum uetera ornamenta deorum,
hic libros dabit et forulos mediamque Mineruam,
hic modium argenti. meliora ac plura reponit   220
Persicus orborum lautissimus et merito iam
suspectus tamquam ipse suas incenderit aedes.
si potes auelli circensibus, optima Sorae
aut Fabrateriae domus aut Frusinone paratur
quanti nunc tenebras unum conducis in annum.   225
hortulus hic puteusque breuis nec reste mouendus
in tenuis plantas facili diffunditur haustu.
uiue bidentis amans et culti uilicus horti
unde epulum possis centum dare Pythagoreis.
est aliquid, quocumque loco, quocumque recessu,   230
unius sese dominum fecisse lacertae.
    plurimus hic aeger moritur uigilando (sed ipsum
languorem peperit cibus inperfectus et haerens
ardenti stomacho); nam quae meritoria somnum
admittunt? magnis opibus dormitur in Vrbe.   235
inde caput morbi: raedarum transitus arto
uicorum in flexu et stantis conuicia mandrae
eripient somnum Druso uitulisque marinis.

si uocat officium, turba cedente uehetur
diues et ingenti curret super ora Liburna   240
atque obiter leget aut scribet uel dormiet intus
(namque facit somnum clausa lectica fenestra)
ante tamen ueniet: nobis properantibus obstat
unda prior, magno populus premit agmine lumbos
qui sequitur; ferit hic cubito, ferit assere duro   245
alter, at hic tignum capiti incutit, ille metretam.
pinguia crura luto, planta mox undique magna
calcor, et in digito clauus mihi militis haeret.
nonne uides quanto celebretur sportula fumo?
centum conuiuae, sequitur sua quemque culina.   250
Corbulo uix ferret tot uasa ingentia, tot res
inpositas capiti, quas recto uertice portat
seruulus infelix et cursu uentilat ignem.
scinduntur tunicae sartae modo, longa coruscat
serraco ueniente abies, atque altera pinum   255
plaustra uehunt; nutant alte populoque minantur.
nam si procubuit qui saxa Ligustica portat
axis et euersum fudit super agmina montem,
quid superest de corporibus? quis membra, quis ossa
inuenit? obtritum uulgo perit omne cadauer   260
more animae. domus interea secura patellas
iam lauat et bucca foculum excitat et sonat unctis
striglibus et pleno componit lintea guto.
haec inter pueros uarie properantur, at ille
iam sedet in ripa taetrumque nouicius horret   265
porthmea nec sperat caenosi gurgitis alnum
infelix nec habet quem porrigat ore trientem.
    respice nunc alia ac diuersa pericula noctis:
quod spatium tectis sublimibus unde cerebrum
testa ferit, quotiens rimosa et curta fenestris   270
uasa cadant, quanto percussum pondere signent
et laedant silicem. possis ignauus haberi
et subiti casus inprouidus, ad cenam si

intestatus eas: adeo tot fata, quot illa
nocte patent uigiles te praetereunte fenestrae.   275
ergo optes uotumque feras miserabile tecum,
ut sint contentae patulas defundere pelues.
ebrius ac petulans, qui nullum forte cecidit,
dat poenas, noctem patitur lugentis amicum
Pelidae, cubat in faciem, mox deinde supinus: 280
[ergo non aliter poterit dormire; quibusdam]
somnum rixa facit. sed quamuis inprobus annis
atque mero feruens cauet hunc quem coccina laena
uitari iubet et comitum longissimus ordo,
multum praeterea flammarum et aenea lampas: 285
me, quem luna solet deducere uel breue lumen
candelae, cuius dispenso et tempero filum,
contemnit. miserae cognosce prohoemia rixae,
si rixa est, ubi tu pulsas, ego uapulo tantum.
stat contra starique iubet. parere necesse est;   290
nam quid agas, cum te furiosus cogat et idem
fortior? "unde uenis" exclamat, "cuius aceto,
cuius conche tumes? quis tecum sectile porrum
sutor et elixi ueruecis labra comedit?
nil mihi respondes? aut dic aut accipe calcem.   295
ede ubi consistas: in qua te quaero proseucha?"
dicere si temptes aliquid tacitusue recedas,
tantumdem est: feriunt pariter, uadimonia deinde
irati faciunt. libertas pauperis haec est:
pulsatus rogat et pugnis concisus adorat   300
ut liceat paucis cum dentibus inde reuerti.
nec tamen haec tantum metuas; nam qui spoliet te
non derit clausis domibus postquam omnis ubique
fixa catenatae siluit compago tabernae.
interdum et ferro subitus grassator agit rem,   305
armato quotiens tutae custode tenentur
et Pomptina palus et Gallinaria pinus:
sic inde huc omnes tamquam ad uiuaria currunt.

qua fornace graues, qua non incude catenae?
maximus in uinclis ferri modus, ut timeas ne   310
uomer deficiat, ne marra et sarcula desint.
felices proauorum atauos, felicia dicas
saecula quae quondam sub regibus atque tribunis
uiderunt uno contentam carcere Romam.
   his alias poteram et pluris subnectere causas,   315
sed iumenta uocant et sol inclinat. eundum est;
nam mihi commota iamdudum mulio uirga
adnuit. ergo uale nostri memor, et quotiens te
Roma tuo refici properantem reddet Aquino,
me quoque ad Heluinam Cererem uestramque Dianam   320
conuerte a Cumis. saturarum ego, ni pudet illas,
auditor gelidos ueniam caligatus in agros.'

SATVRA IV

Ecce iterum Crispinus, et est mihi saepe uocandus
ad partes, monstrum nulla uirtute redemptum
a uitiis, aegrae solaque libidine fortes
deliciae, uiduas tantum aspernatus adulter.
quid refert igitur, quantis iumenta fatiget   5
porticibus, quanta nemorum uectetur in umbra,
iugera quot uicina foro, quas emerit aedes?
nemo malus felix, minime corruptor et idem
incestus, cum quo nuper uittata iacebat
sanguine adhuc uiuo terram subitura sacerdos.   10
sed nunc de factis leuioribus. et tamen alter
si fecisset idem caderet sub iudice morum;
nam, quod turpe bonis Titio Seiioque, decebat
Crispinum. quid agas, cum dira et foedior omni
crimine persona est? mullum sex milibus emit,   15
aequantem sane paribus sestertia libris,
ut perhibent qui de magnis maiora locuntur.
consilium laudo artificis. si munere tanto

praecipuam in tabulis ceram senis abstulit orbi;
est ratio ulterior, magnae si misit amicae,   20
quae uehitur cluso latis specularibus antro.
nil tale expectes: emit sibi. multa uidemus
quae miser et frugi non fecit Apicius. hoc tu,
succinctus patria quondam, Crispine, papyro,
hoc pretio squamas? potuit fortasse minoris   25
piscator quam piscis emi; prouincia tanti
uendit agros, sed maiores Apulia uendit.
qualis tunc epulas ipsum gluttisse putamus
induperatorem, cum tot sestertia, partem
exiguam et modicae sumptam de margine cenae,   30
purpureus magni ructarit scurra Palati,
iam princeps equitum, magna qui uoce solebat
uendere municipes fracta de merce siluros?
    incipe Calliope. licet et considere: non est
cantandum, res uera agitur. narrate, puellae   35
Pierides, prosit mihi uos dixisse puellas.
cum iam semianimum laceraret Flauius orbem
ultimus et caluo seruiret Roma Neroni,
incidit Hadriaci spatium admirabile rhombi
ante domum Veneris, quam Dorica sustinet Ancon,   40
impleuitque sinus; neque enim minor haeserat illis
quos operit glacies Maeotica ruptaque tandem
solibus effundit torrentis ad ostia Ponti
desidia tardos et longo frigore pingues.
destinat hoc monstrum cumbae linique magister   45
pontifici summo. quis enim proponere talem
aut emere auderet, cum plena et litora multo
delatore forent? dispersi protinus algae
inquisitores agerent cum remige nudo,
non dubitaturi fugitiuum dicere piscem   50
depastumque diu uiuaria Caesaris, inde
elapsum ueterem ad dominum debere reuerti.
si quid Palfurio, si credimus Armillato,

quidquid conspicuum pulchrumque est aequore toto
res fisci est, ubicumque natat. donabitur ergo,   55
ne pereat. iam letifero cedente pruinis
autumno, iam quartanam sperantibus aegris,
stridebat deformis hiems praedamque recentem
seruabat; tamen hic properat, uelut urgueat auster.
utque lacus suberant, ubi quamquam diruta seruat   60
ignem Troianum et Vestam colit Alba minorem,
obstitit intranti miratrix turba parumper.
ut cessit, facili patuerunt cardine ualuae;
exclusi spectant admissa obsonia patres.
itur ad Atriden. tum Picens 'accipe' dixit   65
'priuatis maiora focis. genialis agatur
iste dies. propera stomachum laxare sagina
et tua seruatum consume in saecula rhombum.
ipse capi uoluit.' quid apertius? et tamen illi
surgebant cristae. nihil est quod credere de se   70
non possit cum laudatur dis aequa potestas.
sed derat pisci patinae mensura. uocantur
ergo in consilium proceres, quos oderat ille,
in quorum facie miserae magnaeque sedebat
pallor amicitiae. primus clamante Liburno   75
'currite, iam sedit' rapta properabat abolla
Pegasus, attonitae positus modo uilicus Vrbi.
(anne aliud tum praefecti, quorum optimus atque
interpres legum sanctissimus omnia, quippe
temporibus diris, tractanda putabat inermi   80
iustitia?) uenit et Crispi iucunda senectus,
cuius erant mores qualis facundia, mite
ingenium. maria ac terras populosque regenti
quis comes utilior, si clade et peste sub illa
saeuitiam damnare et honestum adferre liceret   85
consilium? sed quid uiolentius aure tyranni,
cum quo de pluuiis aut aestibus aut nimboso
uere locuturi fatum pendebat amici?

ille igitur numquam derexit bracchia contra
torrentem, nec ciuis erat qui libera posset   90
uerba animi proferre et uitam inpendere uero.
sic multas hiemes atque octogensima uidit
solstitia, his armis illa quoque tutus in aula.
proximus eiusdem properabat Acilius aeui
cum iuuene indigno quem mors tam saeua maneret   95
et domini gladiis tam festinata; sed olim
prodigio par est in nobilitate senectus,
unde fit ut malim fraterculus esse gigantis.
profuit ergo nihil misero quod comminus ursos
figebat Numidas Albana nudus harena   100
uenator. quis enim iam non intellegat artes
patricias? quis priscum illud miratur acumen,
Brute, tuum? facile est barbato inponere regi.
nec melior uultu quamuis ignobilis ibat
Rubrius, offensae ueteris reus atque tacendae,   105
et tamen improbior saturam scribente cinaedo.
Montani quoque uenter adest abdomine tardus,
et matutino sudans Crispinus amomo
quantum uix redolent duo funera, saeuior illo
Pompeius tenui iugulos aperire susurro,   110
et qui uulturibus seruabat uiscera Dacis
Fuscus marmorea meditatus proelia uilla,
et cum mortifero prudens Veiiento Catullo,
qui numquam uisae flagrabat amore puellae,
grande et conspicuum nostro quoque tempore monstrum,   115
[caecus adulator dirusque †a ponte† satelles,]
dignus Aricinos qui mendicaret ad axes
blandaque deuexae iactaret basia raedae.
nemo magis rhombum stupuit; nam plurima dixit
in laeuum conuersus, at illi dextra iacebat   120
belua. sic pugnas Cilicis laudabat et ictus
et pegma et pueros inde ad uelaria raptos.
non cedit Veiiento, sed ut fanaticus oestro

percussus, Bellona, tuo diuinat et 'ingens
omen habes' inquit 'magni clarique triumphi.   125
regem aliquem capies, aut de temone Britanno
excidet Aruiragus. peregrina est belua: cernis
erectas in terga sudes?' hoc defuit unum
Fabricio, patriam ut rhombi memoraret et annos.
'quidnam igitur censes? conciditur?' 'absit ab illo   130
dedecus hoc' Montanus ait, 'testa alta paretur
quae tenui muro spatiosum colligat orbem.
debetur magnus patinae subitusque Prometheus.
argillam atque rotam citius properate, sed ex hoc
tempore iam, Caesar, figuli tua castra sequantur.'   135
uicit digna uiro sententia. nouerat ille
luxuriam inperii ueterem noctesque Neronis
iam medias aliamque famem, cum pulmo Falerno
arderet. nulli maior fuit usus edendi
tempestate mea: Circeis nata forent an   140
Lucrinum ad saxum Rutupinoue edita fundo
ostrea callebat primo deprendere morsu,
et semel aspecti litus dicebat echini.
surgitur et misso proceres exire iubentur
consilio, quos Albanam dux magnus in arcem   145
traxerat attonitos et festinare coactos,
tamquam de Chattis aliquid toruisque Sygambris
dicturus, tamquam ex diuersis partibus orbis
anxia praecipiti uenisset epistula pinna.

atque utinam his potius nugis tota illa dedisset   150
tempora saeuitiae, claras quibus abstulit Vrbi
inlustresque animas inpune et uindice nullo.
sed periit postquam cerdonibus esse timendus
coeperat: hoc nocuit Lamiarum caede madenti.

SATVRA V

Si te propositi nondum pudet atque eadem est mens,
ut bona summa putes aliena uiuere quadra,

si potes illa pati quae nec Sarmentus iniquas
Caesaris ad mensas nec uilis Gabba tulisset,
quamuis iurato metuam tibi credere testi.   5
uentre nihil noui frugalius; hoc tamen ipsum
defecisse puta, quod inani sufficit aluo:
nulla crepido uacat? nusquam pons et tegetis pars
dimidia breuior? tantine iniuria cenae,
tam ieiuna fames, cum possit honestius illic   10
et tremere et sordes farris mordere canini?
   primo fige loco, quod tu discumbere iussus
mercedem solidam ueterum capis officiorum.
fructus amicitiae magnae cibus: imputat hunc rex,
et quamuis rarum tamen imputat. ergo duos post   15
si libuit menses neglectum adhibere clientem,
tertia ne uacuo cessaret culcita lecto,
'una simus' ait. uotorum summa. quid ultra
quaeris? habet Trebius propter quod rumpere somnum
debeat et ligulas dimittere, sollicitus ne   20
tota salutatrix iam turba peregerit orbem,
sideribus dubiis aut illo tempore quo se
frigida circumagunt pigri serraca Bootae.
   qualis cena tamen! uinum quod sucida nolit
lana pati: de conuiua Corybanta uidebis.   25
iurgia proludunt, sed mox et pocula torques
saucius et rubra deterges uulnera mappa,
inter uos quotiens libertorumque cohortem
pugna Saguntina feruet commissa lagona.
ipse capillato diffusum consule potat   30
calcatamque tenet bellis socialibus uuam.
cardiaco numquam cyathum missurus amico
cras bibet Albanis aliquid de montibus aut de
Setinis, cuius patriam titulumque senectus
deleuit multa ueteris fuligine testae,   35
quale coronati Thrasea Heluidiusque bibebant
Brutorum et Cassi natalibus. ipse capaces
Heliadum crustas et inaequales berullo

Virro tenet phialas: tibi non committitur aurum,
uel, si quando datur, custos adfixus ibidem,   40
qui numeret gemmas, ungues obseruet acutos.
da ueniam: praeclara illi laudatur iaspis.
nam Virro, ut multi, gemmas ad pocula transfert
a digitis, quas in uaginae fronte solebat
ponere zelotypo iuuenis praelatus Iarbae.   45
tu Beneuentani sutoris nomen habentem
siccabis calicem nasorum quattuor ac iam
quassatum et rupto poscentem sulpura uitro.
si stomachus domini feruet uinoque ciboque,
frigidior Geticis petitur decocta pruinis.   50
non eadem uobis poni modo uina querebar?
uos aliam potatis aquam. tibi pocula cursor
Gaetulus dabit aut nigri manus ossea Mauri
et cui per mediam nolis occurrere noctem,
cliuosae ueheris dum per monumenta Latinae.   55
flos Asiae ante ipsum, pretio maiore paratus
quam fuit et Tulli census pugnacis et Anci
et, ne te teneam, Romanorum omnia regum
friuola. quod cum ita sit, tu Gaetulum Ganymedem
respice, cum sities. nescit tot milibus emptus   60
pauperibus miscere puer, sed forma, sed aetas
digna supercilio. quando ad te peruenit ille?
quando rogatus adest calidae gelidaeque minister?
quippe indignatur ueteri parere clienti
quodque aliquid poscas et quod se stante recumbas.   65
maxima quaeque domus seruis est plena superbis:
ecce alius quanto porrexit murmure panem
uix fractum, solidae iam mucida frusta farinae,
quae genuinum agitent, non admittentia morsum.
sed tener et niueus mollique siligine fictus   70
seruatur domino. dextram cohibere memento;
salua sit artoptae reuerentia. finge tamen te
inprobulum, superest illic qui ponere cogat:

'uis tu consuetis, audax conuiua, canistris
impleri panisque tui nouisse colorem?'   75
'scilicet hoc fuerat, propter quod saepe relicta
coniuge per montem aduersum gelidasque cucurri
Esquilias, fremeret saeua cum grandine uernus
Iuppiter et, multo stillaret paenula nimbo.'

    aspice quam longo distinguat pectore lancem   80
quae fertur domino squilla, et quibus undique saepta
asparagis, qua despiciat conuiuia cauda,
dum uenit excelsi manibus sublata ministri.
sed tibi dimidio constrictus cammarus ouo
ponitur exigua feralis cena patella.   85
ipse Venafrano piscem perfundit, at hic qui
pallidus adfertur misero tibi caulis olebit
lanternam; illud enim uestris datur alueolis quod
canna Micipsarum prora subuexit acuta,
propter quod Romae cum Boccare nemo lauatur,   90
quod tutos etiam facit a serpentibus atris.
mullus erit domini, quem misit Corsica uel quem
Tauromenitanae rupes, quando omne peractum est
et iam defecit nostrum mare, dum gula saeuit,
retibus adsiduis penitus scrutante macello   95
proxima, nec patimur Tyrrhenum crescere piscem.
instruit ergo focum prouincia, sumitur illinc
quod captator emat Laenas, Aurelia uendat.
Virroni muraena datur, quae maxima uenit
gurgite de Siculo; nam dum se continet Auster,   100
dum sedet et siccat madidas in carcere pinnas,
contemnunt mediam temeraria lina Charybdim:
uos anguilla manet longae cognata colubrae
aut †glaciet aspersus maculis Tiberinus et ipse
uernula riparum, pinguis torrente cloaca   105
et solitus mediae cryptam penetrare Suburae.

    ipsi pauca uelim, facilem si praebeat aurem.
nemo petit, modicis quae mittebantur amicis

a Seneca, quae Piso bonus, quae Cotta solebat
largiri (namque et titulis et fascibus olim
maior habebatur donandi gloria). solum
poscimus ut cenes ciuiliter. hoc face et esto,
esto, ut nunc multi, diues tibi, pauper amicis.
anseris ante ipsum magni iecur, anseribus par
altilis, et flaui dignus ferro Meleagri
spumat aper. post hunc tradentur tubera, si uer
tunc erit et facient optata tonitrua cenas
maiores. 'tibi habe frumentum' Alledius inquit,
'o Libye, disiunge boues, dum tubera mittas.'
structorem interea, ne qua indignatio desit,
saltantem spectes et chironomunta uolanti
cultello, donec peragat dictata magistri
omnia; nec minimo sane discrimine refert
quo gestu lepores et quo gallina secetur.
duceris planta uelut ictus ab Hercule Cacus
et ponere foris, si quid temptaueris umquam
hiscere tamquam habeas tria nomina. quando propinat
Virro tibi sumitue tuis contacta labellis
pocula? quis uestrum temerarius usque adeo, quis
perditus, ut dicat regi 'bibe'? plurima sunt quae
non audent homines pertusa dicere laena.
quadringenta tibi si quis deus aut similis dis
et melior fatis donaret homuncio, quantus
ex nihilo, quantus fieres Virronis amicus!
'da Trebio, pone ad Trebium. uis, frater, ab ipsis
ilibus?' o nummi, uobis hunc praestat honorem,
uos estis frater. dominus tamen et domini rex
si uis tum fieri, nullus tibi paruulus aula
luserit Aeneas nec filia dulcior illo.
iucundum et carum sterilis facit uxor amicum.
sed tua nunc Mycale pariat licet et pueros tres
in gremium patris fundat semel, ipse loquaci
gaudebit nido, uiridem thoraca iubebit

110
115
120
125
130
135
140

adferri minimasque nuces assemque rogatum,
ad mensam quotiens parasitus uenerit infans.   145
   uilibus ancipites fungi ponentur amicis,
boletus domino, sed quales Claudius edit
ante illum uxoris, post quem nihil amplius edit.
Virro sibi et reliquis Virronibus illa iubebit
poma dari, quorum solo pascaris odore,   150
qualia perpetuus Phaeacum autumnus habebat,
credere quae possis subrepta sororibus Afris:
tu scabie frueris mali, quod in aggere rodit
qui tegitur parma et galea metuensque flagelli
discit ab hirsuta iaculum torquere capella.   155
   forsitan inpensae Virronem parcere credas.
hoc agit, ut doleas; nam quae comoedia, mimus
quis melior plorante gula? ergo omnia fiunt,
si nescis, ut per lacrimas effundere bilem
cogaris pressoque diu stridere molari.   160
tu tibi liber homo et regis conuiua uideris:
captum te nidore suae putat ille culinae,
nec male coniectat; quis enim tam nudus, ut illum
bis ferat, Etruscum puero si contigit aurum
uel nodus tantum et signum de paupere loro?   165
spes bene cenandi uos decipit. 'ecce dabit iam
semesum leporem atque aliquid de clunibus apri,
ad nos iam ueniet minor altilis.' inde parato
intactoque omnes et stricto pane tacetis.
ille sapit, qui te sic utitur. omnia ferre   170
si potes, et debes. pulsandum uertice raso
praebebis quandoque caput nec dura timebis
flagra pati, his epulis et tali dignus amico.

COMMENTARY

SATIRE 1

1–6 The speaker plunges straight into his self-justification, declaring that he will take revenge for all the recitations he has sat through in the past. Implicit in this *apologia* is a *recusatio*, a 'refusal' to tackle epic, in favour of satire. He begins with a series of four rhetorical questions, the first two introduced by the antithetical extremes *semper* and *numquam*; the second two by anaphora of *inpune* which reiterates *numquam* ... *reponam*. The increasing length of the questions conveys his vehemence.

1 ego auditor: supply *ero* or *sim*; the omission of the verb conveys indignation. *ego* indicates the speaker's self-centredness. He portrays himself as an *auditor* at a recitation (hence 3 *recitauerit* and 13 *lectore*), a regular social event in Rome ranging from the private dinner-party (Mart. 3.45, 11.52.16–18; J. 11.179–81) to grander affairs to which the educated public was invited (Plin. *Ep.* 1.13). The Romans tended to listen to 'literature' rather than simply read it as we do. **tantum** 'only'. This prepares us for his desire for revenge. **reponam** 'retaliate', literally 'repay (a debt)', with no object expressed here. For the idea of taking revenge for recitations, cf. Hor. *Ep.* 1.19.39 *ego nobilium scriptorum auditor et ultor*.

2 uexatus: the past participle has a concessive or causal force, 'though harassed' or 'for having been harassed' (Woodcock §92). **Theseide Cordi:** the poet Cordus is unknown to us and the name possibly fictitious. His poem is an epic about the Athenian hero Theseus (cf. Aeneas – *Aeneid*), a hackneyed subject; *totiens* and *rauci*, 'hoarse', imply that it is very long.

3–4 inpune ... recitauerit ... consumpserit ... : fut.perf.: 'shall he have got away scot-free with reciting ... with taking up ...'. **ergo:** on J.'s prosody see Introduction §8. **togatas:** i.e. *fabulae togatae*, comedies with a Roman setting, as opposed to *fabulae palliatae*, Latin comedies with a Greek setting, such as those of Plautus and Terence. **elegos:** the genre of Roman love elegy bloomed in the first century BC (Gallus, Tibullus, Propertius, Ovid), but elegies were still recited and written in J.'s time (Mart. 8.70.7; Plin. *Ep.* 6.15).

5–6 Telephus, Orestes: tragedies, taking their titles from their heroes; both were popular themes. At *Ars* 96 Horace uses Telephus to epitomise trite subjects. The length of these two plays is emphasised by the enjambment of *Telephus* and by the sheer length of the clause devoted to Orestes, in which *Orestes* is prepared for by the two past participles and postponed until the very end. This effect is accentuated by the framing of lines 5–6 by the two proper names, an example of J.'s verbal dexterity. **summi ... in tergo** 'Orestes, which, when the margin at the end of the roll is already full (abl. abs.), is written as well (*et*) on the back and is not yet finished'. The 'book' until the fourth century AD consisted of a papyrus roll attached to rods (*umbilici*) on which it was rolled. The margin mentioned here was the space normally left at the end of the text before the rod. The back was very seldom used for writing.

7–13 The mythological themes of epic are utterly familiar through constant repetition; cf. Virg. *Georg.* 3.4–8 *omnia iam uolgata*, Stat. *Theb.* 4.536–40 *quis ... nesciat?* The four indirect questions in lines 9–11 suggest by the variation of the question word (*quid, quas, unde* and *quantas*) and by their insistence that the speaker knows every possible theme of epic.

J. is apparently here attacking one particular work and author, the *Argonautica* of Valerius Flaccus: see below.

7–8 'Known better to none is his own home than (is known) to me ...'. A proverbial expression, cf. Cic. *Q.Fr.* 1.1.45 *cum iam tibi Asia sicut unicuique sua domus nota esse debeat.* **lucus | Martis:** the grove in Colchis where the Golden Fleece was kept.

8–9 Aeoliis uicinum rupibus antrum | Vulcani: the Aeolian islands (mod. Lipari islands), here referred to as 'rocks' or 'cliffs', lie to the north of Sicily; Vulcan's workshop ('cave') is placed by Virgil in one of these islands (*Aen.* 8.417–22). According to Valerius Flaccus, the Argonauts called at Vulcan's cave (*antra ... Vulcani* 2.335–6), but he locates it on Lemnos.

9 quid agant uenti 'what the winds are doing'. The storm at sea was a commonplace in epic into which poets often incorporated a description of the winds, e.g. Hom. *Od.* 5.291–332, Virg. *Aen.* 1.81–6, 131–41, Ov. *Met.* 11.474–569, Luc. 5.568–72 and especially 597–614, and not omitted by Valerius Flaccus (1.608–54). Aeolus, god of the winds, also had his home in the Lipari islands.

9–10 quas torqueat umbras | Aeacus 'what shades Aeacus is torturing': Aeacus is one of the three judges of the dead, along with Minos and Rhadamanthys (Plat. *Apol.* 41a, *Gorg.* 524a, 526c, Ov. *Ibis* 187–8, Sen. *Apoc.* 14–15). Curiously, there is no parallel to this scene of the punishments of the dead in Valerius Flaccus.

10–11 unde alius furtiuae deuehat aurum | pelliculae: loaded with disparaging implications. *alius*, 'the other chap', is Jason, leader of the Argonauts; *furtiuae . . . aurum pelliculae* is the object of his quest, the Golden Fleece: *pelliculae* 'little fleece' is a derogatory diminutive and *furtiuae* suggests theft.

11 quantas iaculetur Monychus ornos 'how huge are the ash trees Monychus tosses'. Monychus was one of the Centaurs (Luc. 6.388); the occasion evoked here is the battle of Lapiths and Centaurs (Ov. *Met.* 12.210–535), famous in art and painted on the Argo according to Valerius Flaccus (1.145–6).

12 Frontonis: a rich man who allows his house and gardens to be used by his friends and clients for poetry recitations. For this practice, cf. Mart. 4.6.4–5 *compositos metro Tibulli | in Stellae recitat domo libellos*, Plin. *Ep.* 8.12.2 *domum suam recitantibus praebet*; the practice is satirised at J. 7.40. Given that Book 1 of J.'s *Satires* was published probably during the second decade of the second century AD, this is possibly the Fronto of Mart. 1.55, consul in AD 96 and mentioned by Plin. *Ep.* 2.11 as a renowned orator: these details would certainly combine to produce a picture of an eminent man, not unlike Pliny himself (see Ferguson, *Prosopography*). Such men did not draw a clear line between patronage of the arts and their other spheres of patronage, such as politics, administration, legal affairs: see White (1978).

12–13 platani ... marmora ... columnae: all subjects of the verb *clamant*. Fronto's house is clearly luxurious even by Roman standards. The plane-tree provided shade, most welcome in the Italian heat: Plin. *Ep.* 1.3.1 speaks of shady plane-trees as a pleasant feature of a country villa; cf. Mart. 3.19 for a plane-grove with statues of wild animals. The marble referred to here may be statues (thus Hor. *Ep.* 1.6.17, Stat. *Silv.* 5.1.230, *CIL* XII 1357) or marble walls and pavements (thus Plin. *N.H.* 36.44ff. on marble in houses, J. 3.20, 6.430, 9.104, Ov. *Med. Fac.* 8, Sen. *Ep.* 86.6, 115.9): either would be a sign of conspicuous expenditure in a rich man's house. Either the statues of gods and heroes and muses are shrieking out in agony (*clamant*) from the torture (*conuolsa*) or the walls and pavements are reverberating to (*conuolsa*) and reechoing (*clamant*) the continual reciting (*adsiduo . . . lectore*). The house evidently boasts a colonnade, *peristyla* (on which see Vitr. *De arch.* 6.3.7). On luxurious buildings see Edwards (1993) 150–60.

conuolsa ... clamant ... ruptae: the speaker is characterised as an excitable man who readily exaggerates, with his striking, humorous and vivid picture of the grand house in a state of physical collapse, as if in an earthquake: hence *conuolsa* and *ruptae*. This is a satirical version of the effect of song as portrayed in pastoral, cf. Virg. *Georg.* 3.328 *cantu querulae rumpent arbusta cicadae*. For *clamant* in personification of the inanimate cf. Virg. *Ecl.* 6.10–11 *te nostrae, Vare, myricae, te nemus omne canet.*

13 semper: cf. *semper* 1: J.'s speaker tends to make sweeping generalisations. **ruptae lectore:** the reader is not the agent (that would require *a lectore*) but the instrument, which implies that he does not intend to break the columns; it is the reading which does the damage. There are similar cases of a person as an instrument at 1.54, 6.130; yet this is harsh.

14 All poets are the same. Dobree may have been correct to delete the line, as it simply summarises the sweeping condemnation of poets in the preceding lines. **expectes** 'you must expect' (hortative present subjunctive), addressing no particular person; for this unspecific 2nd person singular cf. *occurras* 18 below and often.

15–17 These lines indicate that J.'s speaker has received a proper Roman education, evoked by the punishments and exercises inflicted on Roman schoolboys: there is nothing to stop him becoming a poet too. Only boys of the élite and of social climbers received an education in rhetoric and literature. Girls usually received at most only an elementary education, the vast majority of the population little or none.

15 et nos 'I too', repeated in anaphora (at the beginning of its clause) for emphasis. *nos* and *ego* are interchangeable in poetry, cf. 3.84 *nostra infantia.* **manum ferulae subduximus** 'I have (in my time) withdrawn my hand from under the cane', cf. 8.77, 11.142, Petr. 98.1 *subducebat Giton ab ictu corpus.* The stem of the giant fennel, *ferula*, was used for canes. Corporal punishment in Roman schools is well attested, e.g. of Orbilius the 'Whacker' Hor. *Ep.* 2.1.70–1 *memini quae plagosum mihi paruo | Orbilium dictare*, Suet. *Gramm.* 9 quoting the poet Domitius Marsus *si quos Orbilius ferula scuticaque cecidit*; see Bonner (1977) 143–5.

16 consilium dedimus Sullae: after learning to read and write and after studying poetry with a focus on the classics, Roman school-boys progressed to rhetoric, usually the final stage of their education. This rhetorical training was designed to prepare them for public speaking in the Senate and in the law-courts. It consisted of two kinds of declamatory exercises: (1) the *suasoria*, 'persuasion', in which the pupil had to compose a speech delivered by a mythological or his-torical character or, as here, addressed to him (see below); (2) the *controuersia*, 'disputation' or 'debate', in which the pupils had to act as prosecutor or defending counsel in a fictitious lawsuit: the subject-matter of the *controuersiae* typically involved pirates and tyrants and magicians, and the pupil's task was to bring some novelty to his handling of his theme. Much of our evidence for the practice of declamation comes from the Elder Seneca's reminiscences of *Suasoriae* and *Controuersiae*. Here, the speaker claims to have delivered a *suasoria* addressed to Sulla the dictator, advising him to resign (*ut* is postponed until after *priuatus*).

L. Cornelius Sulla (138–78 BC) attained sole power in Rome by marching on the city in 88 BC and 'proscribing' his enemies (executing them and confiscating their property). After holding power for several years he retired, became a private citizen (*priuatus*) again and lived a quiet life (*altum dormiret*) until he died. Sulla was a popular theme for *suasoriae*, cf. Quint. *I.O.* 3.8.53.

16–17 altum | dormiret: the neuter *altum* is used adverbially. J.'s expression combines the idea of living a quiet life (*TLL dormio* 2032.36ff.; cf. 'to be inactive', Prop. 3.6.34) with the idea that those of humbler station enjoy deeper sleep (e.g. Hor. *Od.* 2.16.15 with Nisbet and Hubbard).

17–18 'No point ... in sparing paper (it's already doomed to destruction)' (Rudd), sc. by other 'bards'. For similarly facetious tone cf. 6.160 *uetus indulget senibus clementia porcis.* Parker (1983) points out that this is a 'fine sardonic perversion of an heroic commonplace' which begins at Hom. *Il.* 12.322–4, cf. Sall. *B.J.* 106.3 esp. *interiturae uitae parceret.*

18 uatibus: here sarcastic for 'poets'. Originally in early Latin, *uates* denoted a soothsayer; the Augustan poets, especially Horace and Propertius, seem to have been instrumental in elevating the word to mean 'bard' or even 'prophet' (see Nisbet and Hubbard on Hor. *Od.* 1.1.35); thus Tacitus in his *Dialogus* (probably written around AD 100, a decade or more before J.'s first *Satire*) writes *egregium poetam uel, si hoc honorificentius est, praeclarissimum uatem* (*Dial.* 9). For J.'s sarcasm here cf. Pers. *Sat.* 5.1 *uatibus hic mos est* . . . .   **occurras:** indefinite second person sing. involves the audience.   **periturae:** *pereo* is used as the passive of *perdo* 'waste'; cf. 4.56; and for *perdo* in a similar context cf. Mart. 13.1.3.

19-20 The main verb is *edam*, 'I shall explain/Let me explain' (1st person sing. of fut. indic. or pres. subj.), with indirect question *cur* . . . , attached to which is a relative clause (*campo per quem*); a conditional clause (*si* . . .) qualifies the main verb.

Now J.'s speaker indicates his chosen genre and introduces the self-justification for his choice, which occupies the remainder of the poem. The words *magnus* . . . *Auruncae* . . . *alumnus* indicate the satirist Lucilius and hence identify the chosen genre as satire. The words themselves are, however, an epic-style periphrasis (see Essay and Introduction §6(*c*)). C. Lucilius (?180 or ?160–102 BC), born at Suessa Aurunca in Campania, was regarded as the inventor of Roman satire and is depicted by later satirists as outspoken and aggressive (e.g. Hor. *Sat.* 1.10.3–4, 2.1.62–5; Pers. 1.114–5; J. 1.151–3, 165 *Lucilius ardens*). It was common practice for Roman writers to establish their choice of genre by reference to an eminent predecessor or the 'inventor' of the genre. The concept of genre was very important in Roman literature as it provided a framework for the author to work within: Roman literature was very conservative, backward-looking and traditional.

The metaphor in these lines, *decurrere campo* and *equos* . . . *flexit*, portrays Lucilius as an epic hero (see Introduction §6(*c*)), steering his chariot over the battlefield.

decurrere echoes Hor. *Sat.* 2.1.32, also of Lucilius, but in the different sense, 'turn to'.

21 si uacat: impersonal construction as Ov. *Pont.* 1.1.3–4 *si uacat, hospitio peregrinos, Brute, libellos | excipe*; but cf. Hor. *Ep.* 2.2.95 *si forte uacas, sequere et procul audi* and Plin. *Ep.* 3.18.4 of poetry recitations. **placidi:** nom. pl. or gen. sing.? If nom. pl., the speaker asks that his audience be calm (cf. Ov. *Fast.* 1.17, to Augustus *da mihi te placidum*), and flatters them with the hint that they are indeed calm and perhaps asks them to listen in a 'well-disposed' frame of mind (cf. Virg. *Aen.* 4.578 *adsis o placidusque iuues*). If gen. sing., 'hear the reasoning of a calm man', the speaker describes himself as calm, implied by *rationem* too (see below). Of course, he is anything but calm, but this does not stop him making claims which he contradicts, here and throughout the poem (see Essay).   **rationem:** *ratio* has a wide range of meanings; most obviously here 'my account' or 'justification' for writing satire; but it also attributes to the speaker *ratio* in the sense of 'reason-(ableness)', a suggestion which quickly proves to be false.

22–80 A catalogue of wickedness, often designated a 'Gallery of Rogues', supposedly prevalent in Rome.

22–30 Structure. The first four cases are presented in increasing length and detail (three-quarter line, one-and-a-quarter lines, two lines, three lines, accepting Nisbet's deletion of 29: see below) with *cum* repeated four times (22, 24, 26 *bis*) describing the circumstances which impel the speaker to satire. Of the four vignettes, the first two represent perversion of the Roman norms of gender: eunuchs do not marry nor do women normally enter the arena to fight bare-breasted. The second two represent inversion of the social order through money: the speaker's former barber is now a millionaire and the Egyptian immigrant Crispinus (possibly a former slave) has now attained equestrian status and wealth. Sex, money, deviation from norms and inversion of the status quo will be recurrent themes.

22 tener ... spado 'the effeminate eunuch': the surprising *spado* is postponed to the end of the clause. Eunuchs were regarded with contempt by the Romans, e.g. Hor. *Epod.* 9.13. A eunuch might marry for the status a wife might bring him.   **uxorem ducat:** the regular expression for a man marrying: 'to take home a wife'.   **Meuia:** evidently a woman of good family (thus Ferguson (1987)) who disgraces herself by participating in the spectacles of the arena, where the participants were usually slaves or of low rank. The literal degradation (*infamia*: loss of rights and status) resulting from public performances for those of high and noble birth is illustrated by the *senatus consultum* from Larinum (Levick (1983)). For women in the arena, see Grant (1967) 33–5. Mevia participates in the hunt (*uenatio*) staged in the amphitheatre with *bestiarii* (Grant, 10) who were of lower status than gladiators; she is dressed as a virago, an Amazon perhaps (Virg. *Aen.* 1.429), with one breast naked (*nuda ... mamma*).   **Tuscum ... aprum:** the boars who inhabited the woods of Etruria were famed for their size, e.g. Mart. 7.27.9.

24–5 *cum* is postponed from the beginning of the clause. Barbers were generally of low status, e.g. Petr. 46.7. Some identify the barber here with Cinnamus in Martial (7.64, also 6.17). Lines 24–5 are omitted by a substantial number of MSS and not noticed by the scholiast; moreover, line 25 recurs at 10.226, an unusual phenomenon in J. (the only other instances of recurring lines are 10.365–6 and 14.315–16, 13.137 and 16.41). It is possible that line 25 is not genuine; yet line 24 with its stark contrast (*omnis ... unus*) between the entire nobility and one rich upstart is entirely apposite here.

24 patricios: used here to mean 'nobles', as at 4.102, 10.332. The patrician families were a small proportion of the *nobiles*.   **prouocet:** cf. Sen. *Ep.* 120.19 *Licinum diuitiis, Apicium cenis, Maecenatem deliciis prouocant*; J. 6.375–6.

25 Literally 'by whom shaving, my heavy beard sounded to me as a young man', thus 'under whose razor my heavy beard used to rasp in my youth', though *grauis* is probably adverbial (see below), 'rasp deeply'.

This parodies a line early in Virgil's first *Eclogue, candidior postquam tondenti barba cadebat* (1.28). Such parodies and allusions arise from the status of pastoral and satire as the two lowest genres which use the hexameter metre. Here the happy world of Virgil's Tityrus is contrasted with the corrupt world which the speaker sees surrounding him. Parody of pastoral is found again on a larger scale in Satire 3. **grauis:** Latin often uses adjectives where we expect adverbs, so *grauis* here = *grauiter*, qualifying *sonabat*; cf. Virg. *Aen.* 3.70 *lenis crepitans uocat Auster*; Sil. 2.545 *grauior sonuit per litora fluctus* and 17.42–3 *grauior per aures nulla pulsa manu sonuerunt tympana diuae:*   **iuueni mihi:** J. depicts his speaker as a man of somewhat advanced years, looking back to the days of his 'youth' when he wore a beard, up to the age of about 40; cf. 6.105, 14.217. The Romans had no concept of 'middle age'; the transition from *iuuenis* to *senex* was direct.

26–8 Crispinus: an Egyptian (thus *Niliacae* and *Canopi*) who rose to equestrian status and a position of influence (possibly praetorian prefect) under the emperor Domitian: he is attacked again in *Satire* 4 (4.1 *ecce iterum Crispinus*) where he is a member of Domitian's inner 'cabinet of ministers'. The speaker's anger is conveyed in two derogatory phrases (26) and two vignettes (abl. abs. *umero reuocante* and *uentilet ... aurum*).

J. makes his speaker a racist who exhibits the common Roman

contempt for easterners in particular, such as the freedman from the Euphrates 102–9, the Egyptian 130; cf. Umbricius' attitude (3.60–125).

26 pars Niliacae plebis: disparaging, cf. 8.44 *uolgi pars ultima nostri* and, of the Egyptians, 15.46 *barbara ... turba*.   **uerna Canopi:** Canopus was the city at the western mouth of the Nile delta. It had a reputation for moral laxity, cf. 6.84, 15.46, Sen. *Ep.* 51.3 *illic sibi plurimum luxuria permittit. uerna* means both 'slave' and 'native' (from 'home-bred slave'). Although the meaning 'native' is uppermost here, the nuance of 'slave' is insulting to Crispinus.

27 Tyrias umero reuocante lacernas 'with his shoulder hitching up his Tyrian cloak'. The use of the ablative absolute to add a descriptive detail is a typical construction in post-Augustan verse. *Tyrias* = purple. Crispinus is characterised by his liking for purple, 4.31 *purpureus ... scurra.* Tyrian-dyed fabric (from Tyre, Phoenicia) was expensive and might be condemned as a sign of luxury and decadence, e.g. 14.187–8 *peregrina ignotaque nobis | ad scelus atque nefas, quaecumque est, purpura ducit. lacernas* is pl. for sing.

28 'Airs his gold ring in summer on sweaty fingers.' *aurum* denotes the gold ring which was the mark of equestrian status. *aestiuum* should be interpreted adverbially 'in summer', cf. *grauis* 25 and Crispinus' 'morning perfume', *matutino ... amomo* (4.108, *matutino* for *mane*). The evocation of summer is reinforced by *digitis sudantibus* and *uentilet*: he is 'airing' his hand partly to cool his sweating fingers. Crispinus is perspiring again at 4.108, *sudans.*

29 This line should be deleted, with Nisbet (1988) 86–7.

30 difficile est saturam non scribere: J.'s speaker implies that writing satire is a natural reaction to the injustices of life. **saturam:** an explicit reference to Lucilius' genre (19–20).

30–44 A second series of vignettes which reflect and fuel the speaker's anger. Again *cum* is used (at 32 and 37) to introduce the street scenes: (i) of Matho in his litter (*cum ueniat ...*) and the informer (*post hunc ...*) and (ii) of the gigolos who push past (*cum te summoueant ...*).

30–1 iniquae ... Vrbis 'unfair Rome', referring to the injustices and inequalities of city life already mentioned (22–29) and which follow (32ff.). Cf. *saeuae ... Vrbis* 3.8–9 and for *iniquae* cf. 5.3–4. The speaker reveals the chip on his shoulder. For *Vrbs* = the city of Rome, cf. Quint. *I.O.* 6.3.103, 8.2.8.   **ferreus** 'hardened', 'steeled', cf.

Cic. *Amic.* 87 *quis tam esset ferreus qui eam uitam ferre posset* ... *?* The language of indignation.   **ut teneat se:** on the metrically disrupting effect of the final monosyllable, see Introduction §8.

32 causidici ... Mathonis: a lawyer, mocked elsewhere by J. (7.129, 11.34). *causidicus* is not a complimentary way to refer to a lawyer, the normal term being *orator*, e.g. Quint. *I.O.* 12.1.25 and Tac. *Dial.* 1.1 *nostra potissimum aetas deserta et laude eloquentiae orbata uix nomen ipsum oratoris retineat; neque enim ita appellamus nisi antiquos, horum autem temporum diserti causidici et aduocati et patroni et quiduis potius quam oratores uocantur.*

32–3 noua ... lectica ... plena ipso: a vivid vignette: the pompous lawyer shows off in his new litter but appears ridiculous because he takes up the space of two people. The rich in their litters are a recurring object of attack (1.64–5, 158–9, 3.239–42). For *ipso*, 'the great man' or 'his lordship', sarcastic, cf. 5.30n.

33 magni delator amici 'the man who informed on his powerful friend'. Possibly a specific reference to an informer we cannot identify. Informers were rife under various emperors (particularly Tiberius, Domitian): they stood to receive one quarter of the property of anyone condemned on their information (e.g. Tac. *Ann.* 4.20). The victim here is an eminent man (*magni*), the informer's patron (*amici*).

34–5 cito ... superest: the future participle is best translated by a relative clause; *quod superest* follows *de nobilitate comesa* (cf. 3.259): 'who will soon seize the devoured nobility – what there now is left of it'.

34 nobilitate comesa: the noble families had long been in decline and in J.'s day very few remained (cf. 4.97, 151–4; Syme (1958) 574–5, (1939) 490–508); many had lost their ancestral wealth (for an exaggerated example cf. Corvinus 108). *comesa* portrays the informers as carrion crows.

35, 36 Massa, Carus: Baebius Massa and Mettius Carus were two notorious informers under Domitian (see Ferguson (1987); Tac. *Agr.* 45 with Ogilvie and Richmond's note on Carus especially Mart. 12.25.5; on Massa see also Tac. *Hist.* 4.50). Even they are portrayed as in fear of their unnamed rival.

35 palpat 'soothe' or 'soften', cf. Apul. *Met.* 5.31 *palpare Veneris iram*; the informer has to be treated like an animal, cf. Man. 5.701–2 *ille manu uastos poterit frenare leones et palpare lupos.*

36 a trepido Thymele summissa Latino 'Thymele sent private-

ly by the terrified Latinus'; *summissa*, from *submitto*, also has overtones of
the adjective *summissus*, 'submissive, servile'. Latinus was a famous
actor (cf. 6.44) and probably a member of Domitian's court circle
(Suet. *Dom.* 15.3, Marius Maximus in Σ on 4.53: one of *potentes apud
Domitianum*); Thymele was his leading lady (cf. 6.66, 8.197), cf. Mart.
1.4.5–6 *qua Thymelen spectas derisoremque Latinum,* | *illa fronte precor carmina
nostra legas.* The MS reading *et* implies that Latinus has something to
fear from the powerful informer; change of *et* to *ut* makes J. draw an
analogy with a scene of placation and bribery from the stage.

37–9 '... When men who earn legacies on the night-shift shove you
out of the way, men who are raised to the skies by what is now the best
route to the highest advancement, the bladder of a rich old woman'.
For satire of the gigolos of Rome, cf. Mart. 11.87.3, Lucian *Rhet.
praec.* 24.   **summoueant:** technical, of the lictors clearing the
crowd from the path of a magistrate (cf. Liv. 3.48.3 *lictor, submoue
turbam*); here more colloquially, cf. 3.124, Hor. *Sat.* 1.9.48. The word
has another specialised meaning, which is relevant here, as the technical term for excluding someone from a legacy (*OLD submoueo* 5c).
merentur: regularly 'to earn', but with the seedy flavour of prostitution (*OLD* 1b).

38–9 optima summi | **... uia processus:** the 'path' or 'route'
has a philosophical flavour, cf. 10.363–4 *semita certe* | *tranquillae per
uirtutem patet unica uitae,* Hor. *Ep.* 1.17.26 *uitae uia,* Cic. *De leg. agr.* 1.27
quae uitae uia facillime uiros bonos ad honorem dignitatemque perducat. processus
is often used of political advancement, e.g. Sen. *Ben.* 1.11.5, *Tranq. an.*
2.11. The lofty tone is deflated by the next three words, the climax to
lines 37–9 and marked by powerful alliteration of *u.*   **in caelum ...
euehit:** cf. Cic. *De dom.* 75 *in caelum ascendisse,* Hor. *Od.* 1.1.6 *euehit ad
deos,* of supreme happiness.   **uesica:** literally 'bladder', contemp-
tuously for vagina; cf. *uesicam* of homosexual intercourse at Plaut. *Cas.*
455 (although the text may be corrupt); cf. J. 11.170 where semen is
called *urina,* also Hor. *Sat.* 1.2.44, 2.7.52 and 6.73. On cases like this see
Adams (1982) 91–2.

40–1 *uncia,* one-twelfth of a unit, was used with reference to inheritances, cf. Ulp. *Dig.* 28.5.51(50).2 *hereditas ... diuiditur in duodecim
uncias.* Hence *unciolam* (only here in Latin literature) is one-twelfth, the
diminutive underlining the small amount; *deuncem* is eleven-twelfths.
Proculeius. Gillo: unknown to us.

41 'Each heir's share is assessed by the size of his groin.' For *ad* see *OLD* 35 and cf. 6.358. Gillo's erection is implied to be eleven times bigger than Proculeius'. For *mensura* of the penis, cf. 9.34. *inguen*, 'groin', is used euphemistically for 'penis': Adams (1982) 47.

42–4 A sarcastic (*sane*) digression which emphasises the pallor of the gigolos in a double simile. The subject of *accipiat* is *quisque ... heres*. The phrase *mercedem sanguinis* means 'the reward for his vigour', *sanguis* being used metaphorically with reference to his virility (*OLD* 5) and unlike the soldiers who shed blood for their country, 14.164.

The consequence of his nocturnal toils is the pallor (cf. Cic. *Sest.* 16 *libidine exsanguis*) which marks excessive sexual activity (cf. Sen. *Brev. vit.* 2.4 *quam multi continuis uoluptatibus pallent!*); this is the satirical version of paleness, one of the standard symptoms of love (e.g. Ov. *A.A.* 1.729 *palleat omnis amans: hic est color aptus amanti*). Similar is the *pallor* of the reciter at Pers. 1.26, resulting from his sexual exertions and 'uncertainty about attaining his desired goal' (Bramble (1974) 149–50).

Courtney argues that lines 42–44, especially the two similes, relate better to the informers (35–6) than to the gigolos (37–41) and concludes that lines 37–41, as one of the many *cum ...* sentences, have strayed from their original position. However, on this interpretation, *mercedem sanguinis* will have to mean 'the reward for bloodshed', referring to the deaths caused by the informers, not mentioned explicitly (*nobilitate comesa* 34).

Although the sequence of thought does not run entirely smoothly here, it is preferable to retain the text as transmitted.

43 ut nudis pressit qui calcibus anguem: an epic simile for the pallor of apprehension drawn from Hom. *Il.* 3.33–5 and reworked by Virg. *Aen.* 2.379–80 *inprouisum aspris ueluti qui sentibus anguem | pressit humi nitens trepidusque repente refugit.*

44 Lugudunensem rhetor dicturus ad aram: an un-epic simile, referring to the floggings, duckings in the river and other punishments suffered by the losing contestants in Caligula's oratory contests held at Lyon (Lugdunum) (Suet. *Cal.* 20) at the altar (*aram*) to Rome and Augustus (Dio 54.32.1).

45–50 Another outburst of anger (45) followed again by *cum* (46) introducing two more types of rogue (*hic ... hic*) seen on the streets of

Rome, the defrauder and the condemned criminal whose life-style is unchanged.

45 'Why should I tell with what great anger my dry liver blazes ...'. Anger is conveyed not only by *ira* and *ardeat*, but also by *iecur* and *siccum*. The liver was regarded as the seat of the strongest passions, including anger, cf. Hor. *Sat.* 1.9.66 *meum iecur urere bilis*, J. 6.648 and Nisbet and Hibbard on Hor. *Od.* 1.13.4.

46 populum gregibus comitum premit: social status was measured by the size of a man's entourage as he went about the city on business and social calls. The entourage consisted of 'clients', i.e. dependents (*clientes* 132), usually called *comites*, as here (*OLD comes* 2, cf. also 119, 6.353, 7.44, 142, 3.284 *comitum longissimus ordo*). These criminals evidently have enormous bands of hangers-on, whose behaviour is offensive and oppressive (cf. the rich man who *uexat lutulenta balnea turba* 7.131; also the millionaire in Lucian *Nigr.*13 who jostled passers-by with his retinue; *greges*, uncomplimentary, suggests that their behaviour is sub-human: cf. Mart. 2.57.5 *quem grex togatus sequitur*, Cic. *Sull.* 66 *greges hominum perditorum*.

46–7 hic spoliator ... hic damnatus: two types of criminal, 'one ... another', i.e. *hic qui spoliauit ... hic qui damnatus est*. **spoliator ... pupilli:** the defrauder of his ward is a recurring feature of Roman satire, cf. Hor. *Ep.* 2.1.122–3, J. 10.222, 15.135; at Pers. 2.12–13 the greedy man prays *pupillum utinam, quem proximus heres | inpello, expungam* (see Cloud (1989) 51–2); for the converse cf. J. 8.79 *esto ... tutor bonus*. **prostantis:** the ward has been reduced by poverty to prostitution. On male prostitution, see Krenkel (1978).

47–8 damnatus inani | iudicio: cf. 8.94 *sed quid damnatio confert?* in a context of extortion of the provincials, as 49–50 below.

48 quid enim saluis infamia nummis? 'For what is disgrace if he keeps the money?' (Rudd). *infamia* was the official disgrace resulting from conviction in some civil and all criminal trials and involved the loss of certain civic rights (see Crook (1967) 83).

49–50 The speaker amplifies the second type of criminal by citing an example of a noble convicted but continuing to enjoy a luxurious life-style. The conviction of Marius Priscus had relatively recently been celebrated by Pliny (*Ep.* 2.11; see Syme (1958) 500, 776, Townend (1973) 153). Marius was governor of the province of Africa (cf. 8.120) in AD 97–8 and after his return was successfully prosecuted for extortion by Pliny and Tacitus early in AD 100. He was condemned to banishment from Rome and Italy (hence *exul*) and had to repay the money he had extorted, 7,000,000 HS, to the treasury. This did not, evidently, deprive him of all his riches.

49 ab octaua … bibit: as dinner usually began at the ninth hour (thus Mart. 4.8.6), Marius is evidently 'living it up'.

49–50 fruitur dis | iratis 'happily braving the wrath of heaven' (Rudd). A paradox: enjoyment is not usually associated with anger; for a similar paradox cf. 1.74 *probitas laudatur et alget*. The bumpy metre (final monosyllable *dis*) (see Introduction §8) marks the paradox.

50 at tu uictrix, prouincia, ploras: another paradox. Apostrophe of the province, Africa, engages the audience's sympathy still further.

51–62 The catalogue of criminals is again punctuated by an angry outburst (51–2) and a rejection of epic themes (52–4) for contemporary outrages (*cum* 55 … *cum* 58 …) which involve money (*bona* 55 and 59): its acquisition through the prostitution of one's wife and its loss through gambling and conspicuous expenditure. Three questions of diminishing length are followed by a longer, more complex question (52–61) in which mythological themes are outweighed by examples of modern wickedness. Cf. Mart. 4.49 and especially 10.4, e.g. line 4 *quid tibi dormitor proderit Endymion?*

51 Venusina digna lucerna 'deserving the Venusine lamp'. J. sets himself firmly in the tradition of Horace who in a programmatic satire identifies himself as *Venusinus* (*Sat.* 2.1.34–5), from Venusia in South Italy. This complements the earlier reference to Lucilius (19–21), since, in the very passage of Horace alluded to here, Horace declares his own debt to Lucilius. Thus J. declares his literary ancestry; there is no need to suppose that J.'s model in Book 1 is the Horace of the *Odes* and not the *Satires* (Anderson (1982) 103–14). On borrowings from Horace in Satire 1 see Woodman (1983).

The lamp has a dual reference here: (i) the topos of poets working by lamp-light late into the night, often called *lucubratio*, 'burning the midnight oil', e.g. Var. *L.L.* 5.9 *non solum ad Aristophanis lucernam sed etiam ad Cleanthis lucubraui*; Mart. 8.3.17–8 *scribant ista* [sc. tragedies and epics] *graues nimium nimiumque seueri, quos media miseros nocte lucerna uidet*, cf. the *uigilata … proelia* at J. 7.27; Hor. *Ep.* 2.1.112–3 *prius orto* | *sole uigil calamum et chartas et scrinia posco*; (ii) the spotlight cast by satire on the darker aspects of human behaviour. (Cf. Diogenes' lighting a lamp in broad daylight, Diog. Laer. 6.41.)

52 agitem: both 'attack' and 'deal with'.   **sed quid magis?** 'but what should I rather have a go at?' *magis = potius.*

52-4 A list of epic themes, all in the accusative after *agitem*. It commences in grand style with the unusual spondaic fifth foot (*Heracleas* 52) and exotic Greek word (*labyrinthi* 53) but is deflated by *percussum puero* and *fabrumque uolantem* in 54 (see below).   **Heracleas | aut Diomedeas:** the plural of the standard Greek form such as *Odyssea*, designating an epic concerning a hero. The labours of Hercules were popular material for epic; so too Diomedes' return (*nostos*) from the Trojan War and subsequent settlement in Italy. **mugitum labyrinthi:** i.e. a *Theseid*, an epic describing Theseus' killing of the Minotaur in the labyrinth on Crete. The 'bellowing' is the creature's roar before or as it is killed, cf. Sen. *Phaedr.* 1171-2 *Daedalea uasto claustra mugitu replens | taurus biformis.* Mention of the labyrinth, built for King Minos by Daedalus, leads to the story of Daedalus and Icarus.   **mare percussum puero:** Icarus, who, through flying too close to the sun, caused the wax on his wings to melt and fell into the sea. The story was treated in elevated poetry (Mart. 4.49.5, 10.4.5); the expression here, 'the sea hit by a boy', is incongruous and comic: the person is not the agent but the instrument again (cf. *ruptae lectore columnae* 13n.).   **fabrumque uolantem** 'the flying workman', a comic deflation of the master-craftsman and inventor Daedalus.

55-7 leno, moechi, uxori: a husband is depicted conniving at (and even encouraging) his wife's adulterous affairs with rich lovers; because the rewards fall to him he is described as a 'pimp', *leno*. On the background to this scenario, which has more in common with declamation than with contemporary legal provision, see Cloud (1989a) 55-7.   **capiendi | ius nullum uxori:** although the wife is said to have no legal right to inherit, it seems impossible to establish the precise circumstances: see Cloud (previous note).   **doctus:** repeated for sarcastic effect, 'expert at gazing at the ceiling, expert too in snoring over his cups with wide-awake nose'.   **uigilanti stertere naso:** a paradox, cf. Lucr. *D.R.N.* 3.1048 *uigilans stertis.* J. evokes Lucilius' story (recorded by Festus 173,5; see Lucil. 1223M = 251W) about a conniving husband which had the catch-phrase *non omnibus dormio* (quoted by e.g. Cic. *Fam.* 7.24.1): *quod simularet dormientem, quo impunitius uxor eius moecharetur.*

58–62 '... when a man who has lavished his fortune on the stables and is minus his entire ancestral wealth, by racing along the Flaminian Way with speedy chariot, a boy Automedon, thinks himself entitled to have hopes of the command of a cohort?' The young aristocrat who has frittered away his ancestral wealth on horses (i.e.chariot-racing) now seeks a profitable career in the army.   **fas esse putet:** the speaker's indignation arises mostly from the young man's assumption that his course of action is morally irreproachable (*fas*).   **curam ... cohortis:** i.e. a *praefectura cohortis sociorum* (cf. 10.94), normally the first stage in the career of an *eques*, knight. After this he might hold *tribunatus legionis* and the *praefectura alae*, then enter the civil service and become a *procurator*, a lucrative position.

59 praesepibus: horse-stalls; since the word can also = brothel (*OLD* c), there may be a hint of other immoral expenditure here.

60 dum: *OLD dum* 4.

60–1 peruolat ... Automedon: the dactylic rhythm matches his speed.   **Flaminiam:** understand *uiam*: the main road to the north out of Rome.   **puer Automedon:** i.e. a boy charioteer. Automedon, Achilles' charioteer, is from Homer's *Iliad*; cf. Cic. *Rosc. Am.* 98. For similarly ironic use of Homeric names cf. Varro 257 = 248 Cèbe *Automedo meus* (of a slave), Mart. 2.16.5 *dimitte Machaonas omnes*, i.e. the doctors; J. 4.65 *Atriden*.

61–2 nam lora tenebat | ipse: the disgrace inherent in the aristocrat playing the charioteer is now explicated: *nam* explains *Automedon*. Enjambment of *ipse* emphasises the disgrace; cf. 8.147–8 *et ipse,* | *ipse rotam adstringit sufflamine mulio consul.*

62 lacernatae ... amicae: his mistress or girl-friend wears a *lacerna*, a basic cloak worn by soldiers (Prop. 3.12.7) and muleteers (Petr. 69.5) among others. She evidently thinks it fashionable to look 'butch'.   **se iactaret** 'show off'.

63–72 Again the speaker's indignation overflows into an angry question (*nonne ...*) which incorporates a picture of the forger living a life of luxury (*cum ...* 64). There is a temporary lull in indignation as the speaker simply reports his sighting of another criminal, a woman poisoner (69–72). The street setting here is maintained by *medio ...*

quadriuio (63–4); by the forger portrayed in his litter (*feratur* 64); and by the *matrona* passing by (*occurrit* 69; cf. *occurrat* 6.655).

63–4 'Do I not want to fill my roomy notebooks [standing] at the cross-roads, when . . .?'   **ceras:** wax tablets, the Roman equivalent of note-books; wooden slates coated with wax, marked with a sharp point, *stilus*. They could be reused many times by smoothing the wax with a warm knife. Cf. Quint. *I.O.* 10.3.31 *scribi optime ceris in quibus facillima est ratio delendi*.

64 iam sexta ceruice feratur: i.e. *iam sex ceruicibus feratur*, 'he is carried on six necks already'. The forger's litter is very grand. Even more luxurious were litters carried by eight slaves (e.g. Mart. 6.84), to which the forger will evidently soon progress (so *iam*).

65 hinc atque inde patens, ac nuda paene cathedra: both phrases criticise the forger's ostentation: litters could be closed for privacy (e.g. 124, 3.242), but he desires to be seen revelling in his riches. His effeminacy is exposed, since the *cathedra* was specifically a woman's chair, cf. Mart. 12.38.1–2 *hunc qui femineis noctesque diesque cathedris | incedit*; J. 6.91, cf. 9.52 of a homosexual.

66 multum referens de Maecenate supino 'recalling in many ways the languid Maecenas'; for *multum . . . de* cf. 3.123 *exiguum de*. Maecenas, the renowned patron of the arts (cf. 7.94), was also a by-word for effeminacy, cf. 12.38–9. Sen. *Ep.* 114.4–8; see Mayor's note here. *supinus*, the appropriate word to describe the passenger's posture in a litter, e.g. Luc. 9.589, cf. Ov. *A.A.* 1.487 *illa toro resupina feretur*, may comment on his 'laid-back' behaviour (see Mart. 2.6.13).

67 signator falsi: cf. *falsas signare tabellas* 8.142, Sall. *Cat.* 16.2 *signatores . . . falsos*. A *signator* is someone who attests a document (*tabulae*, e.g. a will) by affixing his seal (hence *gemma*, the seal on the ring). The forger makes his fortune by affixing his seal to documents which have been forged or otherwise tampered with. *falsum* is the legal term for fraud, thus *signator falsi* means 'the man who puts his seal to an act of fraud'. For an example see Cic. *Cluent.* 41.

68 gemma . . . uda: the seal was moistened before use to prevent the wax sticking to it (e.g. Ov. *Am.* 2.15.15–17).   **fecerit:** generic or descriptive subj.

69–72 'Along comes the powerful lady, who just before offering her thirsty husband the mellow wine of Cales will add the toad's poison and who, a new improved Lucusta, has taught her simple neighbours

to give their blackened husbands a send-off amid rumour and crowds.'
uiro ... sitiente is ablative absolute, although initially *porrectura uiro*
suggests that *uiro* is in the dative case.   **matrona potens:** a phrase
borrowed from Horace (*Ars* 116) and given a new context.   **molle
Calenum:** a famous, high quality wine from Campania, mentioned by
Horace (e.g. *Od.* 1.20.9, 1.31.9–10, 4.12.14).

70 porrectura: regularly of offering food and drink, cf. *porrexit*
5.67; also in a context of poisoning *porrexerit* 6.632. On J.'s use of the
fut. part. see Introduction §7.

71 Lucusta: a professional poisoner from Gaul allegedly employed
by Agrippina to poison Claudius and by Nero to poison Britannicus
(Tac. *Ann.* 13.15; Suet. *Ner.* 33.2). Cf. the only extant fragment of
Turnus, a satirist writing a few years earlier than J.:

> ex quo Caesareas suboles Lucusta cecidit
> horrida cura sui †uerna nota Neronis   (*FPL* p. 134 Morel)

with Coffey (1979) 89. Tacitus describes her as 'long ... retained as
one of the tools of despotism' (Church and Brodribb), *diu inter instru-
menta regni habita* (*Ann.* 12.66). She is said to have taught her skill (Suet.
Ner. 33.3), cf. *instituit* here.

72 per famam et populum: not hendiadys (saying one thing in
two words connected by 'and' which would here = *per famam populi*) but
syllepsis: funeral processions regularly went through the forum, *per
populum* (*OLD per* 1b), but this procession also takes place 'amid the
rumours' (*OLD per* 16, of attendant circumstance).   **nigros
maritos:** discoloured by poison, cf. *ad Herenn.* 2.8; cf. Prop. 2.27.10
where *pocula nigra* = 'cups of poison'.   **efferre** 'to carry out for
burial' (*OLD* 3), regularly, e.g. 6.175, 6.567, 14.220, Mart. 8.43.1.

73–80 The speaker switches to low-key irony before the anger
explodes again in 77–8. The famous programmatic statement of 79–80
rounds off the catalogue of rogues.

73–4 'Do a daring deed deserving of Gyara and the dungeon if you
want to be somebody.' Sarcastic: these days you have to commit an
outrageous crime to be somebody (lit. 'something', *aliquid*).   **breuibus Gyaris:** deportation to an island was the punishment for many
crimes including forgery of a will. *Gyara* (also *Gyarus*) was a small island
in the Aegean with a poor water-supply (Tac. *Ann.* 4.30).   **carcere:**
Roman criminals were punished with fines, deportation, exile and

execution. Prison was a temporary place of detention and *carcer* is associated with execution, cf. 13.245, hence it might be translated 'death row'.

74 probitas laudatur et alget 'honesty is praised, and shivers' (Rudd). Cf. Sall. *B.J.* 14.4 *parum tuta per se ipsa probitas est*; *Laus Pis.* 121 *probitas cum paupertate iacebit.* For the contrast between the unprofitability of proper behaviour and the rewards of immorality, cf. Mart. 6.50:

> cum coleret puros pauper Telesinus amicos,
> errabat gelida sordidus in togula:
> obscenos ex quo coepit curare cinaedos,
> argentum mensas praedia solus emit.
> uis fieri diues, Bithynice? conscius esto.
> nil tibi uel minimum basia pura dabunt.

This pithy *sententia* ('maxim' or 'epigram') is typical of J.

75-6 'To their crimes they owe their pleasure gardens, mansions, dining tables, antique silver plate, for example, the goat standing outside the cup.' The unnamed subject of *debent* fuels the speaker's anger as he lists the profits of crime. These were all conspicuous signs of wealth. For gardens, situated in the city, cf. 7.79-80 Lucan's *hortis marmoreis*, 10.16 *magnos Senecae praediuitis hortos*; the gardens of Sallust the historian were taken over by the imperial family. On mansions, see Edwards in 12-13n. For tables, cf. 11.117-27; the most desirable dining-table consisted of a single section of the *citrus* tree (Plin. *N.H.* 13.91); others were made of precious metal; they were mounted on a support (*pes*) of ivory or precious metal.

For silver plate, standard in such lists of luxury, cf. Sen. *Helv.* 11.6 (also tables); Mart. 6.50.4 (*argentum, mensas, praedia*); Mart. 11.70.8 (*argentum, mensas, murrina, rura, domum*); J. 7.133 (*pueros, argentum, murrina, uillas*); 12.34. On the cachet of antique silver cf. Plin. *Ep.* 3.1.9, Mart. 8.6.3-16.

One particular cup is adorned with a goat, *stantem extra pocula caprum* (the plural *pocula* may be for metrical convenience or may indicate a pair or set of cups); either the goat is in relief, as generally thought, cf. Mart. 8.51 esp. 9 *stat caper*; or with goats as handles: for arguments and a fine illustration see Griffith (1973) with Plate 1.

77-8 'Who can get to sleep for thinking about the man who seduces his greedy daughter-in-law, about the impure brides and the teenage adulterer?' The speaker invites the world to sympathise with his distress.   **nurus corruptor auarae:** the father-in-law wants sex, the daughter-in-law money. For the combination of sex and greed, cf. 37-41, 55-7.   **sponsae turpes:** even before marriage (*sponsa* = betrothed, fiancée), girls are unfaithful.   **praetextatus:** boys exchanged the *toga praetexta* (white with a purple border) for the *toga uirilis* (pure white) by their sixteenth birthday, so this indicates the youth of the adulterer.

79-80 'If nature says no, indignation makes my verse, such as it can, the sort of verses you can expect from me or Cluvienus.' The famous programmatic statement, disclaiming natural ability and abdicating responsibility to the force of moral indignation, *indignatio*, of which he has shown so many signs. Cf. Catullus' self-deprecation in his programmatic poem, *quare habe tibi quidquid hoc libelli,* | *qualecumque* (1.8-9); cf. Hor. *Sat.* 1.10.58 *uersiculos* of Lucilius' efforts. Line 79 sounds serious enough, but the whole of line 80 is designed to undercut it, with *qualemcumque potest* (the speaker protests too much about the poor quality of his verses to be taken seriously) and with *quales ego uel Cluuienus* (he ranks himself with an amateur poet, Cluvienus, unknown to us). Cf. Horace's humorous self-disparagement through the mediocre Crispinus (*Sat.* 1.1.120-1).

81-146 The second half of the poem presents a programme of the subject-matter of satire, which from an initial declaration of the broadest possible scope (81-6) rapidly narrows down to Roman greed and materialism. See Essay.

81-6 A programmatic statement of his subject-matter. All human activities (85-6) from the very beginning (*ex quo* 81) of history. In deliberate contradiction of the preceding self-deprecation (79-80) and in keeping with the momentous events he is describing, the flood and recreation of humankind, the speaker briefly adopts the grand style (satire *can* replace epic) before deflating it. Green's transposition of lines 85-6 to follow line 80 (Penguin translation) detracts from this effect.

For the story of the flood see Ov. *Met.* 1.253-416. Deucalion and Pyrrha were the two mortals allowed by the gods to survive a universal flood. When their boat finished up on Mount Parnassus, Deucalion consulted the goddess Themis about how to restore mankind and she in reply gave an oracle; acting on this Deucalion and Pyrrha created a new human race by throwing stones over their shoulders; the stones which Deucalion threw became men and those which Pyrrha threw, women. (Cf. J. 15.30: Pyrrha marks the start of human history.) J. selects just three incidents from Ovid's account: (i) the landing on Mount Parnassus, *nauigio montem ascendit* (316–29); (ii) the seeking of the oracle, *sortesque poposcit* (367–83); and (iii) acting on the oracle *anima caluerunt mollia saxa* (390–415). In all three, faint verbal reminiscences suggest that J. evokes Ovid's description: (i) '*nimbis ... remotis*' 328 cf. *nimbis* 81; '*caelo terras ostendit*' 329 cf. 84 'maribus nudas *ostendit* Pyrrha puellas'; 321 'Themin quae tunc oracla tenebat' which prepares for seeking the oracle; (ii) 'auxilium per sacras *quaerere sortes*' 368 cf. 'sortesque *poposcit*'; (iii) '*saxa ... molliri mora mollita*que ducere formam' 400–2 cf. '*paulatim*que anima caluerunt *mollia saxa*' 83 (and for *caluerunt* cf. *percaluit* 418).

81 ex quo 'from the time when', cf. 6.294, 10.77, 14.261. **nimbis tollentibus aequor:** as often in Silver Latin verse, an ablative absolute has an object: 'with the rain-clouds raising the water(-level)'.

82 nauigio montem ascendit: a surprising way to climb a mountain.   **sortes ... poposcit** 'asked for an oracle'; *sortes* originally meant oracles by lot but was extended to include all oracles.

83 anima caluerunt mollia saxa 'the stones grew warm and soft with life' (Rudd); *mollis* is a case of prolepsis, 'anticipation'.

84 maribus nudas ostendit Pyrrha puellas: deflation of the epic tone: Pyrrha is portrayed as the madam of a brothel, displaying her girls to the customers. Ironically, the new race is immediately as corrupt as its predecessor wiped out in the flood. *mas* denotes the male of the species, usually opposed to *femina* (e.g. Laev. *Poet.* 26; Plaut. *Most.* 1047); J. prefers *puella* here because the girls are still virgins and it is the appropriate word for a brothel, cf. 6.127 *lenone suas iam dimittente puellas*.

85–6 'All human activity – prayers, fears, anger, pleasure, joys, hustle and bustle – this is the mish-mash of my little book.' Cf. Mart. 10.4.10 *hominem pagina nostra sapit*, a claim of relevance and realism. **discursus:** futile activity, cf. Plin. *Ep.* 1.9.7 *tu quoque strepitum istum inanemque discursum et multum ineptos labores ... relinque teque studiis uel otio trade.*   **nostri farrago libelli:** often mistranslated, e.g. 'the mixed mash of my verse' or 'the motley subject of my page', ignoring the significance of *libellus*, which indicates that the Book as a whole (Book I = *Satires* 1–5) and not the individual poem is the unit of composition (see Introduction §9). The diminutive *libellus* (cf. Cat. 1.1) and *farrago*, 'animal-feed' (derived from *far*, grain), continue the self-deprecation (cf. 79–80). But *farrago* is also a sophisticated allusion to the etymological derivation of the word *satura* itself: just as *farrago* is literally 'mixed fodder', so *satura* is probably originally mixed first fruits offered to a deity (see Introduction §3 and Coffey (1989) 11–23). So the phrase as a whole is announcing the blend of themes to be found within the Book as a whole.

87–95 A link-passage into the first extended scene, the *sportula*. Here the range of subject-matter is narrowed from 'all human activity' to one vice – contemporary greed. In the first indignant question *et quando . . . copia?* the speaker locates himself in the present (the question invites the answer 'at no other time in history') and confines himself to vices. In the second indignant question *quando . . . sinus?* he further limits himself to greed. In the third, *alea quando . . .?*, he introduces a scene of gambling, expanded in 89–93. Two further indignant questions in 92–5, criticising this behaviour as mad and unprecedented, complete the link passage and provide the jumping-off point for the *sportula* scene (*nunc* 95).

87–9 'And when was the supply of vices richer? When did the purse of avarice gape more widely? When did gambling [arouse] such passions as these?' In the third question the main verb is omitted (ellipse) to convey agitation. For ellipse with *hos animos*, cf. Sen. *Tro.* 339, Luc. 8.544.

88 sinus: the fold in the toga where money could be kept (cf. *gremio* 7.215, 14.327). *Avaritia* is personified, holding open the folds of her toga to receive money. Cf. the foolish man who is eager to receive fortune's gifts at Sen. *Ep.* 74.6 *quae a fortuna sparguntur sinum expandit.*
alea: gambling was prohibited by law, except during the Saturnalia festival in winter; cf. 8.10 criticism of *alea pernox*, 'all-night gambling'; cf. 11.176 and 14.4–5. Sen. *Apoc.* 12.3 with Eden.

89–92 The gambling scene has an epic flavour (cf. 14.5, *Anth. Lat.* 193.7–10R = 184.1–4 Shackleton Bailey) to indicate how these wealthy men should behave and to show that satire is more relevant than epic. Accompanied not by their troops but by their cash-boxes, *loculis comitantibus*, they advance, with the epic-style impersonal passive *itur*

89, to the chance not of war (*ad casum belli*: cf. Cic. *Sest.* 12, Luc. 9.84, Liv. 33.19.4 *casu pugnae*) but of the gaming board (*ad casum tabulae*: *OLD tabula* 3a). They station their forces, *posita* (*OLD pono* 1c) ... *arca*, their treasure-chests, but instead of fighting (e.g. *concurritur*) they play (*luditur*). The analogy is explicit in the sarcastic exclamation *proelia quanta illic* ... *uidebis!* and by likening the steward (*dispensatore*) to the armour-bearer (*armigero*).   **posita:** a multiple pun on 'station' their forces, 'place' their treasure chests and 'stake' money.   **uidebis:** also 5.25; the phrase draws in the audience.

92 simplexne furor: lit. 'Is it pure and simple madness ...', to which can be supplied either the answer yes or the answer no (i.e. 'It is something more than madness ...', e.g. wickedness); -*ne* gives no indication which. The context favours the latter, as the speaker is inviting condemnation of the rich men not only for squandering money (thus *sestertia centum perdere* and *quis totidem erexit uillas*) but also for stinginess (thus *horrenti tunicam non reddere seruo* and *secreto* 95). **sestertia centum** 'a hundred thousand sesterces' (*OLD sestertius* 3b), a fortune; cf. 14.322–8.

93 reddere 'to give back' the *tunica* he has borrowed from his slave to pay for his gambling (thus Heinrich, Lewis).

94–5 quis ..., quis ... auus? 'Which of our forefathers ...?' For the indications of wealth cf. 75–6 (*uillas* ~ *praetoria* and luxurious meals ~ *mensas, argentum uetus*).

95 secreto: the word condemning the selfishness of the rich is prominent at the start of the line.

95–126 The *sportula* scene: the first vignette in the poem, in contrast with the brief glimpses of various rogues and criminals; part of the diary of the poor client's day (95–146).

95 nunc: in contrast with the past (*quis ... auus?*).   **sportula:** literally 'a little basket' but conventionally translated as 'the dole'. This was the reward given by wealthy men to their clients who fulfilled their duties, formerly a portion of food to be carried away in a 'basket'; as time went on a payment in money was substituted. See Braund and Cloud (1981) 197–8.

The patron–client relationship was central to Roman society. The structure of Roman society should be envisaged broadly as a triangle, with the emperor and his courtiers at the top, the senatorial and equestrian families next (these making a small but powerful élite); then the vast majority of the populace in descending order of rank. A man of equestrian rank would be both a patron – to his many dependants and other 'clients' lower in the social structure – and himself a 'client' of senators. The emperor was the supreme patron, inferior to no one.

A patron would act in his client's interests, by defending a member of his family in the law-courts, or nominating him to an important position, or giving him property or smaller gifts of money. In return, the client was expected to act in his patron's interests whenever opportunity arose; in particular, the humbler client boosted his patron's public image by attending him in the morning at the *salutatio* (see below) and, if possible, throughout the day as the patron made his round of business calls, to the forum and the baths and so on.

What is peculiar about J.'s presentation of the *sportula* is that he sets it at the start of the day (128), when other evidence indicates that it took place at the end of the day, in return for services rendered by clients. The event which took place at the start of the day was the *salutatio*, lit. 'greeting', the 'morning call', at which a great man's clients would assemble in his *atrium*, the public part of the house. On this conflation, which creates an entertaining paradox, see Braund and Cloud (1981) 197–8.

95–6 J. introduces various marks of disparagement: the *sportula*, a diminutive form (from *sporta*, a basket or hamper), is described as *parua*; it is given on the threshold, *primo limine*, i.e. the clients are not even admitted to the house; the group is described as a *turba*, 'mob'; *rapienda* is a violent word, suggesting they snatch at the *sportula*.

96 turbae rapienda togatae: gerundive + dat. of agent, regularly. The crowd wears the *toga*, indicating all are citizens, cf. Mart. 6.48.1, J. 3.127, 7.142, perhaps of relatively high status, cf. Sen. *Ep.* 114.12.

97 ille: the patron himself, cf. 5.30n., anxiously overseeing distribution of the *sportula* to avoid being cheated (97–99) and giving priority to the noblest (99–101).

99 agnitus accipies 'once identified, you will receive [your reward]'. The 2nd p. sing. (cf. *uenias* and *poscas* 98, *te* 37), invites identification with the client's viewpoint.

99–101 'He orders the herald to summon even the Trojan families; yes, they too besiege the threshold along with us.'

99 praecone: the slave whose job it was to announce the names of those attending the *salutatio/sportula*, properly called the *nomenclator*, cf. Sen. *Ben.* 6.33.4, *Ep.* 19.11.

100 Troiugenas 'born of Trojan stock', the grand old families who claimed descent from the Trojans who accompanied Aeneas to Italy. The grand word (Cat. 64.355, Lucr. 1.465, Virg. *Aen.* 3.359) is used ironically here and at 8.181, 11.95, cf. *Teucrorum proles* 8.56.

101 nobiscum: now it is made clear that the speaker is one of the humbler clients, not in the category of the *Troiugenae*.

101 'da praetori, da deinde tribuno': the patron's instructions to his herald. The *cursus honorum* ran, in ascending order, *quaestor, tribunus plebis, praetor, consul,* so the patron is apparently observing protocol by giving priority to a praetor. But the satirical force lies in the very presence of a praetor and tribune in the *sportula* crowd (his rush to make the *salutatio* in time is a little less surprising, 3.128).

102 libertinus: a man brought to Rome as a slave but who subsequently gained his freedom. Some freedmen rose to positions of considerable wealth (e.g. Petronius' Trimalchio, *Satyr.* 76 *accepi patrimonium laticlauium*, 'a senator's fortune', strictly at least 1,000,000 HS) and power, especially in the imperial civil service, and a few exercised great influence on the emperor, e.g. the freedman Narcissus under Claudius (14.329–31).

102–9 The freedman's speech, justifying his position at the head of the queue, even in front of the praetor. He justifies his position by reference to his wealth: money rules at Rome. To put these words into the freedman's mouth is designed to alienate the audience through his brash boldness.

102 prior ego adsum: both 'I was here first' and 'I have a prior claim'.

104 natus ad Euphraten: the great river which marked the eastern boundary of the Roman Empire, probably here designating 'the east' in general. Hostility towards easterners is developed in *Satire* 3 (esp. lines 62–6). Many slaves were brought to Rome from the east, e.g. Cappadocia (cf. 7.15) and Syria (cf. 6.351).

104–5 'A fact which the effeminate windows in my ear would prove, although I personally deny it.' *licet* + subj. regularly = 'although'. For the eastern custom of ear-piercing cf. Dio Chrys. 32.3, here satirised with the exaggerated *fenestra*; *mollis* = 'effeminate' (cf. 2.47n., 3.99, 9.38); for this as a classic insult see Plut. *Mor.* 631d.

105 tabernae: a shop, cf. Mart. 7.61.9–10.

106 quadringenta parant 'bring in 400,000 [sesterces]', an enormous amount, equivalent to the property qualification for an *eques*, on which see Wiseman (1970); a recurring motif in J.: 2.117, 5.132, cf. 14.323–4.

106–7 quid confert purpura maior | optandum ...? 'What so desirable does the broader purple [stripe] bring ...?' *purpura maior* = senatorial status, a poetic version of *latus clauus*, the 'broad stripe' on the *tunica* of a senator, contrasted with *angustus clauus*, 'narrow stripe' of the knights. Cf. Stat. *Silv.* 3.2.124 *maioris ... claui* and 4.5.42 *contentus artae lumine purpurae*.

107–9 si ... ego ...: the freedman illustrates his question by contrasting the impoverished noble (*si – ouis*) with his own fabulous wealth (*ego – Licinis*).

107 Laurenti ... in agro: on the coast of Latium (between Ostia and Lavinium, about 16 Roman miles from Rome). Pliny had an estate there with *multi greges ouium* (*Ep.* 2.17.3 with Sherwin-White).

107–8 custodit ... conductas ... ouis: the impoverished noble no longer has estates of his own so enters into a contract whereby he leases (*conductas*) and manages a flock of sheep (cf. *CIL* ix 2438, White (1970) 304–5). This may have been a regular business practice, yet the picture of Corvinus as shepherd, actually minding the sheep (cf. *custos OLD* 1c) is satirical; the noble might be expected to guard a military position (*OLD custodio* 2): the object of the verb is postponed for maximum impact.

108 Coruinus: a cognomen of one of the oldest families (cf. 8.7), the *gens Valeria* (Plut. *Comp. of Solon and Publ.* 1.2). Possibly a specific allusion to M. Valerius Messala Corvinus, consul in AD 58, to whom Nero granted an annual pension because he had fallen on hard times (cf. Tac. *Ann.* 13.34).

109 Pallante et Licinis: Pallas was a freedman of Claudius who amassed a fortune of phenomenal size, 300 million sesterces (Plin. *N.H.* 33.56), from his position *a rationibus*, in the imperial accounts office (see Oost (1958) 128). Licinus was a slave of Julius Caesar, freed by Augustus, who also became very rich as *procurator* of Gaul. Pallas' wealth may have been proverbial; Licinus' name certainly became a by-word for wealth (14.306, Pers. 2.36, Sen. *Ep.* 119.9, 120.19), which explains the plural here, 'people like Licinus'; J. often uses this generic plural, e.g. 2.3n. *Curios*, 8.11 *Numantinos*, 10.108 *Crassos, Pompeios*, 11.91 *Scauros*.

The freedman shows his brashness by claiming greater wealth than Pallas and Licinus and his greed by queuing for a small *sportula*.

109–16 A long sarcastic sentence, presenting the logical consequence (*ergo*) of the freedman's words. Three jussive subjunctives ('let...') are followed by *quandoquidem* ('since') and *etsi* ('although') + 2 verbs, *habitat* and *ereximus*, and finally *ut* 'as' with a list of 5 nouns, the last of which, *Concordia*, is expanded by a relative clause *quae*. The supremacy of money is expressed by *uincant diuitiae, diuitiarum | maiestas, Pecunia templo* and *nummorum ... aras*.

109–11 'So let the tribunes wait, let money rule OK, let the man who recently arrived in this city with whitened feet not give way to sacrosanct office.' *qui* is postponed until late in line 111.

110 sacro ... honori: *honor* means 'office', referring to the magistracies, cf. Mart. 8.8.4 *te colat omnis honos*. At 117 *summus honor* refers to the consulship; *sacro ... honori* here refers to the tribunate (cf. *tribuni* 109); the tribunes of the plebs were sacrosanct (Liv. 2.33.1).   **ne cedat honori:** a reminiscence of Virg. *Aen.* 3.484 *nec cedit honori*.

111 pedibus ... albis: newly imported slaves had their feet chalked when they were put on sale to distinguish them from local slaves: Plin. *N.H.* 35.199–217 *est et uilissima* [*sc. creta*], *qua ... pedes uenalium trans mare aduectorum denotare maiores instituerunt*.

112–13 sanctissima diuitiarum | maiestas 'the grandeur of riches is the most sacred'; cf. 133–4 *longissima cenae | spes*.   **Pecunia:** personified at Hor. *Ep.* 1.6.3–7.

114 The negative words are placed in important positions for emphasis, *nondum* initially and *nullas* immediately after the caesura.

115–16 Vespasian built a temple to *Pax*; the temple of *Fides* is associated with Numa, second king of Rome; there was an altar to *Victoria* in the senate-house and a temple on the Palatine; and there were three temples to *Virtus* in Rome (incl. two to *Virtus* and *Honos*). The temple of *Concordia* was at the entrance to the Capitol. On the monuments in this list see Platner and Ashby (1929). Line 116, 'Concord who clatters when her nest is hailed', humorously deflates the list with its implication that the temple is used only as a bird's-nest. *salutato ... nido* is a typical surprise: see Introduction §7. *salutato* seems to pun on the general context of the *salutatio* (95n.). *crepitat* may indicate that the nest is inhabited by storks, as this verb is used of them elsewhere, at (e.g.) Ovid *Met.* 6.97, *crepitante ciconia rostro*.

For a similar list of good things which are subordinate to money, cf. Hor. *Sat.* 2.3.94–6.

117–20 When the richest men at Rome queue up for handouts, where does that leave poorer people? For *cum* . . . , *quid facient* . . .? cf. 2.65–66 and Mart. 10.10.1–4:

cum tu, laurigeris annum qui fascibus intras,
    mane salutator limina mille teras,
hic ego quid faciam? quid nobis, Paule, relinquis,
    qui de plebe Numae densaque turba sumus?

J. exaggerates in depicting consuls in the *sportula* queue (cf. 101n.).

117 summus honor 'the highest office', i.e. the consulship; 110n.; cf. Stat. *Silv.* 1.2.233 *omnis honos, cuncti ueniunt ad limina fasces*.

118 '. . . what the dole brings in, how much it adds to his income'. *rationes* in a financial context means 'accounts'.

119–20 'What will the dependants do who must buy from the dole their togas, shoes and bread and smoke at home?' *panis* represents food in general (cf. *OLD* 2) and *fumus* firewood (*TLL* 1541.50: metonymic usage). On *comites* see 46n. The client's daily needs are in two contrasting pairs: he needs *toga* and *calceus* to have a respectable image when he is out of the house on business and he needs *panis* and *fumus* at home (*domi*).

120–1 densissima ... lectica 'crowds of litters', singular for plural.   **centum | quadrantes:** *quadrans* is the smallest copper coin, worth one quarter of an *as*. Whether or not this is the actual amount of doles given (cited by Mart. 1.59.1 and often) matters little; it doubtless varied according to the resources of the donor (see Braund and Cloud (1981) 197). The exaggerated picture of crowds of litters surrounding the paltry handout is reflected in the word-order here.

123 hic petit absenti 'this man asks for [a handout] for his absent [wife]'.   **nota iam callidus arte** 'grown cunning at an old trick', of which an example follows (124–6).

124 clausam ... sellam: a woman's sedan chair would normally be closed, which makes this trick easier.   **pro coniuge** 'instead of his wife'.

125–6 The husband's words, first to the slave distributing the dole, then to his wife, then to the slave again.   **Galla mea est** 'It's my [wife] Galla.'   **noli uexare, quiescet** 'Don't disturb her, she'll be resting.' On the idiomatic use of the fut. indic. see McKeown on Ov. *Am.* 1.2.7–8 *sic erit.*

127–34 Line 127 seems to make a promise of a description of the client's day. After the *salutatio*, the clients accompany their patron to the forum, where he might participate in a law-suit or do other business (128–31). The afternoon's activities – normally a visit to the baths – are omitted and we pass directly to the meal, *cena*, in the late afternoon/early evening. This apparent jump between lines 131 and 132 has led to the suggestion that some lines have fallen out here during transmission. This is unnecessary. J. earlier had his speaker give a programme (81–6) then deviate from it (87ff.); the same is happening here. Again the effect is to keep the reader off balance.

127 pulchro ... ordine rerum 'a splendid sequence of events', sarcastic. For ironic use of *pulcher* cf. Cic. *Ver.* 2.154, *Dom.* 108.

128 forum iurisque peritus Apollo: the numerous *fora* in Rome were the focal point for many business activities, including legal activities. The speaker refers to the forum of Augustus (Suet. *Aug.* 29) where stood a statue of Apollo (Plin. *N.H.* 7.183; cf. Hor. *Sat.* 1.9.78), humorously described as 'learned in the law' because he has heard so many cases; for the same joke applied to Marsyas, whose statue stood in the Forum Romanum, cf. Mart. 2.64.8.

129 triumphales: i.e. *statuas.* The main building of the forum was the temple of Mars Ultor, in the colonnades of which Augustus had set up statues of Roman military generals in triumphal regalia.

129–30 'Among which some Egyptian mogul has dared to put his inscriptions.' The *titulus* was the inscription displayed underneath the statue citing the man's ancestry, career and achievements. The expression *nescioquis ... Aegyptius atque arabarches* is contemptuous. For *nescioquis* cf. Petr. 57.3. For scorn for Egyptians cf. 26–9. An *arabarches* was a high-ranking taxation official in Egypt, a term which Cicero used of Pompey (*Att.* 2.17.3 with Shackleton Bailey). The object of attack here is probably Tiberius Julius Alexander, a Jew who rose to the high position of Prefect of Egypt in AD 66–70 and who may have been honoured with a triumphal statue for his support of Vespasian. The speaker implies that he is an impostor in the row of statues.

131 cuius ad effigiem non tantum meiere fas est 'at whose statue it is permitted not simply to piss.' The notion that defecation is permitted – or even appropriate – continues the speaker's scorn. For statues suffering this fate cf. 6.309 (urination), Hor. *Sat.* 1.8.38–9, Petr. 71.8, *CIL* III 1966, Jahn on Pers. 1.112–14.

132–4 After a day of accompanying his patron, the client might expect to be asked to join him at the main meal of the day, as a reward for his support.

132 uestibulis: the client is back where he started, outside the front door, cf. *primo limine* (95–6). Cf. Sen. *Cons. Marc.* 10.1, Gell. 4.1.1. **ueteres lassique clientes:** lit. 'old and tired clients' (i.e. longstanding clients, cf. 3.124–5, 5.13, 64nn., and those who have assiduously performed their duties). The blunt word *clientes* indicates the patron's lack of esteem for them; the clients themselves would prefer to be called the *amici*, 'friends' (5.16n.).

134 caulis miseris atque ignis emendus 'the poor guys must buy their broccoli and fire' (*ignis* here denotes firewood, a rare metonymic usage: *TLL* 291–21); cf. 120, listing the basic needs of the client. *emendus*, understand *est*, is gerundive with dative of agent, *miseris*: the poor client has to dip into his own pocket when he hoped to have earned a free meal. *caulis* indicates the relatively humble status of these clients (as in Satire 5: see 5.87n.), for broccoli was valued low (Plin. *N.H.* 19.136–9), in contrast with the patron's lavish feast.

135–146 The patron's selfish feast and its consequences. Eating alone was a severe offence against social custom since eating was essentially a social activity for well-off Romans at least (cf. *conuiuia* 141; see Essay on Satire 5); hence the stress on his solitude and secrecy: *uacuis . . . toris* 136, *tantum ipse* 136, *una* 138, *sibi* 140, picking up *secreto* 95.

135 optima siluarum ... pelagique 'the choicest products of wood and sea'. A cliché of moralising writers, that Rome's decline into luxury was manifested by rich men scouring the world for its choicest products; cf. Edwards (1993) index s.v. 'food'. The *topos* recurs at 5.93–8 (see Mayor's n.); cf. Luc. 4.373–6:

> o prodiga rerum
> Luxuries numquam paruo contenta paratis
> et quaesitorum terra pelagoque ciborum
> ambitiosa fames et lautae gloria mensae.

optima siluarum here probably anticipates the boars (*apros*, 141).

135–6 uorabit, iacebit: while the client returns home hungry, the patron 'will be devouring . . . and reclining'. *uorabit* is stronger than the simple *edet*.

136 rex: frequently 'the patron', cf. 5.14, 130, 137, 161; 7.45. **toris . . . iacebit:** the Romans reclined at their meals; see 5.17n.

137–8 'Since they consume fortunes at one table chosen from their so many splendid and broad and antique round tables.' *tot* and *una* make a strong contrast.   **pulchris et latis orbibus et tam |
antiquis:** cf. *mensas* 75n. The tables were cross-sections of large trees (hence *orbes*).   **comedunt:** like *uorabit* 135, stronger than *edo*. **patrimonia:** a *patrimonium* was the family's estate, held by the *paterfamilias*; it adds insult to injury that rich patrons eat into their family estates for self-indulgence instead of using them to support the family group (including *clientes*).

139 'Soon there will be no parasite.' I.e. the patron's selfish behaviour will make even parasites redundant. *parasitus*: a very uncomplimentary term, here the extreme version of the client, who makes a profession of living off others. Cf. the client Trebius in Satire 5 (*parasitus* 5.145n.). The Greekness of the word may increase the disapproval.

139–40 'But who can stand such mean extravagance?' Language typical of anger: rhetorical question and verb of enduring; cf. 2.24 *quis tulerit?*, 3.60 *non possum ferre*; cf. Anderson (1982) 278. *luxuriae sordes*: an oxymoron (the combination in one phrase of two opposing ideas).

140–1 'What a huge gullet it is which serves up for itself whole boars, an animal created for parties!' Cf. Mart. 5.70.5 *o quanta est gula centies comesse.*   **gula:** literally 'the throat or gullet', metaphorically 'gluttony', cf. 5.94 *dum gula saeuit*, 157–8 *mimus | quis melior plorante gula?*: both senses are relevant here, as at Mart. 1.20.   **ponit:** regularly of serving up food, cf. 5.51, 85, 146.   **apros:** on eating boars cf. Hor. *Sat.* 2.2.89–92, 3.234, 4.40–2, 8.6–7, with Muecke.   **conuiuia:** the communal activity of eating together: see Essay on Satire 5.

142–6 Death in the bath. J. has already mentioned two of his predecessors in the genre of satire, Lucilius (20) and Horace (51); here he indicates his debt to a third, Persius (AD 34–62), by imitating his 'Death in the bath' scene (Pers. 3.98–106). *turgidus* in initial position (J. 143; Pers. 3.98) and *hinc* introducing the consequences (J. 144; Pers. 3.103) signal the imitation.

The normal time for bathing was just before the *cena*, because of the dangers of bathing *in cruditate* (Celsus 2.17.2); but there was a fashion for gluttons to bathe immediately after eating.

142 'Yet the penalty is at hand'.

142-3 tu deponis, portas: the speaker shifts into the 2nd p. sing. to attack aggressively the stingy patron.

143 crudum pauonem in balnea portas 'you carry an undigested peacock to the baths.' Since *crudus* = 'undigested' (*OLD* 3, e.g. Celsus 2.8.32) is confined to technical medical writers and usually = 'uncooked' (cf. J. 15.83 *cadauere crudo*), some scholars prefer the reading *crudus*, attested in several MSS, which would mean 'stuffed' or 'gorged with food'; cf. Hor. *Ep.* 1.6.61 *crudi tumidique lauemur*, which the present passage may be echoing. As this brings its own problems, it is better to retain *crudum*: J. enjoys playing with language for satirical ends (cf. *farrago* 86; cf. Mart. 3.13, a pun on *crudus*). For the connection between 'undigested' and 'uncooked', cf. Plin. *N.H.* 29.26: 'These [practices] have ruined the morals of the Empire, I mean the practices to which we submit when in health – ... boiling baths, by which they have persuaded us that food is cooked in our bodies, so that everyone leaves them the weaker for treatment, and the most submissive are carried out to be buried ...'.   **pauonem:** a luxury dish introduced to Italy in the late Republic; still bearing exotic connotations two centuries later: Hor. *Sat.* 1.2.116, Petr. 55.2.

144 hinc subitae mortes atque intestata senectus 'hence sudden deaths and intestate old age'. On *intestata senectus* see Cloud (1989a) 57-8: death comes so quickly he does not have time to make a will.

145 noua nec tristis ... fabula 'the new but not gloomy story'.

146 ducitur ... funus: cf. 10.240-1 *ducenda tamen sunt | funera natorum*, regularly of the funeral procession (*OLD funus* 1b), which passed through the streets.   **plaudendum ... amicis:** instead of lamenting the patron, the clients applaud in their bitterness at his selfishness. So *plaudendum* replaces *plangendum*, παρὰ προσδοκίαν (contrary to expectation).

147-9 'There will be nothing worse which posterity can add to our ways, our descendants will do and desire the same things, all vice has reached its peak.' Although generally printed as the start of a new paragraph, this is a transition between the preceding section on the content of satire and the following (149–171), which contains the satirist's self-justification. It balances the questions which ask 'when was vice ever worse?' at 87–9: there the contrast is between present and past; here it is between present and future. Hence lines 87–9 and 147–9 frame the section on the Roman client in ring-composition. **moribus:** here (bad) behaviour, vices.   **minores:** descendants (*OLD* 3c), cf. 2.146, 8.234, as *maiores* = ancestors.   **in praecipiti:** cf. Petr. 55.1; for a similar proverbial expression in Greek cf. Hom. *Il.* 10.173 ἐπὶ ξυροῦ ἵσταται ἀκμῆς, which, however, means 'on the knife's edge'.   **stetit:** the perfect is gnomic.

149–171 This closing passage complements the opening section (1–21): both present self-justification, referring to Lucilius and indicating relationship between satire and epic. On J.'s version of the traditional satiric pattern of *apologia*, see Essay.

149–50 'Use your sails, spread all your canvas', i.e. 'off you go at full pelt'. The speaker exhorts himself to action, i.e. to write satire. The nautical metaphor, though fairly common, sounds grand (Bramble (1974) 166–8, e.g. Plin. *Ep.* 4.20.2, 6.33.10 *dedimus uela indignationi, dedimus irae, dedimus dolori, et in amplissima causa quasi magno mari pluribus uentis sumus uenti*, 8.4.5 *immitte rudentes, pande uela*).

150 dices hic forsitan: an objector immediately interrupts, initiating the dialogue with which the poem closes. J.'s interruptor has a firmer status than Persius', who is openly stated to be a fiction at *Sat.* 1.44 *quisquis es, o modo quem ex aduerso dicere feci.*

150–1 unde | ingenium par materiae? 'From where [will come] the talent equal to the subject?' Ellipse of the verb and hiatus after *materiae* enhance the abruptness. *ingenium* = natural talent, cf. 79 *si natura negat*; Plin. *Ep.* 9.2.2. For *materiae* cf. Ov. *Pont.* 4.13.46 *materiam uestris . . . ingeniis.*

151–3 unde . . . simplicitas? 'From where [will come] that frankness of men of old in writing whatever they desired with blazing soul?', *animo flagrante* abl. of attendant circumstances. Cf. Cic. *Planc.* 33 *ubi illa antiqua libertas?*; Tac. *Dial.* 27.3 *antiqua libertate. priorum* is a generalisation, but the reference to Mucius in what follows indicates that Lucilius is meant. For the vocabulary typical of anger (*flagrante*) see Introduction §6. *simplicitas:* straightforwardness, frankness, outspokenness; cf. Sen. *Ben.* 3.26.1 (negative), Plin. *Ep.* 1.15.4 (positive).

153–4 'cuius . . . non?': the speaker's bold reply to his interlocutor (thus Duff); most other commentators see them as words quoted by the interlocutor which he immediately refutes. Almost certainly a reworking of lines of Lucilius, since Mucius is an object of his attack. After *quid refert* there is ellipse of *utrum*.   **Mucius:** P. Mucius Scaeuola, an eminent Roman politician (tribune of the plebs 141 BC, consul 133 BC), attacked by Lucilius, cf. Pers. 1.114–5 *secuit Lucilius Vrbem,* | *te Lupi, te Muci.*

155–6 'Describe Tigillinus: you will shine on that fire where men stand and burn and smoke with (trans)fixed throat'; lit. 'men who smoke ... standing blaze'. For this punishment, cf. Gell. 3.14.19 (citing Cato), Sen. *Ira* 3.3.6. For the dangers incurred by making political allusions to the living in poetic compositions cf. Cic. *Rep.* 4.11–12 and Hor. *Sat.* 2.1.80–3, referring to the Twelve Tables. **Tigillinum:** C. Ofonius Tigillinus, a favourite of Nero, praetorian prefect in AD 62, depicted as lustful and cruel, abusing his position of power. An example of a powerful man whom it was dangerous to cross; also responsible for punishing the Christians with the torment described in lines 155–7, cf. Tac. *Ann.* 15.44 *crucibus adfixi ... atque ubi defecisset dies in usum nocturni luminis urerentur.*   **fixo gutture fumant:** harsh, with alliteration of *f,* cf. 2.8n.

157 'And [where] it traces a broad furrow across the arena.' There is no obvious subject for *deducit* and the shift from 2nd p. sing. fut. *lucebis* to 3rd p. sing. pres. *deducit* may suggest that the text is corrupt. *deducis* (with two MSS: 'you plough a broad furrow ...') is possible, but the shift from fut. to pres. harsh. Housman's suggestion that a line has fallen out between 156 and 157 is more attractive; the line might have said, 'When the fire has died down, your corpse ...'.

158–9 'So is the man who has given aconite to three uncles to ride by on swaying feathers [= cushions] and to look down on us from there?' Supply '... without my speaking out' or '... with impunity': the speaker's indignant reply, declaring his right to take revenge on those who have profited from crime, is reminiscent of the three indignant questions in lines 1–6.   **tribus patruis:** reference unknown; more likely an allusion to a famous case rather than a generalisation. **aconita:** a deadly type of poison, cf. 6.639 *pueris ... meis aconita paraui,* 8.219, 10.25.   **plumis:** down pillows, a sign of great luxury, cf. 6.88 *in magnis opibus plumaque parenta,* 10.362 *uenere et cenis et pluma Sardanapalli,* Mart. 12.17.   **illinc despiciat nos:** underlines the sharp 'them and us' division between the successful criminals and the ordinary poorer citizens. Disruption of the metre marks the speaker's agitation: see Introduction §8.

160–70 The interruptor's reply: a warning of the danger (160–1); epic is safe (162–4), but satire is dangerous (165–8), so think before you begin (168–70).

160–1 The interruptor picks up the speaker's (previous) point and sketches a scenario of danger: 'Keep quiet when *he* (i.e. the rich poisoner) comes by; if you so much as say, "That's the man who ..." you'll be treated as if you'd accused him in court.'   **'hic est':** taken from Pers. 1.28 *pulchrum est digito monstrari et dicier 'hic est'.*

162–4 'You may pit together Aeneas and the fierce Rutulian without fear, the death of Achilles is harmful to no one nor is Hylas, long sought and gone after his pitcher.' It is safe to write epic. The interruptor refers to three central epic stories, treated in the *Aeneid*, the *Achilleid* (Statius) and *Argonautica* (Valerius Flaccus again: 7–13nn.).

Rutulum ... ferocem: Aeneas' opponent, Turnus.   **committas** 'pit together, match, set fighting', often used of a pair of gladiators, and metaphorically e.g. 6.436 *committit uates et comparat* (Virgil and Homer).   **percussus Achilles:** literally 'Achilles smitten', hence 'the death of Achilles'. This was a common theme for recitation (Epictet. 3.23.35).   **multum quaesitus Hylas urnamque secutus:** Hylas was Hercules' young squire on the expedition of the Argonauts. When he went to draw water he was pulled in by the river-nymphs and, though Hercules searched everywhere for him, he never found him: Theoc. *Id.* 13, Ap. Rhod. 1.1187–1357, Virg. *Ecl.* 6.43–4, Val. Fl. *Arg.* 3.596–7 and 4.18–19. J. alters the order of events here (Hylas ought to fall in before he can be looked for) to create a humorous effect at the end of the line: *urnam ... secutus* strips Hylas of any epic dignity.

165–7 'As often as blazing Lucilius has raged as if with drawn sword, the hearer whose mind is cold with crimes grows red, his heart sweats with silent guilt.' Lucilius recurs in ring composition: see 19–20n. Heat (*ardens*) affects cold (*frigida*) so as to create sweat (*sudant*). **ense uelut stricto:** J. apologises for his imagery with *uelut* again at 5.125. The metaphor depicts Lucilius as an epic warrior: *ensis* is usually found in high poetry and not used elsewhere by J.; cf. Hor. *Sat.* 2.1.39–41, a grand image describing his poetry.   **ardens:** cf. 45

ardeat, 153 *animo flagrante*; the 'warrior' is depicted ablaze with anger, cf. Virg. *Aen.* 10.689 *Mezentius ardens.*   **infremuit:** cf. Stat. *Ach.* 1.855 and for *infremuit* + *stricto ferro* cf. Virg. *Aen.* 10.711–15 which J. may be echoing.   **frigida mens est:** the same phrase at Lucr. 3.299. **criminibus** 'crimes' here, as at 75.   **praecordia:** the area around the heart, regarded as sensitive, cf. Pers. 1.117.

168 inde ira et lacrimae: 'hence rage and tears', meaning, 'if you attack someone who has something to be guilty about, you will make him angry (*ira*) and he will take his revenge on you, causing you grief (*lacrimae*)'. An adaptation of the proverb from Terence, *Andr.* 126 *hinc illae lacrumae.*

168–70 tecum prius ergo uoluta | haec animo ante tubas: galeatum sero duelli | paenitet 'so turn these things over in your mind first before the trumpets [sound]: when the helmet is on, it is too late to repent the battle'. *paenitet*, impersonal verb, takes acc. of person: *galeatum* 'you having been helmeted' + genitive of thing: *duelli*. The warning continues: 'don't write satire unless you're sure you want to face the risks'.   **uoluta | haec animo:** taken from epic, e.g. Virg. *Aen.* 6.157–8 *uolutat* | ... *animo secum*, 185 *haec ipse suo tristi cum corde uolutat*, and from Lucilius: *nonne ante in corde uolutas?* 1017M = 1078W. **galeatum:** the Roman soldier only put on his *galea* when the enemy was sighted: *B.Afr.* 12.3. Cf. 8.238 *galeatum ... praesidium*, 'a helmeted garrison'.   **duelli:** archaic form of *belli*. Horace uses this form (in hexameters at *Ep.* 1.2.7, 2.1.254, 2.2.98), which may point to Lucilius having used it.

170–1 'I will try what I may be permitted against those whose ashes are covered by the Flaminian and the Latin roads', i.e. 'I will attack only the dead'. On the speaker's response to the warnings of danger and death see Essay.   **Flaminia, Latina:** understand *uia* with each, as at 61 *Flaminiam.* The *via Latina* branched off from the great road that led from Rome to the south, the *via Appia.* Since burial within the city of Rome was generally forbidden, the major roads were lined with the tombs of people with the means to afford them.

ESSAY

Satire 1 is a programmatic poem, which provides a declaration of the plan. Programmatic poems are found in the lower genres in the literary hierarchy, because the poet felt obliged to justify the choice of another genre instead of epic, the most prestigious genre which a poet could tackle. They are usually placed at the beginning of the collection, for example, Catullus 1; the first poem(s) in each of Propertius' four books of elegies; Ovid *Amores* 1.1–3; Horace *Satires* 2.1; and Persius Satire 1 (on which see Bramble (1974) esp. 16–23). In these lower genres the themes tend to be drawn from private life and to relate to the individual; they might even be considered subversive, at least in contrast with the celebration of public and national achievements characteristic of epic. The refusal to write epic which typically occurs in programmatic poems we term the *recusatio*. Typical reasons given for not writing epic include lack of talent and lack of inspiration. These negative reasons are sometimes amplified by positive reasons for the choice of another genre, which in scholarly discussion is known as the *apologia*, 'self-defence' (Greek) or 'self-justification'. These two elements, *recusatio* and *apologia*, are prominent in many programmatic poems and, because they represent two sides of the same coin, are often inextricably linked.

As well as these two elements, programmatic poems generally give a foretaste of the style and content of the poetry book, that is, the manner and the matter. All these features are found in J.'s first Satire. The poem is framed by two sections of almost identical length which present his *recusatio*, refusal of epic in favour of satire, and his *apologia*, his self-justification for following in the footsteps of Lucilius, the founder of the genre. The rest of the poem provides a programme of the manner and matter, the style and themes, to be adopted.

Without prelude or introduction, the speaker (for this term, used to designate the *persona* created by J., see Introduction §2) bursts out with a string of indignant questions (1–6) which are remarkable for their extreme manner of expression (*semper, numquam*). He expresses a fierce desire for revenge (1–6n.) and a hatred for contemporary poetry, especially epic on mythological themes, which he regards as boring and silly (7–13n.): this is his *recusatio*. His justification (*apologia*) for raising his voice is not simply a desire for revenge for all the tedious recitations he has sat through; he claims to have had the same training as all those other 'bards' (i.e. poets, sarcastically: 15–17n.) and argues that it would be stupid not to use paper which will be wasted anyway (17–18). This constitutes a variation on the regular theme in the Roman *recusatio* and *apologia* that lack of talent prevents the attempt at epic; exhibiting self-contempt, J.'s speaker claims that the universal lack of talent qualifies him equally with every other poet. After offering this as his defence, he makes a start. Lines 19–21 contain an explicit statement of his chosen genre through the reference to Lucilius and the rest of the poem is an explanation of why he has chosen satire. Lucilius represents the genre of Roman verse satire not only because he was regarded as its founder but also because of his reputation for fiery invective, which suits J.'s speaker well, given the display of anger in the opening lines of the poem (although he may exaggerate Lucilius' fieriness). The portrayal of Lucilius as an epic warrior (19–20n.) glorifies him and at the same time suggests that satire can replace irrelevant and boring epic: again a fusion of *apologia* and *recusatio*.

Lines 22–80 explain why the speaker has chosen satire: because he is morally outraged at what he sees around him. The lines present a catalogue of wickedness (often termed a 'rogues' gallery': a perversion of a feature of epic in which warriors or troops are reviewed), with a cumulative effect designed to justify the speaker's moral indignation. This section of the poem has often been said to lack structure (so Helmbold (1951), for example, attempted to remedy the structure by proposing multiple deletions) and, at first sight, this allegation seems to have some force. The apparently unstructured rantings of the speaker help characterise him as an irrational man carried away by his anger. But further analysis reveals an underlying structure, a recurrent pattern of vignette of vice followed by indignant exclamation containing a programmatic statement:

Vignette	Exclamation
22–29	30
30–44	45
46–50	51–54
55–62	63–64
64–78	79–80

The vignettes of vice are discussed in the commentary; all that need be noted here is that they are commonly introduced as a series of *cum* . . . clauses and that many of them indicate that the speaker's main obsessions are money, sex and status (so Martyn (1970)). This catalogue of vice is punctuated by programmatic statements. The first series of outrages (22–9) causes the explosion of line 30: *difficile est saturam non scribere*. The speaker here claims that to write satire is a perfectly natural response to the vices prevalent in Rome. The same is implied by his next words, *nam quis iniquae | tam patiens Vrbis, tam ferreus, ut teneat se, | cum ...* (30–1), which introduce the second series of criminals (30–44). The series is interrupted by another explosion at line 45: *quid referam quanta siccum iecur ardeat ira, | cum ...* , which explicitly characterises the speaker's mood as one of anger. After two more examples of vice (46–50) the speaker again bursts out with two indignant questions, his anger marked by repetition of *haec ego non* (51–2). He explicitly justifies his choice of genre, this time with a reference to Horace, Lucilius' successor in the genre (*Venusina digna lucerna* 51). The superiority of satire over epic lies in its relevance and seriousness: he depicts themes of epic as silly and irrelevant (52–4) and so suggests that satire is its opposite. This is made more explicit in the next programmatic statement which follows another pair of rogues (55–62): *nonne libet medio ceras inplere capaces | quadriuio, cum ...* (63–4). The speaker's picture of himself standing at the cross-roads with his notebook at the ready, the ancient equivalent perhaps of the camera team making a documentary, is an explicit claim that he is telling the truth. Two more vignettes of criminals visible on the streets of Rome (64–72: *occurrit* at 69 indicates the street setting) are followed by a series of sarcastic generalisations (73–8) which confirm the speaker's anger and obsession with money, sex and status and which may even hint that he is jealous of those who profit from their crimes. All this constitutes the build-up to the last programmatic statement in this part of the poem, the famous lines 79–80:

> si natura negat, facit indignatio uersum
> qualemcumque potest, quales ego uel Cluuienus.

Here the speaker is making two claims. Firstly, that he is a blunt and simple man who lacks talent in versification (a regular element in the *apologia*): this is the implication of the deflationary bathos of *qualemcumque potest* and of the reference to the unknown Cluvienus, who is presumably an insignificant amateur poet. Secondly, and more importantly, that pure moral indignation is his motivation, a claim which he has already made both implicitly and explicitly in the first half of the poem, a claim which seems designed to evoke the claims of impartiality made by historians (e.g. Tac. *Ann.* 1.1; *Hist.* 1.1). This is his *apologia*, his justification for his choice of genre, and at the same time it provides a programmatic statement of his chosen style or manner: a declamatory, epicising, angry style which is an innovation within the genre (see Introduction §6).

His angry manner, revealed in the series of programmatic statements, is apparently provoked by the subject-matter. But there is no explicit programmatic statement concerning subject-matter until the second half of the poem, although the catalogue of wickedness (22–80) obviously provides a foretaste of the themes which attract the speaker. This statement follows immediately after the statement of manner at 79–80, creating a block of programmatic material at the centre of the poem. But at this point the speaker breaks with the style of the preceding lines by adopting a grand epic manner for a moment (81–4). The claim he makes in lines 81–6 is that all human activity and all human experience – whatever humankind has done since the Flood – *uotum, timor, ira, uoluptas,* | *gaudia, discursus* – will be his subject-matter. Whether this sweeping claim is justified will soon emerge.

The programmatic statement is followed immediately by a series of indignant questions (87–95), reminiscent of the opening of the satire. These lines have two functions. Firstly, they give a justification for writing satire NOW (*nunc* 95): because human wickedness has never in the past been worse. Again, this forms part of the speaker's *apologia*. But they also narrow the focus of the speaker's attack from the broad scope of lines 85–6 to, first, vices in general (*uitiorum copia* 87), then to greed and materialism (*auaritia* 88). Moreover, once *auaritia* has been selected as the topic, it is illustrated by brief vignettes (88–95) which give the vice a specifically Roman setting. So within a few lines, the speaker's focus has shifted from 'all human activity' to 'Roman greed'.

Following the brief tableaux of 88–95, lines 95–126 provide a single extended tableau on the same theme of Roman materialism, specifically, the *sportula*, the handout of money to his clients by the great patron (95n.). The scene is at the patron's threshold. First we see the mob awaiting the handout, a mob consisting of those of high and low birth alike: the speaker is outraged by the way the *nouveau riche* freedman pushes aside Roman magistrates (95–111). Then we see some of the noblest and most important men in Rome ousting the humbler clients and even resorting to deception to get as much money as possible (117–26). In between comes the centrepiece of the section, where the speaker declares that money is the highest god of Roman society, *sanctissima diuitiarum | maiestas* (112–16).

J. has been criticised for a lack of proportion or structure, on the grounds that he devotes too much attention to this single scene. This seems a mistaken criticism. So far the poem has contained many theoretical statements about the choice of genre and programmatic indications of the angry manner of presentation, with fleeting glimpses of criminals interspersed. In lines 95–126 J. provides for the first time a sample of his satire: an anticipation or preview of the remaining poems in the Book. It displays a selection of the satirical devices which are J.'s hallmarks: for example, the surprise of finding even *ipsos Troiugenas* (100) in the queue, a surprise capped by another, that the freedman pushes past them (102); the grim irony that although money is revered above all else, there is as yet no temple to *Pecunia* in Rome (112–16); the satiric deflation of the list of temples at 115 by the stork's nest built on top of the temple of *Concordia* (116), where *nido* is typically postponed until final position to deliver the satiric thrust; and the vivid snippet of dialogue in lines 125–6. This passage provides a foretaste not only of J.'s satiric techniques but also of the subject-matter to be treated in the rest of the Book. The *sportula* is an important element in the patron–client relationship which was central to Roman life. This relationship features prominently in Book 1: Satire 3 is, in effect, the complaint of the neglected client, Satire 4 depicts a nightmare version of this relationship between emperor and courtiers and Satire 5 describes a dinner-party to which the client is invited by his patron. The choice of this topic for the only extended vignette in Satire 1 is an indication of its importance.

The topic of the patron–client relationship continues after line 126, which suggests that the 'sample' does not end there but continues through the briefer tableaux up to 146.

Line 127, *ipse dies pulchro distinguitur ordine rerum*, sounds like a programmatic statement announcing a description of the client's day. This programme is manifestly not carried out, since the rest of the day is sketched only in bare outline with large omissions, especially in comparison with the detailed treatment given to the *sportula* scene. This has led some critics to postulate a *lacuna* after 131 (127–34n.). This is unnecessary. Rather, it is typical of J.'s satiric technique to create then disappoint expectations (cf. 81ff., 6.474ff.). So the rest of

the day is briefly evoked by allusions to attendance at the law-courts in
the forum (128–31) and to the invitation-less end of the day (132–4).
This allows the speaker to contrast the humble client and the selfish
patron (135–41) and the deserved and unlamented death of the patron
(142–6). All these scenes illustrate the speaker's central theme: the
degradation of the patron–client relationship through greed.

This ends the 'sample' section of the poem. It is significant that in
the final scene J. pays to one of his predecessors in the genre the
compliment of imitation. Persius, the only Roman satirist between
Horace and J. whose poems survive, included in his third Satire a
graphic and revolting portrayal of 'Death in the bath' (3.98–106).
This J. imitates here, in briefer and less disgusting detail (142–6n.).
This indicates his debt to Persius. So in the course of Satire 1, J. refers
or alludes to all his major predecessors in his chosen genre: Lucilius,
Horace and now Persius (142–6n.).

Most editors begin a new paragraph at 147. This is misleading, as
147–9 form a bridge passage between the 'sample' section and the coda
of the poem. Moreover, in content they precisely balance the lines
immediately preceding the 'sample' section, lines 87–95: lines 147–9
give a justification for writing satire NOW as opposed to in the future
(because nothing posterity can do will be worse), just as lines 87–95
provided a justification in terms of a present–past contrast.

After this elaborate self-justification, the speaker seems on the point
of launching himself into satire: he urges himself with the grand words
utere uelis, | *totos pande sinus* (149–50), which implies a repudiation of
Horace's Callimachean literary principles (see Braund (1992a) 21).
But at this moment, an imaginary interlocutor or adversary (a standard device in satire taken from the Greek diatribe) interrupts with
objections to the speaker writing satire, mostly in the form of warnings
about the risks. The idea that satire is dangerous for its targets is an old
one: the early Greek satirists Archilochus and Hipponax are said to
have caused deaths by their satire (see Elliott (1960) esp. 3–15); the
warning here is that satire will bring retaliation from the target upon
the satirist himself.

The ensuing conversation between speaker and interlocutor constitutes the coda to the poem (149–71), which is another theoretical
passage concerning the choice of genre. This balances the opening
paragraph (lines 1–21): in both passages, the speaker conveys his anger
(1–6, 153–4 and 158–9), in both irrelevant mythological epic is con-

trasted with satire (7–11, 162–7), in both the speaker appeals to the precedent provided by Lucilius (19–21, 153–4) and in both the speaker and Lucilius are associated with martial language and imagery (3,4, 19–20, 165–6, 168–70). The conversation between speaker and interlocutor goes like this:

SP: (addressing himself) Off you go – do your satire! (149–50)

INT: Where will you find the talent and frankness of speech? (150–3)

SP: Whose name don't I dare name? I'll follow in Lucilius' footsteps. (153–4)

INT: It's dangerous to attack important people nowadays. (155–7)

SP: Am I to put up with the contempt of a prosperous criminal? (158–9)

INT: Yes; epic is safe but satire is dangerous and brings trouble. (160–70)

SP: I will attack the dead. (170–1)

The speaker's conclusion, that he will attack only the dead, has seemed to many (e.g. Duff) unsatisfactory. He has twice declared that it is present wickedness which impels him to satire and so led us to expect an attack on his contemporaries. To attack only the dead seems like an evasion. It will be argued below that such inconsistencies are part of the speaker's characterisation. But for the moment another, complementary, explanation of the end of the poem can be offered. (The following reading of the closing section is indebted to Kenney (1962) and Griffith (1970); see also Fredericksmeyer (1990).)

The pattern in the final 22 lines is one established by tradition: a similar pattern of warning and reply is found at the end of the other two programmatic satires which survive in Latin literature, Horace *Satires* 2.1 and Persius *Satire* 1, although the final evasion takes different forms. In *Sat.* 2.1 Horace is discussing with Trebatius, an eminent jurist, the writing of satire. After his last, bombastic, lines, the lawyer warns him of the dangers of satire, as follows:

H: ... In short, whether serene old age lies ahead or death is already hovering near on sable wing, in Rome or if fortune

so ordains in exile, whatever the complexion of my life, I'll
continue to write. (57–60)

T: My lad, I'm afraid you may not be long for this world. One
of your powerful friends may freeze you stiff. (60–2)

H: Why on earth? Lucilius was able to indulge in free speech
and it didn't do him any harm. (62–79)

T: OK, but you'd better beware you're not prosecuted for
defamation. For if a party compose foul verses (*mala
carmina*) to another's hurt, a hearing and trial ensue.
(79–83)

H: Foul verses, yes; but what if a party compose fine verses
(*bona carmina*) which win a favourable verdict from Caesar?
Or snarl at a public menace when he himself is blameless?
(83–5)

T: The indictment will dissolve in laughter and you'll go scot
free. (86)

The main point to notice is that 'Horace' does not take the warning
seriously but sidesteps it with a joke, a pun on the literary and legal
senses of the phrase *mala carmina* (= slander and bad poetry). This is no
real reply to the objections Trebatius has made.

Persius follows in Horace's footsteps at the close of his first, programmatic, satire, in conversation with an imaginary interlocutor:

P: Could such things happen if we had a spark of our
fathers' balls? You're all effete effeminates when it comes
to literature, like morals. (103–6)

INT: Must you scrub delicate ears with truths that bite? Take
care your great friends don't grow cool. I hear a snarling
in the air. (107–10)

P: The whole lot's fine from now. I don't care. Bravo!
Superb! You're all just marvellous. . . . Lucilius crunched
the city – Lupus and Mucius and all – and smashed his
molar. While his friend is laughing, sly Flaccus [=
Horace] lays his finger on all his faults; gaining admis-
sion, he plays on the conscience – so clever at holding the
public up on that well-blown nose. Am I to say nothing?
Not even in confidence? Not even to a hole? (110–19)

INT: Nowhere. (119)

P: I will dig a trench and whisper into it my secret: that
     everyone at Rome has asses' ears. This private secret I will
     keep to myself, for my readers will be a select and dis-
     criminating few. (120–34)

Again Persius evades the issue of offending people with his satire by
overt praise but covert criticism which is 'secretly' confined to his book
of small readership.

   From these two passages a pattern of apology emerges:

(1)   The speaker makes a challenging statement, in bombastic or
      defiant terms, of his mission in writing satire.
(2)   The interlocutor warns him of the risks of satire.
(3)   The speaker appeals to the precedent of Lucilius.
(4)   The interlocutor renews his warning in different terms.
(5)   The speaker evades the issue.

This pattern is visible in J. too. (1) occurs in 149–50, in the overblown
rhetorical cliché of the spreading sail. (2) is the interlocutor's first
warning, that he has neither the talent nor the necessary freedom of
speech (150–3). (3) is the speaker's appeal to the precedent of Lucilius
(153–4). (4) is the interlocutor's warning of danger (155–7). At this
point, the speaker reiterates his intention to attack criminals, a revised
form of (1) (158–9). Then the interlocutor warns of the dangers of
satire, incorporating a reference to Lucilius, as opposed to epic, a
second version of (4) (160–70). Finally (5) the speaker evades the issue
with his determination to attack only the dead (170–1).

   Further, a strong case has been made that this pattern of apology at
the end of a programmatic poem had its origin not with Horace but
Lucilius. Fragments which survive from Book 30 of his *Satires* seem to
bear this out. If this is accepted, all three of Lucilius' successors are
performing variations on what they perhaps saw as an obligatory
theme. And all three contrive ingeniously varied evasions with which
their satiric *personae* (and, by extension, perhaps, they themselves) can
avoid the charge of being a menace to society and thereby putting
themselves in danger.

   But what of the contradiction between the close of Satire 1 and the
speaker's earlier implication that he will attack his contemporaries?
What sort of *persona* has J. created in his opening poem? Is this fiercely

indignant character really a coward in the face of danger, in short, a hypocrite? A closer examination of Satire 1 suggests that J.'s creation is a hypocrite in several other respects. His claims conflict with his practice throughout the poem. Take his claim to be motivated by moral indignation (e.g. 45, 79, also 30). This claim does not sit easily with his evident envy of rich and successful people. Moreover, he exhibits rather too much enjoyment and relish of the sordid details of the shocking sex scenes he describes for his pose of moral uprightness to be really convincing. For example, he reveals that he cannot get to sleep at night for thinking about such outrages (*quem patitur dormire . . .* 77–8). In these manifestations of envy and prurience, J. hints that the speaker's moral indignation is not entirely wholesome: these self-betrayals reveal the speaker's hypocrisy. Another claim he makes is that he is a simple, blunt man without poetic ability (implicit in *si natura negat . . .* 79–80). But this claim conflicts with his earlier claim to have received the same rhetorical training as all the other 'bards' (15–17). A third claim he makes is that he is a reasonable man (*rationem* 21) who is telling the truth (implied by *nonne libet medio . . .* 63–4). Yet his portrayal of life in Rome is marked by distortions in the form of exaggeration of the horrendous and scandalous elements and of suppression of the mundane, boring, undramatic events of everyday life. Rome was doubtless no more crowded with informers, gigolos, husband-pimps, bankrupt young aristocrats and women poisoners than any metropolis of the contemporary western world is with the homosexual spies, corrupt businessmen, serial rapists, vicars eloping with nymphets, suburban madams, and athletes and pop stars on drugs who populate the 'gutter press' (on portrayals of the city in satire see Introduction §9(*a*)). Similarly misleading is his claim to treat the whole of human life and experience (81–6): as suggested above, he is primarily interested in status, sex and money. These gaps between the speaker's claims and his practice combine with his final self-betrayal in the closing lines to hint that he is no paragon of virtue (though he clearly casts himself in this role) but a spineless and petty bigot.

This interpretation of J.'s creation rescues it from the biographical fallacy prevalent in earlier readerships and scholarship. It should, however, be stated that each new reader must make up her or his own mind about the balance between moralist and hypocrite. Above all, satire offers a challenge to the reader, a challenge to react to the *persona* with sympathy or with disapproval. What it defies the reader to do is to stay neutral.

SATIRE 2

1–35 The poem opens with an attack by the speaker on hypocritical moralists who pretend to uphold strict ancient Roman morality and criticise effeminates and homosexuals while indulging in such practices themselves in secret. The theme of this section is *frontis nulla fides* (8), 'you can't trust appearances'. The speaker is immediately established as the raging, indignant, narrow-minded, chauvinistic bigot of Satire 1, who sees Rome as a city seething with corruption. His language is characterised by telling oxymora (3, 8–9, 10, 20–1) and angry questions (8–10, 24–8, 34–5).

1–3 The speaker wishes to flee beyond the edge of the known world, so strong is his desire to escape from hypocritical moralists. For flight from horrors, cf. Pythagoras in Satire 15 (172–3) and Umbricius in Satire 3. **Vltra ... fugere hinc libet** 'I long to flee from here beyond ...'. *ultra* is picked up at 159 in ring-composition. *fugere* initiates the military vocabulary of the poem. **Sauromatas ... et glacialem Oceanum:** i.e. to the far north. The Sauromatae (also called Sarmatae) lived round the Sea of Azov, on the edge of the known world (cf. 3.79, 15.125). The Ocean was thought to surround the entire inhabited world; the 'icy Ocean' is the Arctic and Baltic.

2–3 'whenever those who pretend to be Curii and live like Bacchanals have the gall [to utter] on morals'. The theme of hypocrisy and pretence is introduced; cf. Mart. 7.58.7–9; Bramble (1974) 42 n.3. For *audere* + acc. see *OLD* 4, cf. 82, 10.175. **moribus:** again at 39 and in ring-composition 170; the poem's theme. **Curios:** Manius Curius Dentatus, censor 272 BC and conqueror of Pyrrhus, a typical representative of traditional Roman virtue; so at 153 and 11.78 and in an identical context at Mart. 1.24.3. The plural *Curii* is generic, 'people like Curius' (cf. 8.4, Mart. 9.27.6; also *Scauros* 35). **Bacchanalia uiuunt:** lit. 'live the festival of Bacchus'. In Roman thought, the Bacchanalia represented the starkest antithesis to proper behaviour, *mos maiorum*: hence the drinking, feasting, lust and violence associated with the notorious Bacchanalia of 186 BC (Liv. 39.8).

4–7 Proof no.1 (*primum*) of their hypocrisy: they display the busts of philosophers and sages in their houses, yet are completely uneducated. A man who wished to be thought a philosopher might place such busts in his house and garden (Lucian, *Nigr.* 2). The Greek endings of *Aristotelen*, *Pittacon* and *Cleanthas* help to underline the hypocrites' desire to appear learned. For the contrast between appearance and reality cf. Quint. *I.O.* 1 pr.15 *sub hoc nomine* (sc. of philosopher) *maxima in plerisque uitia latuerunt. non enim uirtute ac studiis, ut haberentur philosophi, laborant, sed uultum et tristitiam et dissentientem a ceteris habitum pessimis moribus praetendebant, ibid.* 12.3.12, e.g. *in publico tristes, domi dissoluti*; for philosophers living badly cf. Cic. *Tusc.* 2.12.

4 indocti: sc. *sunt.* For *indoctus* of those not familiar with philosophy cf. 13.181.   **omnia** 'all [their houses]'.

4–5 plena ... gypso Chrysippi 'full of plaster busts of Chrysippus'. Gypsum or plaster of Paris was regularly used for busts. Chrysippus, a Stoic philosopher of the third century BC, was the third head of the Stoic sect; mentioned as a representative Stoic at Hor. *Ep.* 1.2.4.

5 inuenias 'you may find'.

5–6 perfectissimus horum si quis ... 'the most complete of them is the one who ...'. For *perfectissimus*, 'finished, perfect, complete', cf. Quint. *I.O.* 10.2.24 *perfectissimus Graecorum Demosthenes*, Cic. *Brut.* 118, Cato as *perfectissimo Stoico*.

6 Aristotelen similem 'a life-like Aristotle', i.e. a painted wax mask or portrait, cf. Stat. *Silv.* 5.1.1 *manus ... similes docilis ... fingere ceras*, Mart. 1.109.18–20 *picta ... tabella | in qua tam similem uidebis Issam | ut sit tam similis sibi nec ipsa.* Aristotle (384–322 BC), pupil of Plato, founded the Lyceum.   **Pittacon:** (*c.* 650–570 BC), one of the famous seven sages of the ancient world. For the mixture of sages and philosophers cf. 13.184–5 (Chrysippus, Thales, Socrates).

7 iubet ... pluteum seruare: lit. 'bids his shelf hold'; *iubeo* + infin. often has a weaker sense than 'order', cf. 7.41. *pluteum*, usually the back or side of a couch, here evidently a shelf.   **archetypos ... Cleanthas** 'originals of Cleanthes', as opposed to copies. Greek *archetypos* conveys scorn. Cleanthes (331–232 BC) was the second head of the Stoa, taking over from its founder, Zeno. The plural suggests a collection or may be generic, 'of Cleanthes and his like'.

8–10 A succinct statement of their hypocrisy followed by two indignant questions. The language is typical of indignation, e.g. the generalisations *nulla* and *quis ... non ... ?* and the superlative *notissima.*

8 frontis nulla fides 'you can't trust appearances', a forceful epigram typical of J.; cf. 6.O 20–1 for *fides* in a similar context. Alliteration of *f*, a sound which Quintilian describes as harsh and unpleasant, *paene non humana uoce uel omnino non uoce potius inter discrimina dentium efflanda est* (*I.O.* 12.10.29), conveys disgust. *frons*: the location of *pudor* (cf. 13.242, Pers. 5.104) but also in contrasts between appearance and reality (e.g. 14.56, Pers. 5.116–17).   **uicus:** street, as at 3.236–7 *arto | uicorum in flexu.*

9 tristibus obscenis 'grim perverts'. In this combination of two adjectives, a favourite formulation in J., one becomes a noun, cf. 9.38 *mollis auarus*, 'stingy effeminate'. *tristis*: as usual, stronger than 'sad', hence 'gloomy, despondent, morose' or even 'stern, severe, grim'; cf. Mart. 1.24.2, 7.58.9, and Quintilian quoted above (4–7n.). For *obscenus* as a noun, cf. 6.513.   **castigas ... sis:** in indignation the speaker briefly addresses one of the hypocritical moralists, a technique typical of J. For *castigo*, 'castigate, correct', cf. 35, 14.54, 6.455.

10 Socraticos ... cinaedos: an oxymoron (pointed combination of two opposing or contrasting ideas), one of J.'s favourite devices, cf. 6.118 *meretrix Augusta* (of Messallina), 8.148 *mulio consul*. If J.'s audience recalled Hor. *A.P.* 310 *Socraticae ... chartae*, Prop. 2.34.27 *Socraticis ... libris* or Ov. *Ib.* 494 *Socraticum ... opus*, then the surprise of *cinaedos* is still more brutal.

The contrast between philosophical appearance (the Stoics and other philosophical schools claimed descent from Socrates) and lewd reality (*cinaedus* originally meant 'dancer' but developed to mean a passive homosexual, also called a 'catamite' or a 'pathic') is repeated. *Socraticos* may suggest Socrates' supposed homosexual relations with his pupils (e.g. Lucian, *Am.* 54).   **fossa** lit. 'ditch'; for *fossa* as a sexual term, designating the vagina or anus (as here) see Adams (1982) 86 and cf. 9.45–6 *foderit ... dominum*, where *fodio* is used of the active role in intercourse. The abundance of sibilants in 8–10 conveys hostility.

11–15 Proof no. 2 of their hypocrisy. To outward appearances, their hairy arms and legs are fiercely masculine: removal of hair from the arms and legs was often regarded as a sign of effeminacy (9.95, 8.114–15, Mart. 3.63.6), so their hairiness is intended as a sign of masculinity (cf. 8.116, Mart. 2.36.5). But the hidden smoothness of their depilated bottoms betrays that they are passive homosexuals (cf. Pers. 4.39–41, Mart. 2.62.4). For a similar contrast between appearance and reality cf. Mart 6.56.

11 hispida 'shaggy', a word often used of animals, e.g. goat (Mart. 3.58.37), boar (Phaedrus 5.10.4), bears (Stat. *Theb.* 6.868). **saetae** 'bristles', often of animal hair, e.g. lion (Virg. *Aen.* 7.667), boar (Ov. *Met.* 8.285); monsters like Cacus (Virg. *Aen.* 8.266) and the Cyclops (Ov. *Met.* 13.846) also have *saetae*. For *saetae* as a sign of masculinity cf. Mart. 2.36.5, 6.56.1.   **per** 'all over', cf. Prop. 4.3.26 *per tua colla notas*.

12 atrocem animum 'ruthless mind', a Stoic trait, esp. associated with Cato (cf. Gell. 1.15.8) thanks to Hor. *Od.* 2.1.24 *atrocem animum Catonis*, here recalled.   **podice leui** 'on your smooth anus'. For *leuis* = 'depilated' cf. 8.115, 9.95.

13 caeduntur: more violent than the regular *seco* for the surgeon's cutting.   **medico ridente:** the doctor laughs because he has discovered the hypocrite's secret; cf. Laronia's reaction, *subridens* (38). **mariscae:** probably piles: the usual word is *ficus* (Mart. 1.65, 7.71), and the *marisca* is a large kind of fig. J. makes a regular metaphor (*ficus*) more colourful.

14 rarus sermo: another Stoic characteristic, e.g. Cato is described as a fierce critic of the talkative (Gell. 1.15.8).   **libido tacendi:** almost an oxymoron.

15 supercilio breuior coma: another Stoic characteristic, cf. Pers. 3.54 *detonsa iuuentus* of students of Stoicism, Lucian, *Hermotimus* 18. For cropped hair as an outward sign of an austere life-style, cf. Hor. *Ep.* 1.18.7.

15–23 A comparison of hypocritical with admitted homosexuals: the overt ones can be forgiven, but the hypocrites are unbearable.

15–16 'So Peribomius behaves more frankly and honourably.' Cf. Gell. 10.22.1 *uere ... ingenueque*. A sentence framed by bucolic diaereses.   **Peribomius:** according to the scholiast, a known passive homosexual. The name may be associated with a cult (*IG* xii 3.1126 οἱ περιβώμιοι) and is Greek (*peri + bomos* = about the altar).

16–17 'The behaviour of the man, who admits his disease in look and walk, I ascribe to the Fates.' *imputo* + dative is a financial metaphor meaning 'I lay to the charge of', cf. 5.14n. The Fates are responsible for Peribomius' homosexuality, cf. Manilius 4.518–9 and 5.140–56 for the effeminate walk of some born under Taurus. It was commonly believed that an effeminate or homosexual could be recognised by outward signs: cf. Sen. *Ep.* 52.12 *impudicum et incessus ostendit et manus* *mota et unum interdum responsum et relatus ad caput digitus et flexus oculorum;* Tac. *Hist.* 1.30 of the emperor Otho, *habitune et incessu an illo muliebri ornatu mererentur imperium?*   **morbum:** for *morbus* of effeminacy/ homosexuality cf. 50, 9.49, Hor. *Od.* 1.37.10, and Richlin (1993) 549; Greek νόσος has a similar range: see Courtney's n. Imagery of disease is developed in lines 78–81.

18–19 'The openness of these people arouses pity, their very madness grants them forgiveness.' A generalisation from the individual to the group. Repetition in anaphora emphasises 'these people', *horum ... his,* as does the bucolic diaeresis (cf. 15, 16). For *simplicitas* (as opposed to guile and hypocrisy) cf. Mart. 6.7.6.

19 talia 'such vices'.

20 Herculis: for the Stoics Hercules was a model of correct behaviour (cf. 10.361). To 'attack vices with the words of Hercules' is therefore to condemn fiercely the unmasculine morals of the overt homosexuals. *inuadunt* is a suitably aggressive word for an imitator of Hercules.

20–1 Repetition of the contradiction between appearance and reality of line 3 (and cf. the oxymoron at line 10, *Socraticos ... cinaedos*): the hypocrites 'talking about virtue, heave their buttocks'. For the enjambment see Introduction §7. On *clunem agitant* (Hor. *Sat.* 2.7.50) see below on *ceuentem.*

21 'Shall I be in awe of you, Sextus, when I see you wiggling your arse?' The speaker puts into the mouth of Varillus, evidently a notorious homosexual (see below), an indignant exclamation against a hypocrite, Sextus. Specific names (see below) and direct speech create a striking vignette, cf. 1.125–6 and often. For the idea that the critic should be better than his victim cf. Hor. *Sat.* 2.7.40–2, Cic. *Verr.* 2.3.2. Juxtaposition of *ego* and *te* accentuates the scornful tone.   **ceuentem:** like *clunem agitant,* denoting the movements made by the passive partner during homosexual intercourse; cf. Mart. 3.95.13 *sed pedicaris, sed pulchre, Naeuole, ceues?,* Pers. 1.87 *an, Romule, ceues?* and J. 9.40 *computat et ceuet.*   **Sexte:** a common senatorial praenomen.

22 infamis Varillus: 'notorious Varillus' is not known to us; possibly a satiric fiction. *infamis* indicates that he is an overt homosexual; the name suggests someone with bandy legs (*uarus,* as at Hor. *Sat.* 1.3.47).   **'quo deterior te?'** 'How am I worse than you?' On the disruptive effect of the final monosyllable see Introduction §8.

23 A quieter statement of Varillus' exclamation: to utter criticism you should be above criticism yourself: 'Let a man who limps be mocked by a man who walks upright, let a Negro be mocked by a white man.'   **loripedem:** a deformity of the foot, evidently unattractive, cf. Petr. 45.11; at J. 10.308 linked with swollen glands, a pot-belly and a hump-back.   **Aethiopem albus:** a conventional contrasting pair, cf. Var. *L.L.* 9.42 *si alter est Aethiops, alter albus.* For another black-white contrast cf. J. 8.32–3 *uocamus | Aethiopem Cycnum* (euphemistic naming). For the equivalence of 'Ethiopian' and 'black' see Snowden (1970) 4. Probably a reference to slaves: black slaves in Rome (cf. 5.52–4 *Gaetulus* and *niger Maurus*) were generally not the most highly valued.

24–33 No-one can stand a hypocrite. An elaboration of the point of line 23 with five indignant lines of brief examples and five scathing lines on one over-arching example of hypocrisy, Domitian.

24 quis tulerit ... ?: typical language of indignation, see Introduction §6(*a*). The perfect subjunctive here has the same sense as the present (cf. *misceat* in the next line). For *quis* + perf. subj. thus in poetry cf. Ov. *Her.* 16.7 *quis enim celauerit ignem ... ?*   **Gracchos de seditione querentes:** Tiberius Sempronius Gracchus and his brother Gaius, the high-born grandsons of Scipio Africanus, provoked civil disturbances, in which they died (in 133 and 121 BC respectively) because the measures they sought to introduce seemed to their political opponents threatening to the *status quo. seditio* is especially associated with the Gracchi, cf. Florus, *Epit.* 1.47.8 *Gracchana prima et secunda ... seditio, seditiosus* of one (Cic. *Sest.* 101) or both of them (Cic. *Brut.* 224). A later Gracchus will appear as the ultimate travesty of Roman aristocratic conduct (117–48).

25 quis caelum terris non misceat et mare caelo: i.e. 'who would not turn the world upside down', colloquial, cf. 6.283 *clames licet et mare caelo confundas,* Liv. 4.3.6 *quid tandem est cur caelum et terras misceant?,* Lucian, *Prometheus* 9, Otto s.v. *caelum* 1 and *Nachträge* 263. Similar is Lucr. *D.R.N.* 3.842 *non si terra mari miscebitur et mare caelo,* although this may also refer to the final destruction of the world, see Kenney *ad loc.*

26 Verri: Gaius Verres, governor of the province of Sicily in 73–71 BC, infamous thanks to Cicero's prosecution speeches (cf. J. 8.106). **Miloni:** Titus Annius Milo, tribune of the plebs in 57 BC and a partisan of Pompey. In 52 BC he murdered Clodius and was exiled to Massilia.

27 Clodius: Publius Clodius Pulcher, tribune of the plebs in 58 BC. In 61 BC he had been prosecuted for profane behaviour, entering the women-only Bona Dea festival, dressed in women's clothing, cf. 6.345; hardly the man to accuse *moechos*, 'adulterers'. **Catilina Cethegum:** Lucius Sergius Catilina (Catiline), after failure in the elections to the consulship, resorted to violence in 63 BC, planning a military coup. Gaius Cornelius Cethegus was one of his fellow-conspirators. They recur together at 8.231 and 10.287–8.

28 tabulam Sullae: Lucius Cornelius Sulla (c.138–78 BC) took power by force in 82 BC, had himself elected dictator and massacred his opponents who were named in proscription lists, *tabulae*, cf. Florus 2.9.25. **in ... dicant** 'speak against' i.e. criticise, attack. **discipuli tres:** sc. *Sullae*. The so-called second triumvirate of Antony, Lepidus and Octavian (later Augustus), of 43 BC, which followed Sulla's example in proscribing its enemies (Sen. *Suas.* 6.3, *tabula* Mart. 5.69.2). The disrupting metrical effect (cf. 22) conveys the shock if 'Sulla's three disciples were to criticise his list'.

29–33 qualis ... qui tunc ... cum ... 'This was the sort of man our adulterer ... was recently. He, at that very moment ... when ....' *qualis*: i.e. a hypocrite, looking back to the previous five lines. The hypocritical adulterer is the emperor Domitian who had sex with his niece Julia, his brother Titus' daughter, though to do so was to commit both adultery (she was married) and incest; he allegedly caused her death by forcing her to undergo an abortion in around AD 89 (Suet. *Dom.* 22, Plin. *Ep.* 4.11.6). At around this time, in his capacity as censor, he began to enforce Augustus' legislation against adultery (*lex Iulia de adulteriis*, cf. 37 below). For praise of Domitian as *censor maxime* see Mart. 6.4, specifically preventing adultery, Mart. 6.2, 9.6.

29 nuper: used loosely by J.: at 8.120 of events some twenty years earlier than the date of writing; at 4.9 personalities of Domitian's reign, between ten and twenty years earlier; J. uses *modo* similarly, e.g. at 2.161. (Only at 15.27 might *nuper* denote 'recently' = a couple of years ago.) Here = 'more recently', in contrast with the Republican examples (24–8).

29–30 tragico pollutus ... concubitu 'defiled by a tragic union', i.e. worthy of treatment in a tragedy: for *tragicus* thus cf. Liv. 1.46.3

tragici sceleris exemplum; Prop. 2.20.29 *tum me uel tragicae uexetis Erinyes.* The material of tragedy is often furnished by adultery (e.g. the story of Clytemnestra) and incest (e.g. Oedipus and his mother).

30 leges reuocabat 'he was trying to revive laws', conative imperfect; cf. Suet. *Cl.* 22 *quaedam exoleta reuocauit aut etiam noua instituit*, ibid. *Dom.* 4.1 *quaestoriis muneribus quae olim omissa reuocauerat.* J. implies that these laws had fallen into disuse.

31 'Terrifying to everyone, even to Venus and Mars.' Accusations of adultery, real or fabricated, were regularly used against political enemies. For an allegedly false charge see Stat. *Silv.* 5.2.99–102. Venus and Mars were caught in the act of adultery by Venus' husband Vulcan: Hom. *Od.* 8.266–366, Ov. *Met.* 4.171–89.

32 tot abortiuis 'with so many abortion-inducers', as at 6.368, Plin. *N.H.* 25.25. This phrase, together with mention of her *'fertile womb'* and the plural *offas*, implies that Julia underwent repeated abortions, almost certainly a sensational exaggeration of the single abortion which is said to have caused her death (Suet. *Dom.* 22). **uuluam** 'womb', drawn from everyday speech, occurring in poetry only in satire and epigram, cf. Mart. 11.61.11.

33 patruo similes effunderet offas 'poured out lumps resembling her uncle'. *effunderet* combined with crude *offas*, usually of lumps of food, suggests that she is vomiting, cf. Plin. *N.H.* 23.43 *quorum stomachus in uomitiones effunditur.* Alliteration of *f* (8n.) helps convey disgust.

34–5 A summary of the opening of the poem: overt homosexuals are justified in retaliating when attacked by hypocrites. This paragraph is marked off by ring composition: *fictos … Scauros* ∼ 3 *Curios simulant*; *castigata* ∼ 9 *castigas.*

34 iure ac merito 'rightly and justifiably', cf. Cic. *Marc.* 4 *quod … merito atque optimo iure contigit.*   **uitia ultima:** nominative, lit. 'the worst faults', i.e. overt homosexuals such as Varillus (21–2); for the same phrase referring to homosexual activity cf. Quint. *I.O.* 2.2.15. To be described as a *uitium* instead of *uitiosus homo* was evidently more extreme, as shown by Mart. 11.92 *mentitur qui te uitiosum, Zoile, dicit.* | *non uitiosus homo es, Zoile, sed uitium.* Cf. Sall. *B.C.* 14.1 *omnium flagitiorum atque facinorum … cateruas.*   **fictos** 'false, bogus'.

35 Scauros: generic plural, 'men like Scaurus', as at 6.604 (and cf. *Curios* 3n.). Marcus Aurelius Scaurus, consul in 115 BC, censor in

109 BC, had a reputation for integrity and excellence and became a model of upright morality, cf. 11.90–2, Hor. *Od.* 1.12.37 with Nisbet and Hubbard, Val. Max. 4.4.11. **castigata remordent** 'when criticised bite back'. For *castigo* see 9n. Imagery of biting often conveys the idea of criticism, cf. Hor. *Sat.* 2.1.77–8, Pers. 1.115 and esp. Hor. *Epod.* 6.4 *quid . . . me remorsurum petis?*

36–8 Introduction of a new character, Laronia, who will utter a speech condemning the hypocritical moralists (38–63). This use of a character in addition to the speaker is a preview of Satire 3 where the second character, Umbricius, monopolises the poem. Laronia, though often regarded as a prostitute (thus e.g. Green 76: 'a courtesan'), is evidently a woman who has offended against the laws on adultery (hence *ubi nunc, lex Iulia, dormis?*, see below); she is probably of high birth: a Quintus Laronius was suffect consul in 33 BC. Possibly to be identified with the Laronia in Mart. 2.32.5–6, a rich and influential widow (*orba est, diues, anus, uidua*). LaFleur's suggestion ((1974a) 73 n.4) that her name is Latronia, suggesting a barking bitch, is ingenious but inappropriate: the woman is *not* 'barking'. **non tulit:** typical language of indignation (1.139–40n.), although Laronia's indignation soon gives way to irony (see on *subridens* below). **ex illis toruum . . . quendam** 'Laronia could not stand one of those grim fellows who kept on shouting'; cf. 6.385 *quaedam de numero Lamiarum. illis* refers to *fictos . . . Scauros*, the hypocritical moralists of 11–15. For their stern appearance cf. 9 *tristibus. toruus* is used of Cato (40n.) at Hor. *Ep.* 1.19.12–13 *si quis uoltu toruo ferus . . . simulet . . . Catonem.*

37 'ubi nunc, lex Iulia, dormis?': referring to Laronia's adultery the hypocrite asks, 'Where are you now, Julian law against adultery?' (cf. Cic. *Phil.* 5.8 *ubi lex Caecilia et Didia?*) and implies that the law is in disuse by *dormis* (cf. Fronto p. 216 (Haines) = 68 (van den Hout) *nonnumquam permittendum legibus dormire*). For this double point to the question, cf. Ov. *Her.* 4.150 *heu, ubi nunc fastus altaque uerba iacent?*; the punctuation of both passages is owed to Housman. Further, the wording hints that the law itself is committing adultery, 'In whose bed do you now sleep, Julian law?'

The *lex Iulia de adulteriis coercendis*, enacted by Augustus in 18 BC, made adultery by the wife a criminal act; adultery by the husband was never a crime as such, but illicit intercourse with a respectable woman constituted *stuprum*, which was also covered by the *lex Iulia*. Martial

writing under Domitian speaks of the 'rebirth', or reenactment, of the
law (6.7; cf. Stat. *Silv.* 5.2.101-2) and a letter of Pliny shows the law's
strictest provisions in force under Trajan (*Ep.* 6.31.4-6, *c.* AD 107).

38 ita: sc. *dixit.* For similar ellipse of the verb of saying cf. 2.65 *quid
enim falsi Laronia?*, at the end of her speech; also 13.91 *atque ita secum,*
15.24 *sic aliquis merito.*   **subridens** 'smiling'. Laronia's is a grim,
ironic smile, cf. Virg. *Aen.* 10.742 *ad quae subridens mixta Mezentius ira.*
Irony is her hall-mark.   **felicia tempora** 'what happy times!',
immediately ironic.

38-9 quae te moribus opponunt 'which set *you* up as the enemy
of [corrupt] morality', cf. Cic. *Sest.* 20 *habeo quem opponam labi illi atque
caeno.* Laronia says 'morals' when she means 'lack of morals' or 'corrupt
morality'; cf. Cic. *Cael.* 6 *quod obiectum est de pudicitia*, 'as to the
reproaches cast on his [un]chastity'; *Planc.* 62 *artes in iis reprehenduntur,*
'the [absence of] skill is criticised in them'; Luc. 1.429 *pollutus
foedere*, 'polluted by the [broken] treaty': Friedländer has many more
examples. **te:** any hypocritical moralist (*quendam* 36). *opponunt* maintains
the combative imagery introduced with *inuadunt* at 20.

39 habeat iam Roma pudorem 'let Rome now develop a sense of
shame'.

40 tertius ... Cato 'a third Cato', the first two being those para-
gons of Republican morality, Marcus Porcius Cato (234-149 BC),
censor in 184 BC (cf. 11.90 *durum ... Catonem*), and his great-grandson
of the same name (95-46 BC), a Stoic who committed suicide. Cf. Hor.
Sat. 2.3.296 *Stertinius, sapientum octauus*, similarly ironic.   **e caelo
cecidit:** excellent people, objects and ideas were said to have divine
origin, cf. Cic. *De imp. Cn. Pomp.* 41 *omnes ... Cn. Pompeium sicut aliquem
non ex hac urbe missum, sed de caelo delapsum intuentur*, Stat. *Silv.* 1.1.2-3
caelone peractum fluxit opus? (of a statue), J. 11.27 *e caelo descendit* γνῶϑι
σεαυτόν; Otto *caelum* 8. *cecidit* 'tumbled', with the alliteration *caelo
cecidit Cato*, is rather irreverent.

40-2 Laronia adopts a more beguiling tone of voice, marked by
conspiratorial *sed tamen*, as she disingenuously feigns interest in the
origin of the moralist's perfume. *haec* anticipates *opobalsama* and the
relative pronoun *quae* is postponed until late in the sentence.

41 hirsuto ... collo: the hypocritical moralist has a 'shaggy neck',
supposedly an indication of his masculinity, cf. 11-15n., Mart.
7.58.7-8 *quaere aliquem Curios semper Fabiosque loquentem*, | *hirsutum et dura*

rusticitate trucem.   **spirant opobalsama:** a sensual phrase, a quotation from Mart. 11.8, which describes in terms of fragrance the kisses of a young boy-friend. For *spirant* intransitive, 'is wafted', see *OLD* 4c; cf. 7.208. *opobalsamum* (poetic plural) was the juice of the balsam-tree from Judaea, made into perfume. Balsam might be a suitable perfume for men, Mart. 14.59.1 *balsama me capiunt, haec sunt unguenta uirorum*; yet at 3.63 Martial characterises the *bellus homo* as smelling continually of balsam and cinnamon. For wholesale disapproval of male use of perfume, a sign of effeminacy, see Sen. *Ep.* 108.16 *in omnem uitam unguento abstinemus, quoniam optimus odor in corpore est nullus* and Scipio quoted by Gell. at 6.12.5: *qui cotidie unguentatus aduersum speculum ornetur, cuius supercilia radantur, qui barba uulsa feminibusque subuulsis ambulet . . . eumne quisquam dubitet quin idem fecerit quod cinaedi facere solent?*

42 tibi: virtually = *tuo (collo)*.   **ne pudeat** 'don't be embarrassed'. Use of *ne* + subjunctive where a prose author would write *noli* + infinitive probably imparts a colloquial flavour to Laronia's words; cf. 15.89 *ne quaeras et dubites* and the similar 9.130 *ne trepida.*   **dominum . . . tabernae** 'shop-owner' as at Mart. 1.117.14.

43–4 After disarming the hypocrite with false friendliness, Laronia now begins her attack: if laws are to be invoked, the first should be not the *lex Iulia* (37) but the *lex Scantinia*. The *lex Scantinia de Venere nefanda* was revived by Domitian and enforced energetically (Suet. *Dom.* 8.3); it is reasonably safe to assume that this law outlawed sex with young freeborn males, but our evidence is scanty: see Boswell (1980) 67, Lilja (1983) 112–21. Mention of this law, which is never heard of again, suits the Domitianic flavour of this Satire and is not to be read as evidence that it was still in use at the time of composition: see Cloud (1989a) 55.

43 quod si 'But if'.   **uexantur** 'are to be disturbed', i.e. woken up, continuing from *dormis* 37. Cf. 1.126 *noli uexare, quiescet.*   **leges ac iura:** paired again at 72 in the same position in the line.   **citari:** used in legal contexts; most relevant is the idea of summoning a witness (*OLD* 4b), e.g. J. 8.80 *si quando citabere testis.*

44 omnes: refers back to *leges*, ignoring *iura*.   **Scantinia:** supply *lex*.

44–61 To prove the need to invoke the *lex Scantinia*, Laronia describes the behaviour of effeminate men and asserts that in comparison women's conduct is irreproachable.

44–5 respice primum et scrutare uiros 'Look at and examine men first', i.e. before examining women. *primum* reiterates the idea of *ante omnes*. For *scrutor* in a context of guilt cf. Tac. *Hist.* 1.7 [Galba] *ne altius scrutaretur quoquo modo acta.*

45 faciunt peiora 'their behaviour is worse'. For defence of this emendation see Courtney (1967) 47.

45–7 A parenthetical comment: Laronia alleges that such men escape prosecution thanks to sheer numbers (*numerus*) and solidarity (*iunctae ... umbone phalanges, magna ... concordia*). The military imagery (*defendit, umbone, phalanges*) depicts the hypocrites in a defensive position against Laronia's onslaught.

46 iunctae ... umbone phalanges: lit. 'phalanxes joined by shield-boss', i.e. in a close formation with each man's shield overlapping and protecting the man to his left, cf. Luc. 7.492–3 *densis acies stipata cateruis | iunxerat in seriem nexis umbonibus arma* and Val. Fl. 3.90 *contextis umbonibus; umbo* by synecdoche (part for whole) denotes the shield. *phalanx*, a Greek word used esp. of the Macedonian fighting unit, seems highly appropriate, given its close-knit formation: *Macedonum acies ... clipeis hastisque immobiles cuneos et conferta robora uirorum tegit. ipsi phalangem uocant peditum stabile agmen: uir uiro, armis arma conserta sunt* (Curtius 3.2.13). Laronia's use of a Greek word also invites recollection of the famous Theban 'Sacred Band', an élite fighting force of 300 men composed entirely of pairs of lovers; see Dover (1978) 192.

47 magna inter molles concordia 'Great is the solidarity between effeminates.' Cf. Cat. 57.1 *pulchre conuenit improbis cinaedis. mollis*, lit. 'soft' = effeminate, cf. 9.38, also *mollius* 2.165, 6.O 23, 8.15, Mart. 5.41.1–2. *concordia* was an important political slogan, manifested in Cicero's *concordia ordinum* e.g. *Att.* 1.18.3; CONCORDIA AVGVSTI *BMCI* I 380 no. 65 (a coin of Vitellius), CONCORDIA EXERCITVVM *BMCI* III 1 no. 4 (a coin of Nerva); here used ironically in a trivialising context.

47–8 Laronia resumes from 44–45: women's behaviour is not as bad as men's.

47 non erit 'there will not be', i.e. you will not find; see 1.126n.

48 exemplum ... tam detestabile: strong words, cf. 15.121 *tam detestabile monstrum* (of cannibalism), 13.126–7 *si nullum in terris tam detestabile factum ostendis* (ironically, of the theft of a modest sum of money), Liv. 26.48.11 *nihilominus detestabili exemplo rem agi* (of heated and fraudulent competition for a military decoration).

49 'Tedia does not lick Cluvia nor Flora Catulla.' Laronia alleges that women do not engage in homosexual practices. Evidence for lesbianism at Rome is minimal (Hallett (1989) analyses the ancient evidence); it includes Martial's allegations of a woman's bisexual activity (7.67) and J.'s passing reference in Satire 6, *in . . . uices equitant ac Luna teste mouentur* (6.311, at the altar of Pudicitia). The rarity of accusations of lesbianism in Roman invective against women presumably allows Laronia to make this point.

The names designate women sexually active but heterosexual (LaFleur (1974a)): Flora was Pompey's favourite prostitute (Plut. *Pomp.* 2.3–5); Catulla in Martial is beautiful and immoral (8.53), cf. J. 10.322, perhaps alluding to Catullus' Lesbia; Cluvia evokes the reformed prostitute who assisted Roman prisoners in the Second Punic War; about Tedia no information survives.   **lambit:** use of the tongue to stimulate the sexual organs was more usually conveyed with *lingo*; *lambo* may be more polite (see Adams (1982) 136). For *lambo* in this context cf. Mart. 2.61.2, 3.81.2; *lambenti crustula* at J. 9.5 involves a sexual *double entendre*.

50 Hispo subit iuuenes 'Hispo submits to young men'. *subeo*, virtually unparalleled in this sense in Latin literature (cf. Prop. 3.19.14 *quae uoluit | liquido tota subire deo*, with double meaning 'submit to' and 'be submerged in'; *Priapea* 33.2), indicates the passive position assumed by Hispo, conveyed elsewhere by *supinus* (e.g. Cat. 28.9, Apul. *Met.* 8.29) and *resupinati* (J. 8.176). For the Romans this was a shocking role-reversal: whereas it may have been thought acceptable for boys and young men of certain status to take the passive role in intercourse with an older man, the reverse was regarded as utterly humiliating for the older man: see Richlin (1983) 38, 220–6, Edwards (1993) 63–73, Konstan (1993), Richlin (1993) esp. 541–54 on Satire 2.

Hispo echoes *hispida membra* (11), aligning Hispo with the hypocritical moralists; on this unusual *cognomen*, possibly of an eminent man, see Syme (1970) 72; the feminine version of the name, Hispulla, is chosen as a target for satire at 6.74 (for her lust) and at 12.11 (for her vast size).   **morbo pallet utroque** 'is pale from both diseases', i.e. playing both the active and the passive parts in homosexual intercourse (*paedicator* and *pathicus*). For disease imagery of homosexuality, see 16–17n. Hispo's pallor is caused by the time and effort he devotes to sexual activity; cf. 1.43n. for *pallor* in amatory and homosexual contexts; at Pers. 1.26 Bramble (1974) 150 n. 3 suggests there may also be a medical nuance.

51–7 Pursuing the previous thought that men (passive homosexuals, that is) play the female role in intercourse, Laronia asserts that women do not participate in male spheres of activity but that men usurp female roles. The pronouns *nos* (51) and *uos* in anaphora (54 and 55) enforce a stark contrast.

51–2 In a rhetorical question (her closest approach yet towards indignation) articulated as an increasing tricolon, Laronia suggests that no women engage in litigation. Commentators point out the contradiction with 6.242–5, where female lawyers are added to the catalogue of outrageous women, and cite Valerius Maximus' (short) list (8.3) of women who pleaded cases in court. However, the differing views in Satires 2 and 6 are offered by two very different speakers and in differing contexts for different purposes: it is Laronia's role to defend women; it is the role of the misogynist *persona*, who delivers the invective of Satire 6, to make any allegation thinkable against women (see Braund (1992b)). Neither passage can, or should, be treated as offering reliable evidence about Roman life (as Courtney sees (Commentary, p. 33) by reconciling the two passages in his conclusion that women *could* plead in the courts, but did so rarely).

52 ullo strepitu fora uestra mouemus 'disturb your courts with any uproar'. The Roman *fora* (of which there were five or six by J.'s time) were where legal cases were heard and as such formed part of the 'daily round' (cf. 1.128 *deinde forum iurisque peritus Apollo*); virtually synonymous with 'courts' (cf. 13.135). *uestra* marks the forum as an exclusively male sphere of activity. The uproar (*strepitus*) is the noise made by those pleading cases, cf. Cic. *Orat.* 32 *a forensi strepitu remotissimus*, *Arch.* 12 *ex hoc forensi strepitu*.

53 'Few women wrestle, few women consume the meat-rich diet.' Men of the élite took physical exercise in the form of wrestling and other athletic pursuits, e.g. Tac. *Ann.* 14.59 (Rubellius Plautus) *repertus est certe per medium diei nudus exercitando corpori*; *colyphia* here denotes a cut of pork, evidently the athlete's rich diet: see André (1966) 46–58, 48–9 on *colyphium* in literary texts, e.g. Petr. 70.2, Mart. 7.67.12 (also with *comedit*, echoed by J. here).

Instead of a sweeping denial, Laronia's concession, emphasised by repetition of *paucae*, makes her appear reasonable (cf. her question in 51–2 which implies rather than asserts that no women enter the courts). Female athletes are reviled and mocked at some length by the misogynistic speaker of Satire 6 immediately following his criticism of women in the courts (6.246–67). As with the topic of women in the courts, these passages cannot be used on their own as reliable evidence for female behaviour; such conduct may have been exceptional or may be a projection of male horror or fantasy.

The sexual *double entendre* seen by some in *colyphia* ('slang for the penis' Ferguson) is doubted by Adams (1982) 49–50, correctly, although it is worth noting that Greek κωλύφιον has a possible double sense according to André above; such a word-play would seem to have no role here. Greek terms in Laronia's speech are confined to descriptions of male behaviour (Hallett (1989) 218).

54–7 (Some) men, by contrast, usurp the (for the ancients) quintessentially female jobs of spinning and weaving and surpass even the most renowned female weavers of mythology. For an account of spinning see Forbes (1956) 149–71. This allegation is made against Cleisthenes (Aristoph. *Birds* 831), Sardanapallus (by Ctesias *FGH* III C vol. 1 no. 688 p.444 Jacoby), Midas (Clearchus in Athenaeus 12.516b), Hercules (Ov. *Her.* 9.73); for a Roman example cf. Cic. *De orat.* 2.277 *Egilio qui uideretur mollior nec esset dixisset, 'Quid tu, Egilia mea? quando ad me uenis cum tua colu et lana?'*

These lines fall into three sections: (i) the simple statement, expressed in two verbs, *trahitis* and *refertis*; (ii) the comparisons with weavers of mythology (*melius, leuius, torquetis*); (iii) the expansion introduced by *quale* ('the sort of task which . . .').

54 lanam trahitis 'you pull [the] wool', regularly of teasing (carding) the wool to remove knots prior to spinning, cf. Ov. *Met.* 14.264–5 *nymphae . . . quae uellera motis | nulla trahunt digitis.* On the distinction between carding and spinning see Bennett (1914), esp. 148–50.

54–5 calathis ... peracta refertis uellera 'you bring back in baskets the prepared fleeces', cf. Cat. 64.318–19 *ante pedes . . . candentis mollia lanae | uellera uirgati custodibant calathisci. calathus* often denotes a woman's work-basket for holding wool, cf. Virg. *Aen.* 7.805–6, Ov. *A.A.* 1.693, etc. For *peracta* cf. 5.21 *tota salutatrix iam turba peregerit orbem.*

55-6 tenui praegnantem stamine fusum ... torquetis 'you turn the spindle pregnant with slender thread', i.e. spin. The 'pregnant spindle' is unparalleled besides [Virg.] *Ciris* 446 *grauidos penso ... fusos* (see Lyne *ad loc.*); here it emphasises the men's self-feminisation.

56 Penelope melius, leuius ... Arachne: the names are ablatives. A finely-balanced line. In Homer's *Odyssey*, Penelope's chief occupation is weaving a tapestry. Ovid tells the story of Arachne (*Met.* 6.1-145), a Lydian girl who challenged Athene to a weaving contest, produced such a wonderful tapestry that Athene destroyed it in rage; she then killed herself and was turned into a spider by Athene. *leuius* echoes Ov. *Met.* 6.22 *leui teretem uersabat pollice fusum.*

57 horrida quale facit residens in codice paelex 'the sort of task which the dishevelled mistress does as she sits on the block'. Another mythological comparison which likens the effeminates to women of very low status: the slave-woman concubine who is punished by her master's wife by being made to spin while sitting on the block, a place of punishment. For *codex* meaning the block of wood to which an offender was fastened cf. Plaut. *Poen.* 1153, Prop. 4.7.44 *codicis immundi uincula*; in the previous couplet Prop. mentions as another type of punishment being given extra wool to spin; here J. appears to have conflated the two. A *paelex* was the mistress of a married man (thus Gell. 4.3.3), often but not necessarily a slave (e.g. Tac. *Ann.* 13.46 *Neronem paelice ancilla ... deuinctum*; for relations between *ancillae* and their masters cf. Sen. *Contr.* 6.3, *Ben.* 1.9.4, Mart. 12.58.1). Whatever her status, a *paelex* was held in contempt (Gell. 4.3.3 *probrosam ... habitam*); the story of Antiope (Hyginus 7, 8; Prop. 3.15.11-42; treated by the second-century BC tragedian Pacuvius) presents a mythological illustration of the harsh treatment a mistress might receive. J. may be alluding to the story of Antiope here: like Pacuvius (*ROL* II 14) he describes her as *horrida*, but this alone is insufficient; and no other source locates Antiope *in codice*; yet, such an allusion would be appropriate after the mythological references of line 56, and line 57 would make better sense if it made a specific allusion to a work of literature or, better, to a dramatic production (whether a tragedy or mime: for J.'s interest in mime cf. 8.185-99, also 6.42-4 and 13.110-11; for possible allusions to mime and Atellan farce in Satire 9 see Braund (1988) 173-5).

58-61 Laronia reverts to accusations of homosexuality, suggesting that it is the source of riches for both the homosexual's male paramour (here a freedman) and his wife. Her irony resides in understatement: in *notum est cur ... cur* she does not reveal why but leaves the reader to reach the answer; in *diues erit magno quae dormit tertia lecto* she offers a discreetly-worded explanation; and in *tu nube atque tace* she advises the wife to acquiesce in and profit from the situation – an ironically flavoured argument from expediency like that at 8.95–123, e.g. 97 *iamque tace; furor est post omnia perdere naulum.*

58 notum est: cf. 6.314 *nota bonae secreta deae*, which would be a similarly discreet understatement, if the speaker did not then proceed to describe in graphic detail the alleged conduct of the Bona Dea festival (6.314–41). For *notum est* = 'it is common knowledge' see *OLD notus* 6.

58–9 cur solo tabulas impleuerit Hister | liberto 'why Hister filled his will with his freedman alone', cf. 6.600–1 *heres impleret tabulas.* For *tabulae* specifically of a will cf. 4.19 and Cic. *Inv.* 2.149 *qui heredes in tabulis scripti sunt*, Mart. 5.32.1 *tabulis ... supremis* (*OLD tabula* 8b). *liberto* is abl. after *impleo*, cf. Cic. *Div.* 2.115 *tuis ... oraculis Chrysippus totum uolumen impleuit*, standing for 'the name of his freedman'. The status of sole heir (*solo*) was much coveted cf. 12.124–5 *omnia soli forsan Pacuuio breuiter dabit.* The name Hister in this context of giving legacies recurs in Satire 12 where Pacuvius Hister is a legacy-hunter, *captator* (12.111–30).

59 dederit uiuus cur multa puellae 'why in his life-time he made many gifts to his young wife'. For *puella* of a young married woman cf. 6.258, O32; Hor. *Od.* 3.14.10 *puellae iam uirum expertae*; 3.22.2 *laborantes utero puellas*; Ov. *Fast.* 2.557 *uiduae cessate puellae.* Here, however, the word perhaps suggests that she is still a virgin (cf. 9.72–4 *uxor tua uirgo maneret ... puellam*). *uiuus* contrasts with the reference to inheritance in the previous line: whereas the homosexual can promise his male paramour riches in his will, the legal restrictions on women receiving inheritances (cf. 1.55–6) lead the homosexual to buy his wife's silence with actual rather than promised gifts.

60 'She who sleeps third in a large bed will be rich.' This *ménage à trois* is like that in Sen. *Contr.* 2.1.35 with the difference that the wife is said not to put up with the situation: *arcessitum a domino seruum ut inter se medius et dominam recumberet; illam non esse passam.* In Satire 9 the paramour Naevolus describes how he satisfied both his patron and his patron's wife.

61 donant arcana cylindros 'secrets bestow jewels'; a *cylindrus* was a precious stone cut in the form of a cylinder (Plin. *N.H.* 37.78, 113, *CIL* xi 364, *TLL* s.v. 1586.63ff.). Secrets (*arcana*) reappear in association with homosexuals at 9.116, where, in contrast, the slaves of the household betray the homosexual's secret.

62–3 Laronia completes her speech with a riposte to the hypocrite's exclamation *ubi nunc, lex Iulia, dormis?*, which compelled her to speak. She first (62) reiterates the point made in 43–5, substantiated in the examples of lines 47–61, that men deserve criticism and prosecution before women do, then (63) repeats the implication of 38–42, that male censors are corrupt.   **de nobis ... ?:** cf. 51–2 *numquid nos ... ?* Again the rhetorical question approaches indignation.   **post haec:** i.e. the outrageous behaviour she has just described.   **tristis sententia fertur** 'a verdict of "guilty" is passed', cf. Ov. *Met.* 15.43 *sic lata est sententia tristis* (of the death penalty). For *tristis* as a euphemistic term for an adverse verdict in a legal context see *OLD tristis* 5c. The euphemism is typical of Laronia's understatement. J. picks up 9 *tristibus*: the verdict is not only adverse but (hypocritically) 'severe' in a moral sense.   **dat ueniam coruis, uexat censura columbas** 'judgement acquits the ravens and condemns the doves'. The contrast between ravens/hawks and doves is a proverbial type of formulation: Otto *coruus* 2 + *Nachträge* 266, given extra significance here by the fact that ravens attack doves (Var. *R.R.* 3.7.6). The contrast here is between male (*coruus*) and female (*columba*), aggressor and victim, black and white (possibly inspired by the black and white voting pebbles in the story by Ovid evoked in line 62, *Met.* 15.41–2, 46) and between obscene and pure: the raven was believed by some to have sex by mouth (Plin. *N.H.* 10.32), hence Martial can wittily ask a raven *quare fellator haberis?* (14.74.1); on the chastity of doves see Plin. *N.H.* 10.104, Prop. 2.15.27 with. Enk, Mart. 1.109.2 *purior osculo columbae* with Citroni.   **censura** 'moral judgement', recalling both Laronia's ironic description of the hypocritical homosexual moralist as *tertius ... Cato* (40n.), a name virtually synonymous with censorship, and the speaker's attack in lines 29–33 on Domitian, an archetypal hypocritical censor. Instead of directly criticising the hypocrites, Laronia substitutes the abstract noun *censura* (what she means is, 'you hypocrites pardon the guilty and attack the innocent'), thus maintaining to the end her ironic understatement and distance from emotional involvement.

64–5 The result of the confrontation between Laronia the adulteress and the hypocritical moralists: the hypocrites run away, admitting the truth of her allegations. Epic flavour, cf. Virg. *Aen.* 3.666 *nos procul inde fugam trepidi celerare*, 9.756 *diffugiunt uersi trepida formidine Troes*.   **fugerunt:** highly appropriate military imagery: earlier the hypocrites adopted an aggressive pose (e.g. 20 *inuadunt*, 39 *opponunt*) and formed into a tight-knit military formation (46 *phalanges*); here they are routed by a single woman.   **uera ac manifesta canentem** 'as she utters the obvious truth' (literally 'true things and obvious things'). *cano*, elevated, likens Laronia to a prophetess, cf. Hor. *Carm. Saec.* 25 *uosque ueraces cecinisse, Parcae*; Virg. *Aen.* 6.98–100 *Cumaea Sibylla | horrendas canit ambages antroque remugit, | obscuris uera inuoluens*; 8.49 *haud incerta cano*, spoken by the god Tiberinus. J. satirises the idea of prophetic truth at 8.125–6. *manifesta* is especially appropriate here because it can also describe criminals 'caught in the act, plainly guilty' and 'flagrant' crimes, as in Tacitus (e.g. *Hist.* 4.40 *manifestum reum* etc.) and Gellius (e.g. 11.18.11 *manifestum ... furtum*). The allegation of the hypocrites' guilt continues the legal vocabulary of lines 61–2.   **Stoicidae:** lit. 'descendants of the Stoics', coined by J. to describe the homosexuals who pretend to be moralists; Plautus coins patronymics for similar humorous effect, e.g. *rapacidae* 'descendants of pilferers' (*Aul.* 370) and *plagipatidae* 'descendants of victims of violence' (*Most.* 356). For the designation of the followers of a particular philosophical school as 'children' cf. Sextus Empiricus *Adv. Math.* 6.19 'children of the Epicureans'. The names Chrysippus (5), Cleanthes (7) and Hercules (20) establish that the hypocrites' mask of morality is Stoic. The grand-sounding name contrasts starkly with their flight in panic (*fugerunt trepidi*).   **quid enim falsi Laronia?** 'for what that Laronia said was false?', understand *dixit*, cf. *audent* 2n. *quid ... falsi*: a partitive genitive, lit. 'what of falsehood'. Mention of Laronia's name completes her contribution to the poem (36–65).

65–78 The speaker now turns to Creticus: this section is framed by his name in the vocative in lines 67 and 78. Creticus is accused of patent hypocrisy, shown by his taste in clothing when he goes to court to prosecute adulteresses: he wears a see-through toga. Legal vocabulary is prominent in this section: 67 *perores*, 69 *damnetur*, 71 *agas*, 72 *leges ...ferentem*, 76 *testem*, also 74 *audiret* (a case), 75 *proclames* (*OLD* 3), 76 *quaero* (= hold a judicial enquiry, *OLD* 10). There is considerable emphasis on the offensive garment: 66 *multicia*, repeated at 76, 67 *hanc uestem*, 69–70 *talem ... togam*, 72 *habitum*, 75 *ista*. Creticus resembles the hypocritical moralists earlier, with the important difference that his high moral tone (cf. 1–15, 19–21) makes his hypocrisy clearly visible to everyone; in this respect he is like Peribomius (15–17). This section develops out of the preceding section by the focus on adulteresses and their critics: it was her intolerance of the latter which impelled Laronia to speak (36–7).

65–6 sed quid non facient alii, cum ... ?: this kind of argument, namely that bad behaviour by those at the top gives *carte blanche* to everyone else in society, features elsewhere in J., e.g. 1.117–21 *cum ... quid facient ... ?*, 4.28–33 *qualis ... cum ... ?*, 6.617 *quae non faciet quod principis uxor?*, 8.198–9, and was an element in Roman rhetorical training (*Ad Herennium* 4.18.25).

66 multicia: a rare noun (n.pl.) denoting a fine, thin cloth, evidently transparent (implied by *perluces* 78), characteristically worn by women (11.188): 'gauze'. Cf. *Anth. Lat.* 189.26 (Shackleton Bailey) {*ten*}*uia loricae cedant multicia forti*.

67 Cretice: at 8.38 Creticus denotes an imagined degenerate descendant of the military man Quintus Caecilius Metellus Creticus, conqueror of Crete in 68/67 BC; the Metelli had long since faded out (Syme (1984) 1140). Creticus here too may denote an imaginary degenerate noble; however the scholiast sees it as a reference to a Julius Creticus *qui sub Caesaribus inlustris causas egit*; the name also occurs in *CIL* VI 32409 and at Mart. 7.90.4, a poem which includes two other names used by J. (Matho cf. J. 1.32, 7.129, 11.34, Calvinus cf. J. 13.5). On balance, J. is more likely to be referring to an eminent lawyer; any evocations of military success are ironically appropriate when Creticus the flagrant and hypocritical effeminate shocks the ex-soldiers in the crowd (73). **hanc uestem populo mirante** 'as the people stare in amazement at this garment'. The *populus* here and at 73–4 is the crowd of spectators in the law-courts. Their 'amazement' is an indirect indication of outrageous behaviour, cf. *miratrix turba* (4.62). **perores in** 'you conclude the case against', for *peroro* + *in* cf. Petr. 96.5 *rabiosa ... uoce in ebrios fugitiuosque diu perorauit*. The word probably indicates impassioned speech typical of a peroration (the close of a speech), cf. Quint. *I.O.* 2.4.22 *in ipsa uitia moris est perorare*, hence 'deliver an impassioned climax'.

68 Proculas et Pollittas: evidently adulteresses being prosecuted under the *lex Iulia* (37n.). The plurals sound like throwaway, generalising plurals, as if these names instantly evoked adultery. A Procula occurs at 3.203; see Ferguson (1987) for possible families. Pollitta is a pet-name from Polla; this, like the diminutive *Fabulla*, makes the speaker's tone towards the adulteresses gentler than his savage indignation against Creticus.   **est moecha Fabulla** 'Fabulla *is* an adulteress'. The speaker instantly admits that Fabulla is guilty: his quarrel with Creticus does not rest on the defence of adulteresses. *moecha*: the female equivalent of *moechus* (cf. 2.27). *Fabulla*: the diminutive of Fabia; for an adulteress called Fabulla cf. Mart. 4.9, 12.93, possibly J.'s source.

69 damnetur, si uis, etiam Carfinia 'let even Carfinia be condemned, if you like'. Carfinia is saved until last as a climax. We know nothing about this Carfinia (though see Courtney on similar names).

69–70 talem non sumet damnata togam 'if condemned, she will not put on a toga like that.' Whereas a *matrona* wore the *stola*, a woman condemned of adultery adopted the same dress as the *meretrix* (prostitute), the *toga*; hence Mart. 10.52: 'on seeing the eunuch Thelys in a toga, Numa said he was a convicted adulteress' (*damnatam ... moecham*). Not even a woman so immoral as to commit adultery would stoop so low as to wear such a shameless garment. The unusual punctuation break after the fifth foot places heavy, sarcastic emphasis on *talem*.

70–1 'sed Iulius ardet, aestuo' 'But July is blazing, I am sweltering.' The brief quotation of the wrong-doer's words is regular in satire, cf. 1.102–9n., 125–6, 3.153–8, 5.18, 8.44–6, usually serving to condemn the wrong-doer with his own words. This is no exception: Creticus weakly justifies his garb by complaining of the July heat. The hottest months in Rome were July and August: *feruens Iulius* is mentioned at Mart. 10.62.7; the heat of August at Hor. *Ep.* 1.7.1–13, 1.11.19, J. 3.9. That the courts were generally not at all busy (Plin. *Ep.* 8.21.2) or closed during July and August is suggested by Claudius' boast that he sat in court giving judgement throughout July and August (Sen. *Apoc.* 7). J.'s choice of July rather than August here can be explained as a pun, if the identification of the lawyer as *Julius* Creticus is accepted (67n.): in which case, the words become a double statement of Creticus' warmth, firstly in the third person then in the first person ('but Julius is hot, I am sweltering'). For *aestuo* in this sense, again in direct speech, cf. 3.103.

71 nudus agas 'plead stark naked': the speaker facetiously urges Creticus to behave like a madman. For the jussive subjunctive see Handford (1947) §§40–42. Cf. Mart. 6.77 where the victim is ridiculed for making a greater spectacle of himself by pretentiously riding in a six-man litter *quam nudus medio si spatiere foro*. *ago* = 'plead, go to law', *OLD* 44. **minus est insania turpis** 'insanity is less disgusting', i.e. than effeminacy/exhibitionism/hypocrisy. *turpis*: strongly condemnatory: often used by J. in sexual contexts cf. 1.78, 2.9 and 111, 6.131 and 241, 7.239, 11.177 and *turpissimus* at 2.83 below (virtually the mathematical centre of the poem).

72–4 'What an outfit for the people recently victorious (*populus modo victor*), their wounds bleeding, and for that mountain folk, after laying down their ploughs (*positis aratris*), to hear you citing laws and statutes (*te leges ac iura ferentem*) in!' The outrage at Creticus' garb is highlighted by J.'s introduction of the archetypal uncorrupted Roman *populus*, made up of courageous soldiers and hard-working rustics, groups which evoke the idealised past, before luxury and peace-time decadence corrupted Rome. For a similar idealisation, combining fighting with toil, cf. 6.287–93. The real soldiers contrast pointedly with the military imagery used of effeminates and may hint at the custom of consular candidates speaking in the forum wearing only the toga, to show off battle scars (Plut. *Coriol.* 14.1; cf. Quint. *I.O.* 2.15.7). On the farmer-soldier ideal see Heitland (1921) 316 and Kenney (1984) xxxviii–xxxix and cf. Cato, *Agr.* pref. 4 *ex agricolis et uiri fortissimi et milites strenuissimi gignuntur*, Cic. *S.Rosc.* 50 *accusator esses ridiculus si illis temporibus natus esses cum ab aratro arcessebantur qui consules fierent*. There is also a city/country antithesis here, similar to that in Satire 3 where it is more prominent. Line 74, like 91, is a 'golden line' (see Introduction §7): the form conflicts with content. **en habitum** 'Look at the outfit . . .' *en* is sarcastic here, at 6.531 and 9.50. For *en* + acc., see *OLD* 2c. **leges ac iura ferentem** 'citing laws and statutes' (*OLD fero* 34), cf. 43–4 *si uexantur leges ac iura, citari . . . debet Scantinia*; *ferentem* may also imply 'parading' or 'wielding'. **uulneribus crudis** 'with raw wounds', because 'recently' (*modo*) victorious, cf. Ov. *Pont.* 1.3.16 *horrent admotas uulnera cruda manus*. **populus modo uictor:** echoed in lines 160–2: *modo captas Orcadas* and *populi . . . uictoris in Vrbe*. For *uictor* with adjectival force cf. also Plaut. *Amph.* 188 *uictores . . . legiones reueniunt domum*, Siculus Flaccus, *Agrim.* p.102 *quibus agris uictor populus occupando nomen dedit.*   **illud montanum . . . uulgus:** possibly a reference to rustic folk visiting Rome, but in view of *illud* = 'that (famous)', probably a reference to the early population of Rome who lived on the Seven Hills. For *montani* of the inhabitants of the hills of Rome (at various periods) see *OLD*, Varro, *L.L.* 6.24 on the festival of the Septimontium *feriae non populi sed montanorum modo*, and for *montes* of the hills of Rome cf. J. 8.239 *in omni monte. montanus* bears implications of the tough, simple life, cf. J. 6.5 *montana . . . uxor*, Caes. *BC* 1.57.3 *homines asperi et montani. uulgus* here, often disparaging in J. (e.g. 3.36, 8.44, 15.126), suggests a disorganised crowd.   **positis . . . aratris:** evokes the early Roman heroes who left their work in the fields to take up high office and save the state, e.g. the consul and dictator at 11.89 *erectum domito referens a monte ligonem*; Ov. *Fast.* 1.207 *iura dabat populis posito modo praetor aratro*, 3.781 *et caperet fasces a curuo consul aratro*, Liv. 3.26.6–12 with Ogilvie, and 72–4n. For work on the land as a manifestation of *prisca uirtus* see Wiseman (1971) 113, cf. Virg. *Georg.* 1.43–70 and Wilkinson (1969) 76–7.   **audiret:** the imperfect subjunctive evokes an unreal scene in which the citizens of early Rome 'might hear' Creticus pleading in his see-through toga.

75–6 The speaker attempts to arouse in Creticus a sense of shame and outrage at his own behaviour by inviting him to consider his reaction to a judge or a witness dressed in such a garment.   **quid non proclames . . . ?** 'what outcry would you not raise . . . ?' *proclamo* suggests a noisy outburst which interrupts the proceedings, cf. Sen. *Clem.* 1.9.7 *hoc . . . primum a te peto . . . ne medio sermone meo proclames.* **iudicis:** the judge appointed to decide a dispute in civil law: on the difficulties of translating the word *iudex* see Cloud (1989a) 133 n.7. **ista** 'those (clothes)', n.pl. referring backwards and forwards to *multicia* (66 and 76).   **quaero an** 'I ask if . . .' + indirect question, cf. Val. Max. 7.2 ext. 16 *quaesiuit an . . . .*   **deceant multicia testem** 'if gauze is proper [even] for a witness', cf. Cic. *Orat. Dep.* 14.22 *tu . . . quem decet muliebris ornatus, quem incessus psaltriae, qui effeminare uultum, attenuare uocem, laeuare corpus potes. testem* delivers a pun, meaning both 'a witness' and 'a testicle', in the latter sense virtually equivalent to 'masculinity', cf. Suet. *Ner.* 28.1 *puerum Sporum exectis testibus etiam in muliebrem naturam transfigurare conatus*; more explicitly at Pers. 1.103–4 *haec fierent si testiculi uena ulla paterni uiueret in nobis?* For other puns on *testis* see Adams (1982) 67 and Henderson 112 in Braund (1989a) on Hor. *Sat.* 1.8.44.

77 acer et indomitus: a sarcastic quotation from Luc. 1.146, where the words refer to Julius Caesar, portrayed by Lucan as dynamic and militaristic, a stark contrast with Creticus.   **libertatis ... magister:** sarcastic, meaning both 'teacher of freedom' and 'model of freedom'; Creticus parades as an expert on philosophical *libertas* (such as that advocated by the Stoics: see Wirszubski (1950) 143-7) but reveals that he is nothing more than an example of licentious behaviour (*libertas* of unrestrained conduct (*OLD* 8) rather than of outspokenness (*OLD* 7); Gell. 15.2.5 *libertate per uinum data*). There may be a further echo of Lucan in *magister* here, cf. Luc. 1.326 *Sullam scelerum ... magistrum*, the gulf between Creticus and Sulla serving to highlight Creticus' decadence.

78 perluces 'you are transparent', a brilliant double significance which refers both to Creticus' see-through clothing (cf. Sen. *Ep.* 114.21 *perlucentem togam, Const.* 18.3 *ipse perlucidus, crepidatus, auratus*) and to his revealed hypocrisy (cf. Sen. *Ep.* 79.18 *tenue est mendacium: perlucet, si diligenter inspexeris, Agam.* 148 *perlucet omne regiae uitium domus*). Paradoxically, it is Creticus' choice of garment to 'cover' his body which exposes that he is a hypocrite, because he prosecutes adulteresses while revealing his own effeminacy.

78-81 The centre of the poem presents an image of disease and rot spreading uncontrollably from the centre outwards in images drawn from farming (pigs) and viticulture. The 'disease' here mentioned is homosexuality, not hypocrisy; *contagio* (78) recalls *morbum* (17), from a context describing overt homosexuals. The imagery may be inspired by Ov. *Rem.* 613-14 *siquis amas, nec uis, facito contagia uites;* | *haec etiam pecori saepe nocere solent.* J. here evokes Virgil's classic description of the spread of disease among sheep in *Georgics* 3, *turpis ouis temptat scabies* (3.441, with Thomas), *dira per incautum serpant contagia uolgus* (3.469); also cf. *Ecl.* 1.50 *nec mala uicini pecoris contagia laedent.* The graphic picture of the plague spreading to humans via infected clothing at the close of Virg. *Georg.* 3 may have inspired J.'s focus on clothing immediately before and after these central lines as the symbol of the homosexuals' 'disease'. *dedit* and *dabit in plures* look backwards to homosexuals such as Creticus and Peribomius (15-17) and forwards to the worse depths to be reached by Creticus when he joins the group of homosexuals who celebrate the Bona Dea rites (*foedius hoc aliquid quandoque audebis amictu*). For the idea of the spread from one to many and the words *grex ... unius* cf. Var. *apud* Nonius p.247 Lindsay (= p.168 M) *saepe ... unus puer petulans atque inpurus inquinat gregem puerorum*.

78 contagiŏ: of various sorts of infection or pollution, e.g. Plin. *Ep.* 10.96.9 *superstitionis istius contagio*; cf. Hor. *Ep.* 1.12.14 *inter scabiem tantam et contagia lucri*, Luc. 3.322 *scelerum contagia*. On the prosody see Introduction §8.   **labem** 'stain', cf. Tac. *Hist.* 3.24 *abolere labem prioris ignominiae*.

79 grex: a herd of any domesticated animals, here pigs (*porci* 80).

80 'dies because of the scab and mange of a single pig'. For the combination of *scabies* and *porrigo* cf. Lucil. 1115W = 982M *corruptum scabie et porriginis plenum*, of an old lion, and figuratively at Fronto 2 p.112 (Haines) = 159 (van den Hout) *scabies porrigo ex eiusmodi libris concipitur*. Both words denote forms of eczema (itchy, blistering skin), cf. J. 8.34–5 *canibus pigris scabieque uetusta leuibus*. On the contagiousness of *scabies* see Otto *scabies* 1.

81 'the bunch of grapes takes on discoloration from the sight of another bunch', *conspectā ... ab unā* lit. 'from a bunch of grapes having been seen', J.'s (per)version of a proverb, *uua uuam uidendo uaria fit* (see Otto *uua*). For *uua ... liuorem ducit* cf. Virg. *Ecl.* 9.49 *duceret ... uua colorem*. *liuor* denotes a bluish colour generally caused by bruising, cf. J. 16.11 *nigram in facie tumidis liuoribus offam* and *OLD* 1, interpreting the present passage as 'a taint'. Although *liuidus* can be used to describe the normal process of grapes ripening (Hor. *Od.*2.5.10 with Nisbet and Hubbard), the emphasis here is on disease.

82–3 As a transition to the second half of the poem, the speaker predicts worse behaviour (than wearing a see-through toga) from Creticus some time (*quandoque*) in the future. For a similarly imprecise prediction cf. 5.171–3 *praebebis quandoque caput*. For the linking of sections with a comparative adjective, which places the 'villains' on an ascending scale of disapproval, cf. 6.434 *illa tamen grauior, quae ....* For transvestism see Dio Chrysostom 4.105, Quint. *I.O.* 5.9.14, Sen. *Ep.* 47.7.   **foedius hōc ... audebis amictu** 'you will dare something more disgusting than this clothing'. For *foedus* of disgraceful, self-humiliating behaviour, cf. 4.14, 7.5, 8.225 and 8.183–4 *adeo foedis adeoque pudendis utimur exemplis*. For *foedius ... audebis* cf. 6.97 *turpiter*

audent and 8.165 *turpiter audes.*   **nemo repente fuit turpissimus:**
i.e. no-one ever became utterly disgusting overnight, hence *paulatim*
'little by little' (83), cf. Quint. *I.O.* 7.2.33 *neminem non aliquando coepisse*
peccare, Sen. *Agam.* 153 *extrema primo nemo temptauit loco.*

83–7 The subject of *accipient* is unexpressed *ei,* described in *qui ...*
sumunt ... posuere ... placant, 'men who ... will welcome you'. J. now
moves from hypocrites to admitted homosexuals/effeminates, first
those who practise in private (84 *domi;* 83–116); then those who make
their homosexuality public (117–48).

83 accipient te: suggests admittance into an exclusive club. On the
unsettling metrical effect here see *deterior te* 22n.

84–5 longa ... redimicula sumunt frontibus 'wear long bands
on their foreheads'; *redimicula* were the bands or ribbons which hung
down from a woman's headdress, e.g. Lucil. 535W, Ov. *Fast.* 4.135
aurea marmores redimicula demite collo. Possibly inspired by the taunts of
effeminacy against the Trojans at Virg. *Aen.* 9.616 *habent redimicula*
mitrae. On effeminate headwear see *RAC* s.v. *effeminatus* 631.

85 toto posuere monilia collo 'they have arranged necklaces
over the entire neck'; *posuere,* perfect, 'they have set' therefore 'they
wear'. *monilia:* necklaces or chokers worn by women, cf. Pygmalion's
statue of a beautiful woman which he adorns with *gemmae, monilia, bacae*
and *redimicula* (Ov. *Met.* 10. 264–5). It is to Hercules' shame that he
wore *monilia collo* because of his love for Omphale (Ov. *Her.* 9.57).; cf.
Quint. *I.O.* 11.1.3 *monilibus et margaritis ac ueste longa, quae sunt ornamenta*
feminarum, deformentur uiri.

86–7 Bonam ... placant ... Deam 'they placate the Good
Goddess', cf. Hor. *Ep.* 1.16.58 *deos uel porco uel boue placat. Bona Dea:* a
Roman goddess worshipped exclusively by women. When the rites of
the Bona Dea were infiltrated in 62 BC by Clodius, dressed as a woman,
this was a major scandal, cf. Cic. *Har. Resp.* 44, *Sest.* 116; see Wiseman
(1974) 130–4. In Satire 6 J.'s misogynistic speaker portrays the rites of
the Bona Dea as a nymphomaniacal orgy (314–45), apparently a male
fantasy of women's thrilling and threatening behaviour (see Braund
(1992b) 84). Here J. depicts effeminates dressing themselves as women
to perform a parody of the Bona Dea rites: a travesty by transvestites,
recalling Alcibiades' supposed parody of the Eleusinian mysteries
(Thuc. 6.27–9; cf. Lysias in Athen. 12.551e-f on another religious
parody).   **tenerae ... abdomine porcae:** a sow was an appro-

priate sacrificial victim for the Bona Dea (Macrobius, *Sat.* 1.12.23); the *abdomen* is the udder, the richest part of the animal. *tenera*: strongly suggests effeminacy, cf. 8.16, 9.46. **magno cratere** 'with a large bowl' of wine: a *crater* was a bowl for mixing wine and water. The role of wine in the rites encouraged the accusations of drunkenness against women, 6.315 and 9.117, familiar from Aristophanes, *Thesmophoriazusae*.

87 more sinistro 'in a perverted manner' or 'inverting the normal custom' (Rudd), cf. Luc. 1.450–1 *barbaricos ritus moremque sinistrum sacrorum . . . repetistis*, Tac. *Hist.* 5.5 *cetera instituta, sinistra foeda, prauitate ualuere*, Curtius 7.4.10 *natura . . . sinistra*.

88–90 The effeminates invert the rules of the Bona Dea rites and ban women.

88 exagitata procul 'driven far away'; cf. Ov. *Fast.* 5.141 *exagitant et Lar et turba Diania fures*. **intrat . . . limen** 'cross the threshold'; for *intro* + boundary cf. Afranius, *Com.* 5 *simul limen intrabo*; Nepos, *Dion* 9.4 *ut limen eius intrarent*; Phaedrus 3.10.20–1 *ianuam intrauit*. The threshold was of prime significance in religious ritual.

89 solis ara deae maribus patet 'to males alone the altar of the goddess is accessible'. **'ite profanae':** an inversion of the regular ritual cry *ite, profani* proclaimed before ceremonies to exclude the uninitiated and the impure, cf. Virg. *Aen.* 6.258 *'procul o procul este, profani'*, Calp. Sic. *Ecl.* 2.55 *ite procul – sacer est locus – ite profani*, Sil. 17.28 *procul hinc, quaecumque profanae*.

90 clamatur 'is their cry', impersonal passive verb, chosen to echo Virgil's Sibyl (see previous note), *conclamat uates (Aen.* 6.259). **'nullo gemit hic tibicina cornu':** another inversion of the Bona Dea rites, where everyone present, including the musicians, had to be female (cf. 6.337 *psaltria*). The musician banned from this perverted ceremony (*hic* = 'here') is a female pipe-player, *tibicina*. In the Bona Dea rites in Satire 6, *tibia* and *cornu* are mentioned together (6.314–15 *tibia lumbos* | *incitat et cornu pariter uinoque feruntur*), probably a reference to a double form of musical instrument consisting of one straight and one curved pipe: see Nisbet and Hubbard on Hor. *Od.* 1.18.14. The associations of this double instrument with cults of Asia Minor (*OLD tibia* 1c, e.g. Ov. *Met.* 11.16 *infracto Berecyntia tibia cornu*, cf. *cornu* at Apul. *Met.* 8.26) shed a disparaging flavour on the celebrants of this Roman cult; more explicit links will shortly be drawn between the

Bona Dea rites and the cult of Cybele (111, 115-16). For *gemo* of a musical instrument cf. 7.71 *gemeret ... bucina*.

91-2 A brief comparison with the cult of the goddess Cotyto. 'The Baptae, accustomed to wearing out Cecropian Cotyto, celebrated rites like these with secret torch.' Line 91 is another 'golden line', incongruous in this description of depravity.

Cotyto was a Thracian goddess whose cult was adopted in Athens and Corinth in the fifth century BC for a short time. Her followers were called Baptae, probably derived from a ritual baptism. This mention of the Baptae is probably inspired by Eupolis' comedy of that name (fifth century BC: Hor. *Sat.* 1.4.1, Pers. 1.124), which, according to Probus (first century AD), portrayed Athenian men dancing like women. Lucian regarded the *Baptae* as a shocking play, likely to make its readers blush (*Adv. Indoct.* 27). Its inclusion here suggests that the cult was thought to involve transvestism; cf. also Virg. *Catalepton* 13.19-22.   **secreta ... taeda:** cf. 15.140-1 *face dignus arcana*, also of a mystery cult celebrated at night. The emphasis on secrecy here draws the parallel with the hypocrites earlier whose homosexuality was practised in secret.   **Cecropiam:** i.e. Athenian, after Cecrops, the first king of Attica and founder of the Acropolis.   **lassare:** the goddess is wearied by the excesses of lust practised in her name, cf. Sen. *N.Q.* 4a. pr. 2 *infelicem animum ... uoluptate lassamus.*

93-101 Descriptions of three secret transvestites (*ille*: 93, 95 and 99: 'one ... another ... another'). For a similar description of effeminate followers of the *dea Syria* see Apul. *Met.* 8.27.

93-5 The first picture, of the transvestite applying eye make-up, is acutely observed: blackening and lengthening of the eye-brow and painting a black line along the eyelids next to the eyelashes. Cf. Plin. *N.H.* 11.154 *palpebrae ... mulieribus ... infectae cotidiano; tanta est decoris adfectatio ut tinguantur oculi quoque*; Ov. *A.A.* 3.203 *oculos tenui signare fauilla*.   **madida fuligine tinctum** 'coloured with damp soot', cf. 6.O21 *oculos fuligine pascit*, the ancient equivalent of eye-liner or mascara. For *tinctum* cf. Var. *Sat. Men.* 370 *quos calliblepharo naturali palpebrae tinctae uallatos mobili septo tenent.* Courtney prefers *tactum*, comparing Pers. 3.44 *oculos ... tangebam paruus oliuo*, but the context is significantly different.   **producit:** because long eye-brows were regarded as lovely and desirable (Petr. 126), it was fashionable to extend one's eyebrows.   **trementes ... oculos:** the eyelids tremble involuntarily as the cosmetic is applied.   **attollens:** the transvestite raises both his head and his eyes to apply the make-up.

95–8 The second picture is of the transvestite drinking from an obscene glass, wearing clothing associated with women.   **uitreo bibit ille priapo:** the drinking-vessel is made of glass and is phallus-shaped. The distinguishing mark of the god Priapus was an erect phallus, whether in statues (e.g. Hor. *Sat.* 1.8, Mart. 6.49 and 73) or food (e.g. Petr. 60, Mart. 14.59) or, as here, a vessel (see Courtney's note). Although Pliny says that it is fashionable to drink from obscene cups (*N.H.* 33.4 *in poculis libidines caelare iuuit ac per obscenitates bibere*), since the transvestite appear to be performing *fellatio* as they drink, these cups are indicative of their homosexuality.   **reticulum....
auratum:** 'golden hair-net', as worn by Trimalchio's wife Fortunata (Petr. 67). Cf. *reticulatus adulter*, 6.O22.   **comis.... ingentibus:** the transvestite has long hair and may have an elaborate elevated hair-do, like the woman at 6.502–3.   **indutus** 'dressed in', + acc. of garment (*OLD induo* 26).   **caerulea ... scutulata** 'a check or tartan pattern composed of different shades of blue' (Wild (1964) 263–6); *scutulata* (n.pl. as noun) is connected with *scutula*, a lozenge or diamond shape.   **galbina rasa:** greenish-yellow garments (again, n.pl. used as noun) shorn of their pile, that is, very thin and fine. The colour is associated with women (e.g. Fortunata, *galbino succincta cingillo*, Petr. *Sat.* 67) and with effeminates (e.g. Mart. 1.96.8–9 *habeat et licet semper fuscos colores, galbinos habet mores*).   **per Iunonem domini iurante ministro** 'with the slave swearing by his master's Juno', a woman's oath, equivalent to a man swearing by his *genius* (*OLD Iuno* 4). *minister*: a servant or assistant, often in a religious context: this slave reflects his master's effeminacy.

99–101 The third picture is of the transvestite holding a mirror, with *gestamen* and *spolium* in apposition to *speculum*. Use of mirrors was especially associated with women, and hence with sexual inversion, cf. Scipio in Gell. 6.12.5 ... *qui cotidie unguentatus aduersum speculum ornetur, cuius supercilia radantur, qui barba uulsa feminibusque subuulsis ambulet* .... The mirror is immediately identified as the characteristic mark of the emperor Otho, allegedly effeminate and a travesty of heroic greatness; see Edwards (1993) 69–70.   **pathici gestamen Othonis:** a parody of Virgil's description of Abas' shield, *magni gestamen Abantis* (*Aen.* 3.286); *gestamen* indicates something (characteristically) carried by a person. **pathici:** the passive partner in intercourse. Otho (Marcus Salvius Otho) was briefly emperor in AD 69 after killing Galba; for the allegation that he was Nero's lover cf. Suet. *Otho* 2.2; he is described as *mollis*, 'effeminate' at Mart. 6.32.2.   **Actoris Aurunci spolium:** quoted without alteration and in the same position from Virg. *Aen.* 12.94, describing Turnus' sturdy spear. The quotation from epic is sarcastic and emphasises the gulf between Virgil's martial heroes and effeminates such as Otho.   **quo se ille uidebat armatum** 'in which he used to look at himself when he had put on his armour'. *ille*: Otho.   **cum iam tolli uexilla iuberet:** the speaker alleges that Otho's self-admiration continued even while he was giving orders to his troops. The removal of the standards from the ground (*tolli uexilla*) suggests that battle is just about to begin, cf. Luc. 1.347 *tollite signa*. Repetition of -*ll*- perhaps evokes language of affection, cf. 9.35–7 *labello*, *tabellae* and *sollicitent* of homosexual passion.

102–9 Labelled a parenthesis by Friedländer, but more significant thematically than that label suggests. The speaker sarcastically emphasises the travesty of Roman military excellence which such effeminates present.

102–3 'It is a matter worthy of record in recent annals and modern history, that a mirror was the kit of civil warfare'. Understand *est* with *memoranda*. For *res* in apposition to another phrase cf. 8.198–9 *res haut mira tamen citharoedo principe mimus nobilis*. *sarcina*: regularly of the soldier's kit, *OLD* 1b. The 'civil war' referred to is the intense competition for power in the so-called 'Year of Four Emperors', AD 68–69.

Probably a reference to Tacitus' *Historiae*, an annalistic account which deals with the reign of Otho (Books I and II), published in or soon after AD 105 (see Syme (1958) 118–19). This does not allow us to infer a similarly early date for J.'s *Satires*: as Syme says, designation of the *Historiae* in this passage 'would remain valid for some years, until rendered obsolete by lapse of time or another historical masterpiece', 776; see also Townend (1973) 153.

104–7 Ironic expansion of the picture of a general pampering himself. *summi constantia ciuis | Bebriaci campis* (105–6) should be deleted (following Nisbet (1962) 234–5 and Courtney *ad loc.*): they disrupt the grammatical construction and fine antithetical balance; moreover, mention of the battle of Bebriacum (near Mantua), at which Otho was defeated by Vitellius, is surprising in conjunction with *solium adfectare*

Palati.   **summi ducis est** 'it is the mark of the supreme general', followed by two infinitives. For *nimirum* used with similar irony cf. 7.78, 10.248, 14.54, Tac. *Hist.* 1.33, also of Otho. *summi ducis,* used by Martial to denote the emperor, e.g. 1.70.6, 6.91.1, is here ironical. **occidere Galbam:** Servius Sulpicius Galba, Otho's predecessor as emperor, murdered in January AD 69.   **curare cutem:** taken from Horace, suggests a self-indulgent life-style, *Ep.* 1.2.29 *in cute curanda plus aequo operata iuuentus,* 1.4.15 *me pinguem et nitidum bene curata cute uises,* cf. *Sat.* 2.5.38 *pelliculam curare iube,* and imitated by Pers. 4.17–18 in a similar context, *uncta uixisse patella semper et adsiduo curata cuticula sole.* **solium ... Palati** 'the throne of the Palatine'. *solium* symbolises power and is therefore to be preferred to the reading of the manuscripts, *spolium,* booty or riches, probably influenced by *Actoris Aurunci spolium* (100). *solium* is particularly associated with foreign kings (e.g. Hor. *Od.* 2.2.17 with Nisbet and Hubbard); the hint of 'barbaric' despotism in conjunction with *Palati* is shocking, cf. 4.31 *purpureus magni ructarit scurra Palati* (*Palati* again at the end of the line).   **panem:** a beauty treatment in which a face-pack made of dough was applied to the face (*pressum in faciem*) and spread with the fingers (*digitis extendere*); cf. 6.461–2 *ridenda ... multo pane tumet facies.* Suetonius attributes Otho's use of a face-pack of moist bread (*pane madido*) to his wish never to grow a beard (*Otho* 12.1, part of a list of Otho's 'almost feminine refinements').

108–9 quod 'a thing which....'. Two female leaders contrast with and hence condemn Otho's conduct: Semiramis and Cleopatra did not engage in beautification while conducting military campaigns. For use of female examples to condemn effeminates cf. Laronia's speech, esp. lines 49–53. Each woman is given an adjective and a location and her military activities suggested by *pharetrata* and *Actiaca ... carina* respectively. Both phrases evoke passages of Virgil, the picture of the virago Camilla, *pharetrata* (*Aen.* 11.649) as she plunges into battle, and the scene of Cleopatra on her ship on the shield of Aeneas (*Aen.* 8.707–10). These reminiscences, like those in lines 99 and 100, emphasise the extent to which the effeminate Otho falls short of the heroic standards of epic.   **Sameramis:** more often spelled Semiramis, a legendary queen of Assyria credited with various qualities and achievements (e.g. the building of Babylon, Ov. *Met.* 4.57–8); here perhaps inspired by Cicero's taunt at the effeminate Gabinius, *Semiramis illa* (*Prov.* 9).   **orbe** 'region', *OLD* 13.   **maesta nec:**

nec is postponed, *maesta* agrees with *Cleopatra*.   **Actiaca ... Cleopatra carina:** Cleopatra VII, queen of Egypt, lover of Julius Caesar then of Mark Antony: she joined Antony in his civil war against Octavian (the future Augustus), but after their defeat in the sea-battle near Actium in 31 BC Cleopatra committed suicide.

110–16 hic 'here' (110 and 111) returns to the scene of 86–92 with a further picture of a perverted religious celebration. Cf. Val. Max. 7.7.6 for reaction to religious self-mutilation.

110 nullus uerbis pudor 'no sense of shame in their language', cf. *pudor* 39.   **reuerentia mensae** lit. 'respect for the table', probably the table on which sacred offerings, such as in lines 86–7 above, were placed, cf. J. 6.O4 *sacrae ... mensae*, similarly profaned by effeminates; Naevius *Bell. Poen.* 3 *sacra in mensa Penatium ordine ponuntur*; Macrobius, *Sat.* 3.11.3–8.

111–12 hic turpis Cybeles est fracta uoce loquendi libertas 'here is foul freedom of speech in the effeminate voice of Cybele', reading *est* (Vat. 3286). For *turpis* associated with effeminates and homosexuals cf. 71 and 83 above, 6.O3. Cybele was a goddess whose cult was officially brought to Rome from Phrygia in Asia Minor in 205/4 BC and banned from Rome on several occasions during the next three centuries. Cybele's priests were self-castrated eunuchs called *Galli* (Bramble (1974) 76), hence the association with effeminates here. For *fractus* = 'effeminate' see *OLD fractus* 4, e.g. Phaedrus A10.2 *fracte loquendo*, Plin. *Ep.* 2.14.12 *fracta pronuntiatione*, Tac. *Ann.* 14.20 *fractos sonos et dulcedinem uocum*, cf. *OLD infractus* 2, e.g. Gell. 3.5.2 *uocem ... infractam*. For *libertas* with similar hostility in an analogous context cf. 8.177, *aequa ibi libertas*. For *libertas* + gerund cf. 6.216–17 *testandi ... libertas*, Cic. *Clu.* 118 *libertatem ... dicendi*.

112–14 The priest (*antistes*) of Cybele, described in four phrases. In some respects he resembles the *senex cinaedus* at Apul. *Met.* 8.24. **fanaticus:** a person inspired or entranced by religious cult, particularly a priest or follower associated with the worship of foreign goddesses such as Cybele, Magna Mater, Isis, Bellona (cf. Liv. 37.9.9 *fanatici Galli*, 38.18.9 *Galli Matris Magnae ... uaticinantes fanatico carmine*); used as a substantive at J. 4.123: see note.   **crine ... albo:** for the priest's white hair cf. Ov. *Fast.* 4.339.   **rarum ac memorabile magni | gutturis exemplum:** recalls Luc. 4.496–7 *magnum et memorabile fatis | exemplum*, although here *exemplum* has the meaning 'specimen', cf. 14.120–1 *qui nulla exempla beati | pauperis esse putat*. The priest's throat (*guttur*) is mentioned, probably to indicate the chanting involved in the ritual, cf. 6.517 *grande sonat* and 6.515 *rauca cohors*, also of followers of Cybele. For foregrounding of parts of the body cf. 4.107, a technique possibly derived from Persius (see Bramble (1974) e.g. 34–59).   **conducendus ... magister** 'a master worth hiring, who should be hired'; 'He ought to be paid to give master classes' (Rudd). Cf. 6.558, 15.112 *conducendo ... rhetore. magister* not only means 'expert, master' but also refers in religious contexts to the chief official, e.g. *CIL* 1 581.10 of the presiding official of the Bacchanalia.

115–16 Sarcastic, in effect, 'Why do these effeminates not go all the way and castrate themselves?' The speaker suggests that they should take their effeminacy to its logical conclusion.   **quid ... expectant ... ?** 'What are they waiting for?'   **tempus erat iam** 'it is already time', 'it was a long ago time', cf. Hor. *Od.* 1.37.4. Courtney calls this 'the imperfect of neglected duty' (*debuerant* 3.163n.). For *tempus est* + acc. and infin. meaning 'time for someone to do something' see *OLD tempus* 8c. The accusative after *tempus erat* is *quos*, the effeminates who are the subject of *expectant*: 'Yet what are they waiting for, [when] it was long ago time for them ...'.   **Phrygio ... more:** the cult of Cybele seems to have originated in Phrygia (Asia Minor).   **superuacuam cultris abrumpere carnem:** it is unclear whether the 'superfluous flesh' refers to the testicles (thus *OLD caro* 1) or to the entire genitalia (Adams (1982) 70 n.1). *culter*, 'knife', is often used in religious contexts of sacrifice (e.g. J. 10.269), hence is appropriate in this mock-religious context.

117–120 The attack suddenly changes to Gracchus who has taken the role of bride and married another man: the attack moves from overt homosexuals who practise in private (83–116: *domi* 84) to those who make their homosexuality public. The Gracchus who features in 117–48 and at 8.199–210 is a member of the élite: a Sempronius Gracchus and a Salian priest (124–6n.); if Ferguson ((1987) 105–6) is correct to locate him in Domitian's reign this consolidates the Domitianic flavour of the poem.

The phenomenon of men marrying men is predictably presented with hostile overtones towards both parties, e.g. Suet. *Ner.* 28.1 *puerum Sporum exsectis testibus etiam in muliebrem naturam transfigurare conatus cum dote et flammeo per sollemnia nuptiarum celeberrimo officio deductum ad se pro uxore habuit.* Martial 12.42 features wedding-torches, bridal veil (*flammea*, cf. 124 below) and dowry (cf. 117 *dotem*) and culminates in the mention of pregnancy (cf. 137–142 below). Cf. also *SHA* 17.11.7 *specie philosophi qui caput reticulo componerent, qui improba quaedam pati se dicerent, qui maritos se habere iactarent.* On the Roman wedding ceremony see Balsdon (1962) 181–9.

117 quadringenta ... sestertia: four hundred thousand sesterces, the capital qualification for an *eques:* see 1.106n.

117–18 dotem | cornicini: both words are postponed for maximum impact (cf. 20–1): it is surprising to learn that Gracchus 'gave a dowry' for this apparently combines the roles of the bride and bride's father; the enjambment of *cornicini* is still more surprising, for trumpeters were generally slaves.

118 siue hic recto cantauerat aere 'or it may have been on a straight horn that this man played'. A sarcastic remark with a suggestive *double entendre.* Whereas the *cornu* of the *cornicen* was curved, the *tuba* (*rectum aes*) of the *tubicen* was straight: cf. Ov. *Met.* 1.98 *non tuba derecti, non aeris cornua flexi.* This metaphor for the penis evidently belongs in the category of 'sharp or pointed instruments' (Adams (1982) 14–25).

119 signatae tabulae 'the marriage-contract has been attested', i.e. the *tabulae nuptiales* (Tac. *Ann.* 11.30), which are broken at the end of the marriage, cf. J. 9.75 *tabulas quoque ruperat.* Witnesses to a will or a contract validated it by affixing their seal (*signum*); cf. 10.336. **dictum 'feliciter'** 'felicitations offered', lit. '"good luck" has been said'; cf. Phaedrus 5.1 *'feliciter' subclamant* and *OLD feliciter* 16.

119–20 ingens cena sedat: *cena* here has a wider than usual meaning, 'the company invited to the feast', i.e. the marriage-feast (cf. 6.202). The 'huge' company shows the ostentation of Gracchus and his husband.

120 gremio iacuit noua nupta mariti: for the bride to 'recline in her husband's lap' was indecorous behaviour (see Kenney on Apul. *Met.* 6.24); juxtaposition *nupta mariti* matches the meaning. For a similar scene, cf. Apul. *Met.* 6.24 *accumbebat ... maritus, Psychen gremio suo complexus.* The line-ending here recalls Ov. *Her.* 13.139 *noua nupta marito.*

121–3 The speaker's outrage at the sight of the shameless male bride impels him into an indignant invocation of the Roman élite, followed by a sarcastic question.

121 o proceres 'leading men' or 'nobles' of Rome, from whose number Gracchus has emerged.   **censore opus est an haruspice nobis?** 'do we have need of a censor or a soothsayer?' Gracchus-the-bride requires not denunciation by the censor of morality so much as expiation by a *haruspex*, an expert in prodigies. *censor* recalls Domitian's hypocritical censorship (29–33) and the ironic description of the hypocritical homosexual moralist as *tertius . . . Cato* (40, cf. *censura* 63).

122 scilicet: generally a sign of sarcasm, as at 5.76, 6.239, 7.159, 14.156.   **horreres ... putares** 'you would shudder, you would think'. The vague second person singular draws the reader into complicity with the inaction and acquiescence of the *proceres* over this outrage, Gracchus-the-bride.   **maiora ... monstra** 'greater monstrosities', cf. 9.38 *quod tamen ulterius monstrum quam mollis auarus?* A *monstrum* is an unnatural thing or event: hence a portent, prodigy, freak, horror, atrocity. Repeated at 143 and a key symbol in Satire 4 (2, 45, 115); cf. also 6.286 *unde haec monstra.*

123 ederet 'were to give birth to', with both *mulier* and *bos*. Two freaks of nature, a woman giving birth to a calf and a cow to a lamb, both typical of the lists of prodigies which prelude disaster, e.g. Luc. 1.562–3 *monstrosi . . . hominum partus numeroque modoque membrorum, matremque suus conterruit infans,* Tac. *Hist.* 1.86 *insolitos animalium partus.* A *haruspex* would be called in to interpret such events.

124–6 The speaker lists three items of Gracchus-the-bride's apparel (flounces, long dress, orange veil), then with the periphrasis *arcano qui . . . ancilibus* reveals that he is a holder of high religious office: a Salian priest. The two companies of twelve Salian priests *(Salii)* were young men of patrician birth (Nisbet and Hubbard on Hor. *Od.* 1.37.2, Szemler (1972) 28, 31, 95, Liebeschütz (1979) 64); these priests of Mars played an important part in the ceremonies at the start and finish of the campaigning season (March and October). J. here alludes to their energetic dancing processions (hence *sudauit*) through the city carrying the sacred shields *(ancilia:* small waisted or figure-of-eight shields: see Nisbet and Hubbard on Hor. *Od.* 1.36.12) copied from the shield which fell from heaven as Jupiter's gift to Numa, the second king of Rome (cf. Ov. *Fast.* 3.363–92). Thus mention of a Salian priest carries associations with ancient religious custom, military activity and the Roman élite – all travestied by Gracchus' conduct.

125 arcano ... sacra ferens nutantia loro 'carrying the sacred objects swaying from the mystic thong'; the *sacra* are the shields. The thong is 'mystic' by extension from the general religious context, as at Mart. 6.21.9 (sc. Juno) *arcano percussit pectora loro*, J. 14.102 *tradidit arcano quodcumque uolumine Moyses.*

126 clipeis ancilibus: both nouns, set in apposition, cf. Val. Max. 1.1.9 *arma ancilia tulit*; ablative, indicating the cause of Gracchus' sweat.

126–32 More indignant apostrophes (cf. 121), this time to Romulus (*pater Vrbis*) and then to Mars (*Gradiuus*). The *Salii* were priests of Mars and one of the two companies at Rome was associated with Quirinus, the deified form of Romulus. Understand 'came' with the first *unde.*

127 nefas: a strong word denoting a religious offence, an act of sacrilege, *OLD nefas* 1, cf. J. 15.9, 12.   **Latiis pastoribus:** dative; suggests the early days when the Roman state consisted of 'Latian shepherds', cf. J. 8.275, Justin 28.2.8, Varro, *R.R.* 2.1.9 *Romanorum uero populum a pastoribus esse ortum quis non dicit?*, cf. *montanum . . . uulgus* (74). J. repeats the collocation of Romulus/Quirinus and Latium at 11.100–16.

128 Gradiue: one of the titles of Mars, cf. Liv. 1.20.4 *Salios . . . duodecim Marti Gradiuo legit*, Virg. *Aen.* 10.542 *rex Gradiue*, J. 13.113. **tuos ... nepotes** 'your descendants', a reference to the legendary foundation of Rome by Romulus, son of Mars and Rhea Silvia (Liv. 1.3.10–7.3, Dion. Hal. *A.R.* 1.76–88, Plut. *Rom.* 3, 9–11). The evocation of the pristine days of the state again contrasts with contemporary decadence.   **urtica** 'itch', lit. 'stinging nettle', here metaphorically, as at 11.167–8 *irritamentum Veneris languentis et acres | diuitis urticae.*

129 traditur ecce uiro clarus genere atque opibus uir 'Look: a man illustrious in family and fortune is handed over [in marriage] to [another] man.' The shocking effect of *uiro . . . uir* is fuelled by postponement of *uir* to the end and the disruptive impact of the single final monosyllable (see Introduction §8). For *ecce* second word following a verb, cf. 8.203 *mouet ecce tridentem* (also of Gracchus).

130–1 nec ... nec ... nec ... : a list of the signs of outrage which Mars should (but does not) show. For another unmoved deity cf. Sen. *Phaed.* 671–2 *lentus.*   **galeam quassas:** a sign of disgust and anger; cf. Val. Fl. 7.577–8 *galeam . . . minantem quassat.*   **cuspide:** for the spear as the weapon of Mars cf. Stat. *Theb.* 7.10.   **quereris patri:**

Mars is assimilated to the Greek god Ares, son of Zeus and Hera, hence he might 'complain to his father', Jupiter, as at 13.113, cf. Hom. *Il.* 5.872.

131–2 cede seueri | iugeribus Campi 'withdraw from the acres of the stern Campus', i.e. the Campus Martius. 'The plain of Mars' was an open space just outside Rome used for military musters, for drilling soldiers and for other purposes, including elections; Mars should leave it because he neglects (*neglegis*) its activities and associations. The imperative conveys the speaker's anger.

132–5 A shift from indignant apostrophe to presentation of a snippet of conversation (cf. 1.125–6) which economically sketches a scenario: the time (*cras, primo sole*) and place (*in ualle Quirini*) of a modest (*nec multos adhibet*) wedding ceremony (*officium*) at which a [male] friend (*amicus*) is being married to another man (*nubit*).

132–3 officium ... mihi peragendum: *mihi* dative of agent after the gerundive; for *perago* + *officium* cf. Apul. *Met.* 9.30 *peractis ... feralibus officiis*. An *officium* generally denotes any helpful or supportive act performed out of a sense of obligation between *amici*, patrons and clients, and was a central feature of Roman society, as reflected e.g. in Cicero's *De Officiis*; e.g. 5.13 *mercedem solidam ueterum capis officiorum*, 3.239–40 *si uocat officium, turba cedente uehetur | diues*. Frequently this involved being present at a certain event or ceremony, hence *officio togae uirilis* (Plin. *Ep.* 1.9.2), *nuptiarum officium* (Suet. *Cl.* 26.3) and *feralibus officiis* (Apuleius above).   **primo sole:** cf. Virg. *Aen.* 6.255 *primi sub lumina solis.*   **in ualle Quirini:** unparalleled (probably: at Ov. *Fast.* 4.375 some MSS read *ualle* for *colle*), hence identification of the place in question is difficult: possibly an area adjacent to the Quirinal (*collis Quirinalis*), one of the seven hills of Rome. The choice of a place-name which includes *Quirinus* (see 126–32n.) evokes primitive Roman morality, with which the homosexual wedding ceremony contrasts.

134 quid quaeris?: the casualness of the question (no more emphatic than Eng. 'Oh, ... ') suggests that what follows will be run-of-the-mill, ordinary, conventional. What follows is therefore the more shocking.   **nubit amicus:** an oxymoron designed to surprise, *nubere* being the word appropriate to the bride; cf. Mart. 12.42.1–2 *barbatus rigido nupsit Callistratus Afro | hac qua lege uiro nubere uirgo solet.*

135 nec multos adhibet 'and he invites only a few guests'. For

adhibeo meaning 'invite, summon' see *OLD* 4.　　**liceat modo uiuere**
'if we are allowed only to live (a little longer)'; cf. Ter. *Heaut. Tim.* 980
modo liceat uiuere, est spes.

135–6 fient, fient ista palam: anger is conveyed by repetition
over the line-end (cf. 5.112–13 *esto, esto,* 8.147–8 *ipse, ipse*) and by
disparaging *ista,* 'those deeds'. The speaker's prediction that such
'marriages' will be celebrated openly (*palam*) suggests that this case is
relatively discreet (there are only a few guests, *nec multos adhibet*). The
predicted increase in blatancy is an index of decline, matching the
poem's movement from secrecy to exposure.　　**cupient et in acta
referri** 'they will even want to be reported in the news', cf. 9.84–5
libris actorum spargere gaudes | argumenta uiri; on the *acta* see *OLD* actum 3.

137–42 A sarcastic glimpse of the torment experienced by such
brides: their inability to produce children and thus hold on to their
husbands. Cf. the close of Mart. 12.42.5–6 *nondum tibi, Roma, uidetur hoc
satis? expectas numquid ut et pariat?*

137 nubentibus haeret: i.e. the 'brides' cannot avoid or escape
this torment.

138 quod 'the fact that'.

139–40 'But it is better that nature grants their minds no power
over their bodies.' *nil* goes with *iuris*. For *ius* meaning 'power, control'
cf. Luc. 8.636 *ius hoc animi morientis habebat*; cf. McKeown on Ov. *Am.*
1.1.5, 'jurisdiction'.　　**steriles:** a word used particularly of female
infertility.

140–2 The speaker viciously asserts that any resort to remedies for
infertility is fruitless (*non prodest ... nec prodest*). The Greek name and
noun in *turgida . . . condita pyxide Lyde,* 'swollen Lyde with her box of
medicines', convey scorn (cf. Umbricius' scorn for things Greek and
eastern, 3.60–81). The woman is probably not simply large (Ov. *A.A.*
2.661) but pregnant (cf. Apul. *Met.* 6.9 *turgidi uentris*), a sign of the
efficacy of the medicines in her box (*pyxis*).

The second remedy is *agili palmas praebere luperco,* 'to hold out his
palms to the running Lupercus', a reference to the festival of the
Lupercalia held on 15 February during which young patrician men
(*Luperci*) ran (hence *agili* here) naked along the Sacra Via in the
Forum striking people they met with strips of goat-skin to promote
fertility (Dion. Hal. 1.80.1, Ov. *Fast.* 2.19–36 and Plut. *Caes.* 61.2; also
Ogilvie on Liv. 1.5.1–2). The male 'brides' offer their hands to be

struck, indicating their eagerness to be made fertile. This perversion of ancient Roman ritual heightens the earlier degradation of the Salian priesthood (125–6).

143–8 A final, clinching proof of the shamelessness of Gracchus-the-bride: he appears in the gladiatorial arena as a *retiarius*, the lowest type of gladiator. By doing this, the nobly-born Gracchus courts even more public disgrace than he did as a bride to a smaller audience (117–20, 132–5). For a noble to appear in a gladiatorial show, whether voluntarily or under compulsion, was considered a disgraceful degradation, since gladiators were usually slaves, prisoners of war, condemned criminals or 'volunteers' presumably driven to such an occupation by poverty: cf. 4.99–101, 11.7–8, *senatus consultum* from Larinum (Levick (1983)), Sen. *N.Q.* 7.32.3 where becoming a gladiator is portrayed as the final stage of self-degradation. On the status of gladiators see Hopkins (1983) 20–7, Wiedemann (1992) 102–27, Edwards (forthcoming).

But to appear as a 'net-gladiator' (*retiarius*) was worse still. There was a hierarchy of gladiators dominated by those bearing heavy armour, such as the *murmillo* (helmet, oblong shield, short sword) and the *Thrax* (round shield, curved sword). The *retiarius*, by contrast, was lightly dressed in a tunic (6.O10, *tunicati* here, 143), wore no head-protection (8.203 *nec galea faciem abscondit* and 8.205 *nudum ... uoltum*) and carried as weapons only a trident (here *fuscina*, cf. 6.O11, 8.203 *mouet ecce tridentem*) and a net to entangle his opponent's weapon (*retia* 148, 6.O9, 8.204: hence *retiarius*). This hierarchy of gladiators emerges strongly from 8.200–8 where Gracchus perversely disdains the accoutrements of the heavily-armed gladiator in preference for those of the *retiarius*, and particularly from 6.O7–13 (despite problems with the text) where the trainer (*lanista*) is portrayed as keeping his *retiarii* separate from his other gladiators to avoid pollution. The *retiarius*, then, was regarded as particularly effeminate: the greater the exposure of the body, the greater the disgrace; cf. Sen. *N.Q.* 7.31, e.g. 7.31.3 *alius genitalia excidit, alius in obscenam ludi partem fugit et, locatus ad mortem, infame armaturae genus in quo morbum suum exerceat legit* (on text and interpretation see Housman *CP* II 619–22). J. has followed Seneca's sequence of cosmetics-castration-*retiarius* but inserted between the last two the male bride.

This passage should be read closely with 8.199–210. There Gracchus reappears as a *retiarius* in the arena, sporting his Salian priest's outfit (207–8), which exacerbates the disgrace. Both passages are introduced as extreme examples: 8.199–200 *et illic dedecus urbis habes*, cf. 2.143 *uicit et hoc monstrum tunicati fuscina Gracchi*. In both Gracchus is portrayed as fleeing during the gladiatorial combat (2.144 *lustrauit . . . fuga mediam . . . harenam*, 8.206 *tota fugit . . . harena*), adding to his disgrace. In Satire 2 emphasis is placed upon his high birth (*generosior* 145 + list, his status as Salian priest indicating his patrician origin (see 124–6n.)); in Satire 8 still more emphasis is placed upon his seeking recognition (8.205–6 *nudum ad spectacula uoltum erigit et tota fugit agnoscendus harena*).

143 uicit et hoc monstrum tunicati fuscina Gracchi: the outrage comes at the end of the line; the effect is reproduced in English by changing the construction from active to passive: 'yet even this outrage is surpassed by . . . '. The ranking of types of outrage or villainy (*uicit*) is a mark of J.'s angry speaker, cf. 19 *peiiores qui . . . .* The verb *uicit* indicates Gracchus' failure to meet Roman manly standards: his fighting for entertainment in the gladiatorial arena is a substitute for real military conflict.

monstrum here echoes *monstra* at 122: see n.

144 lustrauit: in context = 'traverse', but the verb puns on its primary meaning, 'purify': Gracchus is manifestly polluting the arena by traversing it as a fleeing gladiator.   **-que** 'for'; *-que* is not always merely connective.

145–8 A list by name and allusion of numerous Romans of noble birth whom Gracchus is said to exceed in nobility (*generosior*). The grand evocations and stateliness of the spondaic fifth foot in line 145 elevate the tone for a moment before the jerky ending of line 146, *et Fabiis et*. The names evoke famous and glorious individuals and families of the Republic: Capitolinus was the *cognomen* of the Manlius who saved the Capitol from the Gauls, the Marcelli were an illustrious plebeian family in the Claudian *gens* (cf. Virg. *Aen.* 6.855–9), there were at least two renowned Republican Catuli (of the *gens Lutatia*), Paulus suggests the L. Aemilius Paulus who fought Hannibal at Cannae, and Fabius suggests Q. Fabius Maximus Cunctator, the hero of the Second Punic War. For a similar collection of evocative names, to indicate the disgrace of a descendant of a noble family, cf. the opening 38 lines of Satire 8.

For *minoribus* = 'descendants' cf. 1.148n.

podium: the front row, where the senators and imperial family sat. **his licet ipsum | admoueas cuius tunc munere retia misit** 'even though you add to these people the man himself at whose show he (i.e. Gracchus) at that time threw his nets'; presumably the emperor, Domitian (117–120n.). Possibly an ironical deflation, given Suetonius' description of the *gens Flauia*: *obscura illa quidem ac sine ullis maiorum imaginibus* (*Vesp.* 1.1). *munus* regularly of a gladiatorial or other public show (*OLD* 4); for the ablative denoting time cf. Lucil. 172W = 149M *Flaccorum munere*. *retia misit* indicates that he has thrown his net, cf. 8.204–5 *uibrata pendentia retia dextra nequiquam effudit* and may echo *reticulum* (96), the hair-net worn by one of the effeminates.

149–52 The epilogue: a hypothetical confrontation between the Roman heroes of the past and an effeminate ghost in the Underworld, commencing with a disclaimer of belief in the Underworld (and by implication in an after-life); contrast the need for belief in consolatory literature, e.g. *Epicedion Drusi* 329 *si non temere haec creduntur*. This disclaimer is designed to present the speaker as sophisticated and to invite the audience to share his view, by asserting that 'not even boys believe' (*nec pueri credunt*), cf. Sen. *Ep.* 24.18 *nemo tam puer est ut Cerberum timeat et tenebras*. Lines 149–51 are accusative and infinitive construction after *credunt*.

Lines 150–1 echo Virgil's description of the Underworld: for Cocytus, one of the rivers of the Underworld, cf. *Aen.* 6.297 and 323 (in initial position); for the adjective *Stygius*, 'of the Styx' (another river of the Underworld), cf. *Aen.* 6.323 *Stygiamque paludem*; for *gurgite* cf. *Aen.* 6.296, 310; for *cumba*, Charon's boat, in final position cf. *Aen.* 6.303; for *uadum* cf. *Aen.* 6.320 *uada*. The insertion of *ranas ... nigras*, however, is an intrusion which indicates the speaker's disbelief: the mention of frogs debunks the epic allusion, particularly because it evokes Aristophanes' irreverent picture of the Underworld in *The Frogs* (cf. 3.44 with Braund (1990)); *nigras* is humorously appropriate to the underworld and finds parallels in several serious contexts: see *OLD niger* 7a. Additional humour may reside in the picture of so many passengers attempting to board a single boat, *una ... cumba*; cf. Petr. 121.117–19 *uix nauita Porthmeus | sufficiet simulacra uirum traducere cumba; | classe opus est.*   **esse aliquos manes** 'that ghosts *do* exist', cf. Ov. *Fast.* 6.366 *putant aliquos scilicet esse deos*. The *manes* are the spirits of the dead. **nisi qui nondum aere lauantur** 'except for those who do not yet pay to bathe' at the public baths, where the admission price was generally a *quadrans* (6.447 *quadrante lauari*) for adults. This qualification to *nec pueri credunt* undermines that statement and provides a final humorous touch.

153 sed tu uera puta 'but suppose this were true'. The direct address to any member of the audience (*tu nube atque tace* 61 is not analogous) draws the audience in.

153–7 The confrontation of the ghosts of Roman heroes, listed in lines 153–6, with the shade of one effeminate ghost of Gracchus' kind, a perversion of Aeneas' vision of the future heroes of Rome during his visit to the Underworld, *Aen.* 6.824–46, which includes Camillus (825: in both, at the line end), *Scipiadas* (843 initial position, cf. J.'s *Scipiadae*), Fabricius (844) and the Fabii (845, in J. *Cremerae legio*: see below). The names collectively evoke the military prowess and achievements of the Republic (cf. 145–6 above), cf. Hor. *Od.* 1.12.37–44 with Nisbet and Hubbard, including Fabricius, Curius and Camillus, Plin. *Pan.* 13.4 *Fabricios et Scipiones et Camillos*, thereby emphasising the effeminates' travesty of Roman virtue. The patriotism aroused in Aeneas by his vision of heroes will shortly be perverted into the heroes' reaction of fear and loathing of the effeminate shade (157–8).

Repetition of *quid* (153, 154, 155) conveys indignation.   **Curius:** cf. 3n.   **ambo Scipiadae:** Publius Cornelius Scipio Africanus elder and younger: two of the great military figures of Republican Rome. The elder (236–184/3 BC) defeated Hannibal at the battle of Zama in 202 BC; the younger, Scipio Aemilianus Africanus Numantinus (185/4–129 BC), his grandson by adoption, conquered Carthage in 146 BC. This form was devised because Scīpiō cannot be accommodated in the hexameter; it first occurs in Lucilius (424W = 394M, 255W = 1139M) and hence in Horace (*Sat.* 2.1.17); it has a grand tone, cf. Lucr. *D.R.N.* 3.1034, Virg. *Aen.* 6.843, Manilius 1.792. The sound echoes *Stoicidae* (65), also in initial position; in sense it contrasts strongly. **Fabricius:** Gaius Fabricius Luscinus, hero of the war with Pyrrhus, censor in 275 BC, cited often as a type of incorruptibility and frugality, cf. 9.142, 11.91, Luc. 10.152 *Fabricios Curiosque graues*.   **Camilli:** Marcus Furius Camillus who captured Veii in 396 BC and saved Rome from the Gauls, another example of Republican heroism; Livy describes him as *parens patriae conditorque alter Vrbis* (5.49.7); Curii and Camilli are coupled at Mart. 1.24.3.   **Cremerae legio:** a reference to the three hundred Fabii who died heroically at Veii on the banks of the river Cremera in 477 BC (Liv. 2.48–50, Ov. *Fast.* 2.195–242). **Cannis consumpta iuuentus** 'the soldiers destroyed at Cannae', referring to the battle of Cannae in Apulia in 216 BC at which Hannibal defeated the Romans. Possibly an echo of Luc. 2.46 *Cannarum ... iuuentus* where too *iuuentus*, lit. 'the young men', specifically refers to men of military age serving as soldiers (*OLD iuuentus* 1b), hence Rudd's translation 'valiant lads'; cf. Gell. 10.28, Varro in Censorinus 14.2 where *iuuentus* designates the years 30–45. **tot bellorum animae** 'the dead of all those wars' (Rudd); embraces all the Republican heroes mentioned and more. Cf. Luc. 1.447 *fortes animas belloque peremptas*, 6.786 *lustrales bellis animas* and Tac. *Hist.* 2.28 *tot bellorum uictores*. **hinc ... ad illos:** i.e. from contemporary Rome to the ghosts in the Underworld. The spread of moral pollution like an infection is developed from 78–81 (see n.). **talis ... umbra** 'such a ghost', i.e. as Gracchus'.

157–8 The ghosts would want to be purified, if they could find the instruments of purification in the Underworld. The *si*-clauses are a reminder that the existence of the Underworld is hypothetical here (149–53). The picture of shades purifying themselves is absurd, if not surreal, because of the corporeal/incorporeal discrepancy; the mundane details add to the absurdity. **lustrari** echoes *lustrauit* 144, but here = 'purify'; purification might be achieved by fire (hence *taedis*) or by water (hence *umida laurus*: see below). Not a reference to the *lustratio populi* conducted by the censors (as argued by Nadeau 1983; for counter-arguments see Braund and Cloud 1983), yet the association of lustration with the censors may subtly maintain the theme of censorship in Satire 2 (explicitly at 29, 63, 121; implicitly at 3, 35, 40). **quā:** with *sulpura*. **sulpura cum taedis:** *sulpura* plural here; burnt as a fumigant in purgation, cf. Servius on Virg. *Aen.* 6.741, explaining three purgations: *aut taeda purgant et sulphure aut aqua abluunt aut aere uentilant.* **umida laurus:** the laurel branch is used to sprinkle water for purification, e.g. Ov. *Fast.* 4.728, 5.677–9. The associations of the laurel with the triumph ceremony will become relevant shortly (see below on *traducimur* 159 and Braund and Cloud (1983) 51).

159 illic heu miseri traducimur 'there, alas, we are paraded in disgrace', i.e. in the Underworld we Romans are miserably exposed to scorn: the hypothetical Underworld of 153 has now become real. *traduco* often describes the parading of captives in the Roman triumphal procession (*OLD* 3); combined with *laurus* (158) it provides a paradoxical contrast with the following statement of Rome's military conquests throughout the world: see Braund and Cloud (1983). Cf. 8.17, the effeminate *squalentes traducit auos*.

159–63 Rome's military might extends to the ends of the earth, yet behaviour in the mother city is worse than that of any of the defeated. *arma* at the head of the sentence emphasises the military image which is disgraced by the effeminacy in Rome.   **arma quidem ... promouimus** 'our troops, indeed, we have advanced ...'; *promoueo* often in military contexts, *OLD* 1b.   **ultra** 'beyond', followed by three phrases in the accusative denoting the area north-west of the Roman Empire. On the significance of *ultra*, see below, 163–70n.   **Iuuernae:** Ireland (also called Hibernia): according to Tacitus, Agricola planned an expedition against Ireland but it did not take place (*Agr.* 24).   **modo captas Orcadas** 'the recently-captured Orkneys', reached and conquered by Agricola in AD 84 (Tac. *Agr.* 10.4). *modo*, like *nuper*, is used loosely by J. (29n.).   **minima contentos nocte Britannos** 'the Britons contented with the shortest of nights', cf. Caes. *B.G.* 5.13.4, Tac. *Agr.* 12.3, Plin. *N.H.* 2.186–7.   **quae ... fiunt ... non faciunt illi quos uicimus** 'those whom we have defeated do not do the things which go on ...' The first relative clause alludes to the homosexual and effeminate practices described earlier; the second makes a pointed contrast between the victorious Roman people (*populi ... uictoris* 162) and the peoples conquered by Rome (*quos uicimus* 163). The purity and nobility of the 'barbarian tribes' on Rome's north-west frontier is epitomised in Tacitus' *Germania*, cf. Sherwin-White (1967) 34–5.   **populi ... uictoris:** repeated from 73 *populus ... uictor* (see n.).

163–70 Proof of Rome's corruption of foreigners. A specific example of the apparent exception proves the rule, which possibly should be attributed to an interlocutor (163–5): the Armenian more effeminate than the other young men, who was seduced by a Roman officer. The speaker explains this apparent exception to his previous assertion that Romans are more corrupt than the peoples they have conquered: his conduct is the result of dealings with Rome. He had been sent to Rome to learn Roman culture and had learned it so successfully that he had gone away fully Romanised, that is, made into a passive homosexual. On the Roman policy of acculturation here satirised, see below on *obses*.

This is clinching evidence that the desire to flee beyond the bounds of the known world (*ultra* 1) to escape the corruption of Rome is futile. Rome's military empire stretches beyond the bounds of the known world (*ultra* 159) and Rome's corruption spreads from the centre to the edges of her empire (see Braund (1989b) 49–51; now with altered view of the words *ephebis* and *homines*). The spread of corruption recalls the image of spreading contagion in lines 78–81, the centre of the poem; for a similar diagnosis of the spread of vices outwards from Rome cf. Plin. *Ep.* 4.22.7 *uitia . . . nostra late uagantur utque in corporibus sic in imperio grauissimus est morbus qui a capite diffunditur.*

163–5 ' "And yet one Armenian, Zalaces, who was more effeminate than all other [eastern] lads, is said to have yielded himself to the impassioned tribune." ' The contradictory force of *et tamen* may suggest that these words are spoken by an imaginary objector who cites an example of a homosexual foreigner from the edge of the empire, contradicting the speaker's previous statement in 162–3 (thus Lewis). Armenia Maior, on the plateau east of the Euphrates, was annexed by Trajan and made into a province in AD 114 for a brief period. As an Armenian, Zalaces might have been regarded as a fierce fighter, unlike other stereotypically effete easterners. As such, he presents a paradox which emphasises the decadence of Rome: the Romans tended to regard the peoples of the east as effete and effeminate, yet in comparison with the young men of Rome, Zalaces is the essence of masculinity – until he is corrupted by Roman morals. For this combination of 'the effete Oriental and . . . the hardy primitive' see Konstan (1993) 13.   **cunctis:** i.e. all other, cf. 11.24–5 *sublimior Atlas | omnibus in Libya sit montibus.*   **ephebis:** a Greek word denoting, when used in Latin, boys at the age of puberty; cf. Isidore (*Orig.* 11.2.10): *pueri imberbes sunt ephebi, id est a Phoebo dicti, necdum . . . uiri, adolescentuli lenes.* The Greek word may suggest decadence (cf. 3.62–70 and nn.); other Latin writers use the word more or less explicitly of the passive homosexual boy, e.g. Varro, *Men.* 205 *hic ephebum mulierauit*, J. 10.306. Cf. Cicero's sneer in his critique of Athenian institutions: *iuuentutis uero exercitatio quam absurda in gymnasiis! quam leuis epheborum illa militia! quam contrectationes et amores soluti et liberi!* (*Rep.* 4.4).   **mollior:** of homo-

sexuals/effeminates see 47n.   **ardenti:** of passionate lust, *OLD ardeo*
5b, 7.   **sese indulsisse:** a rare reflexive use, cf. Stat. *Silv.* 4.6.36–7,
Theb. 6.233; only occasionally of sexual favours (cf. 9.48), hence
possibly euphemistic.   **tribuno:** saved for final position in line and
sentence to create maximum shock impact. The military theme of
Satire 2 in general and of its close in particular, together with *ephebis* in
164, indicates that this is a military tribune.   **aspice quid ... :** cf.
5.80 *aspice quam longo* ..., 6.261 *aspice quo fremitu* ..., a formula inviting
a strong reaction of disgust.   **commercia:** dealings, presumably
implying international dealings (cf. Tac. *Ann.* 2.62 *ius commercii*), but
with a strong hint of the word's sexual usage, of intercourse (*OLD
commercium* 5b).   **uenerat obses** 'he had come as a hostage'. The
English concept of 'hostage' does not do justice to the Roman concept
of *obses*. On the education and acculturation of *obsides*, often young
men, sent to Rome see D. Braund (1984) 12–16. Examples of the
negative effect of this acculturation abound, e.g. at Tac. *Agr.* 21 the
Britons are said to have gradually been seduced into the alluring vices
of Roman 'civilisation' such as *porticus et balinea et conuiuiorum elegantiam*;
Tac. *Ann.* 14.26 *diu obses apud Vrbem fuerat*. For their seduction cf. Suet.
Cal. 36.1 *quosdam obsides dilexisse fertur commercio mutui stupri* (cf. *commercia*
above).   **hic fiunt homines** 'here are created – human beings' or
'Rome is where "men" are produced' (Rudd). *homines* is either a
surprise substitution for, say, *pathici* (which would convey the literal
message: again a euphemism) and for *uiri* (which might be what the
Romans aspired to create) or it is heavily sarcastic, '*real* human beings'
(meaning the reverse), since *homo* often denotes a human being with
the proper moral attitudes (*OLD homo* 2b), e.g. Stat. *Theb.* 12.166 *bello
cogendus et armis in mores hominemque Creon.*

167–9 An explanatory (*nam*) extension of the previous pithy statement, couched as a prediction, that if such boys stay longer in Rome
than Zalaces did, they will become even more Romanised both in the
number of lovers and in their dress. The heavy spondees of line 169
emphasise the grimness of the prophecy.   **mora longior:** implies
that Zalaces' stay in Rome was short.   **Vrbem induerit:** i.e. shall
have Romanised the boys, lit. 'shall have put the city on' the boys.
induerit is Nisbet's excellent emendation of the wholly unsatisfactory
indulsit ((1988) 91), cf. Sen. *Med.* 43 *Caucasum mente indue.* The verb's
image from clothing suits the immediate context (the references to

clothing in *bracae* 169 and *praetextatos* 170) and the entire poem, in which clothing is prominent. This image conveys graphically the process of acculturation of foreign 'hostages': their 'Romanisation' is presented as putting on 'the city of Rome'; *Vrbem* denotes Rome, as at 3.60, cf. Tac. *Ann.* 14.26 (above on *uenerat obses*). *Vrbem* here suggests *urbanitatem*, Roman 'sophistication'.   **pueris:** i.e. boys like Zalaces, compliant with the sexual advances made to them by Rome's homosexuals.   **non umquam derit amator:** cf. the similar prediction made to the client Naevolus who is prepared to gratify his patron's sexual needs: *numquam pathicus tibi derit amicus | stantibus et saluis his collibus* (9.130–1).   **mittentur** 'will be abandoned', probably a case of the simple verb in place of the compound *dimitto* (see Wilson (1900), proposing however (206) that *mitto* here stands for *omitto*). In place of the items abandoned, these boys are envisaged as following Roman 'custom' and adopting women's dress (cf. 83–142).   **bracae, cultelli, frena, flagellum:** a list of the native accoutrements of the Armenians. Trousers, knives, bridle and whip all indicate young Armenian cavalry-men; both *bracae* and *culter* are marks of the barbarian warrior (for *bracae* see *DS* e.g. J. 8.234, Virg. *Aen.* 11.777; for *culter DS* 1584 with n. 25); Zalaces and his like are not slaves but soldiers and aristocrats.

170 A final sarcastic statement: 'that's how they take Roman morality back in triumph to Artaxata' (or, less likely, 'that's how Artaxata recalls (cf. 1.66) Roman morality': see Nisbet (1988) 91). Artaxata was the capital of Armenia. The spread of corruption from the rotten core outwards to the edges renders futile the opening desire to flee.

praetextatos ... mores: cf. *praetextatus adulter* 1.78n.; indicates that the Armenians have taken on the behaviour of Roman boys, who wore the *toga praetexta* until puberty; for speech described as *praetextatus* (*OLD* 3: 'characteristic of youth, i.e. unseemly, obscene') cf. Suet. *Vesp.* 22 *ut ne praetextatis quidem uerbis abstineret*, Gellius 9.10.4. Perhaps they have donned the *toga praetexta* too, as part of their Romanisation. **referunt:** denotes the carrying home in military triumph of spoils captured from the enemy (*OLD* 1b), thus linking with *traducimur* (159), Romans being paraded in triumph in the Underworld: the final element of military vocabulary. The speaker's bitterly ironic conclusion is that Rome's corruption reduces her to the level of peoples she has conquered.

ESSAY

The targets of Satire 2 are often described as hypocrites or homosexuals or hypocritical homosexuals. None of these descriptions exactly
squares with categories of Roman thought: the cultural variations in
taxonomy, especially regarding sexual matters, are notoriously wide.
It is more accurate to say that, in Roman terms, the targets are all men
who forfeit their claim to masculinity, an essentially active, dominat-
ing role, by their effeminate, passive or submissive behaviour (see
Richlin (1993) 541–54). Moreover, they are all Roman aristocrats, the
men who ought to set the moral example to society; their failure to do
so sharpens the speaker's sense of outrage (see Richlin (1983) 201–2).
That is why he starts by expressing a wish to run away (1–3). He
assumes that he is addressing a broadly homogeneous audience which
will agree with his condemnation of this 'out-group' (on the term see
Richlin (1984) 67). In this way he can claim for himself the role of
hero, the moral crusader ridding society of its 'impurities' by exposing
them to ridicule and attack. But in the course of the poem, he reveals
himself to be the same narrow-minded bigot portrayed in Satire 1, his
language full of the marks of indignation (1–35n.) and too suspiciously
'lurid and lip-smacking' to sustain his pose of moralistic preaching (on
the speaker see Henderson (1989) 116–17). From this derives the
humour of the poem, from the way in which J. creates an extreme
position and then still manages to engineer a further twist.

Most of the material in the poem deals with the un-masculine
sexuality of these men. In lines 1–35 the speaker castigates the hypocrisy of aristocrats from old Roman families who publicly uphold the
traditional stern morality and criticise effeminates and pathics (men
who take the passive role in same-sex relationships) but privately
indulge in such practices themselves. The speaker's attack consists of
exploding two of their hypocrisies, the show of morality made by their
display of busts of philosophers (4–10) and the show of masculinity
made by their hairy limbs (11–15). After a venomous condemnation of
moral hypocrites (24–35), the attack is reinforced by a new voice, that
of Laronia (36–8n.), in lines 36–63. (For a detailed study of Laronia's
role in the poem – in particular her subordination to and manipulation
by the speaker – see Braund (1995).) As a result, the hypocrites run
away (64–5). Then the speaker attacks another hypocritical moralist,

but this time one who makes no secret of his effeminacy: this is Creticus, who relishes prosecuting women for adultery while wearing a see-through toga (lines 65–78: the last word, *perluces* 78, brilliantly expresses his bodily and moral self-exposure).

The speaker now abandons the hypocrites and in the second half of the poem criticises men who are self-confessedly unmasculine. He starts by portraying the secret celebration of the (exclusively female) Bona Dea rites by sexual inverts (lines 82–116). Then he attacks the behaviour of Gracchus who takes the bride's role in a same-sex wedding (lines 117–42). Up to this point the victims have been attacked for their adoption of the female role, in terms of both sexual behaviour and clothing. Yet the climax (and signalled as such by 143 *uicit et hoc monstrum*) is a case of public self-humiliation in the arena (143–8). It has been argued that this is a digression (e.g. by Courtney 122), but once it is seen that Roman sexuality is imagined in terms of dominance and submission, it is not difficult to see the analogy: the aristocrat who enters the arena dressed as a lowly type of gladiator is assuming a role that normally falls to a conquered foreigner, a slave. The forms of degradation complement one another (see Konstan (1993) on sexuality and degradation). The poem closes with an epilogue which presents the ultimate example of degradation imaginable to the speaker: the humiliation of the dead military heroes of the Republic in the Underworld by the arrival of unmasculine 'Roman' ghosts (149–59), in a perversion of Aeneas' vision of the future heroes of Rome (153–7n.). The poem closes with an ironic paradox: Rome's military might extends to the ends of the earth, yet behaviour in the mother city is worse than that of any of the defeated (159–63), which the speaker proves with a telling example: the case of the young Armenian sent to Rome to learn Roman culture. He learned it so successfully that he went away fully Romanised, that is, made into a passive homosexual by his dealings with Roman aristocrats (163–70).

The climax of the poem – Gracchus as the net-gladiator (143–8) – presents the most public humiliation imaginable for a Roman aristocrat: defeat in the arena under the gaze of the assembled Roman populace. This climax is prepared for in the course of the poem by a carefully structured sequence moving from secrecy to blatancy. The poem opens with attacks by the speaker and Laronia on hypocritical moralists who publicly deny their desire to play the passive role and

carry out their preferred activities in secret (1–63). Once these hypocrites are driven from the scene (64–5), the speaker turns his guns upon
a hypocrite who displays his vice openly instead of trying to conceal it
(65–78). That is, in the first half of the poem the hypocritical pseudo-
moralists are portrayed first behaving secretively then blatantly. At
the centre of the poem comes the central image of infection spreading
from the core outwards (78–81, developing *morbus* 17). In the second
half of the poem, the speaker turns away from hypocrites to those who
are, paradoxically, worse (82–3n.): those who admit their lack of
masculinity. First he castigates the self-confessed effeminates who
choose to practise in private (82–116). Finally, he attacks the blatant
display of lack of masculinity in the person of Gracchus, who appears
first as bride (117–42) and then as net-gladiator (143–8). This movement from secrecy to exposure to the public gaze which J. executes in
both halves of the poem bears out the Roman concept of the looker as
active and the looked-at as passive: the speaker's voice is that of the
active male, watching in astonishment the behaviour of those who take
the passive role (whether uneasily – in the first half – or happily – in
the second) and vilifying his victims for their self-degradation in their
acceptance of this passive role. The structure which builds towards the
climax conveys an effect of increasing indignation, as one after another
the horrors and outrages are piled up.

That is not all that can be said about the structure. This tightly
controlled poem ends with an epilogue (149–70) which closes by
linking with opening and central passages of the poem (on the circular
movement see Bramble (1974) 43). The speaker's opening wish to flee
beyond the edge of the world is shown to be futile by the closing
picture of the Armenian captive taking back corrupt Roman morals to
the edge of the empire (163–70n.): there is no escape. These framing
passages which together portray the spread of corruption link with the
image of the spread of infection in lines 78–81, appropriately, the
centre of the poem. And on a smaller scale there are several striking
instances of ring-composition within the poem (1–35, 36–65, 65–78:
see 1–3n., 34–5n., 65–7nn.). It is evident (contrary to Courtney 120;
see Braund and Cloud (1981) 203–8) that Satire 2 has a brilliantly
conceived organisation.

Argument and structure are complemented by themes and imagery.
The most striking theme is that of dress and appearance, a classic for

satirists (Bramble (1974) 38–41; on clothing in Satire 2 see Richlin (1993) 545–6). This has two radically different manifestations in the poem. At the beginning, the slogan is *frontis nulla fides* (8), 'you can't trust appearances' (1–35n.). Here the outward appearance of the pseudo-moralists – their hairy limbs and short hair – proclaims their stern morality, an image which is betrayed by their depilated bottoms. By contrast, in the rest of the poem the speaker adheres to the idea that style is the key to character, a concept expressed most famously by Seneca in *Epistle* 114. The first case is Creticus who reveals his effeminacy by his clothing: a see-through toga (65–78). This is followed by the description of the self-confessed effeminates putting on their make-up and clothes for their perversion of the women-only Bona Dea ritual (83–101). Then Gracchus appears in public dressed first as a bride, despite his appearance on other public occasions dressed as a Salian priest (124–6n.), then as a 'net-gladiator' (*retiarius*) (143–8n.). Finally, the corruption of the races on the edge of the empire is revealed by their rejection of their warrior accoutrements – trousers, knives, bridle and whip – and their adoption of *praetextatos . . . mores*, an image from the dress of Roman boys (170n.).

The theme of dress and appearance is deployed to emphasise the aristocrats' abuse of the public roles they should perform with dignity and authority. So it is not surprising that several other thematic strands in the poem appeal to standards of public conduct, primarily in the military and religious spheres. Military symbolism pervades the poem, ranging from single words (e.g. 20 *inuadunt*, 39 *opponunt*, 64 *fugerunt*, 143 *uicit*, 155 *iuuentus*, 159 *traducimur*, 170 *referunt*) through more developed images (e.g. 46, the defensiveness of the pathics; 73–4, real soldiers introduced as a standard; 99–100, literary parody of an epic description of armour; 130–2, the reaction Mars ought to have to such outrages) to more extended passages (e.g. 102–9, depicting the effeminate battle accoutrements of a male general, such as even a woman military leader would not indulge in; 143–8, the travesty provided by Gracchus in the arena; 153–70, the entire epilogue, esp. the names in 153–7). (For full discussion of the imagery see Anderson (1982) 211–16; cf. Walters's discussion (forthcoming 1996) of 'manhood' and soldiers in a pseudo-Quintilianic declamation.) This invites us to measure the decadence described against the militaristic standards of the past: this is especially explicit in lines 153–63 (see nn., esp. 159 *traducimur*). The final paradox of the pathic 'conquest' of the effeminate eastern world (163–70) drives home the irony.

Religious references function in a similar way. The travesty of the venerated Bona Dea rites by the transvestites (83–90) and Gracchus' status as a Salian priest, a position of both religious and military significance reserved only for young men of patrician birth (124–6n.), are two of the pollutions that should make those masculine Roman deities Quirinus and Mars protest (126–32n.) and that might drive the ghosts of Roman heroes to seek religious purification (157–8n.). The position of censor, too, is one of religious, military and legal authority. This is a role abused by the hypocritical Domitian (29–33n.); the theme of censorship reappears in the unfairness condemned by Laronia (*censura* 63) and in the implication that the censor's role is redundant in the face of such monstrosities (*censore* 121) (see Anderson (1982) 209–11). Repeated mention of legislation against adultery (the *lex Iulia*, 30–1, 37, 68) highlights the hypocrisy of the pseudo-moralists with their double standard; Laronia in vain proposes that the *lex Scantinia* (which probably outlawed sex with young freeborn males: see 43–4n.) should be invoked, 43–4. And the prominence of legal vocabulary during Creticus' outrageous performance in court (65–78n.) similarly emphasises the gulf between the ideal and the degradation. All these strands, which are not easily disentangled because in Roman ideology they are closely interconnected, link with the theme of dress and appearance to reinforce the literary texture and complement the argument.

Finally, it is worth noting that although J. presents the same speaker as in Satire 1, there is a development in his satiric technique in his introduction of the ironic voice of the woman Laronia. This prepares the ground for Satire 3, in which he introduces another character – Umbricius – who proceeds to dominate the poem. The flight motif which features at the opening of Satire 2 is also a preparation for the same dynamic in Satire 3. But whereas the speaker in Satire 2, despite his initial wish to run away, by the end sees that escape is impossible because Rome has infected all the world, Umbricius, by contrast, does leave Rome after delivering his tirade against the city.

SATIRE 3

1–20 The speaker swiftly sets the scene for the poem by narrating his meeting with an old friend, Umbricius, who is leaving Rome for Cumae. Lines 1–3, 10–11 and 17 are scene-setting and lines 4–9, 12–16 and 18–20 provide the speaker's commentary: he regrets but approves the decision. This section anticipates themes in Umbricius' speech explaining his reasons which occupies the rest of the poem (see Essay). On difficulties in the text see 10–20n.

1–3 quamuis ... tamen: cf. Apul. *Met.* 6.14 *sic ... Psyche, quamuis praesenti corpore, sensibus tamen aberat.* **digressu ueteris confusus amici** 'distressed by the departure of my old friend'; cf. Plin. *Pan.* 86.3 *quam ego audio confusionem tuam fuisse cum digredientem prosequereris!* For *uetus* = 'long-standing' cf. 1.132, Hor. *Sat.* 2.6.81 *ueterem uetus hospes amicum.* The departure of a friend was a standard occasion for a valedictory speech, known as a *propemptikon* (a 'send-off' speech). On *propemptika* in poetry see Russell and Wilson on Menander Rhetor 304–5 and Cairns (1972) 7–16. **laudo ... quod ... destinet** 'I applaud his decision'. For *laudo quod* cf. 10.28. On the prosody of *laudo* see Introduction §8. *destinet* is subjunctive because this is virtually indirect speech. **uacuis ... Cumis:** Cumae, on the bay of Naples, was an ancient Greek colony (founded in the eighth century BC) which was a favourite resort of the Roman élite (*Princeton Encyclopedia of Classical Sites* 251). Although J. and Statius (*Silv.* 4.3.65 *quieta Cyme* with Coleman) characterise it as quiet, probably relative to Puteoli and Rome, it was not a ghost-town (see *RE* 'Kyme' 2476–8); the calendar of festivals in honour of Augustus suggests a flourishing *municipium* (see Mommsen (1882)). *uacuis* emphasises Cumae's 'emptiness' and thus introduces an important theme, the over-crowding of Rome, a frequent antithesis in Horace, e.g. *Ep.* 1.7.44–5 *mihi iam non regia Roma | sed uacuum Tibur placet.* **sedem figere** 'to establish his home'. **unum ciuem donare Sibyllae:** there were a number of Sibyls, female prophetesses who made ecstatic utterances, throughout the ancient world, of whom the Cumaean Sibyl was the most famous, thanks to Virgil's portrayal of Aeneas' consultation of the prophetess in *Aeneid* 6: see *OCD*². *unum* implies 'one and only', developing *uacuis*. Cumae is an appropriate destination if Umbricius is identified with or evokes the *haruspex* of that name, since it is the home of his fellow-prophet ('fellow-citizen' – *ciuem*), the Sibyl: see Braund (1990), esp. 505–6. Cf. Mart. 14.114 where a plate is described as a *municipem* ('fellow townsman') of the Sibyl.

4–9 Reasons for moving to Cumae: it is pleasant and quiet in comparison with the dangerous and noisy city.

4 ianua Baiarum 'the gateway to Baiae' (*ianua OLD* 2a). Travellers to Baiae ('the Roman fashionable resort par excellence', *Princeton Encyclopedia of Classical Sites* 137) passed through Cumae on the neck of the peninsula. Many wealthy Romans had villas on the Bay of Naples.

4–5 gratum litus amoeni | secessus 'a charming coast with delightful seclusion' (Rudd); the construction is adjective + genitive of quality, unusually not joined by *et*, cf. 10.125 *conspicuae diuina Philippica famae*. On the attractions of this area see Hor. *Ep.* 1.1.83 *nullus in orbe sinus Bais praelucet amoenis*, Stat. *Silv.* 4.7.18–19. The criticism of the city made in *uacuis* (2) is repeated in *secessus*, which denotes withdrawal from Rome and public life (*OLD* 1b). Nisbet ((1988) 91–2) proposes *limen* for *litus* which would give 'the charming threshold of a delightful seclusion', meaning the bay of Baiae. In addition to Nisbet's arguments, this suggestion suitably emphasises Umbricius' liminality; similar is Persius' claim to be *semipaganus* (*Prol.* 6).

5 Prochytam: a small island near Baiae, *aspera* ('rugged') according to Statius (*Silv.* 2.2.76). **Suburae:** the Subura with its shops and brothels was the busiest street in Rome (perhaps like London's Soho), cf. 11.51 *feruenti ... Subura*. Cf. Mart. 12.18.1–2 *dum tu forsitan inquietus erras | clamosa, Iuuenalis, in Subura*, contrasting the disadvantages of Rome with the ease of retirement.

6–7 'For what [place] have you seen so dismal and so lonely that you would not consider it worse to dread fires ... ?' **solum:** links with *uacuis* 2, *unum* 3, *Prochytam* 5. **credas:** indefinite second p. sing. involves the audience, cf. 1.18. **horrere:** for the infinitive treated as neuter noun cf. HS 343, e.g. Sen. *Ep.* 94.40 *uim praeceptorum obtinet frequenter aspici, frequenter audiri*.

7–8 incendia, lapsus | tectorum adsiduos: fires and collapses were two dangers particularly associated with the construction of tall housing blocks (*insulae*) in Rome, often built quickly and of inflammable materials (see Adamietz (1972) 27; Yavetz (1958), esp. 507); cf. Prop. 2.27.9 *domibus flammam domibusque ruinam*; Sen. *Contr.* 2.1.12 *ut anxii interdiu et nocte ruinam ignemque metuant*. Both topics are developed later: collapses at 190–6 and fires in more detail at 197–222. *adsiduos* is satiric hyperbole, cf. 1.13n.

8 ac mille pericula: in English we would say 'and a thousand other dangers'. The theme of *pericula* is developed at 268.

8–9 saeuae | Vrbis: cf. 1.30–1 *iniquae … Vrbis*. Enjambment brings a surprise: *saeua* suggests savage beasts, not *Vrbs*.

9 Augusto recitantes mense poetas: an anticlimax. The hazard of poetry recitations in August, the month when the élite left for their country retreats (Hor. *Ep.* 1.7.1–9), is comically bathetic in comparison with the list of physical dangers. On poetry recitations see 1.1n. and Mayor on 3.9.

10–20 The difficulties in the articulation of this passage (discussed by Nisbet (1988) 92–3 and now Pearce (1992)), are largely resolved by accepting Jahn's transposition of lines 12–16 to follow line 20, giving the sequence: the speaker meets his friend at the Porta Capena, they walk down into the valley of Egeria to the grotto where Numa used to meet Egeria and where the Jews now rent the spring. The abrupt asyndeton between 11 and 17 remains; neither Nisbet's proposal that line 11 is parenthetical nor Pearce's transposition of lines 10 and 11 and proposal of a lacuna after line 9 is satisfactory.

10 tota domus raeda componitur una: Umbricius' possessions (*domus*) are carried to the city gate and there loaded onto a single waggon because (with certain exceptions) waggons were not permitted inside Rome in daylight (cf. 236, 254–6n. below).

11 ueteres arcus madidamque Capenam 'the old arches of the dripping [Porta] Capena' (ἀπὸ κοινοῦ construction). Through the Porta Capena (Platner and Ashby) the *Via Appia* headed south for Capua; over the gate passed part of the aqueduct *Aqua Marcia* built in 144 BC.

17 in uallem Egeriae descendimus: see Platner and Ashby 'Camenae'. On the nymph Egeria see below on line 12. The setting of the poem presents a satiric parody of Plato's *Phaedrus* and Cicero *De Legibus* (see 1.1, 2.1–2): a dialogue between two friends walking in the countryside and halting in a pleasant place, e.g. Cic. *De Leg.* 2.2 *magnificas … uillas et pauimenta marmorea et laqueata tecta contemno.*

17–18 speluncas | dissimiles ueris 'grottoes – but not like natural ones': spondaic *speluncas* and enjambment emphasise *dissimiles ueris*; the theme of artificiality and falseness will be developed in lines

73–108. The Romans' interest in 'natural' scenes included reproductions within their houses, as attested by wall-paintings etc., e.g. Sen. *Contr.* 2.1.13, 5.5 *intra aedificia uestra undas ac nemora comprehenditis.*

18–20 The grove is artificial: the spring is not edged by grass and marble replaces tufa. Cf. Ovid's description of a grotto at *Met.* 3.157–62 where, by contrast, 'nature had imitated art' with tufa (*pumice uiuo | et leuibus tofis natiuum duxerat arcum*) and grass (*margine gramineo*). **quanto praesentius esset numen aquis** 'How much more palpably present the spring's spirit would be!', *quanto* exclamatory adverb 'by how much'. For *praesens* used of divinities cf. *OLD* 3. Egeria's *numen* would be *praesens* because she had been transformed into a spring (Ov. *Met.* 15.547–51). **undas:** often denotes flowing water of springs and rivers (*OLD* 2). **nec ingenuum uiolarent marmora tofum** 'and if marble did not profane the native tufa'. Tufa is a soft volcanic stone readily available in Italy; in contrast marble, which may have been imported, signified luxury and artificiality. *ingenuum*, 'native' or 'natural' (*OLD* 1), and *uiolarent*, suggesting religious profanation (*OLD* 1), both underline the contrast.

12–16 Using a past–present contrast (*constituebat–nunc*) the speaker deplores the invasion of Egeria's grove, a holy place, by Jewish beggars. This displacement of traditional Roman religion, (*Camenae* = Muses) anticipates Umbricius' complaint that he is driven out by the power of money (e.g. lines 21–57) and by eastern foreigners (58–125).

12 ubi nocturnae Numa constituebat amicae 'where Numa used to date his night-time girlfriend'; Latin regularly uses an adjective ('night-time') where English uses an adverbial expression ('by night'). Numa, the second king of Rome, claimed that his religious institutions were inspired by meetings with the nymph Egeria: Liv. 1.19.5 *simulat sibi cum dea Egeria congressus nocturnos esse; eius se monitu . . . sacra instituere*; Livy proceeds to call Egeria Numa's wife (*coniunx* 1.21).

The hint of illicit assignations (cf. 8.144 *nocturnus adulter*, 6.487 *constituit*) conveys the speaker's irreverence.

13 sacri fontis nemus et delubra: for description of the grove see Liv. 1.21.3; cf. Sulpicia 67–8 (spoken by a Muse) *laureta Numae fontesque habitamus eosdem | et comite Egeria ridemus inania coepta*, Mart. 10.35.13–14 *tales Egeriae iocos fuisse | udo crediderim Numae sub antro.* The 'shrine' (*delubra*: plural for singular) is the temple of the Muses, *Camenae* (below 16n.).

13–14 locantur | Iudaeis: the grove has apparently been rented out (hence *mercedem* 15) to Jews, possibly as a place of prayer. The Jewish presence here is confirmed by the reference to the Porta Capena as at 8.160, *Idymaeae portae*; cf. the Jewish cemeteries outside Rome on the Appian Way (Smallwood (1976) 521). The Jews appear in Roman satire chiefly in the context of their superstition: Hor. *Sat.* 1.5.100, 1.9.68–71, Pers. 5.179–84, J. 14.96–106.

14 quorum cophinus fenumque supellex 'whose paraphernalia consists of a hay-lined chest' (Rudd), hendiadys. Cf. 6.542 *cophino fenoque*. The chest of hay may have been for keeping food warm on the Sabbath when cooking was forbidden (*Exodus* 35.3).

15–16 A development of the themes of 13–14. Foreigners have invaded the sacred space and introduced a preoccupation with money. **populo mercedem pendere** 'to pay its rent to the people'. The trees of the grove are assimilated with the Jews who have rented the grove from the treasury.   **mendicat silua:** a graphic personification of the wood begging; the Jews in the grove are implied to be beggars, cf. 6.543 *Iudaea tremens mendicat in aurem*, Mart. 12.57.13 *a matre doctus ... rogare Iudaeus*.   **Camenis:** the specifically Roman name for the Muses, cf. Hor. *Carm. Saec.* 62 *nouem Camenis*, J. 7.2. Egeria was linked with the Camenae: Ovid *Fast.* 3.275 *Egeria est quae praebet aquas, dea grata Camenis*. The expulsion of these Roman deities is a foretaste of the departure of Umbricius.

21–57 Umbricius states his intention to leave Rome for Cumae. This is justified by his condemnation of Rome, which begins with the complaint that there is no longer any place for honourable men in the city, because they have been displaced by the shameless and the criminal.

21 Vmbricius: a name attested in Puteoli (*CIL* x 3142), which may suggest that Umbricius is returning from the metropolis to native haunts; see Ferguson, *Prosopography*. His name suggests an association with the imperial *haruspex* (diviner) of the Elder Pliny's time (44–5n. and see Nisbet (1988) 92 n. 9, Braund (1990) 505–6). On the evocations of *umbra* ('shade' or 'shadow') see Essay.   **quando** 'since', cf. 5.93.   **artibus ... honestis** 'respectable skills', i.e. fitting a man of high rank, honourable; cf. Hor. *Ep.* 1.2.36 *intendes animum studiis et rebus honestis*. The list of 'skills' in 29–38 recalls Martial's list of 'money-making skills' (*artes ... pecuniosas*) at 5.56.8–11; here they amount to sponging off the rich without being prepared for the moral consequences. *artes* is readily loaded with sarcasm in satire, e.g. 4.101, 6.595, 7.36, 8.224.

22 nullus in Vrbe locus: cf. 119 *non est Romano cuiquam locus hic.* **nulla emolumenta laborum:** cf. Hannibal at Liv. 21.43.8 *nullum emolumentum tot laborum ... uidistis.* Umbricius perhaps already betrays his mercenary preoccupations: Seneca suggests that when a person acts in hope of receiving *emolumenti aliquid: non fuit hoc beneficium cuius proprium est nihil de reditu cogitare* (*Ben.* 2.31.3).

23–4 'Today my means are less than yesterday and tomorrow those same means will wear something away from the tiny amount.' For *res ... eadem ... deteret* cf. 16.50 *res atteritur* (*res* = 'property, wealth', *OLD res* 1). The single monosyllable at the end of line 23 is metrically disruptive. **here:** *heri* was by now obsolete: Quint. *I.O.* 1.7.22. **proponimus:** a grand statement of intent, cf. *propositi* 5.1, 9.21, 10.325 'way of life'.

24–5 illuc | ... fatigatas ubi Daedalus exuit alas: an epic-style periphrasis for Cumae, where Daedalus landed after flying from Crete on the wings which he had made. Daedalus here represents escape from the minotaur (elsewhere inventiveness: 80, 1.54n.), so the periphrasis suggests that Rome is like a labyrinth full of unnatural monsters from which Umbricius is fleeing; cf. *fugiam* 59, *migrasse* 163. Cumae, as a Greek foundation, was a paradoxical place of refuge for the xenophobic Umbricius (see below on 61). For *fatigatas* cf. Ov. *Met.* 8.260–1 *fatigatum ... Daedalon.*

26–8 Grandiloquent: four clauses of increasing length with triple anaphora of *dum*, 'while'. Umbricius is perhaps approaching sixty. *recta* contrasts with adjective *curua* frequently found qualifying *senectus*, e.g. Ov. *A.A.* 2.670 *iam ueniet tacito curua senecta pede*; it also hints at Umbricius' high moral stance, cf. *OLD rectus* 10c; cf. Sen. *Ep.* 66.2 *tam rectus corpore quam est animo.* **superest Lachesi quod torqueat** lit. 'there remains something for Lachesis to spin'; cf. Hor. *Od.* 2.3.15–16 *dum res et aetas et sororum | fila trium patiuntur atra* (the three Fates), Mart. 1.88.9 *cum mihi supremos Lachesis perneuerit annos.* **nullo dextram subeunte bacillo** 'with no stick supporting my right hand'; contrast Calp. Sic. 5.13 *baculum premat inclinata senectus.*

29 cedamus patria: the subjunctive conveys his command and encouragement to himself. The phrase indicates (self-imposed) exile;

cf. Tac. *Ann.* 13.47 *quasi conuictus esset, cedere patria et Massiliensium moenibus coerceri iubetur.*

29–38 A catalogue of the shameless people fit to inhabit a Rome where traditional values have been inverted. His use of *istic* ('there', cf. Virg. *Aen.* 10.557; 'in that Rome of yours') indicates his psychological distance from Rome.

29–30 Artorius ... et Catulus: possibly upstarts of the Augustan/ Tiberian period (see LaFleur (1974b)).

30 nigrum in candida uertunt: cf. Ov. *Met.* 11.313–5 *Autolycus furtum ingeniosus ad omne, | candida de nigris et de candentibus atra | qui facere adsuerat.*

31–3 quis facile est 'for whom it is easy'; *quis = quibus.* Umbricius lists activities which he considers degrading, in a progressively more unpleasant sequence. The first five involve taking on contracts: (1) for building/repairing a temple; (2) and (3) for keeping the rivers and harbours clear (cf. Gell. 11.17) or for collecting tolls for water transport; (4) for cleaning up after floods (cf. Plin. *Ep.* 8.17); (5) for disposal of the dead (on the distaste for undertakers cf. Val. Max. 5.2.10). Line 33 suggests that these contractors finally sell themselves into slavery; see below. On the activities regarded as suitable for a man of breeding (*liberales*) and on degrading activities (*sordidi*) see Cic. *Off.* 1.150: the latter include occupations involving taxes, manual labour, retailing and pleasure-oriented occupations (Crook (1967) 193–5).   **conducere** 'to take on contracts for'; *OLD* 5, cf. 38 below. The gerundives indicating the nature of the contracts are expressed in line 32. **praebere caput domina uenale sub hasta** 'to offer themselves for sale beneath the spear of ownership'; the spear was the sign of a public auction (*OLD hasta* 2a), originally of war booty; adjectival *domina* (*OLD* 1b) denotes ownership. Cf. Sen. *Ira* 1.2.1 *principum sub ciuili hasta capita uenalia.* It is not clear precisely what J. means. The surprise introduction of slavery – perhaps they risk being sold into slavery or perpetrate some kind of fraud – makes a suitable climax.

34–7 Articulated by contrasts between past and present, country and city: 'These men, formerly (*quondam*) musicians with travelling country shows, now (*nunc*) put on shows themselves here in Rome', with virtually an extended hendiadys in 34–5 *et ... -que.*

Gladiatorial shows and other entertainments (*munera* 36, *OLD* 4) were regarded by Roman moralists as appealing to the lowest taste; cf.

Tac. *Hist.* 1.4 *plebs sordida et circo ac theatris sueta.* Social upstarts who become rich enough to put on games figure in Martial (3.16, 59) and Tacitus (*Ann.* 4.62, 15.34). Thus Umbricius maps the moral decline of Rome.

34 cornicines: horn-players in the band which gave musical accompaniment to gladiatorial shows, cf. 6.249, hence *buccae* 35, their puffed-out cheeks.

34–5 municipalis harenae | perpetui comites: this show is travelling around the towns of Italy and the rest of the Roman Empire, cf. 6.82–3 *comitata est Eppia ludum | ad Pharon et Nilum. harena:* 'sand' and hence the sand-covered gladiatorial arena. *municipalis* is disparaging, 'provincial' (*OLD*).

36 uerso pollice: the upturned thumb was probably the signal for death, in contrast with our favourable sign of 'thumbs up': Plin. *N.H.* 28.25 *pollices, cum faueamus, premere etiam prouerbio iubemur.*

36–7 uulgus | cum iubet: the man staging the games (the *editor,* cf. *edunt* 36) normally did as the spectators demanded (e.g. Hor. *Ep.* 1.1.6, Sen. *Ep.* 117.7, Mart. *Spect.* 29.3); contrast Caesar (Suet. *Iul.* 26.3).

37 occidunt populariter 'they kill to please', i.e. give the command for death. For *populariter* cf. [Quint. Cic.] *Pet.* 5.

37–8 inde reuersi | conducunt foricas: the sting in the tail: these wealthy men continue to take on contracts for the foulest jobs, here charging for entrance to the public lavatories (a tax instituted by Vespasian). The typical compression suggests that they return immediately to their pursuits.

38–40 Umbricius suggests that such men are prepared to do anything.   **cur non omnia?:** understand *faciant;* the question marks Umbricius' exasperation.   **cum sint quales ... extollit ... Fortuna** 'since they are the sort of men whom Fortune raises up ...'. **ex humili magna ad fastigia rerum:** cf. Sen. *Suas.* 4.2 (of a newborn child) *an ex humili in sublime Iuppiter tulerit.* The line ends grandly, echoing Virg. *Aen.* 1.342.   **quotiens uoluit Fortuna iocari** 'whenever she feels like having a joke'. *uoluit* is generalising perfect (also called aorist). On Fortune's sense of humour in elevating the humble and *vice versa* cf. 6.605–9 esp. *adridens* and 7.197–8 *si Fortuna uolet, fies de rhetore consul; | si uolet haec eadem, fiet de consule rhetor.*

41–8 Umbricius lists the things he cannot or will not do, in effect, a negative definition of the 'skills' (*artibus* 21) essential for success at

Rome; cf. the slave's similar catalogue of versatility at Plaut. *Bacc.* 654–60. Here the list is expressed in a variety of negative words, without repetition: *nescio, nequeo, ignoro, nec uolo nec possum, numquam, norunt alii, nemo, nulli, non.*

41 quid Romae faciam?: cf. Mart. 3.30.2, addressed to another misfit: *quid Romae, Gargiliane, facis?*; 3.38.13 on the impossibility of making a living in Rome: *quid faciam?*

41–2 librum, | si malus est, nequeo laudare: cf. Hor. *Sat.* 2.5.74–5; Mart. 12.40.1 *recitas mala carmina, laudo*; for patrons composing poetry cf. Pers. 1.51–3. For false praise cf. 86–108, *laudat* 86, *laudare* 92 and 106.

42–4 motus astrorum ... nec possum: Umbricius claims that he is no astrologer predicting the day of an individual's death. Astrologers and diviners were regarded with suspicion and consultations about the death of relatives were illegal: MacMullen (1967) ch. 4 and 129–30.   **funus promittere** 'predict the death' (not 'promise the murder'), cf. 6.565 *consulit ictericae lento de funere matris*, Prop. 2.27.1–2 (this observation is owed to Professor Nisbet).

44–5 ranarum uiscera numquam | inspexi: Umbricius declares that he has never performed divination, in which the expert foretold the future by examining the entrails of a sacrificial animal. For *inspicio* in the context of divination see *TLL* 1951.59ff. The 'entrails of frogs' appear here as a surprise satirical substitute for conventional sacrificial victims such as sheep: see Braund (1990).

45–6 quae mittit adulter, | quae mandat 'the lover's gifts and instructions', cf. 6.233, 277, Ov. *Am.* 1.11.

46 norunt = *nouerunt*, 'know how', *OLD nosco* 9b.   **me ... ministro:** ablative absolute, 'with my help', lit. 'with me as accomplice' (*OLD* 3b).

47 fur: Umbricius is thinking of theft particularly in the context of provincial administration, as indicated by *comes exeo* 47 and *Verri* 53, cf. 2.26 *si fur displiceat Verri.*   **nulli comes exeo:** almost technical words relating to provincial governors: the members of the staff of a Roman governor in the provinces were called *comites* (*OLD* 4a; cf. Hor. *Sat.* 1.7.25 and J. 8.127 *cohors comitum*) and *exeo* is one of the verbs regularly used of governors travelling to their postings (*OLD* 1e, *TLL exeo* 1356.48–61).   **tamquam** 'as being', often used by J. and Tacitus to suggest alleged reasons for an action, cf. Tac. *Ann.* 11.36.

Umbricius sarcastically suggests as his disqualification a hand that is disabled, i.e. for theft, bribe-taking, etc.

48 mancus et extinctae ... dextrae: adjective and adjectival genitive of quality. For genitive of quality not dependent on an expressed noun, an idiom typical of Silver Latin, see HS 70, e.g. Apul. *Apol.* 75 *homo iustus et morum.* For *mancus* in a similar context cf. Hor. *Ep.* 2.2.21 *talibus officiis prope mancus.*   **corpus non utile:** in apposition to the rest of the line.

49-57 The only path to success these days (*nunc* 49) is the knowledge of someone else's guilty secret. Umbricius' departure from Rome is motivated by his failure in this department (51-2); his weak formulation of the advice that riches are no compensation for the anxieties which come with corrupt power (54-7) is not convincing (see Essay).

49 conscius: cf. Mart. 6.50 *uis fieri diues, Bithynice? conscius esto* and J. 2.58-61 for the power conferred by secrets.

49-50 'The man whose (lit. to whom) boiling mind seethes with secrets [and things] which must never be told.' In effect, -*que* can be ignored; cf. Rudd's 'unspeakable secrets'. Cf. 1.167 *tacita sudant praecordia culpa,* 4.105 *offensae ueteris reus atque tacendae,* Cic. *Leg.* 2.43 *ardentis ... conscientia.* Secrets are a major theme of satire: cf. Lucil. 672–3W = 651–2M and Hor. *Sat.* 1.4.81–5 (criticism for not keeping secrets); Hor. *Ep.* 1.18.37–8 (advice to keep one's patron's secrets); and J. 9 (Naevolus who reveals secrets); Braund (1988) 163–77.   **cũi:** scan as a disyllable.

51-2 The subject of *putat* and *conferet* is '[the man] who ...', *qui.* **participem ... secreti:** cf. Tac. *Ann.* 1.6 *particeps secretorum,* 15.50 *particeps ad omne secretum.*   **honesti:** echoes 21 *artibus ... honestis.* This ring-composition signals the close of the initial theme of Umbricius' speech, that honourable Romans have been ousted by the dishonourable.

53 carus erit Verri qui ... 'Verres will love the man who ...'. On Verres see 2.26n. On the repetition of Verres' name in this line (*variatio*) see Friedländer on 6.642.

54-6 tanti tibi non sit ... ut ... 'let no riches be worth so much to you that ...', cf. 6.178–9, 10.97–8, Petr. *Sat.* 62 *ut mentiar, nullius patrimonium tanti facio; tanti* is genitive of value. The orotund hyperbole suggests that Umbricius has forgotten the speaker, not readily identified with the *tibi* here; J. develops this characteristic of Umbricius at 60 (see n.).

54–5 opaci | omnis harena Tagi quodque in mare uoluitur aurum: i.e. a huge amount of gold; cf. 14.298–9 *aurum | quod Tagus et rutila uoluit Pactolus harena*. The sands of the river Tagus in Spain and Portugal (mod. Tajo) were thought to contain gold, cf. Cat. 29.19 *amnis aurifer Tagus*, Plin. *N.H.* 4.115 *Tagus auriferis harenis celebratur.* The detail *opaci* echoes Martial's description of the river at 1.49.15–16: *aestus serenos aureo franges Tago | obscurus umbris arborum*; yet Bücheler's proposal ((1874) 637) *opimi*, 'rich' or 'abundant', may be correct (for the adjective in the same position cf. 10.281), since huge wealth is Umbricius' obsession; cf. Martial 10.16.4 *aurea quidquid habet diuitis unda Tagi.*

56–7 A picture of the consequences of success which is achieved through corruption: (1) sleeplessness, whether from anxiety cf. Phaedr. 4.21.10 *ut careas somno* or competitiveness cf. 5.19–20 or a guilty conscience cf. 13.217; (2) rewards which are not lasting (see next note); (3) inspiring fear in your patron – which is dangerous. **ponenda ... praemia sumas** 'you take rewards which must be given up' (*ponenda* for *deponenda*); cf. Sen. *Ep.* 90.30 *ponenda non sumeret*, Hor. *Ep.* 1.10.31–2 *si quid mirabere, pones | inuitus, OLD pono* 10. For *praemia* = bribes see *OLD* 1.

57 tristis: the client's gloom, cf. Domitian's advisers, 4.73–5: *quos oderat ille, | in quorum facie miserae magnaeque sedebat | pallor amicitiae.*   **a magno semper timearis amico:** the dangers are spelled out at 9.96–100: death by sword, club, fire, or poison. The patron's fear is the basis of his affection at 53–4 above. For *magno ... amico*, cf. *magni ... amici* 1.33n., 4.20.

58–125 Umbricius' next complaint is that true Romans have been displaced by foreigners. This section is an extravaganza of xenophobia directed chiefly against the Greeks of the eastern Mediterranean (hence the numerous Greek names and nouns: 61, 62, 63, 64, 66, 67, 68, 69, 70, 74, 76, 77, 81, 98, 99, 100, 103, 115, 118, 120; cf. sarcastic *Graeculus* 78), with a side-swipe at Semites (62–6, introduced by *Syrus ... Orontes*, developing from the prologue, 13–14). This standard theme in satirical attacks on the city has parallels in Lucilius (e.g. a Syrophoenician 540–1W, a Syrian 652–3W, a Hellenomaniac 87–93W), Horace (e.g. *Sat.* 2.2.11) and Persius (e.g. 1.70, 6.38–40). It should not be taken as evidence for Trajanic/Hadrianic Rome, in which Greeks were much better integrated than some other foreign groups whose arrival was more recent; for a different view, however, from a Greek perspective see Lucian *De merc. cond.* Athenaeus at *Deipn.* 1.20b-c praises Rome as an epitome of the civilised world: 'Even entire nations are settled there *en masse*, like the Cappadocians, the Scythians, the Parthians, and more besides.'

58–60 Developing lines 56–7, Umbricius declares that he will name the most successful (*acceptissima*, cf. *diligitur* 49 and *carus* 53) clients of all. 'The race which is now most popular with our rich men and whom I would especially avoid, I shall hurry to tell and shame won't prevent me.'   **diuitibus ... nostris:** i.e. rich Romans, including the *magno ... amico* of 57.   **fugiam:** repeated at 81, explaining Umbricius' flight from Rome.   **properabo fateri:** epic, taken from Stat. *Theb.* 2.342–3 *tua me, properabo fateri,* | *angit amate salus.* On the prosody see Introduction §8.   **nec pudor obstabit:** cf. Ov. *Rem.* 352 *nec pudor obstet.*

60 non possum ferre: language denoting inability to endure, cf. 2.24, is characteristic of the angry man: see Introduction §6(*a*). **Quirites:** the name given to the citizens of Rome when addressed at a public meeting (a *contio*), especially in appeals against injustices suffered; cf. Enn. *Ann.* 112W = 102Sk.; Sall. *B.J.* 31.11 *uos, Quirites, in imperio nati aequo animo seruitutem toleratis?*; Apul. *Met.* 2.27 *per fidem uestram, Quirites, per pietatem publicam.* Umbricius forgets that he is in private conversation with his friend and begins addressing a speech to the citizens of Rome (see Essay). This emotive appeal breaks the rules of speech-making according to Seneca where he states that this appeal should form the climax: *nemo statim Quiritium fidem implorat (Ep.* 15.7).

61 Graecam Vrbem 'a Greek Rome', a paradox. For *Vrbs* = Rome see *OLD* 2.   **quamuis** 'yet': corrects the previous statement, cf. *quamquam* in Ciceronian Latin, KS II 444.   **quota portio faecis** 'how small a portion of the dregs', cf. 13.157 *quota pars scelerum*; Umbricius echoes Lucan's description of Rome, *nulloque frequentem* | *ciue suo Romam sed mundi faece repletam* (7.404–5).   **Achaei:** nom. pl., with *sunt* not expressed. Technically, the word denotes Greeks from the Roman province of Achaia; cf. Plin. *Ep.* 8.24.2 *prouinciam Achaiam, illam ueram et meram Graeciam.* But it probably evokes Homer's Ἀχαιοί, with mock-heroic tone: Homer's Greeks turn out to be parasites.

62 A graphic image of the river Orontes flowing into the Tiber: all the rubbish of the east (listed in lines 63ff.) has reached Rome, a satiric version of Callimachus' use of the dirty Euphrates to symbolise trite epic poetry (*Hymn* 2.108–9.) At 1.104 (see n.) J. uses the Euphrates to evoke the east; here he uses the Orontes, the chief river of Syria, implying Semites; cf. Prop. 2.23.21 *et quas Euphrates et quas mihi misit Orontes | me iuuerint*, meaning eastern prostitutes.   **defluxit:** cf. 6.295–7 of the invasion of luxury from the east: *hinc fluxit ad istos ... colles ...*; Tacitus' description of Rome at *Ann.* 15.44: *quo cuncta undique atrocia aut pudenda confluunt celebranturque.*

63–5 A list of the eastern filth which has invaded Rome. The nouns in the accusative case depend on *uexit*. All the items mentioned are present in a single eastern import: the female musician-cum-prostitute, cf. Plaut. *Stich.* 380 for the importation of *tibicinae*. Livy's attitude is typical (39.6.7–8): *luxuriae enim peregrinae origo ab exercitu Asiatico inuecta in Vrbem est ... tunc psaltriae sambucistriaeque et conuiualia alia ludorum oblectamenta addita epulis.*   **linguam:** Semitic, implied by *Syrus* (62).   **cum tibicine** 'along with pipers', collective singular. Cf. *tibicina* 2.90n., *nigro tibicine* 15.49.   **chordas obliquas:** the 'slanting strings' of the *sambuca*, an Oriental harp; *chordas* is a Greek word.   **gentilia tympana:** another Greek noun; small drums or tambourines associated with eastern cult, especially of Cybele, cf. 6.515, 8.176, and here called 'national' (cf. *gens* 58).   **ad circum:** the Circus Maximus in the middle of Rome where prostitutes could readily be found, cf. Platner and Ashby esp. 116.   **iussas prostare puellas:** i.e. ordered by their pimps. On *prostare* see 1.46–7n.

66–8 Umbricius condemns Romans who prefer things Greek, addressing men who prefer foreign prostitutes (66) and inviting Quirinus to condemn his now degenerate people for their Greek affectations (67–8). The rapid changes of addressee characterise Umbricius as angry: see Introduction §6(a).

66 ite: i.e. to the Circus Maximus; cf. 10.166 *i demens et saeuas curre per Alpes*, similarly scornful.   **quibus grata est** 'men who like ...'.   **picta ... mitra** 'with her bright head-dress'. The *mitra* (Greek) was associated with the east, cf. [Virg.] *Copa* 1 *caput Graeca redimita mitella*; Sen. *Herc. Fur.* 471 *mitra ... barbara* (cf. *barbara* here). According to Servius (on Virg. *Aen.* 4.216 *Maeonia mitra*) the *mitra* was particularly associated with prostitutes.   **lupa barbara:** lit. 'she-wolf'; from

early times it denoted a female prostitute, cf. 6.O16 *flaua ... lupa.*
barbarus, the Greek word for 'foreign', is here turned against easterners.

67–8 The essentially Roman name *Quirine,* i.e. Romulus (see
2.126–32n.), is surrounded by Greek words, *trechedipna, ceromatico* and
niceteria, three words which occur only here in Latin.   **rusticus ille
tuus:** cf. 2.128 *tuos ... nepotes* and 2.73–4 *illud montanum.... uulgus.*
Rustic life is frequently used as a touchstone of morality by J., cf.
6.1–13, 11.78–129, 14.179–88 and 2.74n. Here sarcastic: 'that supposed rustic of yours'.   **trechedipna:** evidently a kind of shoe; with
this meaning only here. The Greek word denotes parasites who 'run to
dinner'.   **ceromatico ... collo** 'on his neck smeared with
wrestling-mud' (*ceroma,* cf. 6.246). Umbricius evokes Roman scorn of
the Greek athletic activities, cf. 115, Sen. *Brev. Vit.* 12.2 and Mayor
and Courtney *ad loc.*   **niceteria** 'prizes'.

69–70 Umbricius lists the origins of the Greeks who invade Rome.
Sicyon was a town in the Peloponnese, Amydon in Macedonia, Andros
an island off Euboea, Samos an island off the coast of Asia Minor, and
Tralles and Alabanda towns near the coast of Asia Minor. The echoes
of epic (including *ast*) underline the gap between the world of the
heroes and the present: *alta* is a traditional epic epithet of cities;
Amydon occurs at Hom. *Il.* 2.849; the hiatus of *Samo, hic* repeats Virg.
Aen. 1.16 (see Introduction §8). *relicta:* ἀπὸ κοινοῦ with all the nouns,
including the plurals.

71 The Esquiline and the Viminal, two of the seven hills of Rome in
the north-east and east of the city. The Esquiline is elsewhere characterised by J. as a pleasant place (11.51) where rich patrons live
(5.77–8); a number of parks were situated here (*Princeton Encyclopedia of
Classical Sites* 769). The Roman *Esquilias* in initial position contrasts
starkly with the preceding Greek names.   **dictum ... a uimine
collem:** *Vīmĭnālis* cannot be accommodated in the hexameter, hence
the periphrasis (cf. Ov. *Fast.* 2.511, for the Quirinal hill) based on the
etymology from 'willow', cf. Varro, *L.L.* 5.51, Plin. *N.H.* 16.37.
petunt: the many singular subjects have a plural verb (cf. *relicta* 69n.).

72 In apposition to the plural subject of *petunt.*   **uiscera** 'the
vital organs' or 'guts', as if the 'great houses' (*magnarum domuum*) were
bodies; cf. Luc. 7.579 [Caesar] *scit cruor imperii qui sit, quae uiscera rerum,*
Curtius 6.9.19 *uidebar enim mihi partem uiscerum meorum abrumpere si in quos
tam magna contuleram uiliores mihi facerem,* Florus 2.9.4 *per ipsius uiscera*

senatus grassante uictoria and *OLD* 2b. *futuri* goes with *uiscera* as well as *domini*, cf. Rudd: 'intent on becoming the vital organs ...'. **dominique futuri** 'and their future masters', a grim prediction that Romans will end up the slaves of these Greek immigrants. The juxtaposition of *domuum* and *domini* is an etymological play: *dominus* derives from *domus*, with basic meaning 'master of a household'; cf. Petr. *Sat.* 76.1 *dominus in domo factus sum.*

73-4 Three brief phrases without connectives or verbs: 'their wit is quick ...'. **audacia perdita** 'their presumption wild'; for *perditus* cf. 5.130, 8.212, 14.269. **Isaeo torrentior:** cf. 10.128 *torrentem et pleni moderantem frena theatri*; for metaphor of a torrent applied to speech e.g. 10.9 *torrens dicendi copia.* Isaeus was a rhetorician from north Syria (Philostr. *Vit. Soph.* 1.20) whose arrival at Rome at the end of the first century AD made a great impact (Plin. *Ep.* 2.3).

74-5 **ede quid illum | esse putes** 'Say what you think he *is*', with emphasis on *esse*; for the Greek's ability to be whatever the occasion demands cf. 75-8 and 93-108.

75 **quemuis hominem secum attulit** 'he has brought with him [i.e. in his own person] anyone you like'. The versatility of the Greeks seems to have been a familiar topic; cf. Hor. *Ep.* 2.1.32-3.

76-7 An astonishing catalogue of nine lowly professions packed into less than two hexameters. Greek words predominate over Latin, even where a Latin equivalent existed, graphically conveying the displacement of Romans by Greeks. **grammaticus:** teacher of grammar and literature; this Greek term replaced the Latin term *litteratus*: Suet. *Gramm.* 4. Many such teachers at Rome were Greek slaves and freedmen: see Rawson (1985) esp. 3-18. **rhetor:** teacher of public speaking, the next stage in education after the *grammaticus* (on the difference see Quint. *I.O.* 2.1.1-6). Another Greek word. **geometres:** geometrician, either a mathematician (e.g. Val. Max. 8.12.ext.1 *ad Eucliden geometren*) or a surveyor (e.g. Sen. *Ep.* 88.10 *metiri me geometres docet latifundia*). Greek word with Greek ending, scanned *gĕŏmĕtrēs*. **pictor:** painter. Many artists in Rome were Greek: Toynbee (1950). **aliptes:** lit. 'anointer', i.e. masseur, hence attendant at the gymnasia or baths (6.422), also a trainer of athletes. The Greek word is preferred to Latin *unctor*. **augur:** i.e. someone who interprets the behaviour of birds for prophetic purposes (cf. 6.585, also lines 43-4 above). **schoenobates:** tightrope walker (cf.

14.266). Greek word and ending again preferred to Latin *funambulus*.
medicus: doctor. Greek physicians were numerous at Rome: Scarborough (1969) 110–12, Plin. *N.H.* 29.17, cf. J. 10.221 *Themison* and
13.98 *Archigenes*.   **magus:** magician.

77–8 A generalisation, perfect *nouit* with present force, as often. The
diminutive *Graeculus* conveys scorn, cf. 6.186 *Graecula*. On diminutives
as sign of anger see Braund (1988) 133–4.   **esuriens:** i.e. when he
wants an invitation to dinner; as Pers. *Prol.* 10–11 *magister artis ingenique
largitor | uenter*.   **in caelum, iusseris, ibit:** the Greek will attempt
the impossible, cf. Otto, *Nachträge* 143, *caelum* 12; *Anth. Lat.* 649.22 *hoc
caelo iubeas ut petat: inde petet* (of a rich man); Dio Chrys. *Or.* 21.9 of
Nero: 'No-one contradicted him in anything, whatever he said, or
affirmed that anything he commanded was impossible to perform ...
even if he ordered anyone to fly.' Understand *si*: 'if you have told him
to ...'.

79–80 Umbricius pursues this last point to its realisation in the
(mythical) person of Daedalus 'who sprouted wings' (*qui sumpsit
pinnas*). The fact that Daedalus was a Greek 'proves' his point. On
Daedalus see 24–5n.   **in summa** 'in short', *OLD summa* 7c, also
Plin. *Ep.* 1.12.12; cf. Hor. *Ep.* 1.1.106 *ad summam*. For the semantic
distinctions between *in summa, ad summam* (some MSS) and *in summam*
(Knoche) see Courtney's n.   **Maurus ... Sarmata ... Thrax:** a
Moroccan, a Sarmatian (from the area between the rivers Don and
Danube) and a Thracian (from the area north and east of Greece).
sumpsit pinnas: cf. Ov. *Fast.* 4.605 *sumptis ... alis*; incongruous,
since the expression more naturally refers to birds growing their
feathers, cf. J. 14.76 (young storks).   **mediis ... Athenis** 'in the
centre of Athens', cf. 10.156 *media ... Subura*, Virg. *Aen.* 7.372 *mediae ...
Mycenae*; implying 'an Athenian of the Athenians': Daedalus was of the
family of Erechtheids (Diod. Sic. 4.76.1).

81–91 Four angry questions expressing detestation of Greeks.

81 fugiam: repeated from line 59: see n. Umbricius the 'true
Roman' (84–5) is ousted by Greeks.   **conchylia:** purple garments,
indicators of wealth, cf. 8.101. Another Greek word, conveying
loathing.

81–2 The key words here are *prior* and *meliore*. Umbricius envisages
two important social occasions when a Greek might be given prece-
dence over him. In the witnessing of a document he might be called

upon to affix his seal first; in the dinner-party he might be placed on a 'better couch'. On witnessing documents see 1.67n. and on the etiquette of the arrangement at dinner parties see 5.17n.; *recumbo* regularly used of reclining at table: *OLD* 3.

83 aduectus: derogatory: the Greek is depicted as a foreign import, cf. 9.23 *aduectae ... matris*, 142.71 *municipes Iouis aduexisse lagonas.*   **quo pruna et cottana uento** 'by the wind by which damsons and figs [are brought]', both products imported from Syria, representing the Greek east (62n.); cf. Mart. 7.53.7 *parua ... cum canis uenerunt cottana prunis.*

84–5 In contrast, Umbricius is a native of Rome itself.   **usque adeo nihil est** 'Does it count for nothing at all?'; cf. Pers. 1.26–7 *o mores, usque adeone | scire tuum nihil est nisi ...?*   **caelum | hausit Auentini** echoes Virg. *Aen.* 10.898–9 *ut auras suspiciens hausit caelum mentemque recepit*; cf. Lucil. 601M = 731W *caelum bibat*, Ov. *Tr.* 4.8.25 *peregrinum ducere caelum.* His childhood on the Aventine Hill makes Umbricius quintessentially *Roman*. It may also suggest his bad luck, for the place was thought to be cursed through its associations with Remus (Gell. *N.A.* 13.14.6, Syme (1979) 314).   **baca nutrita Sabina:** *nutrita* agrees with *infantia*. Cf. Sil. 3.596 *bellatrix gens bacifero nutrita Sabino*: the olive contrasts with the figs and damsons of line 83. The periphrasis evokes the Sabines' reputation for an austere life-style, cf. 169 below and 10.299, Virg. *Georg.* 2.532 with Thomas.

86–91 Umbricius attacks the Greeks' ability to flatter with false praise in four examples (two balanced pairs), cf. 42 *nequeo laudare*, 73–8 on the versatility of Greeks. Cf. Mart. 12.82 e.g. line 13 *omnia laudabit, mirabitur omnia*, echoed in *laudat* and *miratur* here, and more generally the flatterers (*adulatores*) in comedy, e.g. Artotrogus in Plaut. *Miles* 55–71 and Gnathon in Ter. *Eun.* 249–53 e.g. *quidquid dicunt laudo* and 416–33.

86 quid quod 'What of the fact that ... ', again at 147.   **adulandi gens prudentissima:** for the pattern *gens* + superlative cf. 58 *gens acceptissima* and for *gens* see 58n.; for *prudens* + gerund cf. Tac. *Ann.* 3.69 *prudens moderandi*, 'clever at', 'skilled in'.

87 amici: qualified by both *indocti* and *deformis*. The *amicus* is the patron (57n.).

88 inualidi 'a weakling', adjective used as substantive.   **ceruicibus:** plural frequently with singular sense (see *OLD*), often metrically convenient, as here; however, the plural suggests that Hercules is better endowed with neck than the weakling.   **aequat** 'likens' (*OLD* 9), with accusative (*collum*) and dative (*ceruicibus*), cf. Quint. *I.O.* 10.1.101 *neque indignetur sibi Herodotus aequari T. Liuium.*

89 Umbricius refers to the story of Hercules' victory over Antaeus, an invincible giant who took his strength from contact with his mother, Earth. Hercules achieved victory by holding him in the air. Hercules was generally portrayed with a short, thick neck (Philostr. *Vit. Soph.* 552) and his fight with Antaeus featured often in works of art (Philostr. *Imag.* 2.21.25). For the flatterer's use of a mythological comparison to heroise his patron cf. Mart. 12.82.8–9 *exiguos secto comentem dente capillos | dicet Achilleas disposuisse comas.*

90 angustam 'thin' or 'squeaky', cf. Apul. *Fl.* 17 *uox . . . angustior.*

90–1 Umbricius replays a scene in Persius *Satire* 1 where a rich man declares that he wants to be told the truth about himself (1.55–62). Lit. 'than which not even the husband by whom the hen is pecked sounds worse'; i.e. 'which sounds as wretched as that of the cock, which seizes his partner's crest in the act of mating' (Rudd). On the sound effect see Quint. *I.O.* 11.3.52.

The lines are difficult because (i) the 'squeaky voice' and the cockerel-husband are compared where strictly speaking the squeaky voice and the cockerel's *voice* should be compared; (ii) *maritus* is attracted into the relative clause and becomes *marito* agreeing with *quo*. The harsh and awkward expression matches the undignified subject-matter and thus deflates the heroic comparison offered by the flatterer in 88–9.

quo mordetur gallina marito is a mock-epic circumlocution for a cockerel. J. adapts Mart. 13.64: *succumbit sterili frustra gallina marito. | hunc matris Cybeles esse decebat auem*, where Martial puns on *gallus* (a cockerel) and *Gallus* (a castrated priest of the goddess Cybele), into a different pun about voice quality: cf. *fracta uoce* 2.111n.   **nec** = *ne . . . quidem*, cf. 2.152.

92–3 haec eadem licet et nobis laudare, sed illis | creditur 'we too can praise these same things, but it is they who are believed'. *credo* intransitive (followed by dative). For the success of extravagant flattery by Greeks see Suet. *Nero* 22.3. Umbricius' character here admits to participation in the false flattery and ingratiation and indicates his failure.

93–100 Umbricius claims that Greeks are unsurpassed at stage-acting. The scholiast explains *an melius aliquis agit comoediam Graeco, cum aut amicam aut uxorem aut ancillam imitatur?* 'Can there be anyone better than a Greek when he takes the part of Thais or when as a comic actor he plays the wife ...'. I.e. not even a professional actor can beat these parasites at acting; and, moreover, *every* Greek is a born actor.

Male actors played female roles in most of the forms of ancient theatre known to us (except the mime). As the scholiast (above) sees, Umbricius mentions the three main female roles in Greek and Roman New Comedy: the prostitute (*meretrix*), the wife (*uxor* or *matrona*) and the slave-girl (*ancilla*). Thais gave the title to a play by Menander and features in Terence's *Eunuch*; Doris, a standard slave name, features in Menander's *Perikeiromene*.

93 Initial *an* is a mark of indignation, cf. 9.43 *an facile et pronum est ...?*

94–5 nullo | cultam palliolo: *pallium*, here in its common diminutive form for metrical reasons, was the Roman word for the outer garment of Greek men and women. This slave character in the *fabula palliata* (Greek New Comedy) has discarded her *pallium* since she has work to do.

95 mulier ... ipsa: in effect, 'a real woman', cf. *OLD ipse* 5, e.g. Lucil. 669M = 652W *libertinus, tricorius, Syrus ipse.*   **nempe** after a question marks corroboration, cf. 8.180, 10.110: 'without a doubt, of course'.

96 persona: masks were used in New Comedy. Here *persona* by metonymy indicates the masked actor.

96–7 'You would say that below the belly everything is empty and smooth and separated by a thin crack', i.e. the Greek is such a good actor that there is no sign of his (male) genitalia. Cf. Colum. 1 pr. 15 *attonitique miramur gestus effeminatorum, quod a natura sexum uiris denegatum muliebri motu mentiantur decipiantque oculos spectantium.* For *uentriculus* cf. Augustus in Suet. *Vita Hor.* For *distantia* cf. Ov. *Met.* 8.248 [*bracchiis*] *aequali spatio distantibus illis*, Colum. 2.4.8 *inter duos latius distantis sulcos.*

98–9 Four Greek comic actors working at Rome. Of Antiochus and Haemus (also at 6.198) nothing else is known. Quintilian calls Demetrius and Stratocles *maximos actores comoediarum* (*I.O.* 11.3.178–80) and commends Demetrius' portrayal of *matronas et graues anus. mollis* (cf. 6.198 *mollius Haemo*) may imply effeminacy and/or a penchant for female roles.   **nec tamen ... erit mirabilis illic** 'And yet he will not be a marvel there', i.e. in Greece, though he may be here. For *mirabilis*, ἀπὸ κοινοῦ with all the names, cf. Colum. (96–7n.) *miramur*.

100 natio comoeda est: i.e. Greece is a nation of comic actors. The adjective coined from the noun *comoedus* occurs only here.

100–3 With two contrasting pairs of examples (laughter and tears, cold and heat) Umbricius indicates the Greeks' ability to imitate any behaviour, couching the examples as conditions: 'if the patron does this, the Greek does this', although in the first example *rides* and *concutitur* are stated as separate facts where they might have formed the protasis and apodosis of the condition, cf. 13.227, Mart. 12.40.1–3 (a poem depicting the client's ingratiation) e.g. *mentiris, credo ... cantas, canto* and especially Ter. *Eun.* 252 *negat quis: nego; ait: aio*. For the flatterer's exaggerated reaction cf. Cic. *Lael.* 98, Theophr. *Char.* 2.4, Plut. *Quomodo adulator* 54d. The patron is here constructed as 'you' (*rides, poscas* and *dixeris*) and as *amicus* (as often in Satire 3).

100–1 maiore cachinno | concutitur: cf. 11.2; *cachinnus* is more vulgar than *risus* (Cic. *Tusc.* 4.66, *Rhet. ad Herenn.* 3.25). For the physical effect of laughter cf. 13.171 *risu quatiare*, Lucr. 1.919 *risu tremulo concussa cachinnent*.

102 nec: with the sense *nec tamen*, *OLD neque* 5; Schublin (1991) may be correct in reading *ac dolet*: the Greek is the master performer.

103 accipit endromidem: a Greek word: a thick wrap, a garment described by Martial as 'uncouth but not to be despised in cold December' (4.19). *accipit* implies that he is offered the garment by a slave; *arripit* (Scholte), may be preferable, as indicating better his haste.   **dixeris** = *dicas*, see Handford (1947) §108.   **"aestuo":** cf. 2.70–1n.   **sudat:** an exaggerated climax: the Greek flatterer can sweat to order.

104 non sumus ergo pares: cf. 92–3: Umbricius again indicates his participation in false flattery. An echo of an epigram of Martial on clientship in which *iam sumus ergo pares* occurs three times in the build-up to the point (2.18). On the prosody *ergŏ* see Introduction §8.

104–8 A rising tricolon, explaining how the Greek is *melior* (∼ *melior* 93), culminating in a list of the patron's (*amicus* 107) 'achievements' which stimulate false praise.

104–5 semper et omni | nocte dieque: the pleonasm conveys Umbricius' emphasis. For *nocte dieque* cf. 7.61, 13.198.

105–6 aliena sumere uultum | a facie: cf. Stat. *Silv.* 2.6.53 *uultumque tuo sumebat ab ore,* Plaut. *Amph.* 961 *tristis sit, si eri sint tristes; hilarus sit, si gaudeant. uultus* = 'expression'.

106 iactare manus: a gesture of admiration (cf. Mart. 10.10.10, Plin. *Ep.* 6.17.2) but also a characteristic gesture of actors (e.g. Quint. *I.O.* 11.3.179, of Demetrius (cf. line 99)).

107–8 The context suggests that these actions would not normally command praise. The patron's belch is qualified by *bene* and his urination by *rectum* (for neuter adjective used adverbially cf. 1.16 *altum dormiret*); his fart (*crepitus,* fully *crepitus uentris: OLD* c) is simultaneous with his inversion of the now-empty drinking-cup (thus Valla: the best available interpretation of a difficult line). The cup rather than the patron is said to fart: 'if the golden cup turned upside-down gives a fart'. The relative status of belching and farting makes the fart a suitable climax: see Cic. *Fam.* 9.22.5 *crepitus aiunt aeque liberos ac ructus esse oportere*; the edict contemplated by Claudius (Suet. 32) *quo ueniam daret flatum crepitumque uentris in conuiuio emittendi* would overturn the normal disapproval of farting in company. At Mart. 12.40.3 the client humours his patron by pretending not to notice his fart (*pedis, dissimulo*); here the Greek goes further by praising the patron. For the contrast between the gold and the fart cf. Mart. 1.37, a chamber-pot made of gold. For *trulla inuerso...fundo* cf. Lucil. 139M = 132W *uertitur oenophori fundus.*

109–12 Their skill in flattery is dangerous; it paves the way to the seduction or rape of all the vulnerable members of the household, male and female, who fall under the care of the *paterfamilias* (the patron).

109 sanctum nihil †aut† ab inguine tutum: the text is un-metrical; of the solutions proposed, none is entirely convincing; happily, this matters little, as the general meaning of the text is clear. Simplest are *est et* or *est uel* of later MSS; Martyn's more radical *nil restat ab* has some merit, although it involves taking *sanctum nihil* as a noun ('no sacred thing'). For the euphemism *inguen* see 1.47n.

110 matrona laris: the patron's wife; the phrase maintains the idea of the sacred introduced in *sanctum* (the *Lar* was the guardian god of the hearth and home; for *lar* thus = 'home' see *OLD* 3, e.g. J. 14.20,

15.153). For a Greek prepared to seduce/rape his patron's wife cf.
Mart. 4.5.5.

111 **sponsus leuis adhuc:** the daughter's fiancé, so young he does
not yet have a beard (*OLD leuis*[2] 2).   **ante pudicus** 'sexually pure
up to now'; for the social superior to take the passive role in sexual
intercourse with the client, as the son does with the Greek, would be
shameful.

112 **horum si nihil est** 'If none of these is available.'   **resupinat:** *resupino, supinus* and cognates may take on sexual significance, cf.
8.176, *inclino* at 9.26 and 10.224; see Adams (1982) 192.

113 To be deleted as an (irrelevant) conflation of lines 52 and 57 or
as a mistaken gloss on the inferior reading *aulam. amici* (112) forms a
fitting climax.

114–18 The Greeks not only infiltrate the household and seduce the
patron's family but betray and ultimately kill the patron himself: the
key words are *occidit* and *amicum* (116).

114–15 A *praeteritio*, i.e. the (deliberate) omission of a topic, here the
gymnasia, the Greek institution regarded as a hot-bed of immorality
(see above 67–8n.). Umbricius thus indicates his eagerness to utter the
crowning accusation.   **coepit:** intransitive, *OLD coepi* 4.   **transi**
... audi: imperatives; for *transeo* cf. 6.602, 7.190, 10.273.   **maioris**
abollae: possibly a proverb, presumably with the effect 'of a greater
person' or possibly as a metaphor, 'of greater texture'. The *abolla* was a
cloak, cf. 4.76, sometimes splendid in appearance, e.g. Suet. *Cal.* 35.1.

116–18 The subject and object are expressed three times in pairs:
Stoicus + Baream, delator + amicum and *senex + discipulum*. The Stoic professor is P. Egnatius Celer from Berytus who in AD 66 gave evidence
against his patron and pupil Barea Soranus: see Tac. *Ann.* 16.21–33,
e.g. *cliens hic Sorani, et tunc emptus ad opprimendum amicum, auctoritatem
Stoicae sectae praeferebat, habitu et ore ad exprimendam imaginem honesti
exercitus, ceterum animo perfidiosus, subdolus, auaritiam ac libidinem occultans*
(16.32). In short Celer belongs to the type *specie bonarum artium falsos et
amicitiae fallaces* (16.32); cf. *Hist.* 4.10 *Celer professus sapientiam, dein testis
in Baream, proditor corruptorque amicitiae cuius se magistrum ferebat.*
delator amicum: cf. *delator amici* 1.33n. An exaggeration: Egnatius
was not the *delator* but was called as a witness (116–18n.).   **senex:**
indicates the superior morality and wisdom which should have
belonged to the professed Stoic (see Tac. *Hist.* 4.10 cited above).

ripa ... caballi: i.e. Tarsus, a centre for the study of philosophy which produced numerous philosophers who came to Rome (Strabo 14.5.13, p.673). Egnatius evidently was educated (*nutritus*, cf. Hor. *Ep.* 2.2.41) there. A complex periphrasis: Tarsus, on the banks (*ripa*) of the river Cydnus, derived its name from the feather (Greek ταρσός; *pinna* makes this etymological allusion) of the winged horse Pegasus, here called *Gorgonei* because it sprang from the blood of the Gorgon Medusa when Perseus beheaded her (cf. Ov. *Fast.* 3.450 *Gorgonei ... equi*). The grand, epic-style periphrasis (cf. 24–5) is deflated by the more colloquial *caballi* (*OLD*; cf. Pers. *Prol.* 1 *fonte ... caballino*, another irreverent reference to Pegasus).

119 non est Romano cuiquam locus hic: Umbricius concludes his tirade against the Greeks with an echo of 21–2, *artibus ... honestis* | *nullus in Vrbe locus*. Cf. Lucian, *De merc. cond.* 17: 'On top of everything else, this was left for us, to be second in importance even to those who had just entered the household: it is only the Greeks who have the freedom of the city of Rome.' *hic* = 'here', i.e. at Rome, as 127, 131, 160, 180, 182, 232, cf. 22 *in Vrbe.*   **regnat:** the Greek at Rome has supreme power like a king or potentate.

120 *aliquis*, 'some', adj., indicates Umbricius' generalised revulsion for such Greeks.

121 gentis uitio: for the idea of a 'national fault' cf. Ov. *Met.* 6.460 *flagrat uitio gentisque suoque*, Curtius 8.5.17 *nationis uitio*.

121–2 numquam partitur amicum, | solus habet: cf. Luc. 1.290–1 *partiri non potes orbem,* | *solus habere potes*, Mart. 3.26 where *solus habes* is the theme of the epigram. *solus habet* = 'but monopolises him'. Asyndeton.

122–5 The Greek displaces the long-serving client by a few poisonous words in the patron's ear. Umbricius' personal engagement emerges in the first person verb *summoueor* (124): he is jealous of the Greeks' success.

122 facilem stillauit in aurem: cf. 5.107 *facilem si praebeat aurem*, Sen. *Ira* 2.22.3 *ne sint aures criminantibus faciles*. The patron is ready to listen to what the Greek says. For *stillauit*, cf. Hor. *Ep.* 1.8.16 *praeceptum auriculis hoc instillare memento*.

123 exiguum: more often + genitive, here + *de* + ablative, cf. Apul. *Met.* 5.10 *de ... tantis diuitiis exigua*; cf. 1.66 *multum* + *de.*   **ueneno:** i.e. malicious remarks, cf. Cat. 44.11–12 *orationem ... plenam ueneni et* *pestilentiae legi*, Mart. 7.72.13 *carmina quae madent ueneno* and esp. Hor. *Sat.* 1.7.1 *pus atque uenenum.*

124 limine summoueor: the station of the waiting client, cf. 1.96, 100, 132, Sen. *Ep.* 84.12 *illa tumultuosa rixa salutantium limina. summoueor*: 1.37–9n.; the technical sense of the verb prepares for the reference to the praetor and lictor at 128. The verb epitomises Umbricius' experience of displacement.   **perierunt tempora** 'the time has been wasted', cf. Luc. 9.233 *perierunt tempora uitae*; also 4.56 *ne pereat.*

124–5 longi seruitii: echoes Hor. *Sat.* 2.5.99 *seruitio longo.* The metaphorical reduction of the client to servile status is a theme developed in Satire 5.

125 iactura: lit. 'throwing overboard', 'jettisoning', cf. 6.90–1 *famam … cuius … minima est iactura*, Liv. 5.39.12 *facilem iacturam esse seniorum.*   **clientis:** Umbricius' bitterness is conveyed by his blunt reference to himself as a *cliens*: 1.132n.

126–314 Umbricius now alleges that poor Roman clients are displaced by the rich. This displacement is articulated most explicitly at the start of this section (126–30) but recurs at intervals in the form of comparisons between rich and poor in which the rich receive disproportionately favourable treatment.

126–7 Understand *est* with *quod … officium … aut quod pauperis … meritum?*: 'What is the duty or what the service of a poor man … ?' Characteristic vocabulary of the client–patron relationship: for *officium* cf. 239, 2.132–3n., 5.13 and Saller (1982) 15–17; for *meritum* cf. 9.82 *nullum ergo meritum est …* and Saller 20–1; for both, cf. Cic. *Fam.* 12.29.1 *officia uel merita potius.*

126 porro 'furthermore'; marks a change of topic, as at 7.98. **ne nobis blandiar:** lit. 'lest I flatter us [Romans]', cf. Plin. *Ep.* 5.1.11 *nisi forte blandior mihi*, i.e. the Romans must share the blame.

127 hic: 119n.   **curet** 'he takes the trouble'.

127–8 nocte togatus | currere: for the client's haste while it is still dark, cf. 5.19–23nn. and 5.77–8 *gelidas … cucurri Esquilias*; the toga was the appropriate dress for attendance at a *salutatio*, cf. 149, 1.96n. Cf. Mart. 10.82.2 *mane uel a media nocte togatus ero.*

128 praetor lictorem: for the claim that Roman magistrates participate in the *salutatio* cf. 1.99–120 and 1.101n. Lictors were the official attendants of magistrates, such as praetors; it was their role to process ahead to clear the way.

129 dudum uigilantibus orbis: ablative absolute giving the praetor's reason for hurrying his lictor along. The praetor visits child-less patrons because they are more likely to leave him a legacy, cf. 4.19, 5.137–9, 6.548–9, 12.98–101, Hor. *Sat.* 2.5.28–31, 46–7. *dudum* = 'for a long time now', cf. 10.333. *uigilare* = 'to be awake', cf. 10.162. For adj. *orbus* used as substantive cf. 222 *orborum lautissimus*, Quint. *I.O.* 7.4.23 where *patre* and *orbo* are contrasted; feminine here, because of *Albinam* and *Modiam* (130).

130 prior ... collegae salutet: the praetor is anxious that a fellow-praetor will get there before him (see 1.95n., cf. 3.184); cf. 1.102 *libertinus prior est*, Hor. *Sat.* 2.6.24 *ne prior officio quisquam respondeat*. **Albinam et Modiam:** evidently wealthy childless women.

131–2 Umbricius claims that at Rome (*hic*) money has the power to effect role-reversal with the vivid example of the freeborn youth respectfully escorting a rich man's slave.   **cludit latus:** usually *tegere latus*, originally of the protection offered to the soldier's side; a reference to the rules of polite conduct; cf. Hor. *Sat.* 2.5.18 *utne tegam spurco Damae latus?* For the cultivation of rich and influential slaves cf. Sen. *Ben.* 3.28.5–6.

132–6 The slave (*alter*) is much more wealthy than the freeborn man. Umbricius contrasts the slave's casual expense upon gifts for an aristocratic mistress with the poor Roman's unfulfilled desire for a prostitute too expensive for him; this creates bathos and suggests Umbricius' jealousy. The contrast between aristocratic mistresses and ordinary prostitutes is drawn from Hor. *Sat.* 1.2.28–30.

132–3 quantum in legione tribuni | accipiunt: the precise amount of a military tribune's pay (see 1.58–62n.) at this period is not known but was evidently considerable (Plin. *N.H.* 34.11).

133 Caluinae uel Catienae: aristocratic names; the former evokes the Junia Calvina who was condemned for allegedly committing incest with her brother under the emperor Claudius (Tac. *Ann.* 12.4, 8 and Sen. *Apoc.* 8 *festiuissimam omnium puellarum, quam omnes Venerem uocarent*). See Ferguson, *Prosopography*.

134 semel aut iterum: cf. Cic. *Brut.* 308 *saepe ... minus saepe ... raro ... semel aut iterum.*   **palpitet:** usually has as its subject the heart or other bodily organ and means 'beat' or 'quiver'; here denoting the rhythmic movement of the sex act.

134–6 tu ... tibi ... haeres | et dubitas: Umbricius occasionally addresses one imaginary poor Roman client in the second person, here, at 184–5 *quid das ... ?* and 200 *tu nescis.*   **uestiti ... scorti:** some prostitutes were naked, others dressed up, cf. 6.122–3, 11.172–3, Sen. *Contr.* 1.2.7 *stetisti cum meretricibus, stetisti sic ornata ut populo placere posses ea ueste quam leno dederat.*   **Chionen:** a Greek name meaning 'Snow-White' frequent among prostitutes; cf. Mart. 1.34.7, 3.30.4.   **alta ... sella:** her 'high seat' indicates that she is out of the poor client's reach, like the lobster held aloft at Virro's dinner-party (5.81–3).

137–46 Umbricius next 'proves' that the rich man's situation is better than the poor man's with a legal example, concerning provision of a witness and validity of an oath.

137 da testem: lit. 'provide a witness', imperative for conditional clause (*si*), cf. 100–3n.

137–8 tam sanctum quam fuit hospes | numinis Idaei: a periphrasis designating a classic *exemplum* of *sanctitas*: in 204 BC Publius Cornelius Scipio Nasica as the most virtuous man was chosen to escort the image of the goddess Cybele from Phrygia to Rome, cf. Val. Max. 7.5.2 *sanctissimis manibus,* 8.15.3 *sanctissimo uiro.* Cybele is here called 'the deity of Ida' (cf. Liv. 29.14.5–11 *matre Idaea*), a mountain in Phrygia associated with her worship.

138 procedat 'step forward' as a witness, cf. Cic. *Flacc.* 11. **Numa:** king Numa (12n.), the archetypal *exemplum* of *reuerentia,* cf. Mart. 11.5.1–4.

138–9 qui | seruauit trepidam flagranti ex aede Mineruam: another periphrasis designating a classic *exemplum* of devotion to the gods: Lucius Caecilius Metellus, as *pontifex maximus* in 241 BC, lost his sight (6.265) rescuing the image of Minerva (the Palladium) from the burning temple of Vesta, cf. Val. Max. 1.4.5. *trepidam* carries the bathetic suggestion of the goddess herself in a panic.

140–1 The apodosis to the suppressed conditional clause commencing with *da testem* (137n.). For the idea, cf. Sen. *Ep.* 115.14 *an diues, omnes quaerimus, nemo, an bonus* and *quid habere nobis turpe sit quaeris? nihil;* Hor. *Ep.* 1.1.53–4 '*o ciues, ciues, quaerenda pecunia primum est; | uirtus post nummos!*'   **protinus ad censum** '(they go) straight to his wealth'.

141–2 pascit seruos: regularly of keeping slaves, as 9.67; see *OLD pasco* 1d; cf. 167 below *seruorum uentres.*   **quam multa magnaque paropside** 'how many and how lavish [are] the courses'; *paropside* (abl. of Greek word) is a serving-dish; singular for plural, cf. 120–1 *densissima ... lectica.* For abl. after *cenat* cf. 168 *fictilibus cenare.* The number and size of the dishes (cf. 1.94 *fercula septem*) are an index of wealth; the Greek word suggests luxury.

143–4 quantum quisque sua nummorum seruat in arca, | tantum habet et fidei: i.e. people are believed in direct proportion to their wealth; *quantum nummorum* balances *tantum fidei,* both nouns in the partitive genitive construction. The two relevant meanings of *fides* are conveyed by 'credit'. Cf. 14.207 *'unde habeas quaerit nemo, sed oportet habere',* Lucil. 1120M = 1195W *tantum habeas, tantum ipse sies tantique habearis,* Hor. *Sat.* 1.1.62 *'nil satis est' inquit 'quia tanti quantum habeas sis',* Sen. *Ep.* 115.14 *ubique tanti quisque, quantum habuit, fuit.*

144–6 The poor man will not be trusted no matter what oath he swears. The second person verb (*iures*) indicates Umbricius' sympathy. **licet:** + subj. see 1.105n. **iures ... aras:** cf. Hor. *Ep.* 2.1.16 (transitive use: *OLD iuro* 1b). **Samothracum et nostrorum:** understand *deorum.* The two most potent oaths imaginable: the gods of Samothrace, an island in the Aegean, were the Cabiri, worshipped in a mystery cult, cf. Ov. *A.A.* 2.601–2. **fulmina ... atque deos:** hendiadys; for Jupiter's lightning-bolt punishing perjurers cf. 13.78 and 223. **dis ignoscentibus ipsis:** ablative absolute, 'with the forgiveness of the gods themselves'. Either the gods forgive the poor man his perjury because he is insignificant or the gods are as corrupt as mortals nowadays.

147–63 Poverty makes men ridiculous (152–3, with an example, 153–9).

147 quid quod: 86n. **materiam praebet ... iocorum:** cf. Sen. *Vit. Beat.* 27.2 *praebui ego aliquando Aristophani materiam iocorum* (Socrates), J. 10.47 *materiam risus.*

148 hic idem: i.e. the poor man.

148–51 A tricolon (*si ... si ... uel si ...*) conveys Umbricius' indignation at the humiliation of the poor man. For *toga* and *calceus* together cf. 1.119 and Mart. 1.103.5–6 *sordidior multo post hoc toga, paenula peior, calceus est sarta terque quaterque cute.* **toga sordidula:** the toga, formal dress (see 127–8n.), required frequent and expensive cleaning to keep it white. The diminutive adjective conveys derision; cf. the scornful/ comic effect at 5.73 *improbulum,* 6.425 *rubicundula,* 10.82 *pallidulus,* 10.355 *candiduli,* 11.110 *liuidulus,* 11.135 *rancidula.* **rupta ... pelle:** cf. Mart. 1.103 (above) and 12.26.9 *rupta cum pes uagus exit* *aluta.*   **consuto uolnere:** ablative absolute, lit. 'where the wound has been sewn together', i.e. a tear has been mended; the metaphor here and in *cicatrix* suggests that the poor man has been physically attacked.   **crassum | atque recens:** i.e. crudely done and only too obvious.   **non una:** several, as at 6.218, 8.213–14, 14.284. **cicatrix:** literally a scar, continuing the imagery of *uolnere* (150). Cf. 254 *scinduntur tunicae sartae modo* where mended clothes are torn again. Real 'scars' match the psychological wounds (147–53).

152–3 A pithy reworking of the philosopher Crantor's saying (Stobaeus 4.32.33): 'In life there is no misfortune more miserable than poverty: if you are by nature σπουδαῖος but poor, you will be mocked.' *nil ... durius ... quam quod* = 'nothing harsher than the fact that'.

153–9 Humiliation in the theatre. The first fourteen rows of seats behind the *orchestra*, where the senators sat, were reserved for the *equites* in accordance with the *lex Roscia theatralis* passed by Lucius Roscius Otho in 67 BC, a law revived by Domitian (Suet. *Dom.* 8.3, Mart. 5.8.3). Impoverished members of the equestrian class are replaced by *nouveaux riches*, cf. Hor. *Epod.* 4.15–16, hostility towards an upstart who *sedilibusque magnus in primis eques | Othone contempto sedet.*

153 inquit 'says someone', cf. 7.242, possibly the official who assigned seats (*dissignator*).

154 si pudor est: if he has a sense of decency or propriety (*OLD* 2), cf. Mart. 2.37.10 *ullus si pudor est, repone cenam.* On the outrage of someone disqualified sitting in these seats see Cic. *Phil.* 2.44 *illud ... audaciae tuae, quod sedisti in quattuordecim ordinibus.*   **puluino ... equestri** 'knight's cushion', i.e. the seats normally called *equestria* (*OLD equester* 3b) or *quattuordecim ordines*; Martial calls them *bis septena subsellia* and *equitum scamni* (5.41.7).   **surgat:** cf. Mart. 5.25.1 *quadringenta tibi non sunt, Chaerestrate: surge.*

155 cuius res legi non sufficit 'whose wealth does not satisfy the law', i.e. the 400,000 sesterces which was the qualification for the status of *eques* (see 1.106n., 2.117n., 5.132n.), cf. 14.323–4 *summam | bis septem ordinibus quam lex dignatur Othonis.* On the *lex Roscia theatralis* see 153–9n.   **sedeant hic:** the final monosyllabic word disrupts accent and ictus, representing in sound the disruption of social status.

156–8 lenonum pueri ... praeconis filius ... pinnirapi ... iuuenes iuuenesque lanistae: the variation of nouns suggests the massive invasion of the theatre. Cf. 6.216 for *lenones* and *lanistae* together. The pimp, auctioneer, gladiator and trainer of gladiators were all of low (frequently servile) status, and were legally disqualified from holding office; yet these professions could be lucrative (e.g. Mart. 5.56.11, 11.66). The qualification for equestrian rank was not only the possession of 400,000 sesterces but also the free status of the man, his father and grandfather; Umbricius implies that only the property qualification was observed.   **quocumque ex fornice:** *quocumque*, indefinite, 'whatever' (*OLD* 8), as often in Silver Latin. *fornix* lit. arch or vault, hence a cellar or other premises used as a brothel, cf. 11.172–3, Hor. *Sat.* 1.2.30. *ex* presents the *fornix* as the equivalent of their parentage; cf. *nascor* 9, e.g. 9.83 *tibi filiolus uel filia nascitur ex me.* **nitidus, cultos:** denote the elegance of wealth, in contrast with the shabbiness of the client (148–51); cf. the 'smart slaves', *cultis ... seruis* (189), who irritate Umbricius.   **pinnirapi:** lit. 'crest-snatcher', possibly a colloquial term for the *retiarius*, a type of gladiator (2.143–8n.); cf. *senatus consultum* from Larinum 10 *pinnas gladiatorum raperet.*

159 sic libitum uano ... Othoni: understand *est* ; 'that was the liking of foolish Otho': on Otho see 153–9n.   **qui nos distinxit:** i.e. by allocating separate seating areas.

160–2 Three indignant questions highlighting the pre-eminence of wealth and the neglect of the 'poor' in their exclusion from the conventional ways of increasing one's property (marriage, inheritance and patronage) in Rome (*hic*). In the first two, *quis* goes with the adjectives *minor* + *inpar* and *pauper* and the nouns *gener* and *heres* are predicates: 'Who that is less ... has ever found favour as a [potential] son-in-law? Who that is poor is written down as heir?'   **placuit:** 'gnomic' perfect.   **censu minor** 'less in wealth', understand 'than his fiancée' (the *puella*).   **puellae | sarcinulis inpar** 'unequal to the girl's dowry', *puellae* gen., *sarcinulis* dat., lit. 'belongings', referring to the dowry (as 6.146); the diminutive form and literal meaning ('baggage') convey an irreverent tone.

162 quando in consilio est aedilibus? 'When is he consulted [even] by aediles?' A *consilium* consisted of assessors (*OLD* 3b) who might be consulted by magistrates; it is implied that membership of such boards brought material advantages. Not even the aediles, let alone the higher magistrates, would benefit a poor man thus. The aediles had jurisdiction over matters such as public order in religious affairs, traffic regulations, the water supply and the market, particularly weights and measures.

162–3 Umbricius' deduction, halfway through the poem: poor Romans should have emigrated long ago.   **agmine facto** 'in a body' (*OLD agmen* 4b), used figuratively of a crowd of diseases at 10.218.   **debuerant olim ... migrasse:** the pluperfect indicative and perfect infinitive (short form of *migrauisse*) emphasise *olim*, 'long ago'.   **tenues** 'poor', as 7.80, 145, 8.120.   **migrasse Quirites:** the phrase evokes the secessions of the plebs in early Roman history and the proposal to move the capital to nearby Veii after the Gallic sack of Rome in 387/6 BC; cf. the epigram reported by Suetonius as a response to Nero's construction of the Golden House: *Roma domus fiet; Veios migrate, Quirites,* | *si non et Veios occupat ista domus* (*Ner.* 39.2). The idea of withdrawal until happier times also evokes Hor. *Epod.* 16. On *Quirites* see 60n.

164–89 Umbricius contrasts life at Rome with life in a small Italian town. Lines 164–7 provide the link: poverty alone is bad enough (anywhere) but worse still at Rome, where life is so expensive. He condemns the sham and pretence of life in the capital and gives moral weight to his case by idealising country life; for discussion see Braund (1989a) esp. 26–8.

164 emergunt: cf. Plin. *Ep.* 6.23.5 *neque enim cuiquam tam clarum statim ingenium ut possit emergere, nisi illi materia occasio fautor etiam commendatorque contingat.* For poverty as an impediment to success cf. 7.59–71, Ov. *Fast.* 1.218 *pauper ubique iacet, Laus Pis.* 121 *probitas cum paupertate iacebit,* 255 *tenuis fortuna sua caligine celat.*   **quorum uirtutibus obstat** 'whose excellent qualities are impeded by'.

165 res angusta domi: again at 6.357, cf. Cic. *Part. Or.* 112 *angustiae rei familiaris,* Tac. *Ann.* 12.52 *ob angustias familiares*; the opposite at J. 12.10 *res ampla domi.*

165–6 durior illis | **conatus** 'the attempt is harder for them'. *durior* echoes *durius* 152: cf. 5.172–3 *dura ... flagra. conatus* implies a lack of success; the effort is conveyed by the two consecutive lines beginning with two spondees (165 and 166).

166–7 magno ... magno ... magno: i.e. is expensive; ablative of cost. Repetition of *magno* imitates repetition of *rem*, 'money', at Hor. *Ep.* 1.1.65–6: '*rem facias, rem,* | *si possis, recte, si non, quocumque modo, rem*'. For complaints about the cost of lodgings (*hospitium,* cf. 211, 7.69–70) and slaves cf. 9.63–4 (*pensio* and *puer*).   **seruorum uentres:** cf. 3.141 *quot pascit seruos?*, Petr. 57.6. Even 'poor' Romans like Umbricius have standards to maintain; cf. Hor. *Sat.* 1.6.116, frugal fare is served by three slaves.   **frugi cenula:** the diminutive form of the noun and the indeclinable adjective 'frugal' reinforce Umbricius' point.

168–70 The bridge passage is articulated via the contrast between *pudet* and *turpe negabis*.   **fictilibus:** for ablative after *cenare* cf. 142 *paropside cenat*. Earthenware plates symbolised the moral uprightness associated with rustic life and/or the distant past, cf. 10.25–6 *nulla aconita bibuntur | fictilibus*, Plin. *N.H.* 33.142, an old Roman hero *prandentem in fictilibus*.   **quod:** relative pronoun, i.e. *fictilibus cenare*. **translatus subito** 'if suddenly transported', e.g. by a god, as Horace *Sat.* 2.7.24.   **ad Marsos mensamque Sabellam** 'to a Marsian or Sabellan cuisine', hendiadys with disjunctive *-que*; echoes Virg. *Georg.* 2.167 *Marsos pubemque Sabellam*, praise of hardy men of Italy. For the Marsian as a type of primitive frugality cf. 14.179–88 and see Nisbet and Hubbard on Hor. *Od.* 1.2.39.   **contentusque illic** 'and if content there': a second conditional clause parallel with *translatus subito* but introducing a new topic (expanded in 171–9), the contrast in clothing.   **ueneto duroque cucullo:** the dark blue (*ueneto* not *Veneto*) hood associated with the poor man in comedy; cf. Mart. 10.76.8 *pullo ... cucullo*, also of a poor man. The rough cloth (*duro*) symbolises the harshness of his life, as at 9.29.

171 si uerum admittimus: a linguistic gesture designed to emphasise Umbricius' credibility. Cf. Florus 1.42.1 *si uera uolumus* and 2.6.1 *si uerum tamen uolumus*.

172 nemo togam sumit: in the country the toga was seldom worn, cf. Mart. 4.66.3, 10.96.11–12 (he gets through four togas a year in the city but in provincial life one toga lasts four years) and 12.18.5 and 17 (the poem addressed to Juvenal: at Rome *sudatrix toga* but in the provinces *ignota est toga*); Plin. *Ep.* 5.6.45 (one of the pleasures of his country villa is *nulla necessitas togae*); Fronto (Haines II 156 = van den Hout p. 103: the contrast between *rusticatio* and *uita togata*). Augustus forbade Roman citizens to appear in the forum without the toga (Suet. *Aug.* 40.5). On the prosody of *nemŏ* see Introduction §8.   **nisi mortuus:** Roman citizens were dressed in the toga for their funerals; cf. Mart. 9.57.8 *pallens toga mortui tribulis*.

172–9 The idealised scene of the rustic community gathered together to celebrate a holiday contrasts sharply with Umbricius' picture of Rome.

172-4 ipsa dierum festorum ... colitur si quando ... maiestas: lit. 'if ever even the majesty of festival days is celebrated', 'even at the grand celebration of festivals', i.e. at the most important communal occasion of the year. Indefinite *quando* implies that this is not frequently. The significance of festivals in Roman life should not be underestimated: in a society where the weekend was unknown the religious festivals were holidays from work. Cf. Virg. *Georg.* 2.527 *ipse dies agitat festos fususque per herbam*, a passage of significance later (see 309-11n.).   **herboso ... theatro:** Umbricius describes a natural or naturalistic setting for the theatrical element of the festival, either a grassy valley or a theatre constructed of turves, cf. Ov. *A.A.* 1.107 *in gradibus sedit populus de caespite factis*.

174 tandem: i.e. after a long gap, (cf. *quando* above) and contrasting with Rome where more and more days were celebrated as festivals.   **redīt:** contracted from *rediit*, perfect tense, cf. 6.128, 295, 10.118.   **pulpita:** plural for singular; a wooden stage for dramatic performances, cf. 8.225, 14.257.

174-5 notum | exodium 'the familiar farce': audiences in the country welcome an old favourite; by implication, city audiences relish novelty. Probably an Atellan farce (cf. 6.71), a native Italian form of entertainment of crude buffoonery, therefore symbolic of this rustic theatre.

175 personae pallentis hiatum: one of the masks used in the farce. In all forms of Roman/Italian drama except the mime the actors used masks. *hiatus* (cf. 6.636) refers to its gaping mouth (cf. Lucian *Salt.* 27, *Nigr.* 11), *pallentis* to its white colour. Possibly Manducus, one of the stock characters of the Atellan farce, *magnis malis et late dehiscens* (Paul. Fest. p.128M.).

176 in gremio matris formidat rusticus infans: for children's fear of the masks cf. Sen. *Ira* 2.11.2 *timetur ... sicut deformis persona ab infantibus*, Mart. 14.176 *haec timet ora puer*. J. repeats the sentimental picture of *rusticus infans cum matre* at 9.60-1.

177-9 Umbricius states three times the equality of dress which symbolises freedom from the competition of city life: (1) *aequales habitus* is generalised; (2) *similes ... orchestram et populum* indicates the municipal senators and the ordinary people; (3) *clari ... albae* focusses upon the chief magistrates, the aediles.   **orchestram:** the area reserved for the most important members of the audience, in provincial towns the *decuriones*, the provincial senators.   **clari uelamen honoris** 'as the garb of glorious office'; an elevated phrase in apposition to *tunicae ... albae* (179). For *honor* = 'office' see 1.110n.   **tunicae ... albae:** the tunic is symbolic of country life, cf. Mart. 10.51.6 *tunicata quies*. A clean (*albae*) tunic is worn for the festal occasion, cf. Hor. *Sat.* 2.2.60–1 *repotia, natalis aliosue dierum | festos albatus celebret.*   **summis aedilibus:** the title held by the two chief magistrates in some provincial towns (other titles include *praetores* and *duumuiri*; cf. 10.102, Hor. *Sat.* 1.5.34, Pers. 1.130).

180–1 ultra uires 'beyond our means', cf. Hor. *Ep.* 1.18.22 *gloria quem supra uires et uestit et unguit.*   **habitus nitor** 'smartness of dress', *habitus* genitive; cf. *nitor* 9.13, *nitidus* 3.157.   **aliena sumitur arca:** i.e. people run up debts to keep up appearances; for *arca* of metaphorical borrowing cf. Sen. *Ep.* 26.8.

182 commune id uitium est 'It's a universal fault', i.e. 'common' to everyone; cf. Cic. *De orat.* 2.210, Caes. *BC* 2.4.

182–3 hic uiuimus ambitiosa | paupertate omnes: on the need to keep up appearances at Rome cf. 7.136–45 e.g. 138 *finem inpensae non seruat prodiga Roma*, 6.352–9, Sen. *Ep.* 50.3 e.g. *'non ego ambitiosus sum, sed nemo aliter Romae potest uiuere'*; J.'s memorable phrase *ambitiosa | paupertate*, with the pentasyllabic word at the line end emphasising the paradox and the string of spondees at the start of 183, recalls Lucan's *ambitiosa fames* (4.376, reworked by Martial in a Rome/province contrast at 10.96.9 *hic pretiosa fames*) and Quintilian's *pauperes ambitiosos* (*I.O.* 2.4.29). *uiuimus* and *omnes* indicate that participation in the rat-race is a universal phenomenon.

183 quid te moror?: from everyday speech, cf. Plaut. *Stich.* 424 *te nil moror*, Ter. *Andr.* 114 *quid multis moror?*; more elaborate, Hor. *Ep.* 2.1.4 *si longo sermone morer tua tempora, Caesar.*

183–4 omnia Romae | cum pretio: another pithy epigram, adapted from Sall. *B.J.* 86.3 *omnia cum pretio honesta uidentur.* The theme of the venality rife at Rome is also taken from Sallust, *B.J.* 35.10.

184–9 Umbricius cites the necessity of bribing the slaves of important men in order to get their attention; cf. Sen. *Const. Sap.* 14.2 *aliquid impendere ut limen transeat* and Hor. *Sat.* 1.9.57 *muneribus seruos corrumpam.* For the power and arrogance of the door-keepers of rich men cf. Sen. *Const. Sap.* 15.5, Mart. 5.22.10, Tac. *Ann.* 4.74.

184 Cossum: a noble, possibly the son of Gnaeus Cornelius Len-

tulus Cossus, consul in AD 60.   **aliquandŏ:** also at 9.28 of the
client's occasional reward.   **salutes:** on the *salutatio* cf. 130 and see
1.95n.

185 respiciat clauso ... labello 'give a tight-lipped glance', i.e.
nod without deigning to speak to you; cf. Sen. *Brev. Vit.* 2.5 *ille tamen te,
quisquis es, insolenti quidem uultu sed aliquando respexit,* Mart. 10.10.5 *qui me
respiciet dominum regemque uocabo?*   **Veiiento:** another noble, possibly
the Veiiento of 4.133: see n.

186 ille, hic: different patrons who are more concerned with their
favourite slaves (understand *amati* in both phrases) than with their
clients.   **metit barbam:** for the ceremony of the first clipping of
the beard cf. 8.166, Petr. *Sat.* 29.8, 73.6. It was an occasion for
celebration (see 187). The verb stands for 'allow to be done', cf.
4.110n., 16.13 with Courtney, Lucr. 3.490 with Kenney, Mayer's
edition of Horace *Epistles* 1, index s.v. 'causative use of verb'.
crinem ... deponit: for dedication of a young slave-boy's hair cf.
Stat. *Silv.* 3.4, Mart. 9.16, 17.   **amati:** a *puer capillatus*, a decorative
young slave-boy; cf. 5.56-65.

187 libis: cakes used in sacrifical offerings, cf. Hor. *Ep.* 1.10.10.
uenalibus: the clients have to pay for cakes so that they can participate in the occasion.

187-8 accipe et istud | fermentum tibi habe: the client's
angry words to the slave: 'take [your money] and keep your yeast'. A
graphic representation of the situation. For *tibi habe* as an impolite
form of refusal cf. 5.118 (there with *fermentum*, contrasted with truffles);
Sen. *Ben.* 6.23.8 *sibi habeat.* To refer to the sacrificial cake as 'yeast' is
disparaging.

188-9 Umbricius identifies with the clients' viewpoint, 'we clients
are obliged'. On the unflattering term *clientes* cf. 125 above, 1.132n.
For *praestare tributa* cf. Plin. *N.H.* 21.77 *gens ... ea cum ceram in tributa
Romanis praestent. tributum* was the tax paid by the inhabitants of the
provinces to Rome: this ironic use suggests an inversion whereby slaves
= the Roman government and poor Roman clients = provincials.
cultis: cf. *cultos iuuenes* above, 156-8n., Sen. *Ep.* 110.17 *cohors culta
seruorum.* Even slaves are better dressed than wretched clients.
peculia: the money etc. accumulated by a slave or other person not
legally permitted to possess property.

190-231 An extended comparison of the situation of a poor man and a rich man at Rome in which the rich man gets richer and the poor man gets poorer.

190-8 A further comparison of country and city life (cf. 171-81), the dangers presented by the buildings, cf. *incendia, lapsus tectorum adsiduos* (7-8). The incidence of building collapses and fires in Rome is well documented in sources from the late Republic onwards, e.g. Cic. *Att.* 14.9.1 (collapse), Plut. *Crass.* 2.4 (collapse and conflagration), Gellius 15.1.2–4 (fire). More significantly these two dangers were stock worries of the well-off, e.g. at Cat. 23.8–9 *nihil timetis, non incendia, non graues ruinas*, Prop. 2.27.9, Sen. *Ben.* 4.6.2. See Braund (1989a) 33.

190 timet aut timuit 'fears or has [ever] feared'. **gelida Praeneste:** usually neuter, but feminine also at Virg. *Aen.* 8.561. A town in Latium 23 miles south-east of Rome, modern Palestrina, occupying an elevated position on the hills of the Apennines, hence 'cool', cf. Hor. *Od.* 3.4.22–3 *frigidum Praeneste*, a desirable quality in contrast with Rome's oppressive heat. For *gelidus* as a Horatian epithet for the country see Bo s.v., e.g. *Ep.* 1.18.104 *me quotiens reficit gelidus Digentia riuus*; cf. 322n. **ruinam:** the collapse of a building (*OLD* 3). Publilius, *Sent.* 425M *non cito perit ruina qui rimam timet.*

191 Volsiniis: a town in Etruria, north-east of Rome, probably modern Orvieto. Woods (*nemorosa*) and hills (*iuga*) suggest the pleasures of the country.

192 simplicibus Gabiis: another town in Latium, twelve miles east of Rome, epitomising the country at 6.56, cf. Hor. *Ep.* 1.15.9 *Gabiosque petunt et frigida rura*. For *simplex* of a simple, primitive life cf. Mart. 10.33.1 *simplicior priscis … Sabinis*. **proni Tiburis arce:** another town in Latium, 18 miles east-north-east of Rome, modern Tivoli. It was situated on a hill, hence *arce* and *proni* ('sloping', *OLD pronus* 4); cf. Hor. *Od.* 3.4.23 *Tibur supinum*. Coupled with Praeneste at 14.87–8 *summa nunc Tiburis arce, nunc Praenestinis in montibus.*

193 nos: continues the first person plural from *cogimur* (189). A contrast between people ('Who?' i.e. 'No-one' vs. 'We') replaces the earlier there/here contrasts. **tenui tibicine fultam** 'supported by thin props'. For *tibicen* in this unusual sense (usually a pipe) cf. Ov. *Fast.* 4.695 *stantem tibicine uillam*.

194 magna parte sui: more often *magna sui parte*, changed for metrical reasons, cf. Plin. *Pan.* 52.7, *Ep.* 5.6.15. **labentibus:** i.e. 'falling buildings', cf. Sen. *Ben.* 6.15.7 *quantum nobis praestet qui labentem*

domum suscipit at agentem ex imo rimas insulam incredibili arte suspendit!
obstat: i.e. gets in the way of, almost = supports.

195 uilicus: here the agent in charge of the property let by the
landlord, cf. Mart. 12.32.23–4 *quid quaeris aedes uilicosque derides* |
habitare gratis, o Vacerra, cum possis?. **ueteris rimae cum texit
hiatum** 'when he has covered the gape of an old crack'. Cf. Sen. *Ira*
3.35.5 *parietes insularum exesos, rimosos, inaequales.*

196 pendente ... ruina: i.e. in a building on the point of collapse;
ruina is used in a more concrete sense than at 190, cf. 11.13 *iam perlucente
ruina.* For *pendente* cf. Luc. 1.494–5 *iam quatiente ruina* | *nutantes pendere
domos.*

198–222 The contrast between rich and poor is illustrated by their
contrasting experiences of a house fire. Cordus, the poor man, loses
everything whereas Persicus, the rich man, gains more than he lost.
There are many close correspondences between the two.

198–201 Epic borrowing evoking the sack of Troy confers pathetic
dignity on the plight of the poor man in his garret: *iam*, repeated in
anaphora, combined with *Vcalegon* in enjambment and *ultimus ardebit*
(201) recalls Virg. *Aen.* 2.311–12 *iam proximus ardet* | *Vcalegon* (the name
is taken from Hom. *Il.* 3.148). *Vcalegon* then = 'neighbour'; he evidently
lives on a lower storey (*tabulata ... tertia* below). Hor. *Ep.* 1.18.84
proximus ardet similarly exploits this famous passage. The mundane tone
of *friuola* (cf. 5.59n.), 'odds and ends', indicates the gulf between the
Trojan Ucalegon and his Roman counterpart.   **poscit aquam:**
Latin for 'shouts "Fire!"', cf. Prop. 4.8.58 *territa uicinas Teia clamat
aquas*, Sen. *Ep.* 17.3 *aqua conclamata est*, [Quint.] *Decl.* 12.6 *ut arma bello,
ut aqua incendio inclamari publice solent.*   **tabulata ... tertia:** this
high-rise block (*insula*) has at least three storeys. *tibi* = 'for your
information' and *tu nescis* imply that the building is higher than that:
the unspecified addressee, invited to identify with the impoverished
client, does not know that the fire is in the third storey because he lives
higher still. On the height of *insulae* at Rome cf. Gell. 15.1.2 *insulam ...
multis arduisque tabulatis editam* and the two hundred steps mentioned by
Martial at 7.20.20 (doubtless an exaggerated, round number); legislation was passed periodically in an attempt to limit the height of such
blocks.   **trepidatur** 'the alarm is raised', impersonal passive.
ultimus ardebit: J. has 'unpacked' the passage from Virgil (see
198–201n.) by substituting *ultimus* for *proximus.*

201–2   quem tegula ... columbae: pathos is evoked in a variety of ways: the idea that the poor man has little protection from the rain (*tegula sola*: emphasised by the singular and the diminutive formation of *tegula*) and that he shares his garret with nesting doves, specified as 'gentle' (*molles*); the *o* and *u* syllables may evoke the cooing of the doves. Life 'beneath the tile(s)' was a byword for poverty, cf. Suet. *Gramm.* 9 *pauperem se et habitare sub tegulis.* Doves were associated with timidity, cf. 2.62–3n. and Hor. *Od.* 1.37.18 *molles columbas* with Nisbet and Hubbard. *reddunt oua* = 'produce their eggs', *OLD reddo* 15b, more usually of live offspring and thus rendering the dove family more appealing.

203–7 A catalogue of the poor man's paltry possessions, marked by three diminutives, *urceoli, paruulus* and *libellos.* J. adapts a theme from Hor. *Sat.* 1.6.114–18 where Horace characterises his humble life through a list of the modest items at his home (on his exaggeration of his poverty see Armstrong (1986)). The difference in tone here emerges in the ridiculous climax to the catalogue, the books gnawed by philistine mice.   **Cordo:** a poor Cordus occurs in Mart. 3.15 and may be the source for J.; probably to be identified with the poet of 1.2 (thus Z), since he loves literature.   **Procula minor** 'too small for Procula'. For ablative of comparison in this sense cf. 4.66 *priuatis maiora focis.* Procula (plural) at 2.68 denotes 'adulteresses'; here evidently a notoriously diminutive person.   **urceoli:** small jugs; not glamorous items, cf. 10.64 where they feature with basins and chamber-pots. **ornamentum abaci:** in apposition to *urceoli sex.* The *abacus* was a marble slab (cf. Hor. *Sat.* 1.6.116 *lapis albus*), equivalent to the side-board, for the display of silver (Varr. *L.L.* 9.46): Cordus owns no silver.   **cantharus:** usually a large drinking-cup, here specified as a small specimen (*paruulus*). It is kept out of sight (*infra*), indicating Cordus' embarrassment at his poverty.   **recubans ... Chiron:** the slab is supported by a sculpture of the centaur Chiron lying down. The manuscript reading *sub eodem marmore* = 'under the same marble' would refer again to the *abacus*; reference is more likely to the material of the statue, hence the emendations *sub eodem e marmore Chiron* (Matthias, Housman; prob. Courtney) = 'beneath the same, a Chiron [made] from marble' or, better, *sub eo de marmore* (Valesius) = 'beneath it a Chiron [made] from marble'; for *de marmore* cf. *OLD de* 8, e.g. J. 5.165. More luxurious supports were made of ivory: J. 11.123–4.

206-7 Both lines, particularly the second, have the classic 'golden line' pattern: abVAB (see Introduction §7). The incongruity emphasises Cordus' poverty.   **iam:** qualifies *uetus*, 'by now old', cf. 8.153. **cista:** a wicker box usually for keeping clothes. Cordus is too poor to buy a *scrinium* (the ancient equivalent of a bookcase).   **Graecos ... libellos:** prepares for the deflation in 207 where the *diuina ... carmina* contained in these 'little Greek books' are damaged by *opici ... mures.* **opici** 'barbarian', an epithet applied disparagingly by Greeks to Romans (Plin. *N.H.* 29.14 and *OLD* 2; Ὀπικοί denoted the indigenous inhabitants of Southern Italy). Its recurrence in J. (6.455) and in Gellius and Fronto (see Ramage (1973) 144-9) suggests that the word was in vogue. Juxtaposition with *diuina* emphasises the incongruity; for a similar effect cf. 7.28 *parua sublimia carmina cella.*   **rodebant ... mures:** recalls the line of an anonymous poet recorded by Quintilian as an example of inadvertent humour (*I.O.* 8.3.19): *praetextam in cista mures rosere camilli.* The destruction of stored books (i.e. papyrus rolls) by mice and moths is a literary motif (mice: see Courtney *ad loc.*; moths: see *OLD tinea*). For mice as fellow-lodgers in the 'humble hut' see *Moretum* with Kenney (1984) xxxi; Callim. fr. 177 Pf.

208 quis enim negat?: cf. Ov. *Met.* 6.193 *sum felix (quis enim neget hoc?) felixque manebo,* evidently the inspiration for *infelix* in 209.

208-9 illud ... totum nihil 'all that nothing', cf. Ter. *Andr.* 314 *id aliquid nihil est.*

209-10 ultimus ... aerumnae cumulus: cf. Sen. *Phaedra* 1119 *malorum maximum hunc cumulum reor,* Val. Max. 3 pr. *ad summum gloriae cumulum.*

210 quod 'the fact that'.

211 Cf. Martial 5.81.1-2 *semper pauper eris si pauper es, Aemiliane.* | *dantur opes nullis nunc nisi diuitibus.* Anaphora of *nemo* and the chiastic responsion with 210 (*cibo ~ frusta rogantem, hospitio tectoque ~ nudum*) ends the attention to the poor man.

212-14 The contrasting experience of the rich man Persicus (221n.): when his house is destroyed, the reaction is like public mourning. Whereas the destruction of the poor man's house was dealt with in detail (198-202), here the rich man's house is destroyed in a moment and Umbricius dwells upon the scenes which follow. All three elements in 212-13 feature in Luc. 2.16-36, the portrayal of a city in a state of mourning at imminent disaster.   **Asturici ... domus:** the rich man's house is known by the name of a former owner, Asturicus; cf. Nepos, *Att.* 13.2 *domum ... Tamphilianam*, Mart. 12.57.19 *Petilianis ... in regnis*. The name is unparalleled; it suggests an aristocrat descended from an ancestor who enjoyed military success in Asturia, part of Spain; cf. Ponticus, the addressee of Satire 8, and Creticus (2.67n.).   **cecidit domus:** collapse after conflagration, hence *casus* and *ignem* in line 214.   **horrida mater:** *mater* designates *matrona* (*OLD* 1c), singular for plural. Dishevelled clothing was a classic mark of mourning for Roman women, cf. Luc. 2.28–9 *cultus matrona priores deposuit*.   **pullati proceres:** mourners wore drab-coloured clothes, see *OLD pullus*[2] b and cf. 10.245 *perpetuo maerore et nigra ueste*, Luc. 2.18–19. *proceres* is an elevated word designating the 'leading men', cf. 2.121, 4.73 and 144.   **differt uadimonia praetor:** a cessation of judicial and public business, as at Luc. 2.17–18 *ferale per Vrbem* | *iustitium*: the magistrate postpones the hearings at which defendants were bound to appear (*OLD uadimonium* 2d).   **gemimus ... odimus:** the words of consolation offered to the rich: 'we lament and detest'; for consolation offered by a client cf. Hor. *Sat.* 2.8.58–63; for *odimus* thus cf. J. 6.272 *odit pueros*. Umbricius and other clients are complicit in this behaviour.   **casus:** presumably 'disasters' but hinting at 'collapses', cf. 190 *ruinam* and 7–8 *lapsus tectorum*. For *casus* of an 'accidental' fire cf. Mart. 3.52.2 *abstulit hanc* [*sc. domum*] *nimium casus in Vrbe frequens*.

215–20 A catalogue of the gifts brought to the rich man; many correspond with items which the poor man loses (203–7). Repetition with anaphora of *hic* emphasises the number of benefactors. On the perverted generosity and hypocrisy of giving gifts to the rich see Plin. *Ep.* 9.30.1. This incident proves Umbricius' assertion at 143–4.

215 ardet adhuc 'before the fire is out'.   **accurrit:** cf. *occurrit* 1.69n.

215–16 qui marmora donet, | **conferat inpensas:** i.e. to offer materials for rebuilding, a purpose clause with relative pronoun. For marble in houses see 1.12–13n. *inpensae* = building materials: *OLD* 3, cf. Frontinus, *Aqu.* 118.   **nuda et candida signa:** marble statues of nudes, hence Greek (see Plin. *N.H.* 34.18 on the difference between Greek and Roman statues). These expensive items correspond with the poor man's marble Chiron (205), probably run-of-the-mill or second-hand or produced locally; *nuda* echoes the poor man's destitute state

(*nudum* 210).   **aliquid praeclarum** 'a masterpiece' (Rudd).
Euphranoris: a sculptor and painter of the fourth century BC who
worked in Athens, renowned for works of monumental proportions.
Polycliti aera 'bronzes of Polyclitus', a sculptor of the fifth century BC
at Argos, famous for his work in bronze and marble, cf. 8.103. On the
problematic text see, with Housman's *aera* for MS *haec*, Courtney.
Asianorum uetera ornamenta deorum: in apposition to *aliquid . . .
aera*; these works of art were plundered from the temples of Asia, cf.
8.100–7, Cic. *Verr.* 2.4.123, Liv. 26.30.9 and Augustus' claim to have
restored plundered *ornamenta* at *R.G.* 24.1. *ornamenta* contrasts with the
poor man's humble *ornamentum abaci* (204); *uetera* suggests enhanced
value whereas *uetus . . . cista* (206) indicates the poor man's poverty.
libros ... forulos: the poor man's books (206–7) signal his culture,
but the rich man's library is an index of his wealth; cf. Sen. *Tranq. An.*
9.7 *inter balnearia et thermas bybliotheca quoque ut necessarium domus ornamentum expolitur*, Lucian *Adv. indoct. passim.*   **mediam ... Mineruam:**
i.e. a statue of Minerva, goddess of learning, for his library.
modium argenti: cf. Plaut. *Mil.* 1064 *plus mi auri mille est modiorum
Philippi.* A huge amount of money, not counted but measured; cf.
Fortunata *quae nummos modio metitur* (Petr. *Sat.* 37, Hor. *Sat.* 1.1.95–6
diues | ut metiretur nummos).

220 reponit: i.e. puts in place of the objects lost; Cordus receives
nothing to replace his 'nothing' (208–11).

221 Persicus: Umbricius finally utters the rich man's name, possibly a specific individual (a Fabius Persicus, consul in AD 34, is known)
but more likely imaginary or generalised. The name may suggest an
ancestor who won military success against the Persians and/or eastern
luxury; the name recurs as the addressee of Satire 11, where the
evocation of luxury is highly pertinent.   **orborum:** 3.129n.

**221–2 merito iam | suspectus tamquam ipse suas incenderit
aedes** 'who not without reason is now suspected of . . . ' (Rudd). *merito*
gains emphasis from position and metre (the final monosyllable disrupts the rhythm). For *tamquam* see 3.47n. For the suspicion that a
house was deliberately set on fire for profit cf. Mart. 3.52.3–4 *non potes
ipse uideri | incendisse tuam, Tongiliane, domum?*

223–31 Life in the country is advocated on the grounds of comparative cost of housing. This conclusion balances the opening of the
section (190–8n.). On the difference in expense between Rome and the

country see Plin. *N.H.* 14.50, Mart. 4.66 and the literature cited by Courtney *ad* 225.

223 auelli circensibus 'tear yourself (cf. *auelli*, Virg. *Aen.* 11.201) from the races', cf. 11.53 *caruisse anno circensibus uno*; i.e. the chariot races staged in the Circus Maximus, a spectacle unique to Rome; at 10.81 *panem et circenses* are said to be the total desire of the urban populace. On the races see Duff *ad loc.* and *OCD*² 'Circus'.

223–4 Sora, Fabrateria and Frusino were all country-towns in Latium (cf. Silius 8.394–8), near Aquinum, where the speaker has a country house (319).

224 paratur: bought outright, as opposed to rented (*conducis* 225), cf. 14.140–1 *paratur | altera uilla tibi cum rus non sufficit unum.*

225 tenebras: a dark room, cf. Cat. 55.2, Mart. 2.14.12 (of gloomy baths), 3.30.3 *fuscae … cellae.* The shadows inhabited by the poor client reflect Umbricius' 'shadowy' name (see Essay).   **unum … in annum:** for *in* + acc. = 'for (a given period)' see *OLD* 23b.

226–7 A sentimentalised portrayal of a provincial property, conveyed by the diminutive *hortulus*, the modest proportions of the well (*puteus … breuis*), the description of the plants as *tenuis* and the ease of work in the garden (*facili … haustu*). For a similar idealisation cf. 11.78–9 *Curius paruo quae legerat horto | ipse focis breuibus ponebat holuscula.* Horace emphasises the presence of water in his description of his Sabine farm (*Sat.* 2.6.2) and Martial articulates a country–city opposition in terms of water at 9.18.3–4, *de ualle breui quas det sitientibus hortis | curua laboratas antlia tollit aquas,* of a small country house. For *hortulus* of a poor man's garden cf. *Priapea* 85.4 = App. Verg. 2.4 *eri … uillulam hortulumque pauperis.*   **hic:** i.e. in the country; usually in Satire 3 *hic* = here in Rome.   **nec reste mouendus:** i.e. so shallow (*breuis*) that it does not need to be operated with a rope; cf. Columella 10.25–6 *fons illacrimet putei non sede profunda | ne grauis hausturis tendentibus ilia uellat.* **tenuis plantas:** i.e. seedlings; the adjective *tenuis* suggests that the plants are 'poor' (3.162–3n.) like their master.   **diffunditur:** i.e. the well-water.

228–9 Umbricius offers (pseudo-)philosophical advice, perhaps because gardens were the standard setting for philosophical teaching in antiquity, *OLD hortulus* 3; hence the presence of the hundred Pythagoreans here. For the satisfaction gained from the philosophical garden (of Epicurus), expressed in terms of eating simple food and drinking quantities of water, cf. Sen. *Ep.* 21.10. The singular (*hortulus* and *horti*) indicates that this is a functional vegetable-garden and not a pleasure-garden, usually designated by the plural (see *OLD hortulus* 2, *hortus* 2, e.g. J. 10.16).   **uiue:** evokes the philosophical discussions of the best kind of life (βίος); cf. Nisbet and Hubbard on Hor. *Od.* 1.1. **bidentis amans** 'in love with your hoe': a touch of bathos. **uilicus:** an estate-manager, often a slave: 3.195n. and cf. 11.69; the refugee from urban life will care for his little patch (cf. 231 *dominum*). **epulum:** a banquet celebrating a special occasion. The combination of *epulum* and *centum* here recalls Hor. *Sat.* 2.3.85–6, a description of an immensely lavish funeral banquet and entertainment.   **Pythagoreis:** in effect, vegetarians. Pythagoras was a sixth-century BC philosopher from Samos who founded a school in southern Italy. Beliefs included the immortality of the soul and the transmigration of souls (metempsychosis) from one creature to another, including animals, hence the ban on the eating of meat. This ban extended to some vegetables too, including beans, a point treated humorously by Horace at *Sat.* 2.6.62, *faba Pythagorae cognata*, and J. at 15.173–4, *Pythagoras, cunctis animalibus abstinuit qui* | *tamquam homine et uentri indulsit non omne.* Persius characterises the diet of philosophy students as beans and barley (3.55).

230 est aliquid 'it is something', i.e. some achievement (if not a high one).   **recessu:** cf. 1–6 for the theme of withdrawal, retreat and solitude.

231 dominum: ownership/mastery is the prime idea here, emphasised by the strong form *sese*. In Rome, by contrast, the poor man is not 'lord' of anything.   **unius ... lacertae** 'of a single – lizard': the last word delivers a surprise, cf. *mures* 207; 'lord of a single acre' might be expected. Apparently a reworking of Mart. 11.18, a complaint about the tiny size of a farm, e.g. *in quo nec cucumis iacere rectus* | *nec serpens habitare tota possit* (10–11). Johnson interpreted the passage: 'as much ground as one may have a chance to find a lizard upon', i.e. the smallest spot, given the frequency of lizards in Italy. Singleness/solitariness (*unius*) is a theme of Satire 3, cf. 3 *unum ciuem*, 6 *solum*, 314 *uno ... carcere.*

The difficulties of interpretation here disappear if the phrase is viewed as J.'s humorous undercutting of Umbricius' serious declaration of the superiority of country life. However, the presence of textual variants (*lacernae* two MSS: see Knoche; also Heinsius' emendation *lacerti*, cf. Virg. *Ecl.* 2.9) together with the extensive discussion of the phrase in the scholia, suggests emendation to *latebrae*, i.e. 'lord of a single hiding-place'. *latebra* meaning 'hiding-place; hole; lair; hidden place of refuge, escape' (*OLD*) not only fits well with the themes of withdrawal and retreat but also suits Umbricius' name. Moreover, Horace describes his Sabine farm as *hae latebrae dulces* (*Ep.* 1.16.15). For *latebra* (singular) designating a garden a 'refuge' (in the unfavourable context of self-indulgence as opposed to work) cf. Sen. *Ben.* 4.13.1 *intra hortorum latebram*. For *latebra* and *recessus* together cf. Cic. *Marc.* 22 *cum in animis hominum tantae latebrae sint et tanti recessus.* A *latebra* in the country might seem to correspond to a poor man's *tenebrae* (cf. 225) in the city.

232–308 The horrors of city life on the streets of Rome, articulated by two complementary structural devices: the rich–poor contrast, continued from the previous section, and the chronological sequence of a (fictitious) day in Rome, starting with insomnia and the duties of the morning and finishing with the dangers of the evening and the night: see Braund (1989a) 34.

232–8 The difficulties of sleeping at night for the poor (only 235 mentions the rich).

232 plurimus hic aeger 'many an invalid'; for the singular cf. 1.120–1 *densissima ... lectica.* For *aeger* as a noun cf. 9.16, 12.122, 13.124.   **moritur uigilando:** for death from sleep deprivation cf. Cic. *Off.* 3.100 *cum uigilando necabatur.* The gerund has short final -*ŏ*; on J.'s prosody see Introduction §8.

232–4 The cause of the invalid's illness is indigestion: see *OLD imperfectus* d, cf. Celsus 4.23.1 *quicquid adsumptum est, imperfectum protinus reddunt.* On indigestion 'burning' (*ardenti*) the stomach see Sen. *N.Q.* 4.13.5–7, e.g. *cotidianis cruditatibus perustus, stomachus ... aestu suo languidus.*

234–5 meritoria: hired lodgings, like *tenebras ... conducis* (225), in contrast with *paratur* (224) and *dominum* (231).   **admittunt** 'permit, allow', cf. 5.69.

235 magnis opibus dormitur in Vrbe: a grandiloquent declaration (*sententia*) of the inequity of life in Rome, with the grand impersonal passive; cf. Mart. 12.68.6 *uigilatur* (cf. *uigilando* 232); and for the thought cf. Mart. 12.57.3–4 *nec quiescendi in Vrbe locus est pauperi.*

magnis opibus may be ablative of price ('it costs a lot to sleep in Rome') or instrumental ablative ('[only] with great riches is it possible to sleep in Rome'), as at 9.100 *his opibus numquam cara est annona ueneni*. I.e. rich men's houses are large enough to include bedrooms facing inwards, away from the noisy street: see Mart. 12.57.18–25 contrasted with 27 *ad cubile est Roma*.

236 inde caput morbi 'hence the source of disease' [i.e. from the sleeplessness caused by poor accommodation]; 232–4 (*sed ipsum ... stomacho*) is a parenthetical additional complaint.

236–8 For street noise in Rome, one of several carnivalesque aspects of city life prevalent in satire, cf. Lucil. 1145–1151W (= 1228–1234M) and Hor. *Ep.* 2.2.65–86 e.g. 79 *inter strepitus nocturnos atque diurnos*; also Mart. 4.64 e.g. 20 *ne blando rota sit molesta somno*.   **raedarum:** a four-wheeled travelling carriage, cf. 10. Such vehicles were only permitted in Rome at night (see 254–6n.); for the noise cf. Hor. *Ep.* 1.17.7 *puluis strepitusque rotarum*.   **arto uicorum in flexu:** cf. 6.78 *per angustos ... uicos*; narrow streets were characteristic of Rome before the fire under Nero: Tac. *Ann.* 15.38 *artis itineribus hucque et illuc flexis ... uicis*.   **stantis ... mandrae:** the animals being herded through Rome have come to a standstill; cf. Mart. 5.22.7 *uix ... datur longas mulorum rumpere mandras*, perhaps the mules used to haul building materials, as at Hor. *Ep.* 2.2.72.   **conuicia:** possibly the noise of the animals (cf. *OLD conuicium* 1); probably the abuse uttered by the drovers and/or bystanders, cf. Hor. *Sat.* 1.5.11–12 *tum pueri nautis, pueris conuicia nautae ingerere*.   **eripient:** 'gnomic' future; cf. *sic erit* 1.126n. **Druso:** usually explained as a reference to Claudius (Tiberius Claudius Drusus: Suet. *Claud.* 2.1), whose profound drowsiness is mentioned by Suetonius (*Claud.* 8, 33.2); but emendation to *surdo* cannot be ruled out; cf. Courtney's reverse emendation at 13.249.   **uitulisque marinis:** seals (*OLD uitulus* 2), which according to Plin. *N.H.* 9.42 experience a deeper sleep than any other animal (cf. Proteus and his seals at Hom. *Od.*4.400–6). *-que* = 'or'.

239–67 The difficulties of passing through the streets during the day, commencing with the rich (239–43) before elaborating the poor man's discomforts and dangers.

239 uocat officium: echoes Pers. 6.27; on *officium* see 2.132–3n., 3.126–7n.; probably the morning-call (1.95n.).   **turba cedente** 'as the crowd gives way'; ablative absolute.   **uehetur:** the passive verb indicates how effortlessly the rich man travels.

240 ingenti curret super ora Liburna: the effortlessness is continued in *curret*. *super ora* suggests the upturned faces of those less fortunate. The wealthy man's huge litter is described hyperbolically as a warship (see *OLD Liburna*), an image which prefigures the 'wave' of pedestrians (*unda* 244) in the poor man's way and contributes to the mock-epic treatment of the street scene (see Braund (1989a) 35 with n.24).

241 obiter 'on the way, *en route*'; the Elder Pliny did this and rebuked his nephew for wasting time by walking: Plin. *Ep.* 3.5.15–16. **dormiet:** cf. 1.126 *quiescet.* The unfairness is that the poor man cannot sleep even in his bed.

242 A weak line, deleted by Pinzger.   **facit somnum:** cf. 282 *somnum rixa facit.*   **clausa ... fenestra:** by a curtain or the transparent stone known as *lapis specularis*, as at 4.21 (*OLD specularis* 2); see 1.65n.

243 tamen looks forward to the contrast between the rich man and the poor men who have to struggle through the obstacles (*nobis properantibus*).

243–6 The poor man's progress is difficult: there are obstacles in front (*obstat | unda prior*) and behind (*populus premit ... qui sequitur*) and he is assaulted by a variety of objects (*ferit hic ... , ferit ... alter; at hic ... capiti incutit, ille ...*). Much of the vocabulary here would fit a military context and creates a mock-epic tone: *properantibus obstat* is from Stat. *Theb.* 8.350, cf. Luc. 7.153 *uenientibus obstitit*; for *unda* of soldiers cf. Sil. 4.159; *magno ... agmine* evokes epic; and *ferit* typically occurs in epic battles, e.g. Virg. *Aen.* 10.346, Lucan 3.666 etc. Bathos is conveyed by *lumbos* (244: the lower back, often subject to blows, *TLL* 1808.63, e.g. Plaut. *Cas.* 967) and the unglamorous 'weapons' with which the poor man is assaulted: an elbow, a hard pole (of a litter, cf. 7.132), a beam (*tignum*, as Hor. *Ep.* 2.2.73) and a large jar.   **unda:** for the 'wave' of people cf. Virg. *Georg.* 2.461–2 *ingentem ... mane salutantum ... undam.*

247–8 The focus moves downwards to legs and feet. For the combination of collision and dirt cf. Sen. *Ira* 3.6.4 'a man hurrying through the crowded sections of the city cannot help colliding with many people and in one place is sure to slip, in another to be held back, in another to be splashed ...'.   **luto:** for mud in the streets of Rome cf. Hor. *Ep.* 2.2.75 *lutulenta ... sus* and Mart. 12.26.8 *matutinum ... lutum.* **planta ... magna:** collective, lit. 'many a large sole'.   **calcor:** taken from battle-scenes, e.g. Ov. *Met.* 5.88 *extructos morientum calcat* *aceruos.* The passive voice makes Umbricius the hapless victim. **digito:** the toe. **clauus ... militis:** the 'nail(s)' in the sole of the soldier's boot *(caliga)*, cf. 16.24–5 *offendere tot caligas, tot milia.* The climax to this mock-epic catalogue of assaults is appropriately delivered by a soldier.

249–53 This *sportula* differs from the financial rewards to clients who attended the patron (1.95–126); Umbricius describes a gathering of men accompanied by slaves with portable cookers, perhaps for the food distributed to members of a *collegium*: see Tränkle (1978) 171–2. The retinue congests the streets *(centum conuiuae* etc.) and the smoke from the cookers congests the lungs *(quanto ... fumo).* For possibly the same phenomenon cf. Sen. *Ep.* 78.23 and 104.6 *illum odorem culinarum fumantium quae motae quicquid pestiferi uaporis obferunt.* **nonne uides ... ?:** a formula from didactic poetry (Lucretius often, also Virgil *Georg.* 1.56, 3.103). **celebretur:** the appropriate word for the distribution of food, cf. *CIL* xi 379 *sportularum diuisio semper celebretur,* xi 4391, cited by Tränkle (above) 172. **Corbulo:** Cn. Domitius Corbulo, a general eminent under Claudius and Nero, of legendary size (Tac. *Ann.* 13.8 *corpore ingens*): see Ferguson, *Prosopography.* **uasa:** containers for the food to be cooked in; possibly also a pun on 'military kit' *(OLD uasa* 2b). **seruulus:** the diminutive contrasts the tiny slave with the beefy Corbulo. **cursu uentilat ignem:** the slave races along and thus fans the flame which keeps the food warm.

254–6 The dangers caused by the traffic cf. Sen. *Clem.* 1.6.1 *turma ... sine intermissione defluens eliditur quotiens aliquid obstitit.* Day-time traffic was virtually confined to the waggons transporting wood and (in lines 257ff.) marble for public building works: *CIL* 1² 593.56–61, *SHA* 1.22.6; cf. Mart. 5.22.8 *trahi multo marmora fune* (see 236–8n.). For the combination of timber and stone cf. Hor. *Ep.* 2.2.73 *torquet nunc lapidem, nunc ingens machina tignum* and for the types of timber cf. Sen. *Ep.* 90.9 *pinus aut abies deferebatur, longo uehiculorum ordine uicis intrementibus.* The vocabulary here evokes the *topos* of the felling and transportation of trees in epic, e.g. Virg. *Aen.* 2.626–31 inc. *minatur et tremefacta ... nutat,* 6.179–82 inc. *scinditur* at the beginning of the line, 11.135–8 *nec plaustris cessant uectare gementibus ornos.* Lowly *serraco* (see Quint. *I.O.* 8.3.21 *sordidum nomen*) conflicts with the epic associations. **scinduntur tunicae:** cf. 148 *scissa lacerna,* Plin. *Ep.* 4.16.2 *adulescens scissis tunicis, ut in frequentia solet fieri.* The *tunica* was worn underneath the toga.   **sartae modo** 'freshly mended'.   **coruscat** 'quiver, shake', a word often found in elevated military contexts.   **altera ... plaustra:** plural for singular.

257–61 Threat (*minantur*) becomes fatal danger as the poor man is crushed by the load of a collapsing vehicle. The subject of *procubuit* and *fudit* is *axis qui ... portat*. The passage reworks the simile of the miner crushed inside the mountain (cf. *montem* above, 258) at Stat. *Thebaid* 6, esp. lines 876–86 e.g. *... monte soluto | obrutus ac penitus fractum obtritumque cadauer | indignantem animam propriis non reddidit astris.* The idea that the miner's soul does not return to its own stars has a deglamourised equivalent by J. in lines 261–7.   **saxa Ligustica:** high-quality white or green-veined marble from Luna in Etruria, formerly Liguria (cf. Pers. 6.6–9).   **euersum ... montem** 'an overturned mountain'; cf. Virg. *Aen.* 9.569 *ingenti fragmine montis*, 10.128.   **super agmina:** cf. 162 *agmine facto.*   **quid superest de corporibus?:** cf. 1.34–5 *de nobilitate comesa quod superest*, Sil. 10.293 *quod superest de luce.* The plural *corporibus* depersonalises the incident, as do *populo* (256) and *agmina* (258): no identification with the victim(s) is invited.   **obtritum uulgo perit omne cadauer | more animae:** adopting Eremita's emendation *uulgo* (recorded by Knoche and Martyn): 'every corpse, crushed indiscriminately, disappears just like its soul'; *OLD uulgo* 4.

261–7 The scene at the victim's house is contrasted with the victim's plight on arriving in the Underworld. Pathos resides in details such as *secura* (cf. 196 *securos* and Petr. *Sat.* 115) and the diminutives *patellas* and *foculum*. However, the mundane details of household activity (e.g. *bucca, unctis striglibus, pleno ... guto*) combine with echoes of epic to produce a bathetic travesty of the hero's descent to the Underworld: this is no Aeneas but a comic character like Aristophanes' Dionysus (see Braund (1989a) 35). The description of the household preparing for the master's return recalls Hom. *Il.* 22.442–6.

261 domus: i.e. household (*OLD* 6): the slaves (*pueros* 264) are washing dishes and preparing for the bath, usually taken before dinner (11.204).

263 striglibus: usually *strigilibus*, shortened for metrical convenience (syncope). The strigil was a curved, bladed implement used to scrape the oil (hence *unctis* here), sweat and dirt from the skin during bathing; cf. Pers. 5.126 '*i, puer, et strigiles Crispini ad balnea defer*'.

pleno ... guto: massage with oil preceded bathing, hence *unctis* (previous note), cf. Apul. *Met.* 1.23. *pleno* almost stands for a verb, 'having filled'.

264 at ille: the separation of this phrase conveys the master's lonely plight, cf. Virg. *Georg.* 4.513.

265 in ripa: the Underworld scene commences with mention of the bank, i.e. of one of the rivers, Styx or Cocytus or Acheron: cf. 2.150–1n. Descent to the Underworld evokes Aeneas' *katabasis* in Virg. *Aen.* 6 (see notes below).   **nouicius:** lit. 'newly-imported', often of slaves (*OLD* 1), hence here 'a newcomer', alien in tone to the epic and mythological framework.

265–6 taetrum ... horret | porthmea: echoes Virgil's description of Charon, ferryman of the dead, *portitor ... horrendus* (*Aen.* 6.298). The change to the Greek word *porthmeus* (cf. Petr. *Sat.* 121 line 117; *porthmea* is acc. singular) both 'corrects' Virgil's use of *portitor* and recalls the scorn towards Greeks earlier in the poem. This Roman finds even the Underworld populated by Greeks and his own status there diminished (see note on *nouicius* above).

266 nec sperat 'and he has no hopes of', i.e. cannot expect to get, because he has no fare to pay Charon: 267n.   **caenosi gurgitis:** cf. 2.150 *Cocytum et Stygio ranas in gurgite nigras.* The rare adjective *caenosus* echoes Virgil's description of Acheron, *turbidus hic caeno ... gurges* (*Aen.* 6.296) while the idea recalls Aristoph. *Frogs* 145–6 where Dionysus in the parody of a hero's descent into Hades is warned that he will find 'masses of mud and ever-flowing sewage'; cf. *Frogs* 273.   **alnum:** elevated, denoting Charon's boat (*cumba*, 2.150), by metonymy with the name of the wood ('alder').

267 nec habet quem porrigat ore trientem: *nec* is causal, 'since he hasn't ...' The Greek practice of placing a coin (*triens* here; often an obol) in the mouth (*ore*) of the dead person as fare (*quem porrigat* 'to offer') for passage across the river of the Underworld was adopted by the Romans: Aristoph. *Frogs* 270; Prop. 4.11.7; Lucian *De Luctu* 10; Apul. *Met.* 6.18. J. creates a bathetic equivalent of Virgil's mass of the unburied (*Aen.* 6.325–30).

268–308 'The dangers of the night', *pericula noctis*, announced in the programmatic line 268. Cf. *mille pericula* (8n.).

268 respice: used to initiate a new topic, cf. 6.115, *OLD* 6.

269–77 Objects flung from high windows endanger passers-by; at night such objects fall unseen, hence the victim is *subiti casus improuidus* 273. For legislation concerning falling objects see Digest 9.3. Dependent upon *respice* (268) are three indirect questions, *quod spatium [sit]*, *quotiens ... cadant* and *quanto ... pondere signent*. For death caused by a falling chamber-pot see Ehrenberg and Jones (1976) no. 312.

269 quod spatium tectis sublimibus 'what a height there is to the lofty roofs'. On the height of buildings see *tabulata ... tertia* 199n. above.   **cerebrum:** i.e. the top of the head, cf. Hor. *Od.* 2.17.27.

270 testa: a tile (*OLD* 1b). The association with *tectis* determines the meaning 'tile', but the mention of broken pots in what follows expands *testa* in retrospect to include 'fragment of pot' (*OLD* 2). For death by falling tile cf. *CIL* III 2083; Lucian, *Charon* 6 'A man who had been invited to dinner by one of his friends for the next day replied, "Certainly I shall come", and even as he spoke a tile from the roof which someone had dislodged fell on him and killed him. I had to laugh at him because he did not keep his promise.'   **fenestris:** only the upper storeys of city high-rise buildings had windows on the street side, hence windows are associated with heights, cf. 6.31 *caligantes ... fenestrae*.

272 silicem 'pavement', *OLD* 1b, cf. 6.350 *silicem pedibus quae conterit atrum*.   **possis ignauus haberi** 'you may [well] be regarded as careless'.

273 subiti casus improuidus: a pun on *casus*, 'unwary of sudden accident | fall[ing pot]', cf. the ambiguity of *casus* (214n.).   **ad cenam:** 1.132–4n. The spondaic line-ending with this word-division is unparalleled in J.: see Courtney (1980) 50.

274 intestatus 'without having made a will', a pun upon *testa* 270; cf. 1.144n.   **fata** 'deaths' or 'causes of death'. Supply *sunt* with *tot fata*.   **illa | nocte:** ἀπὸ κοινοῦ with *tot fata* and picked up by *te praetereunte = cum tu praeteris*: 'on the night you pass by, there are as many deaths (in wait for you) as open windows'.   **patent uigiles ... fenestrae:** the windows are personified, cf. *sint contentae* (277). *patent* may be used of doors/windows and eyes; for *patent* of unshuttered windows cf. 6.31 *pateant altae caligantesque fenestrae*. For *uigiles* cf. Hor. *Od.* 3.8.14 *uigiles lucernas*.

276 optes ... feras: indefinite 2nd person command, see 1.14n. **uotum ... miserabile:** repeated at 9.147; typical of the victim's life, cf. 166 *hospitium miserabile*.   **uotum feras ... tecum** 'pray as you go'; i.e. a prayer is all the poor man can hope to take with him, since he has no attendant to light his way (286–7).

277 defundere pelues: i.e. empty the contents of the bowls (presumably night-slops), as opposed to hurling down the bowls themselves. Typically, J. reserves the key words for last. On the humour in a drenching from above cf. Plaut. *Amph.* 1034 where Mercury apparently (the text is problematic) tips a bowl of water over Amphitryon below.

278–301 Without introduction Umbricius describes attack by the drunken thug, as the victim returns home from dinner (*deducere* 286n., 292–4 and 301 *reuerti*), progressing further through the twenty-four-hour sequence. The incident is developed with vivid circumstantial detail, commencing with epic parody (see 279–80n.). The motif of comparison between poor and rich is revived in this topic, when Umbricius asserts that the thug will not be so foolish as to attack a rich man with a retinue of attendants (282–5; cf. 235, 239–43).

278 petulans 'aggressive', cf. Sen. *Ira* 3.13.5 *qui ... ebrietatis suae temeritatem ac petulantiam metuunt.*   **qui nullum forte cecidit** 'who by chance has not killed anyone'; by *forte* Umbricius implies (perhaps ironically) that this is unusual. *cecidi* is perfect of *caedo.*

279–80 noctem ... lugentis amicum | Pelidae 'the night of Pelides when mourning his friend'. The epic patronymic denotes Achilles, son of Peleus. On the grief of Achilles at the death of his friend Patroclus; see next n.   **cubat in faciem, mox deinde supinus:** reworks the portrayal of Achilles' restlessness caused by his grief at Hom. *Il.* 24.10–11 'lying sometimes along his side, sometimes on his back, and now again prone on his face'; cf. Sen. *Tranq. An.* 2.12 *qualis ille Homericus Achilles est, modo pronus, modo supinus* (*ille* suggests this is a cliché). Transferral to this context of a thug's anger at his failure to murder emphasises the sordidness of the situation: this thug is utterly unheroic.

281 A spurious line, evidently an explanatory gloss which became inserted into the text; the explanation is unnecessary, the diction feeble and the scansion *érgō* in this position un-Juvenalian.

282 somnum rixa facit: an epigram typical of J.: 'a brawl makes sleep', i.e. the thug cannot get to sleep without a brawl. Cf. 242 *somnum facit clausa lectica fenestra.*

282–3 quamuis inprobus annis | atque mero feruens: i.e.

however insolent and drunk he may be; his insolence comes from his youth (*annis*) and from the unmixed wine he has drunk (*merum* = neat wine; water was usually blended with wine). *inprobitas* is the quality of not conforming to the proper standard, here by going beyond it, cf. 9.63, 4.106, 6.86, 5.73n. *improbulum*; see Braund (1988) 158.

283 coccina laena: a scarlet-dyed thick woollen cloak: the colour (cf. Hor. *Sat.* 2.6.102–3, Petr. *Sat.* 28) indicates the wearer's wealth. Cf. Aeneas' cloak at Virg. *Aen.* 4.262: *Tyrioque ardebat murice laena.*

284 comitum longissimus ordo: 1.46n.; cf. Ammianus, 14.6.16 *familiarum agmina ... post terga trahentes.*

285 multum ... flammarum: noun + partitive genitive, 'plenty of torches' (*OLD flamma* 4). With no street lighting, slaves carried torches to light up the retinue's path. Lines 283–4 echo the description of Pallas' funeral, Virg. *Aen.* 11, e.g. 94 *omnis longe comitum praecesserat ordo* and 143–4 *lucet uia longo ordine flammarum*, thus lending dignity to the rich man.   **aenea lampas:** singular for plural; a lamp made of bronze contrasts with the client's one of clay or a candle.

286–8 me ... contemnit: chiastic contrast with *cauet hunc* (283); initial position of *me* gives emphasis. The shift into the first person is not autobiographical (by Umbricius or J.), since the narrative reverts to the second person at 297 (*temptes, recedas*) and the third person at 300–1 (*rogat, adorat*). For the indefinite first person see Nutting (1924) 377–8. The poor man travels by moonlight or candle-light, accompanied by no retinue at all, not even slaves, an indication of extreme poverty, cf. Cat. 24.   **deducere:** primarily 'to escort' (*OLD* 8b and Hor. *Sat.* 1.9.59), but suggesting the ceremonial use 'to bring home' (*OLD* 10 a, b).   **breue:** although usually taken to mean 'modest' or 'slight', better interpreted as 'brief, lasting a short time', hence the poor man's need to tend the wick (*dispenso et tempero filum*).   **candelae:** the candle (made from string dipped in tallow) was typical of the poor man, cf. Festus 54 *candelis pauperes, locupletes cereis utebantur.*

288 miserae cognosce prohoemia rixae: *prohoemia* is an elevated Greek word, originally a musical term, designating the 'prelude' to an epic poem (*OLD*); *rixae* brings the tone down to earth. The prelude consists of insults (specified in 292–6), cf. 5.26 *iurgia proludunt*, 15.51–2 *iurgia prima sonare* | *incipiunt; animis ardentibus haec tuba rixae.*

289 Qualifies *rixa*: 'if you can call it a brawl when ...', in a lower tone, as if muttered, since *tu* denotes the thug who is not intended to hear. J.'s Latin is wittily concise: 'where you do all the beating and all I do is get beaten'. *uapulo* is the standard plight of slaves in Roman comedy; cf. Ter. *Ad.* 213 *ego uapulando, ille uerberando, usque ambo defessi sumus. tantum* = 'only', as at 1.1.

290 stat contra: cf. Pers. 5.96 *stat contra Ratio*; possibly evoking the confrontation between accuser and defendant in a court of law, cf. 298–9 (Lewis), or evoking combat: *OLD sto* 2a, 3, 11. **stari:** impersonal passive.

291 agas ... cogat: indefinite first person slips into indefinite second person ('for what can you do?', cf. at 4.14) and the thug becomes third person: see 285–7n. above.

291–2 et idem | fortior 'and stronger as well' (*OLD idem* 8, cf. J. 10.331).

292–6 The thug angrily interrogates the helpless victim: *unde, cuius, cuius, quis, nil, in qua.* Cf. the bombardment of questions with which Satire 1 opens. **"unde uenis?":** a standard greeting, cf. Hor. *Sat.* 1.9.62. **"cuius aceto, cuius conche tumes?":** the thug insults both victim and victim's host, by describing the former as 'bursting' with wind (from the beans he has eaten) and assuming that the host can offer only cheap food and drink: *acetum* denotes sour wine (cf. Mart. 11.56.7) and *conchis* a kind of bean (cf. Mart. 5.39.10, Athen. 4.159f: a lentil soup which is associated with poverty). **quis ... sutor:** cobblers were regarded as representative of the poorest and most insignificant, cf. Cic. *Flacc.* 17 and cf. Courtney on 4.153. **sectile porrum:** giant chives (see Kenney (1984) 73, 82), to be distinguished from leeks (*porrum capitatum*). *porrum* typifies humble food at Hor. *Sat.* 1.6.115. The thug implies the victim's breath smells (cf. Mart. 5.78.4, 13.18). **elixi ueruecis labra:** a boiled sheep's head (*ueruex* = castrated ram), cf. Mart. 14.211; *ueruex* also denotes a stupid person (*OLD* b), another insult. **nil mihi respondes?:** at the start of a line cf. Mart. 5.61.7, 6.5.3, 10.41.4. **calcem:** lit. the heel, hence 'a kick' (*OLD* 1b): the Romans used the heel for kicking. **ubi consistas** 'where your pitch is': the thug implies the victim is a beggar. **quaero** 'am I to look for', indicative used in a rhetorical deliberative question, cf. *conciditur* 4.130. **proseucha:** a Greek word denoting a Jewish prayer-house, synagogue: another insult, whether or not this victim is to be identified with the chauvinistic Umbricius. For synagogues at Rome see Smallwood (1976) 133 and on attitudes to Jews see 13–14n.

297–8 Injury is now added to insult: there is no escape from being beaten up. This scene is reminiscent of Mercury's beating-up of Sosia in Plaut. *Amph.* 292–462, e.g. 377 M. *loquere, quid uenisti?* S. *ut esset quem tu pugnis caederes* and 379 M. *quia uaniloquo's, uapulabis.*   **recedas** 'retreat'.   **tantumdem est:** *OLD* 2c; reinforced by *pariter* in the next phrase.   **feriunt:** the thug is generalised into the plural, 'they hit you'.

298–9 uadimonia deinde | irati faciunt: the crowning insult: after beating up the victim the thug will sue for assault; a *uadimonium* is a guarantee that the defendant will appear in court (for *uadimonium facere* see *OLD uadimonium* 2a). Cf. Quint. *I.O.* 6.3.83: a threat to hit a rude inferior then prosecute him for having such a hard head [that he hurt his hand]; cf. J. 16.9–12 where the civilian beaten up by a soldier must keep quiet. The thug is still angry, cf. *petulans* 278 and the comparison with Achilles 279–80.

299 libertas pauperis haec est: sarcasm: Umbricius has already suggested that the poor man has no dignity (147–53) and he now suggests that he has no freedom at all.

300 Uses the same pattern twice for emphasis: *pulsatus* intensifies *pugnis concisus* and *rogat adorat*. For *pugnis concisus* cf. Hor. *Sat.* 1.2.66 *pugnis caesus*. For *adoro* with *ut* + subjunctive = 'beg' cf. Ov. *Pont.* 2.2.53.

301 'that he may be allowed to go home with a few teeth in his head' (Rudd); *liceat* impersonal, *reuerti* deponent. *paucis* carries emphasis: a few teeth as opposed to none at all: the victim accepts that he will lose some. Cf. Athenaeus 6.236a where a man walking home in the dark thinks he is lucky only to be beaten up.

302–8 When the poor man eventually returns home, he still faces attack by robbers or murderers. Mention of the locked houses and shops evokes vividly his vulnerability on the silent streets and may suggest that he is attacked near his home. This is the final event in the twenty-four-hour sequence.

302 'And these are not the only things you must fear.' *metuas:* indefinite second person command, as *optes, feras* 276.   **qui spoliet te:** i.e. a robber. The final monosyllable conveys an unsettling urgency.

302–3 qui ... non derit: cf. 9.112 and on such predictions see 2.168n..

303 clausis domibus: the plural has a general reference, 'after the houses are closed' (Lewis): the victim is still on the street.

303–4 omnis ubique | fixa catenatae siluit compago taber-nae: lit. 'everywhere every shuttering of the chained-up shop, once it had been fastened, fell silent'. Shops, the parts of buildings fronting on to the street, were open across the entire breadth when the shuttering was not fastened and chained (*catenatae*) in place. The tone of line 304 is elevated, presenting a classic 'golden line' of the abVAB pattern (see Introduction §7). The incongruity between style and content is very marked.

305 ferro subitus grassator agit rem: cf. 14.174 *ferro grassatur*; Suet. *Aug.* 32.1 *grassatorum plurimi palam se ferebant succincti ferro*; for stealth and surprise cf. Gell. 20.1.8 *nocturni grassatoris insidiosam uiolen-tiam*. Latin uses adj. *subitus* where English would use adv., cf. Val. Fl. 4.712 *ad subitam stupuere ratem. agit rem* = 'goes about his business' cf. *OLD ago* 38. The final monosyllable suggests the speed of the attack.

306–8 The presence of *grassatores* on the streets is presented as a direct result of attempts to impose military control upon the bands of brigands in the Pontine marshes and Gallinarian forest, both areas difficult to police; cf. Suetonius *Tib.* 37.1 *in primis tuendae pacis a grassaturis ac latrociniis seditionumque licentia curam habuit. stationes militum per Italiam solito frequentiores disposuit.* The Pontine marshes covered a considerable area approx. thirty miles by eight miles along the coast of Latium between Circeii and Terracina through which the *via Appia* passed; Mussolini was the first to drain them successfully, in the 1930s. The Gallinarian forest was a large pine-forest in the west of Campania between the river Vulturnus and Cumae, where Sextus Pompey assembled pirates (Strabo 5.4.4, 243).

Umbricius' closing example of the dangers of the city of Rome arises from population movement from the south into the city (308 *inde huc*), a movement reversed in Umbricius' personal retreat south along the *via Appia* to Cumae. This final case of displacement (poor Romans are either killed or driven out by the brigands) prepares for the coda.

armato ... custode: singular for plural, instrumental ablative, cf. *ruptae lectore* 1.13n.   **tutae:** fem. nom. pl., anticipating *palus* and *pinus*.   **sic ... tamquam:** cf. 6.431, another comparison with the animal world.   **uiuaria:** lit. the game-reserves where game or fish (cf. 4.51) were ·bred and fattened (Gell. 2.20). The brigands are portrayed as predators feeding upon their helpless victims. For similar metaphorical use of *uiuaria* cf. Hor. *Ep.* 1.1.79.

309–11 An exaggerated version of the cliché that in time of war ploughshares and other agricultural implements are melted down into swords, e.g. Virg. *Georg.* 1.508 *curuae rigidum falces conflantur in ensem*, Ov. *Fast.* 1.699–700 *sarcula cessabant uersique in pila ligones | factaque de rastri pondere cassis erat*; for the opposite see Isaiah 2.4. In J.'s version, Umbricius claims that there are so many criminals that ploughshares, mattocks and hoes are melted down to make fetters and chains. On the exaggeration as an indication of Umbricius' obsession and pessimism, see Braund (1989a) 36; cf. 15.165–8 (esp. *ferrum, incude, sarcula, marris, uomere*), the development from agricultural implements to weapons; and contrast Sen. *Herc. Fur.* 930–1 quoted below, 310n. J. possibly evokes the finale to Virgil's second *Georgic* (513–40) where the farmer's life is associated with the ancient idyllic Saturnian age (cf.172–4n.).

309 To be understood as *qua fornace, qua incude non ⟨sunt⟩ graues catenae?*; cf. Virg. *Aen.* 6.92 *quas gentis Italum aut quas non oraueris urbes!* The chains (*catenae*) forged to imprison criminals recall the chains on the shop (*catenatae ... tabernae* 304).

310 maximus in uinclis ferri modus 'most of our iron is used for fetters'; contrast Sen. *Herc. Fur.* 930–1 *ferrum omne teneat ruris innocui labor | ensesque lateant.*   **timeas ne:** indefinite second person singular, see 3.7n.

312–14 A nostalgic idealisation of the distant past, which Umbricius portrays as virtually crime-free. The emotive *felices ... felicia* helps to characterise him as rooted (impossibly) in the past: he is an old-fashioned Roman who does not belong in modern Rome.   **proauorum atauos:** lit. 'great-great-great-grandfathers of great-grandfathers' (see Plaut. *Pers.* 57 for a full list: *pater, auos, proauos, abauos, atauos, tritauos*), so 'distant ancestors'.   **felicia ... saecula:** cf. 2.38 *felicia tempora.*   **quondam:** of the distant past also at 6.288, 11.83, 13.38. For *quondam* + *felices/felicia* cf. Virg. *Ecl.* 1.74 *ite meae, quondam felix pecus, ite capellae.*   **sub regibus atque tribunis:** in the regal and early Republican period of Rome's history. The tribunes are the *tribuni militares* appointed with consular power in the place of consuls during the period 445–367 BC.   **uno ... carcere:** the *carcer Mamertinus* at the foot of the Capitol, said to have been constructed by the fourth king, Ancus Martius (Liv. 1.33.8), to which the sixth king Servius Tullius is said to have added the *Tullianum*, where the Catilinarian conspirators were executed (Sall. *Cat.* 55.3–6). Imprisonment was used primarily as a temporary measure for detention pending and during trials.   **Romam:** not named since line 183; it is appropriate that *Romam* should be the final word of Umbricius' complaint.

315–322 Umbricius announces his departure. The literary texture here is particularly dense. The close of the poem presents a complex set of allusions to the prologue: Cumae is named at 321, cf. 2; transport, *mulio* 317, cf. *raeda . . . una* 10, the restorative effects of the countryside, *refici* 319, cf. *gratum litus amoeno secessus* 3–4, the cool fields as a setting for satire, 321–2, contrasting with banal poetry recitations in the hot month of August, 9; the meeting of the speaker and Umbricius 318–22, cf. esp. 1–3. The effect of this ring-composition is one of closure, suggesting the poet's control of his material.

The first sentence evokes the world of pastoral (316n.), but preludes the gulf between Umbricius and the idyllic potential of pastoral. The language of the last two sentences (318–22) recalls the coda to Hor. *Ep.* 1.18, in which Horace declares a philosophy of contentment and self-sufficiency: *quotiens . . . refici* and *gelidos . . . agros*, cf. *Ep.* 1.18.104 *me quotiens reficit gelidus Digentia riuus*; 190n. Horace evokes a simple country life with appropriate religious observance and intellectual nourishment provided by a good supply of books. J. reworks these features into Umbricius' final words: the simple country life is evoked by *caligatus* (322n.), religious observance in the naming of Ceres and Diana (320), and intellectual food comes from listening to satires (*saturarum*, 321), thus providing a tribute to J.'s predecessor in the genre. But Umbricius hardly measures up to Horace's self-found *aequus animus* (Hor. *Ep.* 1.18.112).

315 poteram: lit. 'I had it in my power', most naturally translated 'I could'; cf. Virg. *Ecl.* 1.79 *hanc mecum poteras requiescere noctem.*   **subnectere:** regularly of composition of speeches/narrative, e.g. by Val. Max., see *OLD* 1b, cf. Sil. 12.603 *subnectere plura conantem.*   **causas:** reasons for leaving Rome.

316 iumenta uocant et sol inclinat: strongly resembles pastoral closure through reference to lengthening shadows and/or the need to fold the herds/flocks, as at Virg. *Ecl.* 1.83, 6.85–6, 10.75–7, Calp. Sic. *Ecl.* 5.120–1. Umbricius figures himself as the herdsman of pastoral who has been displaced.

317 mulio: final *ŏ* is shortened, as often; on the prosody see Introduction §8.

317–18 commota ... uirga adnuit: the driver signals by waving his whip.

318 nostri memor: the phrase suits good-bye contexts, cf. Hor. *Od.* 3.27.14 *memor nostri, Galatea, uiuas,* Ov. *Her.* 11.125 *uiue memor nostri.* If Umbricius is to be an *umbra* (shade), he at least wants to be remembered.

319 tuo ... Aquino: adj. *tuo* may mean 'your favourite' (cf. *OLD* 2b, cf. Suet. *Galb.* 1 *Liuiae ... Veientanum suum reuisenti*) or 'your native' (perhaps supported by *reddet: OLD* 2). It is usually taken to indicate J.'s birthplace; however, this involves identifying Umbricius' interlocutor with the poet Juvenal: see Introduction §2. Aquinum was a town in Latium on the *via Latina* c. 75 miles from Rome. This lover of Rome, who does not leave with Umbricius, may have a country seat in Aquinum.

320 Heluinam Cererem: probably indicates that the temple was built by the Helvii, a family prominent in this area, see *CIL* x 5477, 5585. An inscription from Aquinum, now lost (*CIL* x 5382), records a dedication by a Juvenal, possibly to Ceres; this flimsy evidence has been worked (too) hard to provide biographical detail for the poet. Ceres, like Diana, is a goddess of the countryside.   **uestramque Dianam:** broader than *tuo,* i.e. the Diana of your townsfolk/family.

321 conuerte 'turn', 'bring away', i.e. invite; usually with a plural object (Luc. 9.903, Sil. 12.173, Val. Max. 3.2.ext.9); *conuelle* or Bücheler's *conpelle,* recorded in Martyn's apparatus, are attractive. **saturarum:** Umbricius' interlocutor is a satirist, not crudely to be identified straightforwardly with J. the poet; cf. 1.79n., 4.106n. This seems analogous to Hitchcock appearing incognito in his own films. **ni pudet illas** 'if they are not embarrassed': an audience wearing boots is not like a refined Roman audience.

322 auditor gelidos ... in agros: Umbricius offers himself as a willing audience outside of Rome, in direct contrast with the bathetic condemnation of recitations in the heat of the city (9n.). Ovid describes the role of a listener at *Pont.* 4.2.35: *excitat auditor studium.* On *gelidos* see 190n., 315–322n.; Aquinum at the foot of the Apennines was cooler than Cumae. Appropriately, the final word of the poem is *agros,* locating Umbricius firmly in the country.   **caligatus:** usually a wearer of military boots (*caligae,* 16.24), hence a soldier; the only instance in *OLD* and *TLL* = wearing heavy boots. Umbricius in effect styles himself a soldier, perhaps of the morality which no longer exists in Rome. But it also recalls the soldiers in Persius, specifically the uncouth centurions who sneer (3.77–87 and 5.189–91). Line 322 is a parody of Luc. 1.382 *Hesperios audax ueniam metator in agros*, where the centurion Laelius declares his unquestioning allegiance to Caesar (1.385–6). This confirms the ambivalent status of Soldier Umbricius: he may believe he is acting for the best, but his obsessive hostility to Rome leaves room for doubt.

ESSAY

Satire 3, the longest poem and the centrepiece of Book 1, is one of the most famous of J.'s poems. It presents a powerful condemnation of life in Rome. Satire – 'an urban art' – often has the city as its setting and its subject (Hodgart (1969) 129, cf. 135–7; Kernan (1959) 7–8). J.'s third satire is a classic and an archetype. Its fame and popularity probably come from the readiness of an urban culture such as ours to identify with a complaint against city life. And it is therefore not surprising that J.'s poem has inspired many imitations, of which the most renowned in English is probably Johnson's *London*.

But this identification is only one way of reading the Satire. It is significant that the condemnation of Rome is not delivered by the indignant speaker of Satires 1 and 2 but by his friend Umbricius. The context is a private conversation between the two just before Umbricius leaves the city for a quiet life in the country. From the prologue, in which the scene is set, the speaker appears to sympathise with Umbricius' complaints, yet he remains in the city at the end of the poem, whereas once Umbricius has delivered his tirade he leaves. This distinction between the speaker and Umbricius encourages an objective scrutiny of Umbricius and his motives: perhaps the city is not as entirely bad as Umbricius depicts it if the speaker can bear to remain behind?

Moreover, Umbricius' speech is strongly reminiscent of standard elements in the rhetorical education received by young men of the Roman élite. This too suggests that there is more to Satire 3 than a straightforward loathing for city life. The relative merits of city life and country life were a standard topic of debate in the Roman schools of declamation, particularly criticisms of city life and appeals to the country as a standard of morality (cf. Quint. *I.O.* 2.4.24 'Is town or country life better?'; Sen. *Contr.* 2.1.11–12, 5.5 (criticism of country life); 1.6.4, 2.1.8 (praise of rustic ancestors); see Braund (1989a) 23). Satire 3 reflects this conventional presentation of material with its condemnation of the greed, corruption and selfishness of the urban rat-race punctuated by occasional glimpses of life in the country where traditional morality still prevails: an eloquent counterpoint (Braund (1989a) 28). More specifically, Umbricius' speech can be read as the inversion of a standard type of speech practised in the schools of declamation, the speech termed the 'syntaktikon', that is, the farewell speech of a departing traveller (see Cairns (1972) 38, 47–8). Such speeches contained praise of the place which the traveller was leaving; in this case, the inversion consists of the substitution of attack for praise.

The views expressed by Umbricius find analogues not only in the declamation schools but also in earlier works of Roman satire (see Braund (1989a) 36–9). Comparison with passages in Lucilius and Horace suggests that J. deliberately echoes his predecessors' treatment of the theme of city life. This does not mean that none of these details can be drawn from 'real life', but it establishes that the literary tradition is another important element in the appreciation of Satire 3; circumspection over using satire as a quarry for 'facts' about everyday life in ancient Rome is advisable. Umbricius – whether or not there was a 'real' Umbricius, who might be identified with or at least evoke the imperial *haruspex* of this name (Braund (1990) 505–6) – is a literary creation who should be contextualised within the intellectual milieu of J.'s era.

The prologue of 20 lines uttered by the speaker sets the scene rapidly and economically. Lines 1–3 indicate the dramatic situation: the departure of an old friend for Cumae, a decision the speaker regrets and approves. With all his worldly goods piled on a single cart, they stop at the Porta Capena (10–11) and walk down to the nearby grottoes for a final conversation (17). The remaining material in the prologue serves a different purpose: it anticipates the themes of Umbricius' tirade. Lines 4–9 foreshadow much of the final part of Umbricius' complaint by focussing upon the dangers of city life – the fires and collapses of buildings; in lines 12–16 the speaker contrasts past and present, sacred and profane, foreign and Roman, anticipating the part of Umbricius' tirade against the foreigners who have displaced native Romans; and lines 17–20 present an antithesis of the natural and the artificial which provides a preview of Umbricius' opening theme, the displacement of simple honourable men like himself by crooks and criminals (cf. Fredericks (1973)). After this introduction, the 'conversation' begins as Umbricius gives his reasons for departure. But it soon emerges that this is no conversation at all: Umbricius' indignation carries him away so that he forgets where he is and to whom he is talking and instead delivers a fully-fledged invective against Rome. This becomes explicit at line 60 when he addresses all the citizens of Rome: *Quirites* (see n.).

Umbricius' complaint is, essentially, that there is no (longer) room in Rome for impoverished Roman clients like himself, because they have been displaced by others. In this way he is a development of the treatment of the neglected clients of Satire 1. According to Umbricius, honourable men have been displaced by the shameless and the criminal (21–57); true Romans by foreigners, especially Greeks (58–125); and, in the ultimate paradox, the poor by the greedy rich, both nobles and upstarts, because the power of money reigns supreme (126–314). Hence the only logical decision (according to the mad logic found so often in J.) is to leave (315–22). Throughout his tirade, but particularly at the start, Umbricius appeals to traditional Roman values and arouses conventional prejudices: in his catalogue of the projects undertaken by crooks and upstarts for money (30–8), in the list of the corrupt services he is not prepared to provide as client (41–8), in his evocation of the filthy foreign practices introduced from the east (62–5, see 58–125n. on the abundance of Greek places and words), and in his catalogue of Greek versatility (75–8 and 86–91: see nn.) and plausibility (93–100n.), seduction (109–12) and betrayal (114–18).

It is evident that Umbricius sees himself as a true Roman who upholds traditional values (21–2, 84–5, 119). This reading supports a symbolic interpretation of Umbricius inspired by his name: he is the *umbra*, the 'ghost', of Roman-ness (*Romanitas*) leaving for Cumae on the Bay of Naples, the mythical entrance to the Underworld and (paradoxically) a Greek place, because of his disgust with a Rome that has become un-Roman (*Graecam Vrbem* 61) and in which he no longer has a role (Motto and Clark (1965) 275–6). That is why at the close of his condemnation of Rome he nostalgically longs for the old days, when one prison was enough (312–14). He is a version in satire of the virgin goddess of myth (Astraea) who flees from the world, horrified by human wickedness; but instead of fleeing to heaven, he paradoxically flees to the gates of the Underworld (Motto and Clark (1965) 271–5).

Alongside Umbricius' high moral view of himself and his motives for leaving exists another, less complimentary, view of him as a jealous failure whose anger and departure are inspired by his inability to compete and succeed in the big city (on Umbricius as a case of 'the unreliable satirist' see Winkler (1983) 220–3, LaFleur (1976)). Right from the start, even though he would not contemplate performing such tasks himself, he seems jealous of the money made by the rich upstarts who are prepared to tackle the dirtiest of jobs (30–40) and by those who are able to become conspirators in criminal activity (49–57). Moreover, he is envious of the success won by the Greeks by means of flattery. When he says 'we too can praise these same things, but it is they who are believed' (92–3), he betrays himself. His jealousy continues in the next section of the poem where he complains that poor Romans are displaced by the rich: what annoys him is that he can only afford a cheap prostitute whereas the rich man's slave can lavish gifts upon an aristocratic mistress (132–6). Similarly his complaints that people are believed in direct proportion to their wealth (143–4) and that poverty makes men ridiculous (152–3) are not, perhaps, complaints he would utter were he rich. What annoys him is the humiliation of being asked to move from his seat in the theatre, one of the most public of places in Rome, because his wealth is insufficient to permit him to sit there (153–9n.). At this point he draws the obvious conclusion: that poor Romans (*Quirites* again) should have emigrated long ago (162–3). The double standard revealed here – he condemns the rat-race but up to now has been participating in it – detracts from the dignity of his stance and makes it hard to take his picture of life in Rome at face value (cf. Fruelund Jensen (1986)).

But what does he mean by 'poor Romans'? Umbricius proceeds to condemn the pretentiousness and competitiveness of city life through an antithesis with the simplicity of life in a small Italian country town (164–89), the sort of antithesis which was doubtless a standard feature in rhetorical exercises (Braund (1989a) 28). But the complaint that emerges is that he cannot keep up with the expected standard of living in Rome (e.g. *pudet* 168): *hic uiuimus ambitiosa | paupertate omnes* ('Here we all live in pretentious poverty', 182–3). He then alleges that those who have nothing (among whom he evidently includes himself, despite the evidence that he has, e.g., a number of slaves: 166–7) get nothing: *omnia Romae | cum pretio* ('Everything at Rome has a price-tag', 184–5, cf. 143–4), a point he follows with two examples, one brief, one extended. First, you have to pay to get your patron's attention (184–9). Then, if there is a fire poor Cordus in his garret loses everything (*perdidit infelix totum nihil* 209) whereas rich Persicus receives so much assistance that he is richer than he was before the fire (221–2). Clearly, Umbricius is not as poor as Cordus. Nor is he as wealthy as Persicus – and that is what rankles. Consequently, the remainder of the poem (232–314) consists of a series of antitheses between rich and poor, arranged in a twenty-four-hour chronological sequence from night, through morning and the day to evening and the night-time perils (Braund (1989a) 33–4), and set on the streets of Rome. He has shifted from lamenting the displacement of the impoverished Roman client into attacking the privileges enjoyed by the rich, confirming that he is a jaundiced failure.

His language too shows the linguistic signs of anger familiar from the indignant speaker's rantings (see Introduction §6(*a*)): angry questions (38–40, 49–50, 61, 81–5, 126–30) and exclamations (e.g. 60), vocabulary of 'not enduring' (60, 152) and sweeping generalisations (*nullus, nulla* 22, *omnia* 77, *nihil* 109, *nusquam* 125, *omnes* and *omnia* 182, *nemo* 211, *undique* 247, *tot . . . quot* 274, *omnes* 308, *maximus* 310). The fact that he forgets that he is chatting to his friend, the speaker, and launches into what sounds like a public declamation addressed to the citizens of Rome (*Quirites* 60) confirms this view of him as carried away by his anger. And the sheer length of his tirade indicates his obsession (Braund (1989a) 30–1). These factors together suggest an alternative symbolic interpretation of Umbricius' name as 'Mr Shady' in a less than favourable sense: he is a manifestation of the petty greed and jealousy which haunts the city of Rome.

The tension between these two elements in Umbricius' character emerges clearly at the end of his speech (309–14). He utters an exaggerated version of the cliché that in time of war ploughshares and other agricultural implements are melted down and made into swords (309–11n.). The hyperbole is an important indication of Umbricius' obsession and pessimism. And he closes his complaint with a nostalgic idealisation of the distant past, which he portrays as virtually crime-free, in contrast with the (as he sees it) highly criminalised present (312–14). The emotive words *felices . . . felicia* help to characterise him as rooted (impossibly) in the past: he is an old-fashioned Roman who does not belong in modern Rome: a true 'shade' who has to leave because there is no longer any place for him (cf. Anderson (1982) 219–32). Accordingly, the poem closes with Umbricius' departure (315–22).

It is important to realise that this tension is present throughout the poem and that different readers will respond more fully to one or other element within that tension and therefore have different reactions to Umbricius and different readings of the poem. The reading offered here sees Umbricius' departure from Rome as a parody of the myth of the virgin goddess: in his own eyes he is the essence of Roman-ness leaving an un-Roman Rome; but his greed and envy reveal him to be a covetous failure driven away by his lack of success.

Parody works on another level too in Satire 3. The setting for Umbricius' farewell 'conversation' with his friend is the closest approximation the city can offer to a country setting: the valley of Egeria, with its caves and shady trees and running water and shrine closely resembles the classic setting of pastoral poetry, the so-called *locus amoenus* ('pleasant place'), which provides an ideal(ised) setting for the shepherds of pastoral poetry to rest in and sing their songs, as in Theocritus' *Idylls* and in Virgil's *Eclogues*. J.'s version of the *locus amoenus* has, typically of satire, been corrupted by the city: the caves are unnatural, the spring is paved around with exotic marble and the sanctity of the grotto is disrupted by the Jewish beggars who occupy it. The place symbolises the corrupting power of the city: the attempt to reproduce the countryside is flawed by the invasion of the artificial, the greedy and the foreign. In this way Satire 3 parodies the conventional setting of pastoral poetry; hence it has been termed 'an eclogue for the urban poor' (Witke (1970) 128–34). It also engages with a specific pastoral poem, Virgil's first *Eclogue* (cf. 1.25n.). The opening poem of Virgil's book of pastoral poems establishes the *locus amoenus* setting and within it dramatises the conversation of two friends. One of them is departing sadly from his familiar native fields to go into a kind of exile while the other is fortunate enough to remain behind: in their dialogue the departing herdsman explains why he has to leave and laments his fate while the herdsman remaining explains and celebrates his good fortune. The poem closes with the fortunate herdsman offering an invitation to the miserable one for the night. The similarities between the two poems are striking, particularly in the 'frame' of Satire 3: the description of the setting at the opening and the invitation extended by Umbricius to the speaker to visit him at the close. This parody of pastoral demonstrates yet again that satire works on a number of different levels simultaneously and that an appreciation of as many elements as possible of Roman élite culture is desirable for readers of J.'s Satires.

SATIRE 4

1–33 The first section consists of an attack upon Crispinus, one of Domitian's courtiers, in which the final six lines (28–33) redirect the focus on to the emperor as a preparation for the second, longer, section which consists of a mock-epic attack upon Domitian. The speaker attacks first Crispinus' major faults (1–10) then shifts to 'more trivial matters' (*factis leuioribus* 11), his purchase of an expensive fish for his personal consumption. On the links between the two parts of the Satire see the Essay.

1–3 Crispinus (1.26–8n.) is an extraordinary example (*monstrum*) of vice; the allegation of lust (*libidine* 3) is substantiated in lines 1–10. **Ecce iterum Crispinus** 'Here is Crispinus again'; early Latin uses *ecce* + acc., e.g. Plaut. *Cist.* 283 *ubi tu es? – ecce me*. Vivid *ecce* prepares for the stage metaphor in *uocandus ad partes* (see below). *iterum* does double duty, referring to Crispinus' earlier appearance at 1.26–9 and echoing Hor. *Sat.* 1.4.13–14 *ecce,* | *Crispinus*, where Horace's Crispinus too is making a reappearance from an earlier poem (*Sat.* 1.1.120). *iterum* may allude to a programmatic announcement in Lucilius' second book (possibly the opening) which presented the parody of a trial: *fandam atque auditam iterabimus famam* (53W = 55M); cf. Hor. *Sat.* 1.7.1–3. The phrase suggests the inevitability of Crispinus' appearance in satire, as *ecce iterum fratres* at Stat. *Theb.* 12.429 suggests the inevitability of the brothers' irreconcilability.

est mihi saepe uocandus: gerundive + dative of agent, 'who deserves to be summoned often by me'. **ad partes** 'to play his part', see *OLD pars* 9, with *uoco* cf. Var. *R.R.* 2.10.1, Sen. *Phoen.* 351.

Crispinus is like an actor receiving his cue in this play.   **monstrum:** essentially something unnatural, hence a person of extreme wickedness (*OLD* 4); again at 45, 115: a key word and concept. On *monstrum* in Book 1 of Juvenal see Cloud and Braund (1982) 81 and cf. 2.122n.; typical of *indignatio* (Anderson (1982) 278).   **nulla uirtute redemptum:** cf. Sen. *N.Q.* 6.23.2 *crimen aeternum quod nulla uirtus . . . redimet*; more usually the active *redimo* + acc. + abl.

3–4 Crispinus is a pleasure-seeker (*deliciae*) devoted to lust (*libidine*), especially illicit sex (*adulter*). On Roman attitudes to sensual pleasures see Edwards (1993) 173–206. Use of *deliciae* to denote a voluptuary is unusual; cf. Plin. *N.H.* 22.99, Mart. 8.48.6; J.'s two pictures of Crispinus (here and 1.26–9) recall Martial's thumb-nail sketch there. **aegrae solaque libidine fortes** 'feeble, and strong in his lust alone'; cf. Sen. *Contr.* 1 pr. 10 *nusquam nisi in libidine uiris.*   **uiduas tantum aspernatus adulter** 'an adulterer who rejected only unmarried women'. *uiduus* = 'single', *OLD* 1. Sex with unmarried women was technically *stuprum*, but it seems that *adulterium* and *stuprum* could sometimes be used interchangeably: Edwards (1993) 38 n.10. Crispinus disregards the arguments against liaisons with married women adduced in Hor. *Sat.* 1.2.

5–7 'What does it matter, then, how long are the colonnades in which . . . ?' Three indirect exclamations, anticipating an objection that, despite his immorality, Crispinus is happy (*felix*, 8) because he is wealthy. The dimensions and features of a man's house were an obvious index of his wealth: see Edwards (1993) 143–60; cf. Val. Max. 9.1.4 for colonnades and trees.   **quantis iumenta fatiget porticibus:** cf. 7.178–80, Mart. 1.12 and 12.50 on rich men's lengthy colonnades; Nero's Golden House had three porticoes a thousand feet long (Suet. 31.1). *fatiget* indirectly emphasises their length, cf. SHA 26.49.2 *miliarensem . . . porticum in hortis Sallustii ornauit, in qua cottidie et equos et se fatigabat*; also Pers. 4.26. On *iumenta* = equine animals (and not specifically 'mules') see Adams (1990) 441–2.   **quanta nemorum uectetur in umbra** 'the size of the shady groves in which he is carried', lit. 'in how much shade of groves . . .'. *uectetur* probably indicates conveyance by litter (cf. 6.577).   **iugera quot uicina foro, quas emerit aedes:** 'how many acres and what house close to the forum he has bought' (*uicina foro* goes with *iugera* and *aedes*).

8–10 nemo malus felix 'no bad man is happy'. The thought, possibly a commonplace, sounds Stoic; cf. Plut. *Mor.* 1042a 'vice is the essence of unhappiness' and Long and Sedley 1 394–8.   **corruptor et idem incestus** 'a seducer (polluted at that)' (Rudd). *corruptor* refers back to *adulter* (4), cf. 6.233; *incestus* denotes the religious profanation entailed in the seduction of a Vestal Virgin (see below). For *et idem* cf. 3.291–2n.   **cum quo:** again at 87; *quocum* is usual. **nuper:** 2.29n.   **uittata iacebat ... sacerdos:** a Vestal Virgin, marked out by her headdress of *uittae* (= woollen bands: see *OLD* 2a); cf. Luc. 1.597 *Vestalem ... chorum ducit uittata sacerdos*. For *iaceo* of sexual relations cf. Ov. *Met.* 2.598–9, 3.363. Separation of noun and adjective throws emphasis onto both.

Seduction of a Vestal was regarded as *incestum* and could be punished by entombment alive for the Vestal and scourging, exile or execution for the man: cf. Ov. *Fast.* 6.457–60 (*uittas, sacerdos, uiua defodietur humo, incesta, conditur*); see Dion. Hal. 2.67, 8.89.4–5 for accounts. *uittata* evokes the custom of tearing the *uittae* from the Vestal's head before her entombment. In his capacity as Pontifex Maximus, Domitian tried several Vestals and convicted one Cornelia to death by entombment in AD 93 (Plin. *Ep.* 4.11.6–10, Suet. *Dom.* 8.3–4). Although J. may allude to this case, it is safer to assume that he refers to an incident unknown to us or that he has amalgamated material to portray Crispinus' lust as graphically as possible.   **sanguine adhuc uiuo terram subitura** 'who would go beneath the earth with still living blood' (sc. if convicted); *sanguine ... uiuo* has an epic history (Ov. *Met.* 5.436, Luc. 6.554, Stat. *Theb.* 5.162, 8.761) but here underlines the horror of the punishment.

11 sed nunc de factis leuioribus: understand 'we must speak'. A programmatic announcement, turning to Crispinus' selfish luxury. Contrast the opposite at Ov. *A.A.* 3.499 *si licet a paruis animum ad maiora referre* and compare Tac. *Ann.* 4.32 *pleraque eorum quae rettuli quaeque referam parua forsitan et leuia memoratu uideri*.

11–15 Crispinus led the charmed life of a favourite and his criminality defies description. A parenthesis, stating the relativity of these 'lighter matters'; the example does not commence until 15 *mullum ... emit*.   **alter | si fecisset idem caderet** 'if another had been guilty of the same thing he would now stand convicted'; both verbs technical terms, cf. 6.638 *feci* (also *OLD* 21b); 10.69 *quo cecidit sub crimine?* with *OLD cado* 11 esp. b.   **iudice morum:** i.e. censor, a position which

Domitian took on in perpetuity in AD 85 (Suet. *Dom.* 8.3 *suscepta correctione morum*). The censor regulated expenditure on luxury goods (cf. 9.142 *quae Fabricius censor notet*) through sumptuary legislation; anyone guilty received the censor's 'mark' (*nota*) and was removed from the list of senators or knights. After the criticisms in Satire 2 of Domitian's hypocrisy as censor (see e.g. 2.29–33n.), this phrase is sarcastic and satirical, given the picture of his sumptuary extravagance later in the poem. Cf. Sen. *Ep.* 95.41: 'What is more shameful than an expensive feast which eats away even a knight's income? What so deserves the censor's condemnation as continual indulgence of the self and the "inner man", as those gluttons say? And yet often has an inaugural dinner cost the most careful man a million. The very sum that is called disgraceful (*turpis*) if spent on the appetite is beyond reproach if spent for official purposes!', followed by narrative of the presentation to Tiberius of an enormous mullet (*Ep.* 95. 42). For huge fish as a touchstone of luxury in Roman satire see Hudson (1989) 80–1. **nam ... :** the slight illogicality suits this confiding parenthesis. More logical would have been, 'For what suited Crispinus would have been disgraceful for good men ...'. **turpe ... decebat:** as 8.181–2 *quae | turpia cerdoni Volesos Brutumque decebunt*, cf. 11.1–2 and 176–8. **Titio Seiioque:** ordinary, good (*bonis*) men; standard non-specific names in the Roman jurists (Plut. *Quaest. Rom.* 30). **quid agas?:** 3.291n. **dira et foedior omni | crimine persona est** 'the person himself is appalling and more repulsive than any charge' (Rudd). Language is inadequate to describe Crispinus' wickedness; *dirus* and *foedus* are both strong words. For *persona* = 'person' see *OLD* 5, often in legal contexts, cf. Cic. *Cael.* 30 *sunt autem duo crimina ... in quibus una atque eadem persona uersatur*, and therefore appropriate here, given the legal flavour of *fecisset, caderet, iudice morum, Titio Seiioque* and *crimine*.

15–27 The speaker reveals Crispinus' lesser crime (15–17) and his motivation (18–22) before exploding with outrage at this selfish extravagance (22–7).

15–17 Crispinus' crime is the purchase of a large and expensive fish: a red mullet weighing six pounds and costing six thousand sesterces. For this symbol of extravagance cf. 5.92–8, 6.40, 11.37, Hor. *Sat.* 2.2.34, Mart. 10.33.4, 14.97; Plin. *N.H.* 9.64–8 on sizes and prices; Tiberius enacted sumptuary legislation to control the prices in markets after the sale of three mullets for thirty thousand sesterces (Suet. *Tib.*

34.1).   **aequantem ... paribus sestertia libris** 'equalling the
thousands with as many pounds'. An elevated periphrasis, cf. Stat.
Silv. 2.1.124 *Herculeos annis aequare labores* (i.e. twelve), deflated by
sarcastic *sane* (cf. 1.42n.). For *sestertia* see 1.92n.   **ut perhibent:** the
speaker distances himself from the claim, cf. Sen. *Ep.* 95.42 *mullum
ingentis formae – quare autem non pondus adicio et aliquorum gulam inrito?
quattuor pondo et selibram fuisse aiebant.*   **qui de magnis maiora
locuntur:** the length and weight of the phrase suggest 'who have
nothing better to do than exaggerate (this sort of thing)'.

18–21 Ironic: the speaker would praise Crispinus had he purchased
the fish as a legacy-hunting tactic (18–19) or as a present for a
powerful woman (20–1). Indicatives (*laudo, abstulit*) are more vivid
than the subjunctives of an unreal conditional clause. For mullets
given by legacy-hunters cf. 5.97–8, 6.38–40.   **consilium laudo
artificis** 'I commend a "craftsman's" plan'. *consilium* foreshadows the
mock-epic portrayal of Domitian's *consilium* (council: 73, 86, 145) (see
Essay). For ironic *laudo* cf. 12.121 (same context). For *artifex* = 'perpe-
trator' used absolutely cf. Ov. *Met.* 6.615; usually 'craftsman, artist',
here used ironically of the 'art' of legacy-hunting; ironic also at 14.116,
10.238 and Sen. *N.Q.* 4 pr. 5 of a flatterer.   **praecipuam in
tabulis ceram** 'the first place in the will'. *tabulis*: 2.58–9n. *ceram* here
denotes the page, cf. Hor. *Sat.* 2.5.53–4 *prima ... cera*; see 1.63–4n.
praecipuus is the legal term for the privileged position in the legacy
before distribution of the remainder: *OLD* 1b.   **senis ... orbi:**
pursuit of the childless (*orbi*: 3.129n.), especially when elderly (*senis*),
was potentially lucrative.   **ratio ulterior** 'a further motive' (*OLD
ulterior* 5) or 'an even better ploy' (after Rudd), i.e. surpassing the
previous reason.   **magnae si misit amicae:** as a way of currying
favour; this woman is the female equivalent of *magni ... amici* (1.33n.).
cluso latis specularibus antro: the size of her litter indicates the
woman's status (cf. Sen. *Const.* 14.1): it has 'wide windows' and is
described in grandiose terms as a 'closed cavern'. On *lapis specularis* as
windows see 3.242n.

22 The real reason for the purchase: he bought it for himself. The
stark *emit sibi* completes *mullum sex milibus emit* (15).   **expectes:**
1.14n.

22–5 The many marks of *indignatio* convey outrage at Crispinus'
selfishness: the sarcasm of calling Apicius *miser et frugi* (see below) and

the exaggeration of depicting Crispinus as a worse glutton; anaphora of *hoc* with ellipse in an angry question; apostrophe of Crispinus; and the sarcasm of calling the enormous mullet 'scales'.   **frugi:** 3.166–7n.   **Apicius:** Marcus Gavius Apicius, a wealthy gourmet who lived under Augustus and Tiberius; the cookery-book which survives under his name dates from much later. He was prepared to spend vast amounts on food (though at Sen. *Ep.* 95.42 he is outbid by another gourmet) and committed suicide when he felt his wealth had become too small to support his life-style (Sen. *Cons. ad Helv.* 10.8–9). Hence the sarcasm in the description of him as 'wretched and frugal'.   **hoc tu ... hoc pretio squamas?:** understand 'purchase' (15, 22, cf. 26). Sarcastic 'scales' diminishes the fish.

The transmitted text, *squamae*, which must then be punctuated as two questions, is problematical: it requires that *hoc* has a different grammatical function in each question and that there are two ellipses (*fecisti* and *emptae sunt*). Courtney's analogy with 1.88–9 is not parallel.

succinctus patria quondam ... papyro: formerly in his native Egypt Crispinus performed menial tasks; garments were worn 'tucked up' (into the belt) in readiness for physical work, cf. 8.162 *cum uenali Cyane succincta lagona*. The phrase suggests an epic girding of loins before the bathos of fish wrapping-paper: Gowers (1993) 205 with n. For Crispinus' Egyptian origin 1.26–8n. From the papyrus plant the Egyptians made paper and clothing: Plin. *N.H.* 13.72.

25–7 The speaker gloomily considers the purchasing power of six thousand sesterces: it would buy a slave; land abroad; land in Apulia. *minoris* and *tanti* are genitive of price.   **potuit ... emi:** cf. Plin. *N.H.* 9.67 for fish which cost more than cooks; Mart. 10.31 where the sale of a slave buys a four-pound mullet.   **prouincia:** i.e. land outside Italy (as 5.97, collective singular, *OLD* 3); possibly specifically Gallia Narbonensis, 'the province', Provence.   **sed:** may be translated 'and' to create the list.   **Apulia:** the south-east part of Italy, dry and uncultivated (Sen. *Ep.* 87.7): hence larger estates (cf. 9.54–5) could be purchased for the same sum.

28–33 The poem's pivotal passage. The indignant question with skilful interweaving sets Crispinus in relationship with the emperor as microcosm to macrocosm (see Essay).   **quales tunc epulas ... putamus ... cum ...** 'what sort of banquet must we think ... at that time when ...'. *qualis* acc. pl. with *epulas*, fem. noun always found as plural. Indicative *putamus* with force of deliberative subjunctive is common, e.g. Plin. *Ep.* 4.25.3; cf. *quaero* 3.296n. *tunc* grounds the poem specifically in Domitian's time.   **gluttisse** 'gulp', uneleveted in tone and possibly onomatopoeic (from *gula*: see Maltby), cf. Plaut. *Per.* 94, Pers. 5.112 *gluttu sorbere saliuam.*   **induperatorem:** the archaic form of *imperator*, again 10.138, here = the emperor; Ennius coined the word (e.g. 477W = 577Sk), since *imperator* was metrically impossible in the dactylic hexameter. A dignified word, rendered incongruous by the context of gluttony.

29–30 Crispinus' purchase is set in perspective: his expensive fish is not even the centre-piece of the banquet but a tiny side-dish (*exiguam*, *modicae* and *de margine*); contrast the four-pound mullet at Mart. 10.31.4 *cenae pompa caputque.*

31 A classic 'golden line' (abVAB) with incongruous content. The grand words *purpureus* and *Palati* enclose and conflict with the lowly words *ructarit* and *scurra*; the *u* sounds evoke belching; the oxymoron *purpureus . . . scurra* is typical of J., cf. 6.118 *meretrix Augusta*, 8.148 *mulio consul.*

On Crispinus' liking for purple clothes, 1.27n. Facetiously called the emperor's *scurra*, i.e. court jester (*OLD*; Corbett (1986), cf. 5.3–4n.), perhaps suggesting his subservience.   **ructarit**, i.e. *ructauerit*, 'belch', 3.107n., 6.10; cf. Plin. *Pan.* 49.6 *plenus ipse ⟨et⟩ eructans.* **Palati**: the imperial residence on the Palatine hill.

32–3 A past (*solebat*) – present (*iam*) contrast, in which the 'past' component reworks 24 *patria . . . papyro.* Being called a fishmonger was classic abuse (Plut. *Mor.* 631d), so should not be taken as evidence for Crispinus' profession.   **princeps equitum:** not an official title, cf. *equestris ordinis princeps* (Cic. *Fam.* 11.16.2, Vell. 2.127.3, Plin. *Ep.* 1.14.5). Crispinus perhaps held the highest position available to an *eques* (Suet. *Galb.* 14.2), prefect of the praetorian guard (*praefectus praetorio*), which would accord with the eminence of the other members of Domitian's *consilium* (mostly consular senators); the only other *eques*, Fuscus, was *praefectus praetorio* (111–12n.). Context renders the tone sarcastic, cf. 13.138–9 *gemma . . . princeps | sardonychum.*   **magna . . . uoce** 'in a loud voice'; for the loud voices of sellers cf. Sen. *Ep.* 56.2. **uendere:** a fine reversal: formerly Crispinus was selling fish, not buying them (22n.).   **municipes . . . siluros:** sardonic: both fish and fishmonger are from the Nile (Athen. 3.118f: *siluri* were pickled at

Alexandria). For this humorous use of *municeps* = 'compatriot', cf. 14.271 *municipes Iouis . . . lagonas*, Mart. 14.114 *testam | municipem misit . . . Sibylla suam.* **fracta de merce** 'from a damaged cargo' (Rudd), i.e. the lowest quality of fish; for *merx* cf. Lucil. 317M = 340W *sallere murenas, mercem in frigdaria ferre.* The reading *Pharia*, creating a pointed contrast with *Palati*, may be preferable to *fracta.*

34–154 The remainder of the poem is a mock-epic narrative describing how Domitian summons his *consilium* to advise him what to do with the enormous turbot which has been presented to him. After the invocation (34–6), it falls into three sections: 37–72 narrative of the catching and presentation of the fish; 72–118 catalogue of the members of Domitian's *consilium*; 119–49 narrative of the advice given and ensuing action; 150–4 constitute a coda. Parody is the central satiric strategy: parody of epic language; of a lost epic poem by Statius; and of the *consilium*: see Essay.

34–6 Epic-style invocations of the Muses, *incipe, Calliope* and *narrate, puellae Pierides*, mark the change of tone. Most editors fail to mark a new paragraph here. After the grand invocations, the mock-epic flavour emerges in incongruity at the expense of the Muses. On this technique of alternation, see Essay and Introduction §6(*c*). One or both of the invocations probably appeared in the lost poem of Statius here parodied by J. **incipe:** cf. Stat. *Theb.* 10.628–30 *memor incipe Clio.* **Calliope:** the Muse of epic, cf. Lucr. 6.94, Virg. *Aen.* 9.525, Stat. *Silv.* 3.1.50 *dic age, Calliope*, Sil. 3.222, 12.390; also Sulpicia 12. **licet et considere** 'and you may sit down'; poetry should be recited standing, cf. Ov. *Met.* 5.338–40 *surgit et inmissos hedera collecta capillos | Calliope querulas praetemptat pollice chordas | atque haec percussis subiungit carmina neruis.* The seated position suggests an inferior level of subject-matter. **non est | cantandum, res uera agitur:** cf. 7.152–3 *sedens . . . legerat, . . . stans . . . cantabit*: this is no recitation of elevated poetry but (allegedly) the truth. For the antithesis cf. Pers. 1.88–91 (*cantet si naufragus . . . , cantas cum . . . , nocte paratum* and *uerum*). For satiric claims to truth cf. Sen. *Apoc.* 1.1 *haec ita uera. agitur* = 'is the theme' (*OLD* 40). **narrate:** not a poetic word (*OLD*). **Pierides:** the Muses, associated with Pieria near Mount Olympus; cf. Lucr. 4.1, Virg. *Ecl.* 3.85 with Coleman. **prosit mihi** 'may it be to my advantage', typical of a prayer, cf. Sen. *H.F.* 117 *prosit mihi.* **puellas:** the last word delivers the joke, relating either (1) to the age (probably) or (2) to the virginity of the Muses: (1) the Muses have been inspiring the arts for many centuries and cannot be described as 'young girls'; (2) many Muses have produced offspring, e.g. Calliope Orpheus, and cannot be described as 'virgins'. If Statius' lost poem survived, the force of the joke would probably become clear (Townend (1973) 154).

37–72 The narrative of how a giant turbot is caught, brought and presented to Domitian, with particularly marked alternation between epic- and non-epic-sounding phrases.

37–44 A monstrous 8-line sentence, uncharacteristically long for the genre but matching the monstrous size of the turbot.

37–8 cum iam ... ultimus: epic vocabulary and structure (aVBA/bcVDC) conflicts with non-epic idea, Domitian mangling the world (cf. Plin. *Pan.* 48.3–5). *cum* + subj. is here 'historico–causal', see Deroux (1983) 286–8. For *cum iam* in epic cf. Stat. *Th.* 8.342–3 *cum iam Mauortia contra | cornua, iam saeuos fragor aereus excitat enses*. For mock-heroic *iam*, cf. Sen. *Apoc.* 2.1 and 2.4 with Eden and Sen. *Ep.* 122.12–13. *semianimum* has four syllables, the first *i* being consonantal; it has a strong epic pedigree: Enn. *Ann.* 502W = 484Sk, Virg. *Aen.* 11.635, Ov. *Met.* 5.105, Luc. 3.747, Stat. *Theb.* 6.220. For *laceraret ... orbem* cf. Petr. *Sat.* 121 line 121 *ad Stygios manes laceratus ducitur orbis*; for *lacero* in epic cf. Virg. *Aen.* 12.98, Stat. *Theb.* 5.366.   **Flavius ... ultimus:** i.e. Domitian, last of the three emperors of the Flavian *gens*, after Vespasian, his father, and Titus, his brother.

38 caluo ... Neroni: the bald Domitian wrote a book *de cura capillorum* (Suet. *Dom.* 18.2). He associated his own imperial identity with Nero's, e.g. Plin. *Pan.* 53.4, Mart. 11.33 where he is explicitly called Nero; both were the end of their respective dynasties.

39 incidit 'there turned up' (*OLD* 11); to suppose ellipse of [*in*] *sinus* from 41 seems harsh.   **Hadriaci spatium admirabile rhombi:** an epic-style periphrasis (on this use of the gen. see KS II.1 242, HS 152); for the same feature cf. 81 *Crispi iucunda senectus* and 107 *Montani ... uenter ... abdomine tardus*; recalling [Ov.] *Hal.* 125 *Hadriaco mirandus litore rhombus*. The turbot was an expensive mark of luxury, e.g. Hor. *Sat.* 2.2.95–6 *grandes rhombi patinaeque | grande ferunt una cum damno dedecus*. The best turbot came from Ravenna on the Adriatic (Plin. *N.H.* 9.19), about 100 miles north of Ancona. *Hadriacus* 'Adriatic' is the form favoured in hexameter verse, for metrical reasons. For *spatium* = 'extent, size' cf. J. 6.505, Ov. *Met.* 3.95 *spatium ... uicti ...*

hostis, Luc. 9.732. *admirabilis* invites amazement, cf. 13.53, Sil. 3.685 *admirabile dictu* and links with *monstrum* (2n.).

40 ante domum ... Ancon: the expansive description of the location is another epic-style touch. Ancona was founded in the fourth century BC by colonists fleeing from the tyrant Dionysius I of Syracuse, hence the adj. 'Doric'; cf. Sen. *H.F.* 81 *tellus ... Doris*, i.e. Sicily. Venus (as Aphrodite) was the city's goddess (cf. Cat. 36.13) and her temple stood on a hill, hence *sustinet*, 'supports'.

41 impleuit ... sinus: the fish is so big it 'fills the folds' of the net (*OLD sinus* 7b); the meaning 'bay' may create a glimmer of hyperbole (see Gowers (1993) 206).

41-4 The turbot's size is indicated by comparison with the fish that overwinter in the Sea of Azov; the excessively expansive description reflects its huge size. It is unclear whether *illis* (41) denotes turbot or other fish, e.g. tunny, central in Pliny's discussion of Black Sea fish (*N.H.* 9.50-3). For the description cf. Ov. *Tr.* 3.10.49-50 *uidimus in glacie pisces haerere ligatos,* | *sed pars ex illis tum quoque uiua fuit.* **neque enim minor haeserat illis** 'and it stuck there no smaller than those ...'. *minor* picks up *rhombi*, although neuter *spatium* demands *minus*. **Maeotica:** the Sea of Azov, the north-east part of the Black Sea, called *palus Maeotica*, lit. 'swamp'; its shallow water led to its freezing every winter. **ruptaque tandem | solibus** 'when finally broken by the sun', *rupta* agreeing with *glacies. soles* = sunlight or warmth (*OLD* 4). **effundit ... pingues:** the vigour of the water (*effundit, torrentis*) contrasts with the torpor of the fish (*desidia, tardos, pingues*). For the strong current flowing from the Black Sea cf. Sen. *N.Q.* 4.2.29 *Pontus ... fluit rapidus, semper pronus et torrens. ostia Ponti* (Ov. *Tr.* 1.10.13, Stat. *Th.* 6.328) denotes Byzantium, a major centre for fish, cf. Tac. *Ann.* 12.63 *uis piscium immensa, Pontum erumpens ... hos ad portus defertur*.

45-6 A succinct sentence with epic flavour. Calling the fisherman a 'master of dinghy and line' is incongruously grand, imitating *magister puppis* (e.g. Sil. 4.716-17). *pontifici summo* (dat. after *destinet*, 'earmark') denotes Domitian as Pontifex Maximus, an office held for life by all the emperors. It is ironically appropriate for the supreme religious official to examine any *monstrum*, 'prodigy' (2n.), which turns up (Deroux (1983) 290-1). Further irony resides in the reputation of the pontifical banquets for lavish food (Mart. 12.48.12, Hor. *Od.* 2.14.28 with Nisbet and Hubbard); Macrobius *Sat.* 3.13.10–13 provides an account of such a dinner. *monstrum* explicitly links the turbot with Crispinus (2).

46–56 Epic parody is abandoned temporarily for explicitly dark comments, in explanation (*enim*) of the fisherman's prompt decision.

46–8 An angry question, indicating that either sale or purchase of such a fish would be dangerous because of ubiquitous informers, hence *et litora*, 'even the beaches'.   **proponere** 'offer for sale', often with *uenalis*.   **multo | delatore:** singular for plural; the proliferation of informers is regularly associated with 'bad' emperors: Plin. *Pan.* 34–5, Suet. *Dom.* 12.1. On informers 1.33n., also Mayor on 4.48; here the supposed informers hope to curry favour with the emperor.

48–52 A sarcastic prediction of what would have happened had the fisherman dared to offer the fish for sale.   **dispersi:** lit. 'scattered', in effect, 'ubiquitous'.   **protinus** 'at once' cf. 3.140, with *agerent*.   **algae | inquisitores:** seaweed was proverbially worthless (Otto s.v., e.g. Hor. *Sat.* 2.5.8 *uilior alga*); the 'inspectors of seaweed' represent hyperbolically the pervasiveness of informing under Domitian (cf. Tac. *Ag.* 2.3 *inquisitiones*), while castigating the pettiness of such informers. *inquisitor* is here transferred from its technical usage, denoting the person appointed to collect evidence in a prosecution (*OLD* 2b).   **agerent cum:** i.e. lay a charge against; *TLL* 1396.23ff., e.g. Plaut. *Pseud.* 1231 *cras agam cum ciuibus*.   **nudo:** the fisherman is simultaneously stripped for work (i.e. with tunic removed; not entirely naked; cf. Peter at John 21.7) and without resources (cf. 5.163, 6.232) to combat the 'inspectors of seaweed'.   **non dubitaturi** 'would not have hesitated'; fut. participle, lit. 'not about to hesitate'.   **fugitiuum:** a runaway slave (Crook (1967) 186); the informers would declare the turbot (as anything else remarkable in the world, 54–5) part of the emperor's property. Cf. Mart. 4.30, where a fisherman is warned to avoid fishing from the Lucrine Lake at Baiae in which the fish are 'sacred'.   **depastumque diu** 'and one that had long grazed'.   **uiuaria:** 3.308n., cf. Plin. *N.H.* 9.167 and 10.193 *in Caesaris piscinis*.   **inde | elapsum:** asyndeton: 'and having escaped from there'.   **ueterem** = 'former', with *dominum*.   **dominum:** as at Mart. 4.30.4 (see above); again at 96. Cf. 5.49 and often.   **reuerti:** probably evokes the law concerning the restoration of runaways to their owners (see Griffith (1969) 149).

53–5 The speaker generalises: anything remarkable is liable to be claimed as the emperor's property. For this accusation against Domitian see Plin. *Pan.* 50 e.g. 50.2 *est quod Caesar non suum uideat*, 50.5 *tum exitialis erat apud principem huic laxior domus, illi amoenior uilla.*   **si quid Palfurio, si credimus Armillato** 'if we have any faith in Palfurius or Armillatus'. Probably informers (thus the scholiast), rather than jurists; their claim (54–5) is typically sycophantic (cf. *non dubitaturi* 50). For the oratorical skills of M. Palfurius Sura see Suet. *Dom.* 13.1; Armillatus is not known elsewhere.   **quidquid ... natat:** the grand phraseology conveys the informers' hyperbole; this is an extreme version of the practice of offering to the emperor anything found or acquired by chance (see D. Braund (1983)). On the reservation of the choicest fish for the tyrant/king see Davison (1993) 59–61, Gowers (1993) 202 n. 325. The hyperbole lies in assigning the emperor dominion over the sea, regarded as *commune* (*Dig.* 47.10.13.7), a point emphasised by *aequore toto* and (if Griffith is right, (1969) 149) by the adaptation of *ubicumque latet* to *ubicumque natat.*   **res fisci:** the *fiscus* is the imperial treasury, i.e. the emperor's personal property, cf. Sen. *Ben.* 7.6.3 *Caesar omnia habet, fiscus eius priuata tantum ac sua.*

55–6 The fisherman's necessarily (*ergo*) cynical thoughts are expressed succinctly.   **ne pereat** 'to prevent it going to waste' (Rudd), 1.18n., 3.124n.

56–69 The conveying and presentation of the fish to the emperor is narrated in epic-style diction.

56–9 The epic-style time-setting phrases introduced by *iam* and elevated vocabulary are deflated by incongruous elements. For a similar mock-epic periphrasis describing the season cf. Sen. *Apoc.* 2.1 (cf. repetition of *iam* in anaphora, imperfect tenses, ablative absolute, *deformis hiemps, autumni*; see Eden):

> iam Phoebus breuiore uia contraxerat ortum
> lucis, et obscuri crescebant tempora somni,
> iamque suum uictrix augebat Cynthia regnum,
> et deformis hiemps gratos carpebat honores
> diuitis autumni, iussoque senescere Baccho
> carpebat raras serus uindemitor uuas.

Cf. also Sen. *Ep.* 122.13, where the time-setting periphrasis is mocked for its verbosity.

The story is set in late October/early November. The autumn was a season dangerous to health because of the Sirocco (*auster*, 59), the warm south wind associated with fever: 6.517–18 *metui . . . iubet Septembris et austri | aduentum*, Hor. *Sat.* 2.6.18–19 *me . . . perdit . . . plumbeus Auster | autumnusque grauis, Libitinae quaestus acerbae, Od.* 2.14.15–16 with Nisbet and Hubbard, Cels. 2.1.1–2.   **letifero:** associated with epic poetry, e.g. Stat. *Th.* 1.707 *letifer annus, OLD.*   **quartanam:** understand *febrim*, i.e. a fever recurring every third day, an improvement (cf. 9.17, Cic. *Fam.* 16.11.1) from the *tertiana* which recurred every other day (the Romans counted inclusively) and therefore something for invalids to hope for (*sperantibus . . . aegris*); bathetic.   **stridebat deformis hiems:** epic: cf. Sil. 3.489 for *deformis hiems*; *strido* regularly denotes the whistling sound of winds, e.g. Luc. 9.113, V.Fl. 2.585, Stat. *Ach.* 2.20 *Noto stridente*. For the chill winds of winter cf. 9.67 *bruma spirante*.   **praedam . . . recentem | seruabat** 'kept the booty/ catch fresh'; the idea of the fish going off renders the tone mock-epic. On gourmets' obsession with freshness in fish see Sen. *N.Q.* 3.18 e.g. 2 *ideo cursu aduehebatur, ideo gerulis cum anhelitu et clamore properantibus dabatur uia.*   **tamen . . . auster:** if the fisherman (*hic*) does not present the fish himself, someone else will inform on him and his chance catch will go for nothing (*pereat* 56). The present tense *properat* conveys his urgency.

60–2 The fisherman's destination is Alba Longa in Latium, 13 miles south of Rome; Domitian spent much time in his villa here, e.g. Mart. 5.1.1 *collibus uteris Albae*, Stat. *Silv.* 5.2.168 *ab excelsis Troianae collibus Albae* and 4.2.65 with Coleman, cf. *Albanam . . . arcem* 145n. The length and arduousness of the fisherman's journey (Ancona to Alba is about 150 miles, across the Apennines) reflects the intense fear that permeates society under Domitian.

According to tradition Alba was founded by Aeneas' son Ascanius, hence *Troianum* (cf. 12.70–4: *Iulus, Phrygibus*), and destroyed by the Romans under the third king Tullus Hostilius (*diruta*), although the cult of Vesta survived (Liv. 1.29, Strabo 5.3.4). J.'s choice of words encapsulates the history of Alba.   **lacus:** cf. Hor. *Od.* 4.1.19 *Albanos . . . lacus*, the *lacus Albanus* and *lacus Nemorensis*, visible below (*suberant*) from the *via Appia* on the approach to Alba, which was on a hill, cf. 12.72 *sublimis apex.*   **quamquam** + adjective or participle (as here) is common in Silver Latin, cf. Plin. *Ep.* 1.12.3 *quamquam plurimas uiuendi causas habentem.*   **ignem Troianum, Vestam . . .**

minorem: the sacred fire which Aeneas carried from Troy to Italy and which Ascanius brought to Alba, Virg. *Aen.* 2.293–7 inc. *Vestam* and *aeternum ... ignem.* The temple of Vesta at Alba was smaller (*minorem*) than that at Rome. For the personification cf. Stat. *Silv.* 4.5.2 *prisca Teucros Alba colit lares.*   **obstitit intranti:** the verb's position emphasises that the fisherman is brought to a halt; dat. after *obstitit.* **miratrix turba:** cf. 5.21 *salutatrix ... turba,* 15.81 *uictrix turba;* an unusual word denoting the appropriate response to a *monstrum.* The senators (*patres* 64) are diminished by reference to them as a 'crowd'.

63–5 The fish is admitted to the imperial presence in preference to the senators; *obsonia* shifts the focus from the fisherman (*hic* 59) to the fish. Accessibility was a central issue in ancient kingship treatises: the 'good' ruler was typically *facilis aditu,* the 'bad' ruler secretive, reclusive and accessible only through intermediaries. Thus Seneca urges Nero to be *aditu accessuque facilis* (*Clem.* 1.13.4) and Pliny praises Trajan (*Pan.* 47.3): *in primis laudibus ferat admissionum tuarum facilitatem;* and criticises Domitian (*Pan.* 48.5): *non adire quisquam non adloqui audebat, tenebras semper secretumque captantem.* See Millar (1977) 465–77, Wallace-Hadrill (1982) 35, 42. The terms *exclusi* and *admissa* here are virtually technical terms, cf. Plin. *Pan.* 48.4 *admissis et exclusis. facili cardine* indicates Domitian's perversity: he shows *facilitas* towards the extra-ordinary fish but not towards his senators (*patres*). The pattern of the line graphically has the *exclusi ... patres* surrounding the *admissa obsonia.* Juxtaposition of *obsonia,* an unelevated word of the comic/satiric register (*OLD*), and *patres* emphasises the senators' humiliation.   **ut cessit** 'as it gave way', i.e. the *turba.*   **facili ... cardine:** taken from the amatory context at Hor. *Od.* 1.25.5–6 (*ianua*) *quae prius multum facilis mouebat* | *cardines* to indicate Domitian's passion for extraordinary luxury goods.   **ualuae:** esp. of the grand double doors in a palace, *OLD,* e.g. Pac. *Trag.* 360R^2 = *Inc.* 15W *pandite ualuas.*   **itur ad Atriden:** an epic impersonal passive verb, cf. 144 *surgitur; Atriden* figures Domitian as King Agamemnon of Homer's *Iliad.* On J.'s ironic use of Homeric names, 1.61n. *Atrides* may also evoke the portrayal of the fall of Agamemnon in tragedy, perhaps foreshadowing Domitian's fall at 153–4; cf. 6.660.

65–9 The fisherman's speech of flattery to the emperor. Use of direct speech in this narrative is sparing and occurs at climactic moments; thus the advice of the *consilium* is conveyed in reported

speech until 124–35 (Veiiento's opinion, Domitian's terse question and
Montanus' victorious suggestion).   **Picens:** i.e. the man from
Picenum, a grand way to refer to the fisherman; Ancona was just
within this district.   **priuatis maiora focis** '(a gift) too great for a
private hearth', i.e. the kitchen (*focus OLD* 1b) of a private citizen
(1.16n.); see Davison in 54–5n. For abl. of comparison, 3.203n.
genialis agatur | iste dies 'let this be a holiday', a day devoted to
Domitian's *genius*. The *genius* was a man's spirit, which was indulged on
special occasions, e.g. birthdays, cf. Pers. 2.3 *funde merum genio*; the
emperor's *genius* was an object of worship (*OLD genius* 2b).
propera stomachum laxare sagina 'hurry up and expand your
stomach by cramming'. The fisherman's suggestion imitates the metaphorical expression *animum laxare* (*OLD laxo* 7), 'relax', with mundane
substitution of *stomachum*. *sagina*, the food used to fatten up animals and
the small fry on which larger fish feed (Var. *R.R.* 3.17.7, Plin. *N.H.*
9.14), is similarly incongruous.   **tua seruatum ... in saecula**
'preserved to adorn your glorious epoch' (Rudd), vocabulary typical
of Golden Age imagery associated with each new reign, e.g. Sen. *Apoc.*
1.1 *initio saeculi felicissimi*, 4.1.9 *aurea ... saecula*, Tac. *Agr.* 44.5 *in hanc
beatissimi saeculi lucem*. Pliny at *Ep.* 4.11.6 (the trial of the Vestal Virgin,
above, 9–10n.) uses *saeculum suum* ironically to condemn Domitian's
cruelty, an irony pointed by Domitian's staging of the *ludi saeculares* in
88.   **ipse capi uoluit:** parody of claims such as Mart. 9.31.5–6 (a
goose offered to Mars for Domitian): *ipse suas anser properauit laetus ad
aras | et cecidit sanctis hostia parua focis*. It was a good omen if a sacrificial
victim was willing; the turbot is not precisely a sacrificial victim, but
the analogy is a flattering allusion to the emperor's divine status.

For imagery from fishing in the context of flattery – the emperor is as
ready to be 'hooked' (Gowers (1993) 208) – cf. Hor. *Sat.* 2.5.23–5, Sen.
Ben. 4.20.3.

69–71 The flattery is successful. The speaker utters an indignant
outburst against the fisherman followed by cynical condemnation of
Domitian.   **quid apertius?** 'What could be more blatant?' Cf.
Sen. *N.Q.* 4 pr. 9 *quo apertior est adulatio, quo improbior ... hoc citius
expugnat.*   **illi:** the emperor.   **cristae:** probably a proverb (listed
by Otto s.v.), although no classical analogues survive, which assimilates the emperor with a cockerel whose crest rises; cf. the opposite,
6.198 *subsidant pinnae.*

70–1 I.e. *nihil est quod dis-aequa-potestas non-possit credere-de-se cum-laudatur*: however insincere the flattery, it will be believed. The unusual caesura (see Introduction §8) determines that *dis aequa* goes most closely with *potestas*, but it may also be taken with *laudatur*, 'when power is praised [as being] equal to the gods'. **dis aequa potestas:** i.e. power equal to that of the gods; Rudd's 'virtually' is unnecessary. Cf. Pliny of Trajan, *principem quem aequata dis immortalibus potestas deceret* (*Pan.* 4.4). Domitian preferred to be known as *dominus et deus noster* (Suet. *Dom.* 13.2), e.g. Stat. *Silv.* 4.3.128 *hic est deus*. On imperial cult see Price (1984) esp. 234–48.

72–118 A catalogue of the members of Domitian's *consilium*, his council of advisers: eleven important men are named here (see Highet (1954) 259–61 for a detailed compendium; Vassileiou (1984) 48–59; references to Crook's prosopographical index (1955) are given below). Most emperors preferred to surround themselves with a group of powerful 'friends' (*amici Caesaris*) from whom they could seek advice: on the *consilium principis* see Crook in general and on this poem 50–1.

The catalogue is a feature of epic poetry, usually a catalogue of troops, also ships (Homer's *Iliad*). This catalogue constitutes epic parody, almost certainly of Statius' *De Bello Germanico*, now lost to us. The fragment which survives is quoted in the scholia to 4.94:

> lumina; Nestorei mitis prudentia Crispi
> et Fabius Veiento (potentem signat utrumque
> purpura, ter memores implerunt nomine fastos)
> et prope Caesareae confinis Acilius aulae.

'... lights/eyes; the gentle wisdom of Nestor-like Crispus, and Fabius Veiento – the purple marks each as eminent, three times have they filled the recording annals with their names – and Acilius, near neighbour of Caesar's palace'.

The fragment names three of the same advisers and is evidently part of a longer catalogue; moreover, J.'s use of an epic periphrasis in the case of Crispus (*Crispi iucunda senectus*, 81) indicates intertextuality. This poem is probably the one with which Statius won the prize at the contest held at Alba by Domitian (AD 90: see Coleman xvii), which he mentions at *Silv.* 4.2.65–7: *Troianae ... sub collibus Albae, | cum modo Germanas acies modo Daca sonantem | proelia Palladio tua me manus induit auro.* In Statius' epic poem, the members of the *consilium* were presumably summoned for serious debate on a matter of military urgency (lines 147–9 of Satire 4 hint as much).

72 sed resumes the narrative of the fish.   **patinae mensura:** i.e. a dish big enough; *patina* again 133. Cf. Hor. *Sat.* 2.2.95 *grandes rhombi patinaeque*, Mart. 13.81 *quamuis lata gerat patella rhombum,* | *rhombus latior est tamen patella.* A gourmet might think it outrageous to serve a large fish on a plate too small: Hor. *Sat.* 2.4.76–7 *immane est uitium dare milia terna macello* | *angustoque uagos piscis urgere catino.*

72–5 Domitian's *consilium* is therefore summoned early in the day to Alba to advise on this crisis. Cf. Plin. *Ep.* 4.11.6 *pontifices non in Regiam sed in Albanam uillam conuocauit*: the location and timing of the meeting is part of Domitian's tyrannical humiliation (on the unexpected morning summons see 108n.). The relationship between emperor and courtiers is portrayed as one of loathing and fear, a classic feature associated with a tyrant, cf. *oderint dum metuant*, 'let them hate me so long as they fear me', a line of Accius quoted at Cic. *Off.* 1.97; cf. *Off.* 2.23 *quem metuont oderunt* (= *TRF* 379). There is ring composition with 144–5, the dismissal of the *consilium*. The passive verbs separate Domitian from the action and reflect his self-elevation to a higher plane.   **proceres:** 3.213n., also 2.121; a grand word, cf. Virg. *Aen.* 6.489 *Danaum proceres Agamemnoniaeque phalanges*, denoting the 'leading men' at e.g. Plin. *Pan.* 26.6.   **quos oderat ille:** Domitian's hatred implies scorn and perhaps fear (cf. Cic. *Off.* 2.24–5 on the mutuality of fear). Ironically these *amici Caesaris* (cf. 75) are *inimici*. *ille* = Domitian (cf. 69): the pronoun conveys hostility.   **facie:** English would require 'faces'.   **miserae magnaeque ... amicitiae:** i.e. friendship with the great which is 'miserable' because dangerous; cf. *magni ... amici* 1.33n. The relationship between emperor and advisers here termed *amicitia* is one manifestation of a relationship central to Roman society: see Introduction §9(b). See Plin. *Pan.* 85.1–2 on the withering of *amicitia* under Domitian, e.g. *in principum domo nomen tantum amicitiae, inane scilicet inrisumque remanebat*; cf. Tacitus on the fear induced by Nero's friendship, *nec minus sibi anxiam talem amicitiam quam aliis exilium* (*Hist.* 4.8).   **sedebat | pallor:** cf. Ov. *Met.* 2.775 *pallor in ore sedet.* According to Tacitus, Domitian watched for people to change complexion: *denotandis tot hominum palloribus* (*Ag.* 45.2). Pliny contrasts life under Trajan with life under Domitian (*Pan.* 48.1): *itaque non albi* [Madvig] *et attoniti* (cf. 146 below) ... *sed securi et hilares*. Cf. Hor. *Ep.* 1.1.61: the best life is *nulla pallescere culpa*.

75–81 Adviser no. 1: Plotius Pegasus. (Crook no. 251; *PIR*[1], P 164.) An eminent jurist of whose writings fragments survive (see Courtney's n.), consul under Vespasian, governor of provinces and prefect of the city at some date (Syme (1958) 805): i.e. an aristocrat who attained high office and eminence in the most respected profession.

Pegasus' speed and eagerness to respond to the emperor's summons is emphasised: by initial position of *primus*; by present participle *clamante*: 'while the slave was [still] shouting ...' (abl. abs.); by the second ablative absolute *rapta ... abolla* (he grabs his cloak without pausing to put it on) and by *properabat*.

75 Liburno: an Illyrian slave serving as usher, cf. Mart. 1.49.33 with Howell.

76 abolla: 3.115n.

77 attonitae ... Vrbi: Rome's 'astonishment' is caused by Domitian's reign of terror, the appropriate reaction to a *monstrum*. The advisers themselves will be labelled *attonitos* at 146. **positus modo uilicus Vrbi:** satirical reference to the *praefectus Vrbi*, a magistracy held by a senator whose duty was to keep order in the city with his own court of law and a standing police force (*cohortes urbanae*); see Tac. *Ann.* 6.10–11. A *uilicus* was a slave (3.228n.), hence Rome is presented as Domitian's household controlled by his chief slave, cf. 38 *caluo seruiret Roma Neroni*. *positus* = 'appointed' (*OLD pono* 12b).

78–81 A parenthesis, providing a brief character-sketch of Pegasus as a good man but weak because of his fear of Domitian. 'Well, what else were the prefects then, [given that] the best of them and the most upright of jurists thought, as is natural in terrible times, that every case should be handled by justice unarmed?' The text follows Courtney in adopting Housman's suggestion *quippe*; this gives the required sense, unlike the transmitted *quamquam*. **praefecti:** the plural refers to Pegasus' predecessors in the post and/or to the other positions *praefectus annonae, praefectus praetorio, praefectus uigilum*. **interpres legum:** again at 6.544. **temporibus diris:** the same phrase, of Nero's reign, 10.15; cf. 151 below *tempora saeuitiae*. Contrast Mart. 12.6.11–12 *sed tu sub principe duro | temporibusque malis ausus es esse bonus*. **inermi | iustitia:** justice without a sword, her conventional accoutrement (*LIMC* III.1 390. 7–9), is justice without any impact on the criminality rife under Domitian; 'unarmed justice' is the manifestation of Pegasus' servility.

81–93 Adviser no. 2: Quintus Vibius Crispus. (Crook no. 340; *PIR*[1], V 379.) A rich and eminent man, consul three times, governor of Africa around 71 and a survivor in the company of emperors. Tacitus places him *pecunia potentia ingenio inter claros magis quam inter bonos* (*Hist.* 2.10) and praises his eloquence (*Dial.* 8); Quintilian also praises his wit: *uir ingenii iucundi et elegantis* (*I.O.* 5.13.48) and *compositus et iucundus et delectationi natus* (10.1.119); for an example see Suet. *Dom.* 3.1.

81 Crispi iucunda senectus: a grand epic-style periphrasis (39n.), evidently a parody of Statius' phrase *Nestorei mitis prudentia Crispi* (72–118n.): both refer to his gentleness and old age. Crispus' *iucunditas* is mentioned by Quintilian (*I.O.* 12.10.11, also previous note). Translate 'pleasant old Crispus'.

82 cuius erant mores qualis facundia 'whose moral character was like his eloquence', an inversion of Sen. *Ep.* 114.1 *talis hominibus fuit oratio qualis uita.* See Bramble (1974) 23–5.

82–3 mite | ingenium 'a gentle soul' (Rudd), in apposition to *Crispi iucunda senectus*; *mite* is inspired by Statius, see 81n. Crispus is as weak as Pegasus, see 89–91.

83 maria ac terras populosque regenti: cf. Pliny on the ideal emperor *cuius dicione nutuque maria, terrae, pax, bella regerentur* (*Pan.* 4.4).

84 quis comes utilior 'Who would have been a more useful companion?'. *comites* denoted the emperor's *amici* who accompanied him (Crook (1955) 24–5), developed from the practice of provincial governors (3.47n.). **clade et peste:** literally 'disaster' and 'plague', strong words of abuse, combined at Cic. *Prov. Cons.* 13 *pestes sociorum, militum clades*; cf. [Sen.] *Oct.* 240 *pestis* of Nero; Pliny's abuse of Domitian at *Pan.* 48.3 *immanissima belua.*

85 saeuitiam: the classic mark of the tyrant, hence *tempora saeuitiae* (151); the opposite is *clementia*, e.g. Seneca's *De Clementia* addressed to Nero. See Braund (1993) 65–7. **liceret** 'he had been allowed', imperf. for plupf. subj.

85–6 honestum … consilium 'honourable advice', the function of the council of advisers (*consilium*) under an ideal emperor.

86 sed quid uiolentius aure tyranni 'But what is more savage than the ear of a tyrant …': explicit condemnation of Domitian's style of kingship. *uiolentia*, arbitrary aggression, is another hallmark of the tyrant.

87–8 cum quo ... amici: lit. 'with whom hung in the balance the fate of a friend about to talk about the rain or the heat or the showery spring'. The future participle functions as a conditional clause, 'even if he were simply to talk ...'. On the triteness of weather-talk see Sen. *Ep.* 67.1; Sen. *Ep.* 23.1 *ineptias*. On the dangers of even trivial conversations because of informers cf. Tac. *Ann.* 6.7 *perinde in foro, in conuiuio, quaqua de re locuti incusabantur*. For weather imagery of the emperor's potential for unexpected outbursts of anger, cf. Plin. *Pan.* 66.3 *erant sub oculis naufragia multorum, quos insidiosa tranquillitate prouectos improuisus turbo perculerat*. The spondaic line-ending of 87 (*aut nimboso*) may sound sinister. *amici* is reserved for final position, emphasising the dubious nature of 'friendship' with the emperor.

Spring showers are a feature of Italian weather, cf. 5.78–9, 9.51 *madidum uer*, Sen. *N.Q.* 4.4.2 quoting Virg. *Georg.* 1.313 *imbriferum uer*. For *cum quo* 9n. For *fatum pendebat* cf. Luc. 6.632 *fata ... pendent*.

89 ille: Crispus.

89–90 derexit bracchia contra | torrentem: i.e. swam against the stream, a proverbial idea, Otto *flumen* 7 and *Nachträge* 163, cf. Fronto II 46 Haines = 133 van den Hout *aduerso, quod aiunt, flumine*. *torrentem* implies that Domitian's power is irresistible.

90 nec ciuis erat qui 'and he was not a citizen who ...'. *ciuis* is used intensively to mean 'good citizen', 'patriot', 'real Roman', cf. Tac. *Ann.* 12.11 *ut non dominationem et seruos, sed rectorem et ciues cogitaret*. **qui ... posset:** generic subj. (Woodcock § 155–9), i.e. 'of the sort who'.

90–1 libera ... uerba animi: freedom of speech is one of the first casualties under tyranny. On freedom, a major theme of Book 1, see Introduction §9(*b*).

91 uitam impendere uero 'risk his life for the truth', cf. Luc. 2.382 *patriae ... impendere uitam*.

92–3 I.e. he survived life at court to the age of eighty by not speaking his mind. For the combination of *hiemes* and *solstitia* cf. Virg. *Georg.* 1.100. *octogensima ... solstitia* (lit. 'eightieth summers'), probably poetic plural.   **his armis** 'with this armour'; the military metaphor is sarcastic.   **quoque:** with *illa ... in aula*, 'even'.   **aula:** often in contexts of danger and despotism, e.g. Tac. *Hist.* 1.7 *eadem ... nouae aulae mala*; J. echoes Luc. 10.55 *Pellaea tutus in aula*.

94–103 Advisers nos. 3 and 4: the Acilii, father and son, members of an eminent plebeian family which claimed descent from Aeneas

(Herodian 2.3.4). (Crook nos. 2 and 3; *PIR*[2], A 49,62.) The father may be M'. Acilius Aviola, consul AD 54 and member of Claudius' *consilium* (Crook (1955) 44). The son, M'. Acilius Glabrio, was consul with Trajan in AD 91, but was exiled and executed in 95 (Suet. *Dom.* 10.2).

The epic-style expansiveness of the first two items in the catalogue is continued; *proximus* (i.e. next to Crispus) is a reminder of the catalogue format.

The (future) execution of the younger Acilius conveys criticism of Domitian for his removal of eminent men. A ruler's tolerance of the noble, wealthy and able (i.e. of potential rivals) is a standard feature of treatises concerning kingship; hence Pliny's praise of Trajan for choosing *amicos ex optimis* (*Pan.* 45.3) and Seneca's criticism of Claudius for his executions of members of the élite (*Apoc.* 11.5, 13.5, 14.1).

94 eiusdem ... aeui: of the same age as Crispus: Acilius is another survivor.   **properabat:** for the fourth time in Satire 4: 59 (of the fisherman), 67 (spoken by the fisherman), 76 (of Pegasus); again 134 (like 67, addressed to Domitian); cf. *festinare* 146.

95 iuuene indigno quem mors tam saeua maneret: lit. 'the undeserving young man whom a death so savage would await', i.e. 'the young man who did not deserve the death so savage which would await him'. Dio attributes Domitian's execution of Acilius Glabrio to jealousy of his prowess in fighting wild beasts in the arena (67.14.3); see below on 99–101. *iuuene* serves for *filio*, impossible in hexameter verse (again 10.310).

96 domini: like a slave-owner, cf. Plin. *Pan.* 2.3, 7.6 *non seruulis ... dominum ... sed principem ciuibus ... et imperatorem. dominus* was a title adopted by Domitian: Suet. *Dom.* 13.2.

96–7 Cf. Sen. *Ira* 2.33.2 *notissima uox est eius qui in cultu regum consenuerat. cum illum quidam interrogaret quomodo rarissimam rem in aula consecutus esset, senectutem, 'iniurias,' inquit, 'accipiendo et gratias agendo.'* Similar is Tacitus' cynical comment on the rarity of a natural death (*Ann.* 6.10). *in nobilitate senectus* is a paradox epitomising life under a tyrant; cf. *nobilitate comesa* 1.34n.   **olim ... est** 'has long been' (and still is).   **prodigio:** dat. after *par*, according with the theme of *monstra* (2n.).

98 An unusual personal intervention (*malim*) into the epic-style narrative. The speaker declares that he would therefore (*unde fit*) prefer to be a nobody. *fraterculus ... gigantis* is a contrived circumlocution for the proverbial *terrae filius*, 'son of the earth', meaning 'a nobody' (Otto *terra* 2, e.g. Petr. *Sat.* 43, Pers. 6.59, cf. Pers. 6.57 for another satiric variant, *progenies terrae*); 'little brother of a giant' functions in that the Giants of mythology were sons of Ge, the Greek goddess equivalent to *Terra* (*filii Terras*, Naevius, *Pun.* 46W).

99–101 The younger Acilius' efforts at pleasing Domitian by self-humiliation were therefore useless (*profuit ergo nihil*). For Acilius' appearance in beast-fights held at Alba (*Albana … harena*), see Dio 67.14.3 (he killed a lion without injury to himself). Whether or not such appearances were voluntary, they brought disgrace: 2.143–8n.; a beast-fighter (*uenator*) was considered lower in status than a gladiator (1.22–3n.), hence the forceful enjambment of *uenator*.   **misero:** dative after *profuit*, 'to the unfortunate man'.   **quod** '[the fact] that …'; the entire *quod* clause is the subject of *profuit* (*OLD prosum* 2b). **ursos … Numidas:** on bears in beast-fights see Toynbee (1973) 93–100. The noun *Numida* (African) is used adjectivally, cf. Ov. *A.A.* 2.183 *Numidas … leones*.   **Albana … harena:** Domitian himself performed in beast-fights at his amphitheatre at his Alban villa (Suet. *Dom.* 19; cf. 4.4).   **nudus … uenator:** display of the body, esp. the face, exacerbated the disgrace for a noble in the arena, cf. 1.23 *nuda … mamma*, 6.O12, 8.205 *nudum … uoltum* and 2.143–8n.

101–3 Such tricks by the nobility to curry favour are unsuccessful because everyone is familiar with them; hence the premature death of the younger Acilius (95–6). The two rhetorical questions invite the answer, 'No one.'   **quis enim … patricias?** 'For who these days would not recognise the tricks of the nobles?' For *artes* = 'tricks, ruses' cf. 7.36. For *patricias* = 'noble' see 1.24n.   **quis … miratur** 'Who is amazed at … ?', the indicative bolder than the subjunctive *intellegat* (101). This links with the theme of marvels (cf. *miratrix* 62); here, unusually, the speaker's cynicism denies the element of amazement. **Brute:** Lucius Junius Brutus, traditionally the founder and first consul of the Roman Republic in 509 BC, following his expulsion of the kings. His *cognomen* Brutus is said to have come from his pretending to be 'stupid' to escape the attention of the Tarquin rulers (Liv. 1.56.7–8). The juxtaposition of *acumen* and *Brute* is an oxymoron: 'sharpness' and 'bluntness'; Accius quoted at Cic. *Div.* 1.45 = *TRF praet.* 32 calls Brutus *hebetem*.   **facile est barbato imponere regi** 'it is easy to fool a bearded king' (*OLD impono* 16, + dative, cf. Sen. *Apoc.* 6.1 *imposuerat*

Herculi minime uafro), i.e. Tarquin, as opposed to Domitian; an old-time king as opposed to the (then) contemporary ruler. For the beard as a mark of the early Romans cf. 16.31–2 *et credam dignum barba dignumque capillis | maiorum*; 5.30 *capillato ... consule*. On the Roman history of shaving see Var. *R.R.* 2.11.10 and Plin. *N.H.* 7.211: from the third century BC it was the convention and fashion to shave (3.186n.), until Hadrian popularised beards once more.

104–6 Adviser no. 5: Rubrius Gallus, a military man and another survivor. (Crook no. 285; *PIR*[1], R 94.) He first comes to notice during the civil wars of AD 68–9, when he fought as general for Nero against Galba, for Otho against Vitellius and for Vespasian (Tac. *Hist.* 2.51, 99).

After the expansive catalogue of the first four members of the *consilium*, the remaining seven are dealt with more succinctly, continuing the same themes of terror, weakness and corruption.

104 nec melior ... ignobilis 'looking just as ghastly in spite of his humble background' (Rudd) (*nec* closely with *melior*). I.e. although Rubrius is less eminent in birth than the others (94–103n.), he has the same look of fear on his face (cf. *magnae ... pallor amicitiae* 74–5n.). **ibat:** the advisers are still rushing into Domitian's presence.

105 offensae ueteris reus: the 'ancient offence' Rubrius supposedly committed (Σ) was the seduction of Domitia, presumably the empress, when she was a child. Cf. Crispinus' sexual offence (cf. 3–4n., 8–10).   **tacendae** 'which must not be mentioned'. Rubrius' guilt puts him in Domitian's power. Guilty secrets are prominent in satire, cf. 3.49–54nn.; cf. the secret in Persius 1 (with Reckford (1962) 483, 500–1, Bramble (1974) 136–7).

106 'and yet with all the nerve of a sodomite writing satire' (Rudd). Rubrius is described as shameless nevertheless (*tamen*): presumably he either brags about the crime which should not be mentioned or flagrantly attracts attention in other ways. On *improbitas* see 3.282n. *saturam scribente cinaedo* constitutes a paradox, almost an oxymoron: a *cinaedus* (2.10n.) writing satire (in which *cinaedi* might be the victims of attack) is chosen as a striking instantiation of hypocrisy (here *improbitas*), which Rubrius is alleged to exceed.

The fleeting self-referentiality here in 'writing satire' affirms the robust masculinity of the speaker, who evidently regards 'a sodomite writing satire' as far removed from his self-image.

107–18 The remainder of the advisers are introduced in one largely paratactic sentence, *et* (108), *saeuior illo* (109), *et* (111), *et* (113), *cum* (113), thus speeding through the catalogue with narrative ease. Those dealt with most briefly play the most prominent part in advising Domitian in the final section of the poem: Catullus, Veiiento and Montanus (the last two in direct speech).

107 Adviser no. 6: Montanus, specific identity uncertain. (Crook no. 232; *PIR*[1], J 512; M 494.) Possibly Curtius Montanus, influential with Nero (Tac. *Ann.* 16.33); cf. 136–9: evidently another imperial survivor. He is presented as a long-time gourmand (136–43nn.), hence his paunch: he represents the luxurious side of court life.

Another epic-style periphrasis, 39n., 81n., deflated by the mundane words and picture: 'Montanus' belly too is present, slow because of his paunch'; *abdomine* abl. of cause, cf. Stat. *Theb.* 2.8 *uulnere tardus*. For a similar effect cf. 6.326 *Nestoris hirnea*.

108–9 Adviser no. 7: Crispinus. (Crook no. 129; *PIR*[2], C 1586.) The object of attack in the opening lines (1–33) is a member of the *consilium* catalogued in less than two lines. On Crispinus see 1.26–8n., 4.1–3n. To the earlier attack on his sexual depravity (1–10) and self-indulgent gluttony (11–33) is added another manifestation of *luxuria*, Crispinus' excessive use of perfume, cf. Sen. *Ep.* 86.13. The excess is conveyed primarily by *matutino ... amomo* (for *mane*, 1.28n.): the use of perfumes, along with garlands of flowers etc., was associated with the *cena* and *comissatio* held in the afternoon/evening, cf. 9.128, 11.122. *amomum* was an eastern perfume and a symbol of leisurely self-indulgence, e.g. 8.159, Mart. 5.64.3. *matutino* implies that the *consilium* is called in the morning, which would take the advisers by surprise. The largely spondaic line conveys Crispinus' leisurely response to Domitian's summons.   **sudans:** cf. *digitis sudantibus* 1.28n.   **quantum uix redolent duo funera:** lit. 'to the extent two funerals hardly smell of', i.e. 'more overpoweringly than two funerals', or possibly 'corpses'. For lavish use of perfume at Roman funerals, a necessity, to conceal the smell of putrefaction, cf. Pers. 3.104 *compositus lecto crassisque lutatus amomis*, Stat. *Silv.* 2.4.34 *Assyrio cineres adolentur amomo*.

109–10 Adviser no. 8: Pompeius, characterised here as an informer; possibly one of the Pompeii who had held or were soon to hold consular office. (Crook no. 266; *PIR*[1], P 461.) Back to the terror, danger and cruelty of court life.   **saeuior illo ... aperire:** abl. of comparison; for *saeuus* + infin. cf. Hor. *Ep.* 1.15.30 *quaelibet in quemuis opprobria fingere saeuus*; Sil. 11.7 *saeuior ante alios iras seruasse repostas*. Like the other advisers, Pompeius reflects Domitian's character; on Domitian's cruelty (*saeuitas*) see 85n.   **tenui iugulos aperire susurro:** Pompeius' *saeuitas* is expressed graphically, as if he slit throats personally; cf. 3.37n. For *aperire iugulum* cf. Sen. *Ira* 1.2.2; also *fuste aperire caput* J. 9.98; on the elevated tone see Duff. On the power of whispers into an autocrat's ear cf. 86 *quid uiolentius aure tyranni?* and Plin. *Pan.* 62.9 *huic aures huic oculos intende: ne respexeris clandestinas existimationes nullisque magis quam audientibus insidiantes susurros*. Adj. *tenui* creates expectation of 'dagger', hence *susurro* is a surprise.

111–12 Adviser no. 9: Cornelius Fuscus. (Crook no. 113; *PIR*², C 1365.) Another military man, another survivor and the second *eques* in the catalogue; he renounced senatorial for equestrian status early in his career, supported Galba and Vespasian (Tac. *Hist.* 2.86) and was appointed *praefectus praetorio* (32n.) by Domitian. He was (later) killed by the Dacians (hence line 111) while leading the Roman army against them in AD 86–7 (Suet. *Dom.* 6.1; cf. Mart. 6.76: an epitaph).

Postponement of *Fuscus* until after the relative clause is unusual, providing variation in the catalogue sequence.   **qui uulturibus seruabat uiscera Dacis:** Fuscus is diminished both by the allusion to his (future) defeat and by evocation of unburied corpses on the battlefield as vulture fodder.   **marmorea meditatus proelia uilla:** he is further diminished as an armchair general. For *meditatus proelia* cf. 7.128 (of a decrepit military statue). His luxurious 'marble villa' is like a premature tomb, cf. 7.79–80 *iaceat Lucanus in hortis | marmoreis* with Rudd (1976) 100.

113–18 Advisers nos. 10 and 11: Aulus Didius Gallus Fabricius Veiiento and Lucius Valerius Catullus Messalinus: the two most dangerous men, appropriately enough interwoven in 113, form the climax to the catalogue. (Crook no. 148; *PIR*², F 91 and Crook no. 328; *PIR*¹, V 41.) Catullus will be the first to offer advice (119–22) and Veiiento will immediately compete with him (123–9). The two are mentioned together at Plin. *Ep.* 4.22.4 and [Aurelius Victor] *Epit.* 12.5.

Fabricius Veiiento (perhaps the same as 3.185) was another survivor in imperial circles: an *amicus* of Nero, Domitian, Nerva (Pliny above) and Trajan (Plin. *Pan.* 58.1 with Syme (1979) 8 n.2) and consul three times (discussed by Syme (1991) 532–4); one of the three advisers named in the fragment of Statius (72–118n.) where he is called Fabius Veiiento instead of Fabricius in an allusion to his Fabian-type caution (hence *prudens* 113): see Bücheler (1884) 283.

Catullus Messalinus twice held the consulship with Domitian (AD 73 and 85); presented as an informer in several texts. For his influence with Domitian cf. Tac. *Agr.* 45 *intra Albanam arcem sententia Messalini strepebat*; for his blindness and cruelty cf. Plin. *Ep.* 4.22.5 *luminibus orbatus ingenio saeuo mala caecitatis addiderat: non uerebatur, non erubescebat, non miserebatur; quo saepius a Domitiano non secus ac tela, quae et ipsa caeca et improuida feruntur, in optimum quemque contorquebatur*. Had he survived Domitian, he might have been one of Nerva's advisers, *ibid.* 6 *de huius nequitia sanguinariisque sententiis in commune omnes super cenam loquebatur, cum ipse imperator: 'quid putamus passurum fuisse si uiueret?' et Mauricus: 'nobiscum cenaret'*.

This Catullus may be a descendant of the Republican poet (see Wiseman (1987) 361–6); on J.'s allusions to the Catullan tradition here see LaFleur (1974a) 73–4.

113 mortifero: very rarely of a person (in classical literature only here and 9.95: see *OLD*, *TLL* 1518.36).

114 'Who blazed with passion for a girl he had never seen.' *numquam* goes closely with *uisam*. For mockery of blind lovers cf. Mart. 3.15, 8.49, *Anth. Lat.* 357.

115 The deadly informer is singled out as 'a great and remarkable prodigy even in our age', an age full of *monstra; monstrum* (2n., 45) sets Catullus on a par with Crispinus and the giant turbot. Ironically, though blind himself, he is the centre of attention, *conspicuum*. For *grande . . . monstrum* cf. 6.645 *grandia monstra*; J. recalls the Cyclops at Virg. *Aen.* 3.658 *monstrum horrendum, informe, cui lumen ademptum*.

116 Although *caecus adulator* and *dirus . . . satelles* appear to be oxymora characteristic of J. (cf. 31 *purpureus . . . scurra*, 6.118 *meretrix Augusta*, 8.148 *mulio consul*), the line is probably an interpolation formed from material glossing what precedes and/or what follows (see Courtney for a full discussion). This proposal has the merit of removing the unsolved textual problem in *a ponte*.

117 dignus ... qui mendicaret 'who deserved to be a beggar'. The comparison, drawn from the opposite end of the social scale, emphasises Catullus' servility towards Domitian; cf. 5.8–11.   **Arici-nos ... ad axes:** carriages approaching Aricia on the via Appia had to pass down a steep hill very slowly, thus affording ample opportunity for beggars. For beggars on hills cf. Pers. 6.56; at Aricia cf. Mart. 2.19.3.

118 blanda ... iactaret basia: a beggar would 'blow obsequious kisses' in gratitude for the alms given him; cf. Tac. *Hist.* 1.36 *nec deerat Otho ... iacere oscula et omnia seruiliter pro dominatione.* The adj. *blanda* denotes the beggar's (and Catullus') desire to ingratiate himself, cf. 6.125, 9.36. Possibly an echo of Pers. 4.15 *blando caudam iactare popello*, given the ingratiating -*ll*- sound in the lines describing Catullus. The abVAB structure conflicts with the subject-matter.   **deuexae ... raedae:** i.e. travelling down the hill to Aricia: see above.

119–54 J. glides almost invisibly into the final section of the poem, a narrative of the advice given at the *consilium*. Use of direct speech marks the climax of the deliberations of the *consilium* (124–35; see 65–9n.). Epic parody continues in the allusions to procedure (see 130n., 136n., 144–5).

119–22 Catullus links the catalogue and the account of the advice given by the members of the *consilium*: the last to arrive is the first to utter advice. There is no explication of the nature of the 'crisis' for which the advisers have been summoned, which makes the narrative economical.   **rhombum stupuit:** the fish is mentioned again in the resumption of narrative from 71. For *stupeo* + acc. cf. 13.16 *stupet haec* and 164; here probably with the ring of epic. For Catullus' reaction of 'amazement' cf. *admirabile* 39n., *miratur* 102n.   **plurima dixit:** like *nemo magis*, indicates that Catullus was the most fulsome of all the speakers.   **laeuum:** Catullus' mistake appropriately involves turning to the left, since this side was usually thought unlucky by the Romans, cf. *OLD* 4.   **at:** marks the change in tone to ironic commentary; virtually 'unfortunately', cf. Cic. *Att.* 7.21.2.   **illi:** Catullus; dative, indicating his disadvantage.   **belua** 'beast, monster', repeated by Veiiento at 127, implying the abnormal size of the fish, cf. *monstrum* 45. Enjambment increases its impact.   **sic ... laudabat** 'that's the way he used to praise', i.e. Catullus had a habit of eulogy of things he could not see.   **Cilicis:** evidently a type of gladiator from Cilicia, cf. *Thraex* and *Syrus* Hor. *Sat.* 2.6.44.   **ictus:** the 'thrusts' of the gladiator as he fought, cf. 6.261 *monstratos perferat ictus.*   **pegma et pueros inde ad uelaria raptos:** the *pegma* was a wooden platform used for theatrical effects involving height and flying, Sen. *Ep.* 88.22 *pegmata per se crescentia*, Mart. *Spect.* 2.2 *crescunt media pegmata celsa uia*, hence the 'boys whisked up to the awning', the actors/acrobats playing the relevant parts, e.g. Icarus (Suet. *Ner.* 12.2). *uela* is the more usual word for the awnings hung across the amphitheatre to protect the audience from the sun's heat.

123–9 Veiiento does not yield (*non cedit*). To surpass the blind man's praise he bursts into prophecy (*diuinat*), boldly addressing the emperor directly (*habes, capies, cernis*). J.'s use of direct speech (124–8) is an epic touch.

123–4 ut fanaticus oestro | percussus, Bellona, tuo diuinat: Veiiento is compared with a priest of Bellona in a frenzied trance. The name Bellona, the Roman goddess of war, was given to the Cappadocian goddess Ma, whose followers were called *fanatici* (from *fanum*, 'temple'). Her cult involved noise, ecstasy and self-mutilation. Cf. 6.511–12 *ecce furentis | Bellonae matrisque deum chorus intrat* and 517 *grande sonat*; Tib. 1.6.45–50 *ubi Bellonae motu est agitata ... canit*; Luc. 1.56–6 *quos sectis Bellona lacertis | saeua mouet cecinere deos*. Apostrophe of Bellona is an epic-style touch. The language of inspiration here is also associated with Bacchus, e.g. *percussus* cf. Lucr. 1.922–3 *acri | percussit thyrso laudis spes magna meum cor*, Sen. *Oed.* 442 *thyades oestro membra remissae*. J.'s wording recalls Livy's description of the Bacchanalian frenzy which overtook Rome in 186 BC, e.g. *uiros, uelut mente capta, cum iactatione fanatica corporis uaticinari* (Liv. 39.13.12).

124–5 As befits a prophet, Veiiento interprets the giant turbot as an omen, with size again prominent (*ingens, magni*). *triumphus* here denotes both 'victory' and, more specifically, the triumphal procession through Rome in which the emperor would parade his captives and spoils.

126–7 More specifically, Veiiento foresees the capture of a king (*regem aliquem*) or the defeat of Arviragus in Britain. Arviragus is otherwise unknown in classical texts; in Geoffrey of Monmouth (4.16) he is one of Cymbeline's sons, which fits the dramatic date of this poem, when there was considerable interest in Roman involvement in Britain, during the governorship of Agricola.   **de temone Britanno:** the Britons fought by running out upon the pole of the chariot, Caes. *B.G.* 4.33 *per temonem percurrere ... consuerint.*

127–8 The appearance of the turbot is 'proof' of Veiiento's prophecy: like the king Domitian will conquer, the turbot is foreign (*peregrina*) and hostile (*erectas ... sudes*).   **peregrina:** though caught off Ancona (39–40), the fish is alleged to be of foreign origin. **erectas in terga sudes** 'the spikes that march up his spine' (Rudd): the spiky dorsal fins are referred to as weapons (*sudes* = 'stakes' or 'pikes') to 'prove' the prophecy of military victory. The phrase works by analogy with *erigere aciem/agmen in collem*: see Bower (1958) 9–10.

128–9 After Veiiento's grand prophecy, the speaker points out his one omission (*hoc defuit unum*) in a sarcastic comment. For the gourmet's interest in the age and provenance of food cf. 140–3nn. and Hor. *Sat.* 2.4, e.g. 45 on *aetas*. *Fabricio*: dat. after *defuit*; i.e. Veiiento: 113–18n. *ut ... memoraret*: 'to mention'.

130 Domitian's only direct speech in this poem is ruthlessly abrupt: ignoring the fulsome flattery, he presses the *consilium* for practical advice. *quidnam igitur censes?* is the formula with which the chairman asked committee members for their recommendation in the Roman senate and other council meetings: *OLD censeo* 4; cf. Sall. *B.J.* 31.18 '*quid igitur censes?*'; Sen. *Apoc.* 9.3 with Eden. On the procedure see Crook (1955) 113.   **conciditur?:** for indicative instead of subjunctive in a deliberative question cf. 3.296n.: 'is it to be cut up?'

The absurdity of praising a huge fish then cutting it up is satirised at Hor. *Sat.* 2.2.33–4 *laudas, insane, trilibrem | mullum, in singula quem minuas pulmenta necesse est.*

130–5 The gourmand Montanus' (107n.) clever proposal is carried (136 *uicit ... sententia*): direct speech lends him authority. First he subtly rejects Domitian's suggestion with a periphrasis (*absit ... hoc*), then he recommends that a huge dish be made specially (*testa ... properate*); finally he suggests that the emperor's entourage should henceforth include potters (*sed ... sequantur*). His proposal recalls the problem which provoked the summoning of the *consilium, sed derat pisci patinae mensura* (72).

130–1 absit ab illo | dedecus hoc: grand, cf. Val. Max. 3.2.20 *absit istud dedecus a sanguine nostro*.

131–2 'Let a deep dish be prepared to contain its ample circumference with a delicate wall.' Absurdly grandiose: *spatiosum* recalls *Hadriaci spatium admirabile rhombi* (39); *orbem* evokes the circular shape of the turbot. The 'delicate wall' of the dish is a sign of high quality, cf. Plin. *N.H.* 35.161.

133 debetur 'is required'.   **subitus:** cf. 59, the fisherman's haste.   **Prometheus:** grandiose for 'potter': Prometheus is the original potter, from the creation story in which he formed humans from clay (Paus. 10.4.4), cf. 14.35, Mart. 14.182.

134–5 Montanus can command Domitian's slaves, hence the imperative *properate*, but not Domitian himself, hence the iussive subjunctive *sequantur* combined with the vocative *Caesar*.   **rotam:** a potter's wheel, Pers. 3.24.   **citius:** comparative adverb, in the common sense, 'pretty sharpish'.   **castra sequantur:** i.e. be among the camp-followers, i.e. entourage; later *castra* means 'court'. Montanus flatters Domitian by presenting him as military leader (cf. *dux magnus* 145). For *castra* used ironically cf. 6.419–20 *conchas et castra moueri | nocte iubet*. Military imagery indicates Domitian's travesty of his position.

136 uicit ... sententia: more technical language (130n.), in parody of the Roman senate, e.g. Liv. 2.4.3 *cum in senatu uicisset sententia quae censebat*; in parody Sen. *Apoc.* 9.6 *uariae erant sententiae, et uidebatur Claudius sententiam uincere*.   **digna uiro:** Montanus' proposal is 'worthy of him' thanks to his experience of imperial banqueting (136–9) and his knowledge of luxury food (139–43); hence his 'victory' (*uicit*). Montanus' expertise in self-indulgence makes him 'heroic' (*uir*).

137 luxuriam inperii ueteris 'the extravagance of the old imperial court'. On Montanus' capacity for survival see 107n.

137–8 noctes ... Neronis | iam medias: cf. Suet. *Ner.* 27.2 *epulas a medio die ad mediam noctem protrahebat*; Nero courted publicity for his midnight revels, Tac. *Ann.* 16.20. *iam*, lit. 'already', suggests that the feasting continued beyond midnight, cf. 6.302 *mediis iam noctibus*. On the link with Nero, 38n.

138–9 aliam ... famem, cum pulmo Falerno | arderet: the appetite was thought to be renewed by wine: Mart. 5.78.17–18 *post haec omnia forte si mouebit | Bacchus quam solet esuritionem*. The brutal term 'a second hunger' exposes the luxury. *aliam* for *alteram*, as at 6.437, 7.114.

Association of the lung with drinking may evoke the Greek idea e.g. τέγγε πλεύμονας οἴνωι (Alcaeus in Page (1955) 303); the idea found currency in philosophical and scientific writers, hence the report at Gell. 17.11. Falernian was a fine wine from Campania (Plin. *N.H.* 14.62, 23.33). For 'burns with Falernian' cf. Hor. *Od.* 2.11.19 *ardentis Falerni* with Nisbet and Hubbard. For the metaphor cf. 5.49 *stomachus domini feruet uinoque ciboque*.

139 nulli maior fuit usus edendi 'no one had greater experience in eating'.

140 tempestate mea: cf. 6.25–6 *nostra* | *tempestate*, 7.2 *hac tempestate*; *tempestas* for *tempus* was considered by Cicero (*De Orat.* 3.153) a poetic feature.

140–1 Oysters are associated with extravagant banquets, e.g. 6.302, 8.85–6; see André (1961) 108. Three possible provenances of oysters (*ostrea*) in three varied constructions are presented succinctly in an indirect question marked by *forent an.* (1) Circeii, on the coast south of Rome; praised by a gourmand at Hor. *Sat.* 2.4.33. (2) The Lucrine lake near Baiae, on the coast of Campania, mentioned again at J. 8.85–6, 11.49 *Baias et ad ostrea currunt*; Martial uses *Lucrina* alone to denote oysters (6.11.5). (3) Rutupiae, mod. Richborough on the coast of Kent, England, a site yielding many oyster-shells.

Circeiis evokes the *Odyssey*: Montanus' experience as a gourmet parodies Odysseus' experience of many cities and peoples (Gowers (1993) 208).

Rutupino edita fundo 'produced from the Rutupian depths' (of the sea); the adj. may be inspired by Luc. 6.67 *Rutupina . . . litora.*

142–3 The imperfect tenses indicate Montanus' enduring ability to identify immediately (*primo . . . morsu* and *semel aspecti*) the origins of exotic foods. For interest in provenance cf. 129 *patriam . . . rhombi*, Hor. *Sat.* 2.2.31–3, *ibid.* 2.4 throughout and perhaps Lucil. 357–8W = 328–9M. For criticism of such 'precious and sterile debates in which gourmets engage' see Stat. *Silv.* 4.6.8–11 with Coleman. Oysters and sea-urchins are combined as exotic delicacies at Var. *Sat. Men.* 173, Hor. *Sat.* 2.4.33. On sea-urchins see André (1961) 106.   **callebat** 'he had the skill' + infin., *OLD* 3b, cf. Pers. 5.105 *ueri speciem dinoscere calles.*   **deprendere** 'to detect', *OLD* 4b.

144–5 The *consilium* is ended and the advisers dismissed. Ring composition with 72–5 includes passive verb, *proceres* and *consilium. misso . . . consilio*: abl. abs., lit. 'the council having been dismissed'.

145–9 The speaker indicates an acceptable reason for summoning the *consilium*, i.e. to deal with a military emergency. This indicates the debasement of the *consilium*. Such abuses of power are regular complaints brought against 'bad' rulers, cf. Plin. *Ep.* 8.14.8 of Domitian e.g. *cum senatus aut ad odium summum aut ad summum nefas uocaretur, et modo ludibrio modo dolori retentus numquam seria, tristia saepe censeret*; Dio 67.9

(Domitian); Dio 63.26.4 of Nero: 'One night he suddenly summoned in haste the foremost senators and knights, as if to make some communication to them about the political situation, and then said to them (I quote his exact words): "I have discovered a way by which the water-organ will produce louder and more musical tones."' Domitian's military image is satirised by his substitution of fish for war, hence the ironic: *dux magnus* (cf. 2.104n.) and *Albanam ... in arcem* (145). To depict the villa on the hill (60n.) as an *arx* (Tac. *Agr.* 45, quoted above, 113–18n.) is to depict Domitian as a tyrant (cf. 10.307 *saeua ... in arce tyrannus*). Word order situates the 'great general' inside his 'Alban fortress'. **dux magnus:** of Domitian, Stat. *Silv.* 3.1.62; cf. *induperatorem* 29n. for similar irony. **attonitos:** the bad emperor renders his subjects *albi et attoniti* Plin. *Pan.* 48.1, 76.3, cf. 75n. on *pallor amicitiae* and Rome's reaction to Domitian, *attonitae ... Vrbi* (77). **festinare:** haste is a repeated motif, cf. *properat* 59, *propera* 67, *properabat* 76 and 94. **tamquam ... dicturus:** parallel to the following clause, *tamquam ... uenisset,* 'as if he had been about to deliver a communication ...'. **de Chattis ... toruisque Sygambris:** the adjective goes ἀπὸ κοινοῦ with both proper nouns, German peoples who conveniently signify the threat of barbarians on the empire's frontiers; cf. Tac. *Germ.* 30–1 on the warlike nature of the Chatti (e.g. *Chattos ad bellum*) and Hor. *Od.* 4.2.34–6 *feroces ... Sygambros* and *ibid.* 14.51.

Mention of the Chatti inevitably evokes Domitian's campaign against them in AD 83 after which he celebrated a triumph (Suet. *Dom.* 6.1) and took the name Germanicus. Contemporaries praise Domitian's generalship in Germany (e.g. Frontinus, *Strat.* 1.1.8, etc.; Stat. *Silv.* 1.1.27, etc.), but later sources deny him credit, e.g. Tac. *Agr.* 39.1 *inerat conscientia derisui fuisse nuper falsum e Germania triumphum.* The campaign referred to here was presumably eulogised by Statius in the lost *De Bello Germanico* (72–118n.): see Coleman on Stat. *Silv.* 4.2.66.

There is no evidence for a campaign against the Sygambri, hence their appearance here may hint at the bogus military claims made by Domitian. **tamquam ... pinna:** the apparent vagueness of the second *tamquam* clause is surprising, but may conceal a specific allusion lost to us. It sounds elevated, with personification of the letter as 'anxious' and the 'Golden Line' patterning of 149; the grandiloquence may allude to Statius' lost poem (72–118n.). The context demands

that the 'anxious letter' announces a defeat, recent or imminent. For a
contrasting snapshot of happy communications from all parts of the
empire cf. Stat. *Silv.* 5.1.88–91.   **diuersis:** probably 'distant', cf.
Virg. *Aen.* 12.708 *genitos diuersis partibus orbis*, or possibly 'opposite',
presumably meaning the south (opposite to the northern barbarians).
praecipiti ... pinna: an elevated metaphor denoting the speed of the
message, reminiscent of Virg. *Aen.* 9.473–4 *pauidam uolitans pinnata per
urbem | nuntia Fama ruit*, of bad news (cf. 'Bad news travels fast'); of a
letter cf. Cic. *Att.* 6.4.3 *fac ut mihi tuae litterae uolent obuiae.*

150–4 In a fiercely indignant tone the speaker condemns Domitian's behaviour. J. reserves *utinam* (only here and at 6.335 and 638) for
moments of strong personal emotion. The personal note marks the end
of the epic-style narrative; the level of diction becomes more colloquial
with the strictly unnecessary emphasis in *potius* (reminiscent of Catullus' portrayal of conversation in poem 10) and *nugis* (see below). The
speaker's expression of regret that Domitian did not spend all his time
on such 'frivolities' does not mean that the degradation of the élite
through abuse of the *consilium* is insignificant, *except* in comparison with
his murders of members of the élite. Seneca similarly presents different
aspects of Claudius' outrageous conduct, ranging from stupidity to
murder, throughout the *Apocolocyntosis* (see Braund (1993) 61–4).

Domitian's outrages are on a rising scale of risk: the debasement of
advisers (*his ... nugis*), the murder of members of the élite (*claras ...
animas* and *Lamiarum caede*), the murder of artisans (*postquam ...
coeperat*). Though this may reflect Suetonius' account of Domitian's
death at the hands of men of lowly status (*Dom.* 17.1–2), it is more
importantly an indirect condemnation of the élite for acquiescing in
their own humiliation. Significantly, the catalogue of Domitian's outrageous tyranny ends only with his death: *periit* (153) and *hoc nocuit*
(154).   **nugis** 'silly amusements' (Rudd), perhaps an allusion to
the 'gags' of comic actors (*OLD* 3). On the poem's chiastic structure
(*nugis* of Domitian's fish story as *de factis leuioribus* 12 of Crispinus' fish
story) see Essay.   **tota illa ... tempora saeuitiae** 'the *whole* of
that savage time'. Domitian's reign is portrayed as above all else cruel,
see 85n. Suetonius characterises Domitian's reign as one of *saeuitia*
(*Dom.* 10.1, 5).   **abstulit Vrbi:** echoes *abstulit orbi* (19), again
linking Crispinus and Domitian. *Vrbi* = Rome, cf. 77.   **animas:**
both spirits (cf. 8.254) and lives (cf. 8.83); *inlustres ... animas* echoes

Virg. *Aen.* 6.758 *inlustres animas nostrumque in nomen ituras.* Some of
Domitian's eminent victims are catalogued at Suet. *Dom.* 10.2–5.
inpune et uindice nullo: the emphasis on revenge recalls the indignant opening of Satire 1; *inpune* occurs only there and here in J. *uindice*
probably puns on Vindex, a leading figure in rebellion against Nero
(8.222; note that Domitian was styled a *caluus Nero* at 38); for the pun
cf. Suet. *Ner.* 45.2.   **postquam ... esse timendus | coeperat** 'as
soon as he had begun to be a cause of fear'.   **cerdonibus:** a figure
used almost exclusively by satirists to represent lowly status, hence
'artisans' or 'workers'; the name *Cerdo* is associated with slaves, cf. Petr.
Sat. 60. Possibly here a proper name; see Jahn on Pers. 4.51 *respue quod
non es; tollat sua munera cerdo.* At 8.181–2 *quae | turpia cerdoni Volesos
Brutumque decebunt* the proximity of noble names makes *Cerdoni* almost
certain; here *cerdonibus* sits between the unspecified *claras ... inlustresque
animas* and the named *Lamiae* (154). For Domitian's assassination see
Suet. *Dom.* 17.1–2.   **hoc nocuit** 'it was this that destroyed'; Domi-
tian follows in the dative case (*madenti*).   **Lamiarum:** one of
Domitian's victims was the consular Lucius Aelius Plautius Lamia
Aelianus, whose wife Domitian had earlier married: the pretext for
execution was some 'ancient and harmless jokes' (Suet. *Dom.* 10.2).
This was regarded as an aristocratic family, cf. 6.385, Hor. *Od.* 3.17,
Tac. *Ann.* 6.27; the plural is generic (cf. 8.11 and often), 'Lamia and
his type'. Another Lamia, Lucius Aelius Lamia Aelianus, was consul in
AD 116, roughly contemporary with J.   **caede madenti:** the lasting
image of Domitian is with his hands dripping with gore, cf. Cat. 64.368
alta Polyxenia madefient caede sepulcra. caede connects with *conciditur* (130):
in Gowers's words ((1993) 209), Domitian's 'instincts have always
been for cutting up'.

ESSAY

The satire starts with an indignant attack on Crispinus. He is
announced immediately as a good subject for satire (1n.) and introduced as a *monstrum* (2). With fervent indignation (see Sweet (1979)
292) the speaker first attacks Crispinus' major faults (1–10): he is a
Casanova who does not stop at sacrilege. Then he shifts to 'more trivial
matters' (*factis leuioribus* 11), namely, Crispinus' purchase of an expensive fish, a mullet, for his personal consumption (15–27). This shifting

focus reinforces the impression of spontaneity which is central to *indignatio* (see Introduction 6§(a)). The next six lines (28–33) direct the focus on to the emperor as a preparation for the mock-heroic attack upon Domitian which follows (examined below), while driving home the speaker's hostility towards Crispinus. In a reprise of the chauvinism and bigotry shown by the speaker in Satire 1 and by Umbricius in Satire 3, Crispinus is portrayed as a foreign, wealthy upstart who is enslaved to the emperor (see 31–3nn.).

At this point (34), the tone changes radically. The speaker utters an epic-style invocation of the Muses, *incipe, Calliope* and *narrate, puellae Pierides*, in lines 34–6, and then delivers a lengthy mock-epic narrative describing how Domitian summons his cabinet of advisers (his *consilium*) to advise him what to do with the enormous fish which has been presented to him. This narrative falls into three sections. Lines 37–72 describe how a fisherman lands a huge turbot at Ancona and races across Italy to Alba Longa to present it to Domitian. In lines 72–118, because there is no dish big enough to hold the turbot, Domitian summons his *consilium* to offer advice: there follows a catalogue of the eleven members of Domitian's *consilium*. Lines 119–49 narrate the advice given by some of them and the ensuing action: the decision is to make a dish big enough and the *consilium* is then dismissed. Finally lines 150–4, a comment on Domitian's frivolity, constitute a coda. The narrative thus has a balanced structure in which the first and third sections dealing with the fish frame the central section which presents a catalogue of Domitian's advisers.

The central issue in the interpretation of Satire 4 has long been the relationship between the two parts of the poem (discussed by Stegemann (1913) 30–6; Helmbold & O'Neil (1956); Kenney (1962) 30–1; Anderson (1982) 232–44; Kilpatrick (1973), 230–5; Sweet (1979) 283; Flintoff (1990); Jones (1990)). The problem lies in the apparent disjunction between the opening lines with their indignant attack on the courtier Crispinus for his vices and selfish gluttony and the longer mock-epic narrative attacking Domitian's abuse of his courtiers. A secondary issue is where the division between the two parts occurs. Most editors place the new paragraph at line 36, failing to appreciate that the mock-epic portion commences with the epic-style invocations at 34. In concentrating upon these issues, critics have perhaps neglected other aspects of the poem which deserve attention. This Essay will attempt to redress the balance by indicating the coherence of material with the rest of Book 1 as well as considering the thorny question of the poem's unity.

What strikes critics as unusual about Satire 4 is the narrative of Domitian and the fish which occupies the bulk of the poem. This is the first extended narrative in J.'s Satires; there is nothing comparable in Satires 1–3 nor in earlier extant verse satire. (Horace includes first-person narratives with mock-heroic touches in *Sat.* 1.5 and 1.9 and an epic parody in dialogue form in *Sat.* 2.5, but has nothing like this third-person narrative; the only extended third person narrative in Horace is the extended version of the Aesop fable of the city mouse and the country mouse with which *Satires* 2.6 closes.) Moreover, J.'s narrative adopts a lofty, mock-heroic tone. This is achieved primarily by the technique of tonal alternation: grand-sounding phrases, which might be appropriate to epic poetry, are debunked by mundane and incongruous comments (on J.'s technique of parody see Anderson (1982) 237–43, Sweet (1979) esp. 288, 296). Often, this variation is almost one of volume, with the epic-sounding phrases inviting declamation at top volume (e.g. lines 37–46, 56–69: see nn.) while the diminishing comments are best muttered behind the sleeve (e.g. lines 46–56, 69–71: see nn.). By appropriating the 'grand style' for this narrative, the poem fulfils the programmatic declaration of Satire 1 that satire can replace epic (see Essay on Satire 1).

J.'s choice of epic parody revitalises the relationship between satire and epic which was present virtually from the inception of the genre (see Introduction §6(c)). In the sister genre of Menippean satire, epic parody is still more prominent, notably in the debate in heaven about whether or not the emperor Claudius should be deified which forms the centre-piece of Seneca's *Apocolocyntosis*. There, as here, procedural formulae are central to the parody: the language of the Roman Senate is parroted (see 130n., 136n., 144–5; cf. Eden on Sen. *Apoc.* 9.1, 2, 6, 11.6). Moreover, J.'s is not the first parody of a *consilium* in Roman satire. The precedent was set by Lucilius. In a poem in his first book apparently called *Concilium Deorum*, Lucilius used parody of the divine council narrated in the opening book of Ennius' epic poem, *Annales*, to attack a dead politician. Similarly, J. here uses parody to attack both Domitian and his subservient courtiers.

Moreover, there is sufficient evidence to suggest that J. is debunking a specific epic poem, now lost to us, Statius' *De Bello Germanico* (see 72–118n., also 34–6n.). The fragment which survives, quoted by a scholiast on J., is part of a catalogue of advisers which names three of the men who feature in Satire 4. Catalogues are an intrinsic feature of epic poetry and lend themselves to parody by a satirist (on catalogues in J. see Griffith (1969) 147–8; J. will return to epic parody in Satire 12, where he debunks another standard element of epic, the storm). In Statius' panegyrical poem about Domitian's campaigns in Europe, the members of the *consilium* were presumably summoned for serious debate on a matter of military urgency and given heroic treatment by the epic poet. In Satire 4 the parody is achieved by substituting the trivial matter of the fish, thus denigrating Domitian's military achievements (see Ramage (1989) 692–704). The satiric force lies in Domitian's humiliation of his advisers by his flexing his autocratic muscles and exploiting their subservience to the corrupt imperial system. J. attacks both emperor and courtiers for their collusion in that system.

The direction of J.'s satire becomes evident when we examine the presentation of the *consilium*, which was not an official body but had become a fixture, virtually an institution, from Augustus onwards, and had its precursors under the Republic (on the phenomenon of the emperor's council of advisers, the *consilium principis*, see 72–118n.). Domitian's chosen eleven comprise men prominent through birth and position, nine of whom are senators, mostly consular senators, and the remaining two prominent *equites*. The mixture is of diplomats, military men and jurists, and several had long experience as imperial advisers. That is, on a more favourable view, Domitian's *consilium* is a sensible collection of advisers for an emperor. But since this is satire, the advisers are presented as a collection of the weak and the depraved. The picture of their corruption, flattery, cruelty and terror conveyed in the catalogue and in the narrative of the advice they give serves to condemn not only them but also Domitian. His advisers' faults convict the emperor of classic charges against the bad ruler: of *saeuitia* (cruelty), of *dominatio* (tyranny) and of the absence of *libertas* (freedom) manifested particularly in his encouragement of *adulatio* (flattery) (cf. 145–9n., 150–4n.; see Braund (1993) esp. 64–7). Appropriately, the poem ends on a note of indignant condemnation of Domitian with the speaker deploring his murderous tendencies (150–4n.); this is the first manifestation of outright indignation since the opening condemnation of Crispinus. Indignation thus provides a frame for the mock-heroic narrative.

The issue of the relationship between the indignant attack upon Crispinus and the (largely) mock-heroic attack upon Domitian and his courtiers may now be tackled. The fact that both parts feature the consumption of fish is an obvious link, yet it does not take us very far. The expensive mullet which Crispinus purchases for himself is an indication of his selfish gluttony, while the enormous turbot symbolises Domitian's absolute control over all his subjects, ranging from the fisherman who feels compelled to offer the emperor his catch (see 54–5n.) to the courtiers who try to ingratiate themselves with him. The multifarious symbolism of fish as food does not on its own provide an adequate account of the poem as a unity.

Crispinus offers more fruitful ground. This victim of the speaker's indignation in the opening section recurs in the catalogue as no. 7 in the list of members of the *consilium*, where he is relegated to a relatively minor role, receiving a mere two lines. At the same time, we noted above that Domitian, the chief object of attack in the mock-epic narrative, features at the close of the section on Crispinus, in lines 28–33. This permits an analysis which sees Crispinus as prominent in the shorter, opening section where Domitian features in a minor role, while in the longer main section Domitian is the prominent figure and Crispinus features in a minor part. That is, the poem presents a kind of balance: Cd : Dc.

A further development of this analysis is to see the poem as structured on a chiastic pattern of crimes and folly, folly and crimes. According to this, Crispinus' crimes are tackled, rather briefly and obliquely, in lines 1–10, then his fishy folly (introduced with the words *facta leuiora* 11) attacked in much more detail (lines 11–33); Domitian's folly, as demonstrated in his reaction to the gift of the fish and epitomised as *nugae* 150, occupies most of the mock-epic, which is rounded off by a brief and oblique condemnation of Domitian's crimes (lines 150–4). This analysis, though intellectually appealing, does not adequately explain the disparity in treatment afforded to the two protagonists. This disparity is partly explained by an appreciation of the literary substrata to J.'s satires, specifically in accounts of the emperor Nero in whom 'the themes of extravagance, sexual ruthlessness, tyranny and violent death all converge' (as Townend (1973) 153–8 argues).

The most convincing reading of the poem is to see Crispinus as a microcosm of Domitian, an image which is invited by lines 28–33, the pivotal passage which paves the way for the mock-epic narrative and in which Domitian is introduced in the archaic, epic term *induperator* (29n.). Gowers piquantly suggests that Crispinus' behaviour 'is a mere hors d'oeuvre to Domitian's cruelty' ((1993) 206: in her discussion (202–11) she emphasises J.'s use of understatement). The similarities between the two characters support this view. Both are excessively concerned with fish, both exhibit an element of frivolity and both are characterised as vicious, Crispinus in his adultery (1–10) and Domitian in the *saeuitia* mentioned at the close (150–4). And running through the poem is the key word and idea, *monstrum* (used at 2 of Crispinus, at 45 of the turbot and at 115 of Catullus; see nn.). Its recurrence implies that Domitian's reign is marked by the extraordinary, the portentous and the ominous (on the vocabulary of prodigies and portents see Gowers (1993) 207).

The view of Crispinus as a miniature Domitian accounts for his minor role in the catalogue of advisers (he is dealt with in two lines, 108–9, as the seventh in the list of eleven) and for the disproportionate length of the two parts of the poem and the difference in tone: only the emperor may be treated in mock-epic narrative. The difference in length and tone indicates the gravity of discovering such faults in the emperor; satire now takes on the epic mantle prepared for in the comparisons with epic in Satire 1 and delivers a fully-fledged (mock-) epic narrative in which the speaker condemns the source and centre of what is wrong with Rome: the emperor. Crispinus pales into insignificance in comparison.

J. might have devoted the entire poem to mock-epic narrative (although to launch straight in at line 34 would have been difficult); instead he uses the opening section on Crispinus to reinforce the characteristic indignant tone, to create a perspective and to set up the themes of the attack before shifting into mock-heroic mode. Just as we settle into the speaker's attack upon the selfish Crispinus, J. surprises us by shifting up a gear and attacking the power-crazed and manipulative Domitian. Satire 4 thus bears a close resemblance to Satires 2 and 3 in terms of the technique of surprise: in Satire 2, it is unclear whether the speaker or Laronia will be the chief voice in the condemnation of pathics; and although Satire 3 is introduced as if it will be a dialogue, Umbricius does not permit the speaker to get a word in and delivers a monomaniacal tirade. Surprise is one of the chief weapons in the satirist's armoury and Satire 4 does not disappoint.

It is not only in satirical techniques that Satire 4 coheres closely with the other poems of Book 1, but in themes too. The poem depicts and condemns the uneven relationship between emperor and courtier, the powerful and the subservient, which links with the theme of patron and client elsewhere in Book 1: patrons are portrayed as tyrants and clients as, in effect, slaves, but voluntary slaves who revel in their humiliation (this theme will be developed more explicitly in Satire 5). The emperor is, of course, the ultimate patron, all powerful over his 'clients', however exalted their status in society's normal terms. All the speaker's victims in this poem are members of the élite, as in Satire 2; the poem exemplifies the same diagnosis that society's malaise spreads from the rot at the centre. And, like the patron we shall shortly meet in Satire 5, Domitian exploits food as an instrument of power. Finally, the sequence from Satire 3 to Satire 4 is executed excellently. Satire 3 closes with Umbricius' departure from Rome, leaving the speaker behind. The next person to walk on to the now-empty stage (*ad partes* 2n.) is the Egyptian Crispinus, an upstart foreigner, precisely one of the types criticised by Umbricius. J. has ordered the sequence of poems to play out Umbricius' complaint, that good, old-fashioned Romans like himself are displaced by corrupt and depraved foreign upstarts (Braund (1988) 15). So despite its superficial difference from the remaining poems of Book 1, differences attributable primarily to the mock-epic narrative format adopted for the main section, it seems clear that Satire 4 develops and anticipates major themes explored elsewhere in J.'s first book of Satires and is an integral element in the composition of the Book.

SATIRE 5

1–11 The opening section establishes the relationship between speaker and addressee. The speaker attacks somebody, as yet unnamed, for his continuing and voluntary acceptance of humiliation from dinner hosts when he could behave otherwise. Trebius (19, 135) is evidently a parasite (1.139n.), a lowly *cliens* (16) who lives in hope of an invitation to a *cena* (24). The closing lines of the poem will present a reprise of the vocabulary and ideas of this opening (170–3nn.).

After the measured opening with two elaborate *si* clauses of two lines each, the speaker becomes agitated with anger in lines 6–11, marked by the shorter sentences and indignant questions.

1–2 The vocabulary of ethical discussion (*propositi, mens, bona summa, uiuere*) emphasises the humiliating treatment to which Trebius exposes himself. This is not the first time that the speaker has attempted to dissuade Trebius from his life-style (*nondum, eadem*). **Si te proposititi nondum pudet** 'If you are not yet ashamed of your plan'; for *propositum*, i.e. 'life-plan', cf. 9.20–1 *igitur flexisse uideris | propositum et uitae contrarius ire priori*, Hor. *Sat.* 2.7.5–6 *pars hominum uitiis gaudet constanter et urget | propositum*; Sen. *Ep.* 95.46 *uita sine proposito uaga est.* **atque eadem est mens | ut ... putes** 'you persist in your view that ...'. J. echoes Hor. *Ep.* 1.1.4 *non eadem est aetas, non mens*. Postponement of *mens* to the final position dislocates the emphasis, perhaps as a reminder that this is satire and no regular ethical treatise, an impression confirmed by the remarkable metre here, possibly an archaising touch: *átqu(e) éă | d(em) ést mens*. **bona summa** 'the highest good'; n. pl.; usually singular, *summum bonum*, plural here for metrical convenience (*bonum* only once but *bona* six times in J.); further vocabulary drawn from ethical philosophy; cf. Lucian *Parasit.* 7–12, 14. **aliena uiuere quadra:** *aliena* is central to the parasite's situation, cf. Plaut. *Capt.* 77 *quasi mures semper edimus alienum cibum*; Ter. *Eun.* 265 *uiden otium et cibus quid facit alienus?* J. replaces *cibus* with the more graphic *quadra*, a quarter of a round loaf of bread, i.e. a tiny amount, cf. Hor. *Ep.* 1.17.49 *diuiduo findetur munere quadra*, Sen. *Ben.* 4.29.2 *quis beneficium dixit quadram panis?*, perhaps connecting with παράσιτος, which refers to food, specifically bread (LSJ: παράσιτος = 'one who eats at the table of another', from σῖτος = 'grain, bread, food'). *uiuere*, instead of 'to eat', continues to evoke the vocabulary of ethical debate; juxtaposed with *aliena* it hints at the life of enslavement chosen by the parasite.

3–4 si potes illa pati: the parasite's role is the epitome of passivity, cf. 173 *flagra pati*; cf. Mart. 11.23.15 *si potes ista pati, si nil perferre recusas.* **illa ... quae nec Sarmentus ... nec ... Gabba tulisset** 'treatment which not even Sarmentus nor Gabba would have put up with'; the first *nec* means 'not even' (*OLD neque* 2b).

Both Sarmentus and Gabba were *scurrae*, i.e. professional buffoons (4.31n.), associated with Maecenas and Augustus (hence *Caesaris* 4). For contests of witty abuse involving Sarmentus and Gabba see Hor. *Sat.* 1.5.51–70 (Sarmentus) and Mart. 10.101 (Gabba). Both were of lowly origin: Sarmentus was the slave or freedman of Marcus Favonius; Gabba is designated *uilis* (echoed *uilibus ... amicis* 146). Quintilian cites Sarmentus' wit (*I.O.* 6.3.58); the Galba of *ibid.* 27, 62, 80 is probably this Gabba, cf. Mart. 1.41.16. *tulisset*: echoed by *ferre* 170.

iniquas | Caesaris ad mensas: i.e. at Augustus' feasts the *scurrae* were treated as inferior. Hence *uilis* denotes not only Gabba's origin but also his place at table. In contrast, Pliny commends Trajan's *mensa communis* (*Pan.* 49.5) and asserts his own parity of practice (*Ep.* 2.6.3 e.g. *cunctis ... rebus exaequo*).

5 The idiomatic Latin for 'I would not trust you under any circumstances'; cf. Plaut. *Amph.* 437 *nam iniurato scio plus credet mihi quam iurato tibi*, Cic. *Att.* 13.28.2 *iurato mihi crede.*   **quamuis iurato** 'even though you were on oath'; the past participle is here active in meaning.

6 frugalius 'less excessive'; a cliché of Stoic and Epicurean homily, cf. 14.318–20, Sen. *Ep.* 60.3; *uentre* abl. of comparison.

6–7 hoc ... aluo 'However, suppose you lack the little it takes to fill the void' (Rudd). For *puta* = 'suppose', functioning as the protasis, cf. 2.153, also followed by a question.

8–11 I.e. 'Would it not be preferable to beg rather than submit to such humiliations?', expressed in three indignant questions of increasing length and varied metrical pattern. Cf. 14.134 *inuitatus ad haec aliquis de ponte negabit*: even the lowest of the low have their standards. The locations are typical of beggars (8–9): *crepido* denotes a raised platform e.g. the pavement/sidewalk or the steps outside a public building such as a temple, cf. Val. Max. 4.3.*ext.*4 (the chosen stand of Diogenes the Cynic); any bridge (*pons*) made a good situation for beggars because of the funnelling of traffic at that point, e.g. J. 14.134 above, Sen. *Vit. Beat.* 25.1 *in sublicium pontem me transfer et inter egentes abice*; the *teges* is the beggar's woven mat, cf. 9.139–40 *sit mihi tuta senectus | a tegete et baculo*, diminished by the formulation *tegetis pars*, 'a share in a mat' (not 'a bit of mat'). The final monosyllable in 8 is disturbing, cf. *mens* 1n.   **dimidia breuior:** understand *parte*, 'less than a half'.   **tantine iniuria cenae** 'Is the insult of a dinner worth so much?', i.e. the dinner *is* the insult. Cf. Plin. *Pan.* 49.6 of conduct at dinner *superbam illam conuictus simulationem*; *Laus Pis.* 116

nullius subitos affert iniuria risus. iniuria cenae recalls *iniquas ... mensas* (3–4) and, since the legal meaning of *iniuria* is physical as well as psychological, anticipates the brawl of 24–9. *tanti:* 3.54n.   **tam ieiuna fames** 'is your hunger so famished?', a quotation from Ov. *Met.* 8.791.   **cum possit honestius illic ... tremere** '[that it endures the insulting dinner] when it could more honourably be shivering there', i.e. on one of the beggars' pitches. *fames* as subject implies that there is nothing else to Trebius besides his hunger. For hunger + cold cf. 14.318 *in quantum sitis atque fames et frigora poscunt*; for *tremens* of a beggar cf. 6.543. *honestius* evokes a value-system of respectability, cf. 3.21n., 4.85n., and ends the *propositio* as it began, with the language of ethical debate: to describe a beggar's lot as more honourable would seem paradoxical to a Roman audience.   **sordes farris ... canini:** lit. 'filth of dog's grain', i.e. scraps of coarse bread, *panis sordidus* (*OLD sordidus* 4), specifically *far caninum*, bread made from barley and bran (Phaedr. 4.19.1; Lucil. 711M = 768W for *canicae* = 'bran'). For *far caninum* as beggars' fare cf. Mart. 10.5.4–5 *inter ... raucos ultimus rogatores | oret caninas panis inprobi buccas*, 4.53.6 *latratos ... cibos* (also part of the build-up to a pun on *Cynicus*).   **mordere:** favoured by satirists, cf. 6.302, 7.19, Pers. 4.30, probably because it emphasises the physicality of the action: the parasite becomes dog-like as he gnaws the bread; for dogs see Otto *canis* 2.

12–23 The first insult is the invitation itself: the speaker sarcastically portrays the gulf between the host's attitude to Trebius and Trebius' attitude to his host. Their mercenary relationship is reflected in the vocabulary associated with counting and accountancy: *primo* 12, *mercedem* 13, *fructus* 14, *imputat* 14 and 15, *duos* 15, *tertia* 17, *una* 18, *summa* 18.

12 primo fige loco: appears to herald a logical argument, cf. Quint. *I.O.* 5.12.14 *potentissima argumenta primone ponenda sint loco. fige*, 'fix', is a stronger form of *pone*; 9.94 *nostras intra te fige querellas* is similar: 'In the first place, get this stuck in your head ...'.   **discumbere iussus:** i.e. 'by [merely] being invited to dinner': the participle is causal, with *iussus* in a weak sense; cf. Virg. *Aen.* 1.708 *toris iussi discumbere pictis*, Petr. *Sat.* 21 *iussi ergo discubuimus. discumbo* denotes the reclining position adopted at table by the Romans.

13 'you are getting payment in full for your long-standing services': vocabulary of *amicitia* relationships: on *ueterum* 1.132n. and on *officiorum*

2.132n. *solidus* regularly thus of payments 'in full': *OLD* 9b. For *merces* denoting 'payment' or 'reward' see 1.42n. The pentasyllabic word ending the line is an archaic touch (J. tends to confine his use of words longer than three syllables to Greek words), ironically suggesting the debasement of the patron–client relationship.

14 fructus amicitiae magnae cibus: understand *est*. 'The reward of great friendship is – food'; the rhythm, i.e. bucolic diaeresis and strong punctuation, contributes to the satirical effect: anticipation of the reward (*fructus*, figurative, *OLD* 5) is disappointed by the swift pyrrhic *cibus*, which is nonetheless put down in the ledger. 'Great friendship' = friendship with the great, 4.74n.

14–15 imputat: from accountancy, 'enter as a debt' (*OLD* 1), 2.16n. The host insists on counting; cf. the similar cluster of number words in the client's condemnation of the stingy patron at 9.39–42:

> 'haec tribui, deinde illa dedi, mox plura tulisti.'
> computat et ceuet. ponatur calculus, adsint
> cum tabula pueri; numera sestertis quinque
> omnibus in rebus, numerentur deinde labores.

rex: the patron (1.136n.) is also the autocrat. The bucolic diaeresis and two final monosyllables (cf. 1) emphasise *rex*.   **quamuis rarum** 'however infrequent'.

15–16 ergo: on the prosody, see Introduction §8.   **post:** another final monosyllable (cf. *pars* 8), again following a bucolic diaeresis, with double clash of ictus and accent.   **si libuit:** both words emphasise that the invitation is the patron's whim.   **neglectum ... clientem:** cf. 3.125 *nusquam minor est iactura clientis* and Naevolus in Satire 9 who styles himself a *cliens* (59, 72) and 'neglected' (*neglegit* 92). *cliens* is a stark word, rare in J. and generally confined to references to 'humble members of the lower classes' (Saller (1982) 9).   **adhibere:** 2.135n.

17 Lit. 'to prevent the third cushion on the empty couch being unused', i.e. left empty; the Romans reclined three to a couch (*lectus* or *torus*, cf. 3.82), leaning the left elbow on a cushion (*culcita*). For a classic arrangement of guests cf. Horace's *cena Nasidieni* (*Sat.* 2.8) where three couches (*triclinia*) accommodate the nine guests according to status (see Muecke on lines 20–3). Perhaps Trebius is summoned to take the lowest place on the third and lowest couch; however, the double menu served in *Satire* 5 suggests that a larger number of guests is envisaged here; cf. Plin. *Ep.* 2.6. The abVAB pattern (Introduction §7) contrasts sharply with the patron's inappropriate motives for the invitation.

18 'una simus' ait: direct speech features rarely in this poem; significantly this is the only direct communication between patron and client (cf. 76–9n., 130, 135–6n., 166–8n.) and it ironically conflicts with the double menus: patron and client are never really 'together' (*una*), contrast Cic. *Att.* 7.4.2 *fuimus una*, a tête-à-tête.   **uotorum summa** 'It's a dream come true!' (Rudd); ellipse of *est* conveys Trebius' excitement. Cf. Plin. *Pan.* 74.4 *summa uotorum*, *Ep.* 7.26.3 *summa curarum, summa uotorum*. The idea is mirrored at *spes bene cenandi* 166n. and echoes *summa bona* 2n.; cf. 1.132–4 *clientes uota ... deponunt, quamquam longissima cenae spes homini*.

19 habet Trebius: the shift into the third person marks the speaker's sarcasm; cf. 13.16. Specific reference unknown; the name Trebius occurs in Aquinum (*CIL* x 5528–9) and from several consuls under Hadrian (see Ferguson, *Prosopography*).

19–20 propter quod ... debeat 'has a good reason for', lit. 'has a reason why he must'. *propter quod* is repeated at 76–9. The idea of obligation (*debeat*), emphasised here by enjambment, is central to the patron–client relationship: here the humble client is obliged to race to the morning *salutatio* (*salutatrix ... turba* 21); cf. 3.126–30, 1.95nn.   **rumpere somnum:** likewise Sen. *Breu. Vit.* 14.4 *illis miseris suum somnum rumpentibus ut alienum expectent*, Mart. 12.26.7 *medios abrumpere somnos*; cf. 3.127–8 *si curet nocte togatus currere*.   **ligulas dimittere:** a sign of haste, 'letting his laces fly about', because he has not the time to fasten them. For the client's haste to attend, cf. *horridus* 'unkempt' at Mart. 3.36.3.   **sollicitus ne:** Trebius' haste indicates his anxiety, a picture reinforced by the metre, monosyllabic conjunction and strong enjambment (8n., 1n.). The competitiveness of Roman society is evoked graphically, cf. 3.130 *ne prior ... salutet*.

21 salutatrix ... turba: *turba* is dismissive, cf. *turbae ... togatae* 1.96n.; cf. *miratrix turba* 4.62n.   **peregerit orbem** 'completed the round' of visits to different patrons.

22–3 I.e. early in the morning (cf. Plin. *Ep.* 3.12.2 *officia antelucana*) or even at midnight: the exaggeration (cf. 7.222–3) attacks Trebius for subjecting himself to such harsh conditions.   **sideribus dubiis:** i.e. fading in dawn's light; for *dubius* cf. Luc. 3.7 *dubios cernit uanescere montes*; Sen. *Ag.* 457 *dubia pereunt montis Idaei iuga* with Tarrant.   **quo se |**

frigida circumagunt pigri serraca Bootae 'when the frosty cart of sluggish Bootes is wheeling round', i.e. midnight, if J. recalls *Anacreontea* 33.1-3. This constellation, known to us as the Plough or Great Bear (and in the US the Big Dipper), is called *frigida* because of its proximity to the northern pole; its drover Bootes is *piger* (cf. Ov. *Fast.* 3.405 *piger ille Bootes*, Mart. 8.21.3-4 *placidi ... pigra Bootae plaustra*) because it changes position gradually and in winter is slow to set. *serraca* (3.255n.), instead of elevated *plaustra* (see Martial above), is bathetic. *frigida* also evokes the chill endured by Trebius; *pigri* contrasts with his frantic haste.

24-155 With the words *qualis cena tamen!* the speaker announces the commencement of the meal in parallel menus, a form of catalogue (see Essay).

24-37 The first item is the wine served to the two types of guest, first the client's wine (24-9), then the patron's (30-7).

24-5 The short sentences and ellipse convey indignation. **uinum quod sucida nolit | lana pati** 'wine which fresh wool would not put up with [is served to you]'. *sucida lana*, wool with the natural oil in it, was used in ancient medicine to apply wound treatments of wine or vinegar (Plin. *N.H.* 29.30). Trebius' wine is worse than that (cheap stuff) used for medical purposes. **de conuiua Corybanta uidebis:** a generalising prediction, as 1.91. *conuiua* expresses the ideal of the Roman banquet, where civilised people 'share their lives' (cf. Cic. *Fam.* 9.24.3), whereas *Corybanta* (Greek acc. sing.) denotes a fanatical priest of Cybele (see Nisbet and Hubbard on Hor. *Od.* 1.16.7); cf. *fanaticus* 4.123n. *de* = 'out of' (*OLD* 9), indicating change, cf. 7.197 *fies de rhetore consul*.

26-9 The consequence is verbal then physical violence, committed (*pocula torques*) and suffered (*saucius*) by Trebius. For brawls at dinner see Nisbet and Hubbard on *Od.* 1.27.1, Plaut. *Capt.* 88-9 *colaphos perpeti | potest parasitus frangique aulas in caput*, Lucil. 223-7M (= 226-7, 230-1W), Lucian *Symp.* 43-5. Military vocabulary, some of it associated with high poetry, contrasts with the drunken brawl described: *proludere* = 'to skirmish'; *torquere* fits hurling a spear, e.g. Virg. *Aen.* 11.284; *saucius* and *uulnera* evoke the battlefield; *cohortem* suggests military organisation; *pugna ... commissa*, 'battle joined', is formulaic (*OLD committo* 8). The balanced structure of 29 (AbVaB) heightens incongruity. **iurgia proludunt** 'abuse is the skirmishing'; cf. 15.51-2 *iurgia prima sonare | incipiunt.*   **saucius:** ambivalent, both 'drunk' (*OLD* 4) and literally 'wounded'.   **rubra ... mappa:** the napkin, supplied by the host (Hor. *Sat.* 2.4.81) or brought by the guest (Mart. 12.29.11), reddened by blood (proleptic: 1.83n.).   **inter uos ... libertorumque cohortem:** plural *uos* (again at 166, *uos decipit*) indicates that Trebius is one of a group. Their lowly status is confirmed by the overt hostility of Virro's 'squad' of freedmen, who would be unlikely to brawl with more elevated guests. For status gradations cf. Plin. *Ep.* 2.6.2 (three categories: host and peers, lesser friends and freedmen). Augustus did not invite freedmen to dinner (Suet. *Aug.* 74).   **quotiens** 'when' or 'if', not 'whenever' (*OLD* 3d).   **Saguntina ... lagona:** earthenware crockery from Spain, presented as the antithesis to antique silver plate at Mart. 8.6.1–3.

   30–1 In contrast, the patron drinks a fine old vintage.   **ipse:** i.e. the host, *T.L.L.* 344.14–33; again at 37, 56, 86, 107, 114, 142; conveying sarcastic respect for 'the master' (cf. *OLD* 12), Virro (not named until 39).   **capillato diffusum consule:** understand *uinum*: '[a wine] bottled under a long-haired consul', i.e. in the ancient era when consuls had long hair, antiquity (4.103n.). Cf. Mart. 3.62.2 *sub rege Numa condita*, of vintage wine. *diffusum* refers to the stage when the wine was transferred to *amphorae* labelled with the year (expressed as consuls' names) and place of production. Cf. Luc. 4.379 *nobilis ignoto diffusus consule Baccho*.   **bellis socialibus:** the so-called Social War, fought between Rome and her Italian allies in 91–87 BC. A wine (lit. 'grape', *uuam*) from this period would be approximately two hundred years old. For wine of this age which was virtually undrinkable cf. Plin. *N.H.* 14.55. J.'s phrase may allude to Hor. *Od.* 3.14.18 *cadum Marsi memorem duelli* (from the Social War).

   32–7 The speaker predicts the patron's behaviour on the next day (*cras*): he will continue to drink the finest wines while his client will be suffering from indigestion (*cardiaco ... amico*), presumably from the meal, yet will receive no relief from the patron; *amico* is ironic, as often. Wine was considered the only remedy in extreme cases of dyspepsia: Plin. *N.H.* 23.50 *cardiacorum morbo unicam spem hanc esse certum est*; cf. Sen. *Ep.* 15.3 *bibere et sudare uita cardiaci est*. For justification of the punctuation of 31 and 32 see Housman *ad loc.*   **numquam ... missurus** 'he would never send': the future participle stands for a conditional clause, i.e. 'if his friend were suffering from indigestion, he would never

send'.   **cyathum** 'even a spoonful'; a ladle, to convey wine from the mixing-bowl to the drinking-cup, and hence a measure of liquid, cf. Celsus 3.19.5 *uini cyathum*.   **Albanis aliquid de montibus aut de |
Setinis:** fine wines produced in Latium at Alba (cf. 6.O15, 13.213–14) and Setia (cf. 10.27). Both types would give relief from indigestion (Plin. *N.H.* 23.35–6). Pliny's ranking of wine runs Setine, Falernian, Alban and Surrentine (*N.H.* 14.59–65), whereas Dionysius of Halicarnassus (*R.A.* 1.66.3) considered Falernian the best, followed by Alban.
cuius patriam titulumque senectus | deleuit 'whose country and label old age has effaced'. The *titulus* included both place and date of origin (expressed in terms of the consuls: 30), hence *patriam* is technically redundant. Cf. Petr. *Sat.* 34 *allatae sunt amphorae uitreae diligenter gypsatae, quarum in ceruicibus pittacia erant affixa cum hoc titulo: 'Falernum Opimianum annorum centum.'* For the *patria* of an object cf. 4.129. For the 'old age' of wine cf. 13.214 *Albani ueteris pretiosa senectus*.
fuligine: wine was matured in a smoke-room (*fumarium*: Mart. 10.36.1, Hor. *Od.* 3.8.11–12 *amphorae fumum bibere institutae | consule Tullo*, Stat. *Silv.* 4.8.39 with Coleman), hence a sooty jar (*testa*: the clay amphora) indicates a mature wine.

36–7 Virro's fine wine evokes the assertion of political independence, hence is incongruous for a tyrannical host like Virro. Publius Clodius Thrasea Paetus (consul AD 56) and his son-in-law Helvidius Priscus were leaders of the senatorial opposition to Nero and Vespasian; in AD 66 they were, respectively, condemned to death and exiled; Vespasian later put Helvidius Priscus to death. *libertas* was their slogan and they were associated with Stoicism (Thrasea wrote a book on the Stoic Cato and committed suicide in Stoic fashion), hence the celebration of the birthdays of the Bruti and Cassius. Marcus Brutus, Decimus Brutus and Gaius Cassius Longinus were chief figures in the assassination of Julius Caesar in 44 BC and were thereafter seen as champions of *libertas*; cf. Tac. *Ann.* 1.10 *Cassii et Brutorum exitus*, 16.22. For celebration of birthdays of the dead cf. Sen. *Ep.* 64.9, Suet. *Dom.* 10.3 where commemoration of the emperor Otho is seen as a political threat by Domitian.   **coronati:** the wearing of garlands was usual at any party, cf. 6.297, 15.50.

37–48 Following the contrast of wines, the wine-cups, the host's (37–9 and 43–5) and humble guest's (39–41 and 46–8). Virro's cups are large and gorgeous and have exotic and heroic associations, whereas Trebius is likely to be given a small, mundane and broken item. For contrasting cups concealing different wines see Mart. 4.85. Hence *inaequales* 38 (lit. 'embossed') also suggests 'unfair'.

37 ipse: cf. 30n., here adj. with *Virro* 39, contrasting with *tibi* 39.

37–9 Virro's cups are magnificent: *capaces* indicates their generous size; they are decorated with amber (*Heliadum*) and beryl (*berullo*) which make the surface uneven (*inaequales*; cf. 14.62 *uasa aspera*); Greek *Heliadum*, *berullo* and *phialas* evoke eastern riches. A *phiala* was a broad shallow bowl. For jewels on cups see 43n.

crusta usually means the outer casing but here unusually denotes the cups themselves, i.e. 'casings of Helios' daughters'. The Heliades were the daughters of the sun god Helios and sisters of Phaethon: when lamenting their brother's death they were turned into poplars and their tears turned into amber (see Ov. *Met.* 2.1–366); cf. Mart. 9.13.6 *gemma ... Heliadum*. The three spondees of *inaequales berullo* make a unique line-ending in J., an effect taken from Ov. *Met.* 1.117 *inaequalis autumnos*.   **Virro:** finally the patron is named; cf. the delay in naming Trebius (19). A rare name from the same area of Italy as Trebius', according to Syme (*JRS* 39 (1949) 17; if Virro is to be connected with the *scurra* Vibidius who attends the *cena Nasidieni* with Maecenas (Hor. *Sat.* 2.8.22) this would add the further piquancy of social climbing). The name evokes manliness, *uir-ro*, ironically, in that Virro is no epic hero, despite the epic evocations of his food; J. repeats the name at 9.35 even more ironically of another mean patron, who is also a pathic: see Braund (1988) 242 n. 32.

39–41 Two humiliations: either the client is not entrusted with a gold cup or a guard is stationed nearby to ensure he does not remove the encrusted jewels with his fingernail. For jewelled cups cf. 10.26–7 *pocula ... gemmata*, Luc. 10.160–1 *gemmae ... capaces | excepere merum*. **aurum:** i.e. the gold cup (again 10.27 *lato ... auro*), into which the amber and beryl (above) are set. The word has an epic pedigree, e.g. Virg. *Aen.* 1.738–9 *ille impiger hausit | spumantem pateram et pleno se proluit auro*. For a thieving guest cf. Mart. 8.59 esp. 7.   **adfixus:** of guards, attendants, *OLD affigo* 4b.   **qui numeret ... obseruet:** subjunctive denoting purpose, 'to count ... to watch'.

42 Probably sarcastic comment by the speaker (fiercer than the irony in Rudd's translation), rather than direct speech of Virro or his slave: the speaker ironically adopts the host's materialistic standards

for a moment to expose them. *illi*: dative of advantage.   **iaspis:**
three syllables; mention of this jewel prepares for the allusion to Virg.
Aen. 4.261–2 *illi stellatus iaspide fulua | ensis erat* at lines 44–5.

43–5 Virro's cups are adorned with jewels taken from rings, cf.
Mart. 14.109 *gemmatum Scythicis ut luceat ignibus aurum | aspice. quot digitos
exuit iste calix!* The jewels are given an ancient, heroic, epic pedigree in
the periphrastic relative clause: they are such as the *iuuenis* Aeneas
(might have) had adorning his scabbard; cf. Virg. *Aen.* 4.261–2 (cit.
42n.). For *quas* equivalent to *quales* cf. *quod* 153 and Courtney here.
Transferral of jewels from military to luxurious context marks the
breakdown of Roman morality portrayed in the dysfunctional patron-
client relationship in Satire 5; cf. 11.100–9.   **zelotypo … Iarbae:**
evokes Virg. *Aen.* 4.36 *despectus Iarbas*, the African suitor scorned by
Dido in preference for Aeneas. The Greek word, = 'jealous', is post-
Augustan and used by J. at 6.278 and 8.197 (of a role in mime). *z* is
sometimes treated as a single consonant for metrical convenience; cf.
15.114 *cladē Zacynthos*; *Iarbae* three syllables.

**46–7 Beneuentani sutoris nomen habentem … calicem
nasorum quattuor:** the bathetic periphrasis designates Vatinius
(metrically impossible), originally a 'shoemaker at Beneventum', who
rose to power in Nero's court through informing (Tac. *Ann.* 15.34).
So-called 'Vatinian cups', *calices Vatinii*, had four long spouts resem-
bling his nose: Mart. 14.96 *uilia sutoris calicem monimenta Vatini | accipe;
sed nasus longior ille fuit.* In the phrase *nasorum quattuor* the genitive gives
the specific measurement (Roby §1308). For *siccabis calicem*, cf. Hor.
Sat. 2.6.68 *siccat inaequalis calices conuiua.*

47–8 iam quassatum 'already cracked'.

48 rupto poscentem sulpura uitro: the glass should be sold to
the pedlars who exchanged sulphur-tipped matches for broken glass
(Mart. 1.41.3–5); *rupto … uitro* is abl. abs.

49–52 Water follows readily from wine (24–37), hence *non eadem …
uina* 51. The host's water is pure and cool, the client's not.

49–50 The host's dyspepsia is described in an epic-style phrase,
uinoque ciboque (cf. 6.424, 7.34, 10.152, 14.219, 222, all elevated contexts). The water served to him is exotically cool (*frigidior Geticis …
pruinis*). Cool water was at a premium in the days before mechanical
refrigeration and condemned as luxurious (e.g. Sen. *N.Q.* 4.13.5–8
stomachus … cotidianis cruditatibus perustus, niuem … bibunt, ne niue quidem

contenti sunt, sed glaciem . . . exquirunt).   **domini:** again 71, 81, 92, 137, 147; cf. 4.52n. on imagery of slavery.   **feruet:** cf. *pulmo Falerno* | *arderet*, 4.138–9n.   **Geticis ... pruinis:** cf. Mart. 11.3.3; the Getae were a Thracian people on the Danube whose winters became a byword for coldness, particularly in Ovid's exile poetry (*Tristia*, *Ex Ponto*).   **decocta:** i.e. *aqua*, purified by boiling (hence its name) then cooled with snow, cf. Mart. 14.116.2 *decoctae nobile frigus aquae*.

51–2 A shift from singular (*tu* 46) to plural (*uobis*, *uos*): Trebius is not alone in his humiliation. Metre and punctuation of 52 contribute to the emphasis upon *aquam*, final word before the caesura, an effect repeated by J. at 158. Cf. 1.95, 105, 120, 139.   **poni** 'are served', as at 85, 135, 146, *OLD pono* 5.   **modo:** with *querebar*, 'Was I complaining just now . . . ?'   **aliam** 'different', i.e. inferior.

52–65 Water leads to waiters. The client is served by a lowly or ugly African slave (52–5, 59–60, 62–5), but the patron by an expensive and pretty boy from the east (55–9, 60–2). The speaker reverts to the singular (*tibi* 52) to point the contrast with the host (*ante ipsum* 56).

52–5 The client's waiter is an African footman, hence low in status, or a Moroccan whose ugly and threatening appearance evokes a sordid picture of robbery or possibly suggests a ghost.   **pocula:** cups (of wine and water), picked up from 37–48.   **cursor | Gaetulus:** a slave whose job was to run ahead of his master's litter (Petr. 28.4), here from NW Africa, adjacent to Mauretania. On the fashion for Numidian *cursores* cf. Sen. *Ep.* 123.7.   **ossea:** the slave's boniness makes him more sinister, cf. Ov. *Ibis* 144 *insequar et uultus ossea forma tuos*. **Mauri:** 3.79n.   **et cui per mediam nolis occurrere noctem** 'and a character whom you would not want to run into in the middle of the night'; cf. Sen. *Apoc.* 13.3 *ut illum uidit canem nigrum, uillosum, sane non quem uelis tibi in tenebris occurrere*; a black creature might seem more frightening at night because invisible and an omen of doom (for the latter see Hall (1983)).   **cliuosae ... monumenta Latinae:** the tombs which lined the hilly *via Latina*, 1.171n., a likely hiding-place for muggers. For fear of night journeys cf. 10.19–22.

56–9 The patron's waiter, a boy given attractive and exotic associations. *flos Asiae ante ipsum* responds chiastically to *tibi ... cursor* 52. **flos Asiae** 'the flower of Asia', i.e. choicest specimen, *OLD flos* 10, as at e.g. Cat. 63.64 *ego gymnasi fui flos*, implying sexual attractiveness; cf. 9.45–7. Eastern slaves were often seen as exotic indices of luxury, cf.

11.147 *non Phryx aut Lycius.*   **ante ipsum:** the host displays and
enjoys looking at his pretty slave; for *ipsum* 30n.   **pretio maiore
paratus:** cf. 60 *tot milibus emptus*, 4.25n.; for *paratus* 3.224n.   **Tulli
census pugnacis et Anci:** the slave-boy's price evokes the romantic,
distant past: higher than the entire fortune (*census*) of two early kings of
Rome (the third and fourth) of legendary wealth, Hor. *Od.* 4.7.15 *diues
Tullus et Ancus.* Adj. *pugnacis* recalls Virgil's portrayal of military
prowess (*Aen.* 6.813–15).   **ne te teneam** 'to cut a long story short';
the conversational phrase (cf. Sen. *Ep.* 124.20) prepares for the dismissive close to the sentence.   **friuola:** worthless junk, as 3.198n.;
delayed into final position, emphasised by enjambment, to create a
surprise effect in place of 'riches'.

59–60 Back to the client and back to earth, with a phrase characteristic of prose, *quod cum ita sit.*   **Gaetulum Ganymedem:** a paradoxical combination of lowly black African slave (53n.) and beautiful
boy of Greek mythology: Ganymedes was abducted from Asia by Zeus
to be his waiter and lover (cf. 9.47, 13.43, Mart. 9.73.6). The striking
oxymoron, typical of J. (2.10n.), marked by alliteration, conveys
sarcasm: Trebius' waiter is neither beautiful nor young enough to be
anybody's boyfriend.   **respice:** the waiters stood behind the guests,
except the host's *flos Asiae.*

60–2 Back, briefly, to the patron's waiter, through this connexion of
thought: 'You must catch the eye of your black Ganymede, since the
flos Asiae is too grand for you. There is some excuse for *him* . . . ', namely
his youth (*puer, aetas*), good looks (*forma*) and price (*tot milibus emptus*).
pauperibus: clearly marks the division in the *cena*, cf. 146 *uilibus . . .
amicis.*   **miscere** 'to mix' the water and wine, as was normal in
Roman drinking.   **sed forma, sed aetas:** cf. Ov. *Met.* 3.455 *nec
forma nec aetas.*   **digna supercilio:** (sc. *est*); 'justify his pride', i.e.
make his haughtiness appropriate. Cf. Sen. *Const.* 14.1 *contumeliam
uocant ostiari difficultatem, nomenclatoris superbiam, cubiculari supercilium.*
Haughty attendants are the mark of a tyrant: Mart. 9.79.2; cf. J. 6.169.

62–5 In contrast with the *flos Asiae* who has some excuse for ignoring
Trebius, the black slave (*ille*) has no such excuse. His lofty attitude
makes Trebius' humiliation even more pointed.   **rogatus** 'reques-
ted', *OLD* 6.   **calidae gelidaeque:** i.e. *aquae*: both hot and cold
water were mixed with wine, according to taste, cf. Mart. 14.105,
Athen. 3.123e.   **indignatur:** cf. *digna* 62, *indignatio* 120, *dignus* 173

(the penultimate word); this root often conveys humiliation. *indignatur* is followed by two different constructions: infinitive *parere* and two *quod* clauses.   **quippe** 'for', as always in J.   **ueteri ... clienti:** echoes *ueterum ... officiorum* 13; on the uncomplimentary tone 1.132n. **quod ... poscas et quod ... recumbas:** the verbs are subjunctive because they represent the waiter's thoughts rather than the speaker's statement of facts.   **se stante:** abl. abs. = waiting at table (*OLD* 1b).   **recumbas:** 3.82n.

66–79 The breads enjoyed by client (67–9) and patron (70–5), leading to contemplation of the toils and the rewards of the system (76–9). For different qualities of bread cf. Sen. *Ep.* 119.3 *utrum hic panis sit plebeius an siligineus, ad naturam nihil pertinet*, Mart. 9.2.3–4 *illa siligineis pinguescit adultera cunnis,* | *conuiuam pascit nigra farina tuum.*

66 Heinrich's deletion is accepted by Housman and Clausen; Courtney and Martyn retain the line, ending it with a colon so that it introduces the example of *superbia* which follows. Generalisations such as this are often suspected, not always justifiably, e.g. the lines about bad slaves at 9.120–3 (discussed by Braund (1988) 254 n. 117).

Line 66 assists the transition from waiters to bread by highlighting the superiority (*superbia*) typically shown by slaves of wealthy households.

67–9 Another slave grumbles (*quanto ... murmure*) as he hands the lowly client his rock-hard and mouldy bread. Cf. the *panis secundus* with which a poet must content himself (Hor. *Ep.* 2.1.123).   **ecce alius quanto ... murmure:** lit. 'See with what a loud grumble another [slave] ...'; better 'Here's another. Grumbling audibly, ...' (Rudd). **uix fractum** 'hardly breakable', hence *solidae ... farinae.*   **mucida frusta:** again 14.128 *mucida caerulei panis ... frusta.*   **quae genuinum agitent:** *quae* picks up *frusta*: 'to keep your molars busy': the subj. indicates purpose or quality. The sheer physicality of this picture of the client chewing in vain degrades him; contrast Persius' portrayal of Lucilius (*genuinum fregit*, 1.115), where physicality indicates his satirical ferocity.   **admittentia:** 3.235n.

70–5 The patron's bread is described in terms of sexual attractiveness (*tener, niueus, mollis*), as if it were a beautiful slave-boy; it is the object of almost religious awe (*reuerentia*). Whiteness (*niueus*) of the bread contrasts with the client's mouldy morsel (*mucida*). Apostrophe to the impertinent client (*dextram cohibere memento*) and quotation of

direct speech by an attendant emphasise the client's humiliation.
niueus: for flour whiter than snow and white bread see Archestratus
fr. 4 in Athen. 111e.   **siligine:** a fine type of wheat; cf. Sen. *Ep.*
119.3 (cit. 66–79n.).   **fictus** 'kneaded', 'shaped', *OLD* 1c.   **seruatur** 'is kept (back), reserved'.   **salua sit artoptae reuerentia:**
lit. 'respect for the bread-pan must be maintained' (Lewis). *artopta*,
Greek, designates the bread-pan in which the bread was baked. For
reuerentia, see 2.110n.   **finge tamen ...** 'But suppose ...', functioning as conditional clause.   **improbulum:** the diminutive suggests
'rather': 'rather cheeky'. Lack of tact was not the way to ingratiate
oneself with a patron, cf. 129–30n., 9.63 *'improbus es cum poscis'* with
Braund (1988) 162.   **superest illic** 'there is [always] someone
there standing over you'.   **ponere:** i.e. *deponere*, 'to put down' (cf.
3.56n.) the bread which you have hybristically taken.

74–5 The slave's rebuke to the humble client deepens his humiliation.   **uis tu:** peremptory in tone, 'Kindly ...'.   **consuetis:**
the client ought to know which are the baskets (*canistris*) from which he
must take his bread: he has been a guest here before.   **conuiua:** an
ironic misnomer, in that there is no sharing here (25n.).   **impleri:**
i.e. fill yourself, cf. Petr. *Sat.* 16.1 *nos impleuimus cena.*   **panis ... tui
... colorem:** i.e. black (cf. 66–79n.).

76–9 The client is left muttering sarcastically (*scilicet*) to himself,
that this is an inadequate reward for the privations he has endured for
the patron; cf. Mart. 3.36, 12.26. For guests muttering at the table cf.
Hor. *Sat.* 2.8.77–8.

These lines rework 19–23, also introduced by *propter quod*. Here the
mock-epic touches of 78–9 convey Trebius' indignation, before the
bathos of his dripping cloak.   **hoc fuerat propter quod ...** 'it was
for this that ...'.   **montem aduersum gelidasque ... Esquilias:** hendiadys: 'the Esquiline's freezing slope' (Rudd). It was a steep
climb up from the Subura to the Esquiline (Mart. 5.22.5), an area of
expensive housing (cf. 11.50–1). *gelidas* recalls *frigida* 23.   **cucurri:**
like the client at 3.128.   **uernus | Iuppiter:** cf. Calp. Sic. *Ecl.* 5.45
peragit uernum Iouis inconstantia tempus. Jupiter was the Italian sky-god,
hence can designate the sky (*OLD* 1 and 2). A more elevated translation than 'the spring-time sky' is required, cf. Ceres = corn, Bacchus =
wine, etc. On spring showers see 4.87–8n.   **paenula:** a close-fitting,
weather-proof, hooded cloak.

80–91 An abrupt return to the sequence of the *cena*, announced by *aspice* 80. The starters, seafood in an oil dressing. The patron's is a huge lobster garnished with asparagus (80–3), the client's half an egg stuffed with one prawn (84–5); next, the oil on the patron's dish is the finest (86) whereas that on the client's dish is of the lowest quality (87–91). The descriptions emphasise again the social divide and highlight the patron's lordly lobster and the client's rancid oil.

80 quam longo ... squilla 'with what a long breast the lobster marks out the dish which is carried to my master'.

80–1 quibus undique saepta | asparagis 'with what asparagus it is walled in on all sides', cf. *constrictus* 84. *saepta* figures the lobster as a king or a prisoner surrounded by a bodyguard; the asparagus was perhaps presented erect like spears.

82 qua despiciat conuiuia cauda 'with what a tail it looks down upon the company'. For ironic *conuiuia* (1.141n.) cf. *conuiua* 74.

83 excelsi manibus sublata ministri: the lobster's lofty position is metaphorical too: even the seafood scorns the humble clients, repeating the superciliousness of the patron's slaves (60–5).

84 dimidio constrictus cammarus ouo: the crayfish, an inferior and cheaper seafood dish (e.g. Mart. 2.43.12, contrasted with huge mullets). Fish served with halved boiled eggs was standard in a modest meal, e.g. Mart. 5.78.5 *diuisis cybium latebit ouis*; the singular *ouo* and *dimidio* and *constrictus* (which seems not to have the military connotations of *saepta* 81 above) diminish the size and significance of this dish.

85 ponitur: 51n.   **exigua feralis cena patella** 'a funereal supper on a tiny dish', in apposition to *cammarus*. Reference is to the *nouemdialis cena*, a frugal meal which often included eggs left on the grave nine days after burial. The careful patterning (VabBA) conflicts with the content.

86 Venafrano: sc. *oleo*: olive oil from Venafrum on the border of Latium and Campania was of the highest quality.   **piscem perfundit:** cf. Hor. *Sat.* 2.4.50 *perfundat piscis ... oliuo*. The verb suggests lavishness: 'drench'. *piscem* refers to the lobster.   **at hic qui:** the three monosyllables (an unusual feature at the end of a line) mark the stark contrast.

87 pallidus ... caulis: broccoli is humble food (1.134n.), in contrast with the patron's asparagus (82), and pale broccoli is utterly

unappetising, cf. Mart. 13.17.1 *tibi pallentes moueant fastidia caules.*
adfertur: cf. Hor. *Sat.* 2.6.109, 2.8.42–3 *adfertur squillas inter murena
natantis | in patina porrecta.*   **misero tibi:** cf. 1.134, but here the
sympathy is at least partially ironic.

87–8 olebit | lanternam: here *oleo* = 'stink' (*OLD* 1c). *lanternam*,
lit. 'lamp', connotes the poor quality oil used in lamps; the patron has
emptied his lamps to provide the salad dressing for the humble guests,
a reworking of the insult at Hor. *Sat.* 1.6.123–4 *unguor oliuo | non quo
fraudatis immundus Natta lucernis.* Enjambment increases the impact of
the unexpected *lanternam* (cf. *friuola* 59), which introduces the lengthy
description of this oil (88–91).

88–91 A threefold description of the unpleasant associations of the
oil offered to Trebius, delivered with relish. For this expansive description cf. 34–7. There is poor MS support for line 91, yet it provides a
suitable climax, incorporating an echo of Virg. *Georg.* 1.129.
uestris ... alueolis 'your dishes'; for the plural 51–2n.   **canna
Micipsarum:** lit. 'a reed of the Micipsas', disparaging; *canna* suggests
a reed-boat (cf. Val. Fl. 2.108) associated with the Nile (Plin. *N.H.*
7.206); the name suggests African origin, since Micipsa was the son of
Masinissa, king of Numidia.   **subuexit** 'has conveyed upstream'
(*OLD* 2), i.e. up the Tiber to Rome, the opposite of *deuexit* (cf. 7.121
uinum Tiberi deuectum).   **propter quod:** an extra facetious point: no
one at Rome will bathe with this African (Boccar is the name of an
ancient Mauretanian king) because he anoints himself with this oil.
quod ... etiam: the climactic element is that the oil wards off black
snakes. Poisonous snakes were particularly associated with Africa, e.g.
Hor. *Sat.* 2.8.95 *serpentibus Afris*, Plin. *N.H.* 7.14; Luc. 9.619–937.

92–106 The seafood dishes, with contrast in numbers and origins.
The host is served with two fish, a mullet (92–8) and a moray
eel/lamprey (99–102), the client with one (103–6, although two possi-
bilities are mentioned, *aut* 104); the host's seafood is of exotic provenance, the client's of local and unpleasant origins.

92 mullus erit domini quem 'the master's mullet will be one
which ...'. On mullet 4.15n.; for *domini* 49n.

93 Tauromenitanae rupes: i.e. Taormina, Sicily. The grand
phrase lends dignity to the fish. The mullet from here was probably the
saxatilis mullus, Mart. 10.37.7, Sen. *N.Q.* 3.18.4.   **peractum** 'used
up', *OLD* 7.

94 nostrum mare: usually the Mediterranean, here specifically the Etruscan sea (*OLD Tyrrhenus* b), between Italy, Sardinia and Sicily.   **dum gula saeuit:** *dum* is causal (*OLD* 4b), explaining the depletion of local seafood: 'since gluttony rages', cf. Gell. 6.16.6 *peragrantis gulae et in sucos inquirentis industriam*; Petr. *Sat.* 119.33 *ingeniosa gula est. gula:* 1.140n.; *saeuit* cf. 14.148–9 *saeuos ... uentres.* On scouring the world for choice produce: 1.135n., and cf. esp. Sen. *Ep.* 89.22 *gula ... maria scrutatur.*

95–6 retibus ... proxima: *scrutante macello*, ablative absolute, stands for *dumque scrutatur.* Here 'the market' is personified, cf. Hor. *Sat.* 2.3.229–30 *cum scurris fartor, cum Velabro omne macellum | mane domum ueniant. proxima* n. pl. = 'the closest [places]'. *adsiduis, penitus* and *scrutante* convey the vigour of the fishing.

96 nec patimur Tyrrhenum crescere piscem: also after *dum* 94; i.e. the fish are caught young. The first person plural verb suggests that the speaker identifies with this ransacking of the environment. For *Tyrrhenum* see *nostrum mare* 94n.

97–8 Provenance of exotic foods is connected with legacy-hunting, an archetypal focus of the debasement of relationships in Roman satire. The chiastic word order of 98 makes *uendat* surprising (we expect 'eat' not 'sell'), repeating Mart. 7.20.22 where a miserly glutton takes home scraps of food from dinners not to eat them but *postero die – uendit.*
        focum: 4.66n.   **prouincia:** 4.26n.   **captator ... Laenas:** an unknown Popilius or Octavius. On inheritance-hunters (usually called legacy-hunters), a standard feature of Roman satire, see 3.129n., 4.19n., Champlin (1991) esp. 87–102.   **Aurelia:** evidently a wealthy widow, probably not that at Plin. *Ep.* 2.20.10.

99–102 A large (*maxima*) *muraena* from the straits of Messina, Sicily, to be identified as a moray eel or as a lamprey (on the differences between the two, see Thompson (1947) 162–5 and Wilkins and Hill (1994) 54). The *muraena* was a delicacy, Hor. *Sat.* 2.8.42, particularly that from Sicily: Plin. *N.H.* 9.169, Mart. 13.80; here described in a grandiloquent style.   **gurgite de Siculo:** the whirlpool is the Charybdis (102) of Homer and Virgil; J. uses *gurges* when evoking epic at 2.150, 3.266.

100–2 The weather conditions under which lampreys may be caught in the straits of Messina, i.e. when there is no south wind. Grand style (line 102 has the pattern VabBA), with personification of

Auster. Cf. Ovid's description of Aeolus at *Met.* 11.431–2 *qui carcere fortes | contineat uentos.* On the dangers of the south wind in these straits see Ov. *Met.* 8.121 *austro . . . agitata Charybdis*, Sen. *Ep.* 14.8.   **se continet:** lit. 'contains himself', i.e. is inactive.   **madidas:** cf. Virg. *Georg.* 1.462 *umidus Auster.*   **carcere:** cf. 10.181 *Aeolio . . . carcere*, likewise of the winds.   **contemnunt . . . temeraria lina:** the 'nets' (personified) 'disregard' (cf. 6.90 *contempsit pelagus*) the dangers of the sea. *linum* lit. 'flax', hence things made from flax (*OLD* 2d).

103 uos (cf. 52) in asyndeton marks the contrast with the clients' dish, the eel. The link with the snake (Lat. *anguis:* see Var. *L.L.* 5.77), brought out in *longae cognata colubrae* in apposition, makes the eel unpleasant. Other sources indicate that the eel was acceptable fare or even singled out (see André (1961) 99; Wilkins and Hill (1994) 54).

104–6 The alternative (*aut*) is river-fish, usually identified as pike or sea-bass (*lupus*). On the problems of text and interpretation here see Courtney *ad loc.* and Gowers (1993) 215; Campbell may be correct in reordering the lines 103, 106, 104, 105. *glacie aspersus maculis* is probably corrupt, a reminiscence of 4.42, concealing a noun in agreement with *Tiberinus,* cf. Lucil. 603W = 1196M *hunc pontes Tiberinus duo inter captus catillo,* Hor. *Sat.* 2.2.31 *lupus . . . Tiberinus.* The fish's blotches (*maculis*) and the sewage and sewer through which it swims introduce unsavoury associations.   **Tiberinus:** caught from the river at the heart of Rome, around the *insula Tiberina* (see Platner and Ashby 281–2) *inter duos pontes* (see Lucilius and Horace above).   **et ipse | uernula riparum** 'himself a slave native to the banks'; unclear reference: *et ipse* links fish with client: both are slaves who feed on shit. The diminutive of *uerna* ('home-grown') emphasises the fish's lowly status.   **pinguis:** bloated not by the cold (*longo frigore pingues* 4.44) but by the sewage it has fed upon.   **torrente cloaca** 'the gushing sewer', cf. 4.43n. The *cloaca maxima* flowed into the Tiber a little downstream of the *insula Tiberina.* On the Roman sewer system see Plin. *N.H.* 36.104–8.   **mediae cryptam . . . Suburae:** a verbal parallel with *mediam . . . Charybdim* (102) which emphasises the un-exotic nature of this fish. For *Subura* with associations of bodily appetites as last word in the line or sentence, cf. 3.5n., 10.156.

107–113 The speaker interrupts the menu to attack the patron with increasing directness and rising indignation: *ipsi* and *praebeat,* third person; *nemo petit . . . quae mittebantur,* ellipse of direct reference to the patron ('no one asks [you to send] the gifts sent . . . '); *poscimus ut cenes*, the second person with the politeness of the indirect command; *hoc face et esto*, direct imperative. The patron is not required to behave like the legendary patrons of the past, but is desired to show certain standards of decency. On the antithesis between wholesome past and corrupt present in Satire 5 see Cuccioli (1990).

107 ipsi: the patron, 30n.   **pauca uelim:** understand *dicere*; cf. Ter. *Andr.* 29 *paucis te uolo.*   **facilem ... aurem:** 3.122n.; the line-ending *praebeat aurem* repeats Hor. *Sat.* 1.1.22. Accessibility is typical of the good patron/emperor, cf. Plin. *Pan.* 47.2–3.

108 modicis ... amicis: gradations of *amicus* were expressed through adjectives, e.g. 146 *uilibus ... amicis*, Plin. *Ep.* 2.6.2 *minoribus amicis (nam gradatim amicos habet)*; cf. Saller (1982) 11–12.

109 Seneca ... Piso ... Cotta: Neronian Piso and Seneca are paired by Martial in a poem nostalgic for the good patrons of the past (12.36.8). L. Annaeus Seneca is the famous Stoic philosopher, millionaire (10.16) and tutor to Nero; C. Calpurnius Piso, addressee of the *Laus Pisonis* which praises his generosity, was executed after the so-called Pisonian conspiracy of AD 65. Cotta is probably Cotta Maximus, Ovid's patron, praised as a model patron at 7.95.

110–11 'For then the honour of giving was prized more highly than titles and symbols of office.' (Rudd) *titulis*: 1.130n. The *fasces* were the bundle of rods which symbolised a magistrate's power.

111–12 solum poscimus: contrasts with *nemo petit* 108; the collective request (first person plural) and the limitation of *solum* (this is our only request) make this plea persuasive.   **ciuiliter:** i.e. as equals, without insult, 'unpretentiously'; for this language and idea cf. e.g. Plin. *Pan.* 2.4 *nec minus hominem se quam hominibus praeesse meminit*; see Wallace-Hadrill (1982). Ovid uses this word of Augustus' treatment of him at *Tr.* 3.8.41 (see Luck *ad loc.*); cf. Tac. *Ann.* 1.54 *ciuile rebatur misceri uoluptatibus uulgi* (Augustus).

112 hoc face et esto: veils a conditional, 'if you do this, then you may'. For this imperative cf. Cat. 36.16, V.Fl. 7.179, Quint. *I.O.* 1.6.21.

113 esto: repetition of the last word of the previous line, as 2.135–6.   **ut nunc multi:** cf. 43 *ut multi*.   **diues tibi, pauper amicis:** provided the patron observes the appearance of courtesy he can be stingy to his humble clients and lavish to himself, cf. the oxymoron *luxuriae sordes* 1.140n. Cf. Cic. *Off.* 3.63 *neque enim solum nobis diuites esse uolumus sed liberis, propinquis, amicis maximeque rei publicae*, Mart. 9.2, e.g. 1 *pauper amicitiae cum sis, Lupe, non es amicae*. A stinging comment on contemporary hosts and on clients' passive endurance of discrimination provided it is practised tactfully.

114-16 The arrival of the meat dishes in front of the patron (*ante ipsum* 114). His three dishes to Trebius' none shows that he ignores the speaker's intervention. The meat dish was conventionally the centre-piece of the *cena*, yet here is dealt with briefly, in two and a half lines. All three dishes served to Virro were delicacies: (1) goose liver (foie gras), from force-feeding geese on figs, cf. Hor. *Sat.* 2.8.88 *ficis pastum iecur anseris albae*; for the Romans' enthusiasm for this see Athen. 9.384c; (2) fattened fowl, i.e. a chicken fattened in the dark on sweetened meal, cf. Var. *R.R.* 3.9.19–21, Sen. *Ep.* 122.4; (3) boar (1.141n.), a dish which ought to be shared, cf. 1.141 *animal propter conuiuia natum*. The language describing Virro's food is elevated by polyptoton *anseris ... anseribus* and the boar's heroic associations.

par 'as big as'. The final monosyllable and enjambment of the noun create a moment of suspense. **flaui ... Meleagri:** the Latin for ξανθὸς Μελέαγρος, Hom. *Il.* 2.642, slayer of the Calydonian boar which ravaged his land (Aetolia); see Ov. *Met.* 8.270–429 (a burlesque treatment). For comparisons with the Calydonian boar at *cenae*, e.g. Mart. 7.27.1–2 and often. *ferro* is his hunting-spear. **spumat:** cf. Mart. 14.221.2 *spumeus in longa cuspide fumet aper* (perhaps the source of the variant *fumat*). J. may envisage the boar served up foaming at the mouth, as if still alive direct from the hunt (cf. Virg. *Aen.* 4.158); for 'realistic' presentation of a boar at *cena* cf. Petr. *Sat.* 40.

116-19 Truffles (*tubera*) are served to the patron; again, there is no equivalent dish for Trebius. These fungi were (and still are, esp. in Italy) another delicacy, cf. 14.7, Mart. 13.50, Plin. *N.H.* 19.33–5. 'Truffles are a kind of underground fungus or mushroom, mostly about the size of a golf-ball, blue-black in colour when fresh, turning to brown-black. The outside has a somewhat warty appearance and inside the flesh is yellow-white.' (Mabey (1972), quoting from an article in *Country Life* 'Truffle hunting in England'.)

116-18 'If it is then spring and the longed-for thunder makes feasts larger.' J. incorporates gastronomic lore that truffles grow most tender in spring and most vigorously in thunderstorms (Plin. *N.H.* 19.37), a tradition rejected by Plutarch at *Qu. Conv.* 4.2 = *Mor.* 664b–665e. This detail is on a par with Montanus' gourmandise at 4.140–3nn. **facient ... cenas maiores:** i.e. by adding a dish to the menu.

118–19 Alledius is an epicure otherwise unknown. His pompous apostrophe to Libya refers to the fact that Rome's chief grain supplies came from Africa, Sicily and Egypt. For truffles from Africa cf. Plin. *N.H.* 19.34. The Libyan truffle differed from the native Italian kinds: André (1961) 45–6. *Libye*: three syllables, Greek form; north Africa, west of Egypt. *dum*: 'provided that'.   **tibi habe frumentum** 'keep your corn to yourself', 3.188n.   **disiunge boues** 'unyoke your oxen', i.e. the oxen used for ploughing the land and hence producing cereal crops.

120–4 The humble client is compelled to watch the carving of the meat while the others are eating (*interea*). *spectes* emphasises his role as mere spectator, cf. Mart. 1.20, 43.11 *et nihil inde datum est; tantum spectauimus omnes.* Carving was part of the entertainment at lavish dinner-parties and is here presented as an art form; cf. Trimalchio's carver at *Sat.* 36. The description of the carver ends with a sarcastic jibe (123–4).   **structorem:** properly the slave who lays the food on the trays (7.184, Petr. *Sat.* 35) but by extension the carver, as at 11.136–41.   **ne qua indignatio desit** 'that no cause of anger may be missing'; the client considers this treatment less than worthy (*dignus*) of him (cf. *ciuiliter* 112n.), but the patron understands the client well (see *dignus* 173n.).   **chironomunta** 'gesticulating' (as 6.63), hence *gestu* 124, cf. Petr. *Sat.* 36 *scissor ... gesticulatus ... lacerauit obsonium*; the Greek word conveys scorn.   **uolanti | cultello** 'with flourishes of the knife' (Lewis).   **peragat dictata magistri | omnia:** the carver is thorough in following his teacher's instructions; for teachers cf. 11.137 *discipulus Trypheri doctoris*, Sen. *Ep.* 47.6.   **nec minimo ... discrimine refert:** ironic understatement, *nec minimo = nam maximo. refert = interest*, as 6.657, 11.21.   **sane:** 1.42n., 4.16n.   **secetur:** i.e. is carved, as 11.135; often *carpere* is used.

125–31 The speaker pauses to deplore the fact that Trebius is not even permitted to protest at this uncivilised treatment because of the threat of violence (125–7); he portrays a total communication barrier between rich and poor (127–31).

125 duceris planta 'you will be dragged by the foot', a rephrasing of Virg. *Aen.* 8.264–5 *pedibus ... informe cadauer | protrahitur* (Cacus' ejection). **uelut ictus ab Hercule Cacus:** a reference to Virgil's story (*Aeneid* 8) of the monster Cacus who lived in a cave on the future site of Rome and who stole Hercules' oxen but was beaten and killed by the hero. Only here is Trebius linked with mythology, unlike Virro, whose choice food is laden with exotic mythological associations; for Trebius the associations are not food-focussed but evoke an unceremonious removal and defeat; cf. the similar associations of *Corybanta*, 25n.

126 ponere foris 'dumped out of doors'.

127 hiscere: precisely the right word: *OLD* 2: 'to open the mouth to speak (esp. as the first or minimal action in speaking)', cf. Liv. 45.26.7 *nemo aduersus praepotentes uiros hiscere audebat*. **tamquam habeas tria nomina:** i.e. as if you were free, ironically, since Trebius is. This refers back to *ciuiliter* 112 and anticipates the theme of freedom at 161–73. A free man had a *praenomen, nomen* ^nd *cognomen* (cf. Sen. *Ben.* 4.8.3, Quint. *I.O.* 7.3.27), whereas a slave had only one name. **quando:** the question invites or implies the reply, 'Never!' **propinat:** the proposer of a toast drank first himself then passed the cup to the friend to whom he was drinking. Toasts between Virro and Trebius are impossible (127–9).

128 contacta 'polluted, contaminated'.

129 quis uestrum: the plural generalises the speaker's complaint. **usque adeo:** with *temerarius* and *perditus*; after its adjective again at 6.181–2.

130 perditus: 3.73n., cf. 8.211–12 *quis tam | perditus ut dubitet Senecam praeferre Neroni?*; for the same idea cf. *inprobulum* 73n. **'bibe':** an invitation to drink, 'Cheers!' (Rudd); cf. *CIL* III 293 *dum uixi bibi libenter bibite uos qui uiuitis*.

131 pertusa ... laena 'when they have holes in their coat', abl. abs.; for status diminished by damaged clothes cf. 3.147–51; for *laena* 3.283n.

132–6 Virro's different reaction to a sudden change in his client's fortune is abruptly pictured. For *si quis deus* initiating the hypothesis cf. Hor. *Sat.* 1.1.15, typically undermined here by an alternative donor, a *homuncio*.

132 quadringenta: 1.106n. For gifts to bring the recipient up to the equestrian census cf. Plin. *Ep.* 1.19.2, Mart. 4.67, 5.25.

133 melior fatis ... homuncio 'a mere man ... kinder than fate';

homuncio is a diminishing term, cf. Petr. *Sat.* 34 *diutius uiuit uinum quam homuncio.*

133–4 quantus | ex nihilo ... fieres 'from a nobody what a great man you would become', cf. Petr. *Sat.* 38 *de nihilo creuit.*

134 quantus ... amicus: i.e. a valued, close and powerful friend, *magnus amicus* (1.33n.), opposite to the *uilibus ... amicis* 146.

135–6 The speaker puts words into Virro's mouth, first to the slave then to Trebius himself. Direct speech is rare in this poem: 18n.; significantly, this speech is purely hypothetical. Repeated use of Trebius' name marks his change into favour.   **frater:** a complimentary mark of familiarity, cf. Hor. *Ep.* 1.6.54.   **ilibus:** the loin, the most prized part of the boar, Mart. 10.45.3–4.

136–7 A grand apostrophe to riches (*nummi*), which are central to J.'s portrayal of life in Rome, cf. 1.111–14. Anaphora *uobis ... uos* is elevated and emphasises Virro's allegiance to money, as does the run of spondees.   **frater:** virtually quoted from 135; cf. Mart. 8.81.6 (of pearls) *hos fratres uocat.* For mixed singular + plural cf. Plin. *Ep.* 4.27.2 *unus Plinius est mihi priores*, Mart. 5.38.7 *unus cum sitis, duo, Calliodore, sedebis?*

137–9 A logical if cynical rider: children are an obstacle to anyone with ambitions, an allusion to legacy-hunting, in which the childless are pursued for their riches (3.129n.; cf. 6.38–40).   **dominus ... et domini rex:** two terms of absolute superiority used earlier are here combined; on *dominus* 49n., on *rex* 14n.; cf. 8.161 *dominum regemque.* The final monosyllable is metrically disruptive again.   **tibi paruulus aula | luserit Aeneas:** reworking Virg. *Aen.* 4.328–9 *si quis mihi paruulus aula | luderet Aeneas* (Dido). *Aeneas* here stands for 'son'; the heroic reference is ironic. *luserit:* perf. subj., as regularly in 3rd person prohibitions. *paruulus* is famously the only diminutive adjective used in the *Aeneid* (see Austin *ad loc.*).   **dulcior illo:** *dulcior* is to be construed with both *Aeneas* and *filia:* the client is advised to have no child which is 'dearer than [Virro]', i.e. who would come between Virro and a legacy.

140 'A barren wife makes your friend pleasant and close.' I.e. the hope of inheritance makes 'friends' behave affectionately. For complementary advice to a legacy-hunter cf. Hor. *Sat.* 2.5.31 *sperne domi si gnatus erit fecundaue coniunx.*

141–5 The speaker imagines (*licet* = in effect 'if') the antithetical situation (hence *sed . . . nunc*, 'but as it is'): if Trebius' wife produces many children, the patron will not be distressed (because he already knows that he can gain nothing from impoverished Trebius) and will be happy to give the children gifts of insignificant value. The vocabulary of affection (*in gremium patris*) including the imagery of the nest (*loquaci . . . nido*) sharpens the speaker's cynicism: the patron gushes sentimentally over this pretty scene, a sardonic contrast with the cheap-skate beneficence he actually offers. The wife's fertility is emphasised by the final position of *tres* and by *fundat semel*: she produces triplets. **Mycale:** Trebius' wife (77 *coniuge*), probably a freedwoman, since the name sounds Greek or Jewish. **tres:** the existence of three heirs rules out hopes of a legacy, cf. 12.95. **loquaci ... nido:** cf. Plin. *N.H.* 35.12; another echo of Virgil, *Aen.* 12.475 of the swallow, *pabula parua legens nidisque loquacibus escas.* **uiridem thoraca:** a green jacket, the colour of one of the most popular chariot-teams, cf. 7.114, 11.198 *uiridis . . . panni.* This gift resembles the gift of a shirt or scarf of the child's favourite soccer team. **minimas ... nuces:** children were often given nuts to play with (like marbles) and then eat; cf. Hor. *Sat.* 2.3.171, Pers. 1.10. The small size of the nuts (*minimas*) emphasises Virro's meanness. **assem:** a small coin, 'a penny', *OLD as* 2, cf. J. 14.301. **parasitus ... infans:** Trebius' son, taught to follow his father; cf. Lucian, *Paras.* 13. On *parasitus*, 1.139n.; cf. Corbett (1986). Almost an oxymoron, disparaging tone, cf. Ter. *Ad.* 779 *parasitaster paullulus.*

146–8 Here the speaker resumes the double menu with mushrooms, first those served to the humble clients then that served to the host. The vocabulary corresponds with Martial's attack on dual menus, *sunt tibi boleti, fungos ego sumo suillos* (3.60.5). **uilibus ... amicis:** cf. *uilius* 4n., *modicis . . . amicis* 108n., *quantus . . . amicus* 134n. **ancipites** 'of dubious quality' (*OLD* 1ob), hardly qualifying as food, like the wine at 24–9; cf. Plin. *N.H.* 22.97 *quae uoluptas tam ancipitis cibi?* **boletus ... quales Claudius edit | ante illum uxoris, post quem nihil amplius edit:** inspired by Mart. 1.20.4 *boletum qualem Claudius edit edas.* J. alludes to the story that the emperor Claudius was poisoned by his wife Agrippina who served him *boletus*, a favourite dish (6.620–1 *Agrippinae | boletus*, Suet. *Cl.* 44.2). This suggests that the emperor's death would suit this tyrannical host too. For the demonstrative pronoun + gen. cf. Cic. *Att.* 13.45.1 (sc. *epistula*) *quae . . . ante data erat quam illae Diocharinae.*

149–55 The final course is apples, the regular *mensae secundae* of fruit, again articulated as a contrast between the delectable fruits served to Virro and his like (149–52) and the rotten item given to Trebius (153–5). The picture of the performing monkey (153–5) symbolises Trebius' degradation and servile status; cf. 8–11nn. for similar implications. Cf. Lucian, *De merc. cond.* 24 of the parasite: 'with your neck in a collar like a monkey you are a laughing-stock to others, but seem to yourself to be living in luxury because you can eat figs without limit'.

149 reliquis Virronibus: the 'other Virros', the guests who share Virro's menu.

150 poma: fruit, specified as apples by lines 151–2. **quorum solo pascaris odore:** the smell is a meal in itself. Cf. Mart. 1.92.9 *pasceris et nigrae solo nidore culinae.* Generalising second person singular.

151 perpetuus Phaeacum autumnus: Virro's apples are linked with the mythological produce of Alcinous' ever-fertile orchard (Hom. *Od.* 7.114–21); cf. Virg. *Georg.* 2.87 *pomaque et Alcinoi siluae. autumnus* translates ὀπώρα = 'fruit-time', 'ripeness', cf. Sen. *Thy.* 167–8 *totus in arduum | autumnus rapitur siluaque mobilis.*

152 subrepta sororibus Afris: a second mythological allusion, to Hercules' theft of the golden apples of the Hesperides (the nymphs here called 'African sisters') from their garden located in north west Africa, which was Hercules' final labour. The apples of the Hesperides are linked with Alcinous' at Mart. 10.94, 13.37, *Priap.* 16.

153 tu: with stark asyndeton the speaker turns to Trebius. **scabie ... mali** 'a scabby apple', metonymically for *scabioso malo*, cf. 11 *sordes farris . . . canini.* **frueris:** ironic, since Trebius is unlikely to enjoy any of this *cena.* **quod:** *quale* would be more accurate; for this loose use of the relative pronoun cf. *quas* 44n. **aggere:** the embankment running from the Esquiline to the Colline gate, a pleasant place for a promenade (cf. 8.43 *uentoso ... aggere,* Hor. *Sat.* 1.8.15 *aggere in aprico spatiari*); consequently, it attracted fortune-tellers (6.588) and other entertainments, as here, a performing monkey. The client has refused to live off dog biscuits as an independent beggar (*crepido,* 8) and ends up chewing a wizened apple like a performing monkey. **rodit:** typically of animals (*OLD* 1), cf. 3.207 (mice).

154–5 qui tegitur ... capella: this monkey, dressed like a soldier, sits upon a goat and throws a javelin, fearing his owner's whip (*metuens ...flagelli*) and rewarded for a good throw by a rotten apple (*scabie ... mali*); cf. Aelian's claim to have seen a monkey holding the reins, using a whip and driving a chariot (*H.A.* 5.26). For *metuens* + gen. cf. 7.210 *metuens uirgae*.

156–73 This closing section resumes and develops themes of the opening section, 1–11nn.: the speaker attacks Trebius for his willingness to endure degradation at Virro's hands and portrays him as deluded about his autonomy: he has reduced himself to the status of Virro's slave. At the same time, Virro's behaviour assimilates him to the bad emperor whose conduct at feasts is contrasted with Trajan's ideal(ised) behaviour at Plin. *Pan.* 49.6: 'You do not arrive already gorged with a solitary feast (*solitaria cena*) before midday to sit menacingly over your guests, watching and noting all they do, nor when they are fasting and hungry do you belch from a full stomach and present or rather throw at them the food you disdain to touch'.

156–60 Virro's motivation for serving up a horrible meal to Trebius is due not to stinginess but to his desire to mock Trebius, cf. 3.147–53, Plaut. *Stich.* 217 *ridiculus aeque nullus est quam quando esurit* (of the parasite). Mart. 4.67 *inuitas centum quadrantibus et bene cenῦs.* | *ut cenem inuitor, Sexte, an ut inuideam?*

156 inpensae ... parcere 'practising economy', 'saving money'.

157 hoc agit ut doleas 'he does it deliberately to annoy you'. For *hoc agit* cf. Sen. *Ep.* 100.10 *eloquentiam uelut umbram non hoc agens trahit.*

157–8 quae comoedia, mimus | quis melior plorante gula?: Virro prefers the spectacle of Trebius' discomfiture to the regular comic entertainments of dinner-parties; cf. Hor. *Ep.* 2.1.197–8 where Democritus is entertained more by the audience than the performance they are watching. For *comoedia* performed after the *cena* cf. Plin. *Ep.* 9.36.4, 40.2. For the range of after-dinner entertainments (lascivious to intellectual) cf. 11.162–82. The gullet (*gula* 94n., 1.140n.) is personified by *plorante* (cf. 14.10 *cana monstrante gula*), so that it is 'whining', like a dog, cf. Lucr. 5.1072. Hiatus after *gula* and before *ergo* emphasises both.

158–9 omnia fiunt ... ut 'his whole intention is to ...' (Rudd).

159 si nescis 'let me tell you', assertive in tone.   **effundere bilem:** also at Sen. *Ira* 2.26.3; Trebius is inevitably angry, cf. *indignatio* 120n., but it is too risky to express this openly, hence *per lacrimas* and

160. For the clients' inability to respond to the host's arrogance cf. Var. *Sat. Men.* 102 *discumbimus mussati*, Mart. 3.82.32 *hos Malchionis patimur inprobi fastus,* | *nec uindicari ... possumus.*

160 presso ... diu stridere molari 'to gnash long with grinding teeth', a classic sign of anger, cf. Sen. *Herc. Fur.* 693 *frendens Dolor. diu* goes with *stridere*; for *strido* of grinding the teeth cf. Cels. 2.6.5. Mention of his teeth is a reminder that they have been exercised only on bread (69n.), not meat (13.212).

161–5 The speaker explains to Trebius his self-delusion and the reality of the situation (pronouns *tu ... te ... ille* mark the antithesis) and condemns Trebius for this voluntary humiliation with a rhetorical question. The vocabulary of 161–2 recapitulates central themes of the poem. Thus Trebius considers himself (*tibi ... uideris*, mistakenly, cf. Mart. 1.41 esp. 1 *urbanus tibi, Caecili, uideris*) a free man (*liber homo*; cf. 127n.) and a fellow-diner of the patron (*regis conuiua*), whereas he is really like an enslaved animal (153–5), not on equal terms with his host (on <u>conuiua</u> see 25n., 74n.), hence *captum te* ('you are enslaved') in emphatic position, contrasting with *liber*. For the intrinsic contradiction between independence and greed cf. Mart. 2.53.3 *liber eris, cenare foris si, Maxime, nolis*, 9.10.4 *liber non potes et gulosus esse*, Epict. 4.1.55. For vocabulary of slave and king in the context of dinner-invitations cf. Mart. 2.18.

162 captum ... nidore ... culinae: cf. Mart. 5.44.7–8 *captus es unctiore mensa* | *et maior rapuit canem culina*, also Hor. *Sat.* 2.7.38 inc. *nidore.* For *nidore ... culinae* cf. Mart. 1.92.9 (150n.).

163 nec male coniectat 'and he's not far wrong'; understatement.

163–5 No free man would subject himself to such treatment more than once (*bis* is emphasised by position): a condemnation of Trebius, who persists in this life-style: 1–11nn.   **quis enim tam nudus ut ... :** cf. 1.30–1 *nam quis ... tam patiens Vrbis, tam ferreus, ut .... nudus* = 'destitute' (*OLD* 10), cf. 7.35 *nuda senectus.*   **illum:** the patron. **bis:** emphasised by position: once should be enough.   **Etruscum puero si contigit aurum** 'if as a child he wore the Tuscan gold (*bulla*)', i.e. if he is free-born. The amulet hung around the neck of freeborn children until puberty and for the affluent was contained in a gold locket, *bulla*, cf. J. 14.4–5 *heres* | *bullatus*, Stat. *Silv.* 5.3.120 *nobile pectoris aurum. Etruscum*: this was regarded as an Etruscan practice. **nodus tantum et signum de paupere loro:** for those who could not afford a golden locket (hence *paupere*), the amulet consisted of a knot (*nodus*) in a leather thong (*loro*). *de paupere loro*: 'of poor man's leather'. This too is an indication (*signum*) of free status.

166–9 A glimpse of the poor clients (*uos*, 28n.) still waiting, in empty hope, for the meat course (cf. *uotorum summa* 18n.); cf. 1.133–4 *longissima cenae | spes homini*. Direct speech in 166–8 by any or all (*omnes* 169) of the humble clients makes the scene vivid; they mutter among themselves, out of Virro's hearing.   **decipit:** the self-deception of 161–2.   **ecce dabit iam:** a phrase full of expectation; the final monosyllable, metrically disruptive, reflects the mismatch between the clients' hopes and the stark reality. *iam* conveys 'any minute now', repeated 168.   **semesum leporem ... apri:** the humble clients' best hope is for the remains of a dish served to the elevated guests, hence 'half-eaten hare'. Cf. Mart. 3.82.20–1 *partitur apri glandulas palaestritis | et concubino turturum natis donat*, 9.48 esp. 11–12 *nulla | de nostro nobis uncia uenit apro. leporem*: cf. 124; *apri*: cf. 116n. For *clunibus*, 'haunches, buttocks', cf. Plin. *N.H.* 10.140.   **minor altilis:** for *altilis* 115n.; possibly 'too small [for Virro]', or 'smaller' hence inferior or 'smaller [because so much of it has already been served]'. **parato | intactoque ... et stricto pane:** 'bread' is the surprise final word where 'sword' (e.g. *ensis*) might be expected, after the three participles. *intacto* is especially witty: a sword would be 'untouched', i.e. unbloodied, before the fighting commenced; the bread is 'untouched' because the clients have no gravy into which to dip it. The clients are like soldiers waiting to fight: this *cena* is a battle-field, cf. Var. *Sat. Men.* 102 *dominus ... cenam committit.*   **tacetis:** the silence of anticipation and fear (cf. 159n.): Virro's feast is staged as a spectacle to incite the envy of the humble clients.

170–3 The final condemnation of Trebius resumes points made at 1–11nn., particularly the comparison with the *scurrae* at 3–4.

170 sapit: appropriately 'has good sense' and referring to the sense of taste: Virro is 'a discriminating host'.

170–1 omnia ferre | si potes, et debes 'if you *can* endure anything, then you deserve to endure anything'. Cf. 3–4 *si potes illa pati quae nec ... tulisset.*

171–2 pulsandum ... caput: the ultimate consequence of self-abasement: Trebius will some day (*quandoque*) turn into a clown (*morio*), an entertainer with a shaven head (*uertice raso*) receiving blows to the head (*pulsandum ... caput*). The bad patron has such butts of laughter, *Laus Pis.* 126–7 *miserum parua stipe focilat, ut pudibundos | exercere sales inter conuiuia possit.* This figure resembles the *stupidus* in the mime, whose role is likewise to be slapped, cf. 8.192 *alapas.* Cf. Plin. *Ep.* 9.17 for a complaint of *scurrae cinaedi moriones* at a grand dinner-party (*lautissimam cenam*). Cf. Plaut. *Capt.* 88–90: 'If a parasite gets fed up with being beaten (*colaphos perpeti*) and having crockery smashed on his head, he can go off to the far side of Three Arch Gate', Ter. *Eun.* 243–4 *at ego infelix neque ridiculus esse neque plagas pati | possum.*

172–3 nec dura timebis | flagra pati 'and will not hesitate to endure the harsh whip', i.e. a flogging, a slave's punishment (6.479) which it was illegal to apply to a free man, cf. Sen. *Apoc.* 15.2 *testes qui illum uiderant ab illo flagris, ferulis, colaphis uapulantem,* thus proof of servile status. *pati* is repeated from 3. *pati, his*: elided.

173 his epulis et tali dignus amico: very pointed: since Trebius' meal can hardly be described as a 'banquet' (cf.4.28) and his host hardly a 'friend', it is clear that he thoroughly deserves (*dignus*) the degradation he gets. Appropriately the last word of Book 1 represents its central theme, *amicitia,* the patron–client relationship and its corruption and perversion.

ESSAY

Satire 5 is the final poem in Book 1 and appropriately it features the final event of the Roman day, the dinner-party (*cena*). The prominence of food in Roman satire has long been acknowledged but until recently (starting with Hudson (1989)) has met with a reaction from scholars that verges on embarrassment. But now it is appreciated that satire, perhaps more than any other literary genre, deals with the body and bodily functions, of which the consumption of food and drink are primary examples, as part of its celebration of the carnivalesque (Bakhtin (1968)) and its focus upon the 'animal' or appetitive part of human beings.

Several of the etymologies of *satura* invite a connection with food (see Introduction §3) and the texts of Roman satire do not disappoint, with their treatment of food, as in Ennius' didactic *Hedyphagetica* and Varro's *Peri Edesmaton,* and their particular focus upon the *cena* (see Shero (1923)). Lucilius described *cenae* in several of his thirty books of satires (Fiske (1920) 408: in books 4, 5, 13, 20 and 21), of which Book 20 seems to have been especially important. Four of the eight poems of Horace's second book of satires concern food: in 2.2 the countryman Ofellus (whose name = 'Mr Cutlet', see Rudd (1966) 143–6) urges moderation of diet (a theme which J. will take up in Satire 11); in 2.4 the gourmand Catius repeats to Horace as if it were philosophical wisdom a lecture on gastronomy which he has heard; during the *cena* at his Sabine farm in 2.6 a neighbour tells the fable of the town mouse and the country mouse, a fable which uses the contrast between the two meals to suggest conclusions about life-style; and 2.8 narrates the 'feast of Nasidienus' (*cena Nasidieni*), a disastrous dinner-party thrown by a social climber who so fails to impress that his elegant guests finally run away. Prose (Menippean) satire too took the *cena* as a theme, as is evident from fragments of Varro (Gell. 6.16, 15.19.2) and from Petronius' 'feast of Trimalchio' (*cena Trimalchionis*), part of his huge work, the *Satyrica*, which satirises a host still more vulgar and pretentious than Horace's Nasidienus. And besides these dedicated treatments of the *cena*, the texts of Roman satire are full of passing references to food and feasts.

Feasts feature prominently in Roman satire because they offer an opportunity to portray human beings interacting: the *cena* is above all a socio–politico–economic occasion (Gowers (1993) 25–6), central to the operation of *amicitia*, which in turn is a central theme of Roman satire. In 'normal' society, it represented the reward to social inferiors for their attendance and a chance to impress social superiors with lavish expenditure; it fostered social bonding through observance of decorum (cf. Elias (1978)). But in the hands of satirists the *cena* becomes a nightmare in which folly, vulgarity and viciousness are paraded, or, much more rarely, a vehicle of fantasy in which simplicity and a return to traditional values are advocated (as in Horace *Sat.* 2.2 and J.'s Satire 11). As usual, satire tends to polarise. It is difficult, and would be rash, to attempt to reconstruct real Roman feasts from the pictures provided by satire.

A further reason for the prominence of the *cena* in Roman satire is the influence of Greek literature, in which the symposium was a serious literary form exploited by philosophical writers as a vehicle for conversation (Gowers (1993) 29). The most familiar example of this is Plato's *Symposium*, which purports to be the conversation of a number of famous people on the topic of love. Philosophical dialogues such as this exercised an important influence on Roman satire (most obviously in the case of Horace, including several of the poems of *Satires* Book 2), so it is not surprising to find the same kind of setting adapted into a more anecdotal format for satirical purposes. Significantly, J.'s fifth satire commences with sarcastic use of the terminology of ethical discourse (1–2n.) and uses the feast as a vehicle to deal with how people of unequal power behave towards one another (cf. Morford (1977) 227–9 who relates Satire 5 to Horace's *Epistles* on this theme).

With characteristic extremism, both host and guest are attacked by the speaker, who retains his indignant personality from the earlier poems in Book 1 (e.g. 8–11, 24–5, 107–13nn.). Virro, the patron, is criticised throughout the poem for serving up two menus, one consisting of fine food for himself and guests of like status, the other consisting of grotty, inferior food – or, at some stages of the meal, of no food at all (a witty stroke, as we come to expect correspondence) – for guests such as his lowly client Trebius. This is not a novel theme in Roman literature: there are similar criticisms of the unequal feast at Martial 3.60, 3.82, 4.68, 6.11 and 9.2 (also, on specific items 1.20 (mushrooms), 1.43 (boar), 3.49 (wine), 4.85 (wine and cups)); Pliny *Ep.* 2.6; and, later, Lucian, *Saturnalia* 22 where the quantity of food, the boar, the wine-cups and the wine are all contrasted, with incidental reference to the different attitudes of the slaves (see Adamietz (1972) 85–96, Morford (1977) 221–6, Gowers (1993) 211–12). But J. develops this idea, which lends itself to Martial's treatment thanks to the antithetical tendency of epigram, into a bravura piece which portrays the breakdown of society in terms of alienation.

The patron's conduct contradicts a central point in the Roman system of values that sharing is the essence of the feast, an idea reflected in the etymology of *cena* from Greek κοινωνία, 'fellowship' (reported by Plutarch *Qu. Conv.* 8.6.5 = *Mor.* 726e-f). Instead of behaving like one of the generous patrons of the past (107–13n.), the host is portrayed behaving like a petty tyrant, a miniature Domitian (cf. Satire 4), lording it over his helpless and humiliated guests (cf. 156–73n.) whose only wish is to be treated as equals (*ciuiliter*, 112n.). This is the central passage of the poem (as Morford (1977) 219 and Gowers (1993) 212) perceive), with its focus upon equality at the table (on which see D'Arms (1984) and (1990)). So it is entirely apposite that the patron is referred to rarely by name (in fact, he is not named until line 39) but instead as *ipse* (37, 56, 86, 107, 114, 142), *dominus* (49, 71, 81, 92, 137 twice, 147) and *rex* (14, 130, 137, 161), all terms which reinforce the gap between patron and client and characterise the relationship as the perversion of *amicitia* into that of master and slave. It seems no accident that the final word of the poem is *amico* (173n.). It is also highly appropriate that the poem ends in silence, the silence of the clients still waiting and hoping (*tacetis* 169). This absence of conversation (see Morford (1977) 221) represents the alienation and separateness of patron and client and thereby displaces the poem's energies onto the food. The words of the invitation, *una simus* (18), the only direct communication between patron and client, are shown to be an utter travesty.

The parallel menus – the items are dealt with methodically, one by one – constitute the major structuring device of the poem. Consequently, it is streamlined and controlled, but without being predictable, thanks to the speaker's disruptions of the menu sequence (76–9, imagining the client's sarcastic muttering; 107–13, attacking the patron; and 132–45, emphasising the supremacy of money). The menus reproduce the sequence of a Roman *cena* (see Gowers (1993) 17), but are dealt with more and more economically and elliptically as the poem accelerates to the crowning humiliation, that the humble clients never receive the main meat dish and are left still sitting there in hungry anticipation at the end of the poem (166–9). This may be conveyed graphically by setting out the parallel menus as follows:

VIRRO VIRRONIBVS : VNA SIMVS	VIRRO TREBIO : VNA SIMVS
Fine Wine	Cheap Plonk

Served in Bejewelled Goblets
  with Ice-cold Water to Mix
	Served in Cracked Crocks
	  with Grade Two Water

Served by a pretty Asian Slave-boy	Served by an Ugly Black Slave
Soft White Bread	Hard Mouldy Bread

Lobster with Asparagus in
  dressing of Choice Olive Oil
	Egg Stuffed with Prawn, with
	  Cabbage in dressing of Lamp Oil.

Specially Imported Mullet
  & Sicilian Eel/Lamprey
	Tiber-bred Sewer-fed Eel
	  OR River-Pike

Foie gras	

Fattened Fowl
Gigantic Boar
Choice African Truffles
Magnificent Mushrooms   Dubious Toadstools
Exquisite Apples   A Rotten Apple

The stark contrast between the two menus is conveyed by the imagery and associations with which the food and drink, implements and servers, are invested (discussed by Anderson (1982) 244–50, Morford (1977) esp. 233–7 and 245, Gowers (1993) 213–17). For example, Virro's meal is endowed with epic and exotic mythological associations (see 37–9, 43–5, 56–7, 100–2, 115, 151–2nn.), whereas Trebius' meal is connected with sordidness and violence (see 26–9, 46–8, 52–5, 88–91, 104–6, 125–6, 153–5nn.).

The poem is not simply an attack on the patron's shoddy and uncivilised treatment of his lowly client. The speaker's criticisms of Trebius frame the poem (1–23 and 156–73) in prominent positions which render them still more memorable. Gone is the speaker's sympathy for impoverished clients expressed in earlier satires in the Book and in its place direct, sarcastic (12–23n.) and angry criticism of a parasite who is prepared to subject himself to humiliations which effectively place him in the position of a hired buffoon (3–4, 171–2) or a slave (161–5, 172–3, cf.127). A similar effect is created by the animal imagery which occurs through the poem: he is lower than a beggar fed on dogs' scraps (8–11); he is despised by the lobster dish (80–3); and he resembles a performing monkey (153–5). Patron and client perform a mutually reinforcing dialectic of corruption into master and slave. In sum, the poem is presented as a *suasoria*, in effect: a dissuasion from the degrading life-style of the parasite. And the treatment of Trebius in Satire 5 shows graphically how in the course of Book 1 J.'s speaker has shifted a long way from his sympathy for the client into an altogether bleaker outlook which emphasises the breakdown of society (see Introduction §9).

BIBLIOGRAPHY

(1) Abbreviations

ANRW	*Aufstieg und Niedergang der römischen Welt* edd. W. Haase and H. Temporini (Berlin, 1972–)
CIL	*Corpus inscriptionum Latinarum* (Berlin, 1863–)
DS	C. Daremberg and E. Saglio *Dictionnaire des antiquités grecques et romaines* (Paris, 1877–1919)
Ferguson, *Prosopography*	J. Ferguson *A prosopography to the poems of Juvenal* (Brussels, 1987)
FGH	*Die Fragmente der griechischen Historiker* ed. F. Jacoby (Leipzig, 1940–58)
GLK	*Grammatici Latini*, ed. Keil (Leipzig, 1857–70)
Housman	*The classical papers of A.E. Housman* 3 vols. edd. J. Diggle and F.R.D. Goodyear (Cambridge, 1972)
HS	J.B. Hofmann and A. Szantyr *Lateinische Syntax und Stilistik* (Munich, 1965)
KS	R. Kühner and C. Stegman *Ausführliche Grammatik der lateinischen Sprache*, zweiter Teil (Hanover, 1971)
LIMC	*Lexicon iconographicum mythologiae classicae* edd. H.C. Ackermann and J.-R. Gisler (Zurich and Munich, 1981–)
LSJ	*Greek-English lexicon* H.G. Liddell, R. Scott, rev. H.S. Jones (Oxford, 1968)
Maltby	R. Maltby *A lexicon of ancient Latin etymologies* (Leeds, 1991)
OCD	*Oxford classical dictionary* 2nd edition, edd. N.G.L. Hammond and H.H. Scullard (Oxford, 1970)
OLD	*Oxford Latin dictionary* ed. P.G.W. Glare (Oxford, 1982)
Otto	A. Otto *Die Sprichwörter und sprichwörtlichen Redensarten der Römer* (Leipzig, 1890)
Otto, *Nachträge*	R. Häussler *Nachträge zu A. Otto, Die Sprichwörter ...* (Darmstadt, 1968)
PIR	*Prosopographia Imperii Romani* von Rohden and Dessau (1897–9), 2nd ed. by E. Groag and A. Stein (1933–)
PL	*Patrologia Latina* ed. J.-P. Migne (Paris, 1878–90)

Platner   S.B. Platner and T. Ashby *A topographical dictionary of*
and Ashby   *ancient Rome* (London, 1929)
The Princeton encyclopedia of classical sites ed. R. Stillwell (1976)
RAC   *Reallexicon für Antike und Christentum* ed. T. Klauser
               (Stuttgart, 1950–   )
RE   *Realencyclopädie der klassischen Altertumswissenschaft* edd.
               Pauly–Wissowa–Kroll–Mittelhaus–Ziegler   (Stuttgart,
               1893–   )
SHA   *Scriptores historiae augustae*
TLL   *Thesaurus linguae Latinae* (Leipzig, 1900–   )
TRF   *Tragicorum Romanorum fragmenta* ed. O. Ribbeck 2nd ed.
               (Leipzig, 1871)

(2) Editions, Commentaries, Translations

Juvenal

Clausen, W.V., *A. Persi Flacci et D. Iuni Iuuenalis Saturae* (Oxford, 1959,
    rev. 1992)
Courtney, E., *A commentary on the Satires of Juvenal* (London, 1980)
Duff, J.D., *D. Iunii Iuuenalis Saturae XIV* (Cambridge, 1898, repr. 1970)
Ferguson, J., *Juvenal: the Satires* (New York, 1979)
Friedländer, L., *D. Iunii Juvenalis Saturarum libri V* (Leipzig, 1895)
Green, P., *Juvenal: The sixteen Satires* (Harmondsworth, 1967)
Housman, A. E., *D. Iunii Iuuenalis* (New York, 2nd ed., 1931)
Knoche, U., *Juvenal: Satiren* (Munich, 1951)
Lewis, J.D., *D. Iunii Iuuenalis Satirae* (London, 1873)
Martyn, J.R.C., *D. Iuni Iuuenalis Saturae* (Amsterdam, 1987)
Mayor, J.E.B., *Thirteen Satires of Juvenal* (London, 4th ed., 1886–9)
Rudd, N., *Juvenal. The Satires* (Oxford, 1992)

Other authors

Austin, R.G., *P. Vergili Maronis Aeneidos liber quartus* (Oxford, 1955)
Coleman, K.M., *Statius Silvae IV* (Oxford, 1988)
Eden, P.T., *Seneca Apocolocyntosis* (Cambridge, 1984)
Kenney, E.J., *Lucretius De rerum natura III* (Cambridge, 1971)
Luck, G., *Ovid Tristia* (Heidelberg, 1967–77)

Marx, F., *C. Lucili carminum reliquiae* (Leipzig, 1904)

Mayer, R., *Horace Epistles Book I* (Cambridge, 1994)

McKeown, J.C., *Ovid Amores I* (Leeds, 1989)

Muecke, F., *Horace Satires II* (Warminster, 1993)

Nisbet, R.G.M. and Hubbard, M., *A commentary on Horace, Odes Book I* (Oxford, 1970)

A commentary on Horace, Odes Book II (Oxford, 1978)

Ogilvie, R.M. and Richmond, I., *Tacitus Agricola* (Oxford, 1967)

Rudd, N., *Horace Epistles Book II and Epistle to the Pisones ('Ars Poetica')* (Cambridge, 1989)

Russell, D.A. and Wilson, N.G., *Menander Rhetor* (Oxford, 1981)

Warmington, E.H., *Remains of old Latin* III (Cambridge, Mass. and London, 1979)

Other works

Adamietz, J. (1972), *Untersuchungen zu Juvenal* (*Hermes Einzelschriften* 26)

Adams, J.N. (1982), *The Latin sexual vocabulary* (Baltimore)

(1990), 'The meaning and use of *subiugale*' *R.F.I.C.* 118: 441–53

Anderson, W.S. (1965), 'Valla, Juvenal and Probus' *Traditio* 21: 383–424

(1982), *Essays on Roman satire* (Princeton)

André, J. (1961), *L'alimentation et la cuisine à Rome* (Paris)

(1966), 'Notes de lexicologie', *R.Ph.* 40: 46–58

Armstrong, D. (1986), '*Horatius eques et scriba*: Satires 1.6 and 2.7' *T.A.Ph.A.* 116: 255–88

Bakhtin, M. (1968), *Rabelais and his world* (tr. H. Iswolsky, Cambridge, Mass.)

Balsdon, J.P.V.D. (1962), *Roman women* (London)

Bennett, C.E. (1914), 'Notes on Horace', *C.Q.* 8: 145–50

Bo, D. (1965), *Lexicon Horatianum* (Hildesheim)

Bonner, S.F. (1977), *Education in ancient Rome* (London)

Boswell, J. (1980), *Christianity, social tolerance and homosexuality* (Chicago)

Bower, E.W. (1958), 'Notes on Juvenal and Statius' *C.R.* 8: 9–11

Bramble, J.C. (1974), *Persius and the programmatic satire* (Cambridge)

Braund, D. (1983), 'Treasure trove and Nero' *G. & R.* 30: 65–9

Braund, D.C. (1984), *Rome and the friendly king* (London)

Braund, S.H. (1988), *Beyond anger: a study of Juvenal's third book of satires* (Cambridge)

(ed.) (1989a), *Satire and society in ancient Rome* (Exeter), including 'City and country in Roman satire', 23–47

(1989b), 'Juvenal and the east: satire as an historical source', in *The eastern frontier of the Roman Empire* edd. D.H. French and C.S. Lightfoot (Oxford) 45–52

(1990), 'Umbricius and the frogs' *C.Q.* 40: 502–6

(1992a), *Roman verse satire* (Greece & Rome New Surveys in the Classics No. 23) (Oxford)

(1992b), 'Juvenal – misogynist or misogamist?' *J.R.S.* 82 71–86

(1993), 'Paradigms of power: Roman emperors in Roman satire' in *Humour and history* ed. K. Cameron (Oxford) 56–69

(1995), 'A woman's voice? – Laronia's role in Juvenal Satire 2' in *Women in antiquity* edd. B. Levick and R. Hawley (London) 207–19

Braund, S.H. and Cloud, J.D. (1981), 'Juvenal: a diptych' *L.C.M.* 6: 195–208

(1983), 'Juvenal's traducement again (2.153–163)' *L.C.M.* 8: 50–1

Brink, C.O. (1963), *Horace on poetry: prolegomena to the literary epistles* (Cambridge)

Bücheler, F. (1874), 'Iuvenalianum' *Rh.M.* 29: 636–8

(1884), 'Coniectanea' *Rh.M.* 39: 274–92

Cairns, F. (1972), *Generic composition in Greek and Roman poetry* (Edinburgh)

Campbell, A.Y. (1945), 'Pike and eel: Juvenal 5, 103–6' *C.Q.* 39: 46–8

Champlin, E. (1991), *Final judgments: duty and emotion in Roman wills, 200 BC–AD 250* (Berkeley, Los Angeles and Oxford)

Cloud, J.D. (1989a), 'Satirists and the law', in Braund (1989a) 49–67

(1989b) 'The client–patron relationship: emblem and reality in Juvenal's first book' in *Patronage in ancient society* ed. A. Wallace-Hadrill (London) 205–18

Cloud, J.D. and Braund, S.H. (1982), 'Juvenal's libellus – a farrago?' *G. & R.* 2: 77–85

Coffey, M. (1979), 'Turnus and Juvenal' *B.I.C.S.* 26: 88–94

(1989), *Roman satire* 2nd ed. (Bristol)

Corbett, P. (1986), *The scurra* (Edinburgh)

Courtney, E. (1967), 'The transmission of Juvenal's text' *B.I.C.S.* 14: 38–50

Crook, J. (1955), *Consilium Principis* (Cambridge)

Crook, J.A. (1967), *Law and life of Rome* (London)

Cuccioli, R. (1990), 'The "banquet" in Juvenal Satire 5' in *Papers of the Leeds International Latin Seminar Sixth Vol.* edd. F. Cairns and M. Heath (Melksham) 139–43

D'Arms, J.H. (1984), 'Control, companionship, and *clientela*: some social functions of the Roman communal meal', *Echos du Monde Classique* 28: 327–48

(1990), 'The Roman *convivium* and the idea of equality', in *Sympotica* ed. O. Murray (Oxford) 308–20

Davison, J. (1993), 'Fish, sex and revolution' *C.Q.* 87: 53–66

De Decker, J. (1913), *Juvenalis declamans: étude sur la rhétorique déclamatoire dans les satires de Juvenal* (Ghent)

Deroux, C. (1983), 'Domitian, the kingfish and the prodigies' in *Studies in Latin literature and Roman history* ed. C. Deroux (Collection Latomus) (Brussels) 283–98

Dessen, C.S. (1968), *'Iunctura callidus acri': a study of Persius' Satires* (Urbana, Chicago and London)

Dover, K.J. (1978), *Greek homosexuality* (London)

Duckworth, G.E. (1967), 'Five centuries of Latin hexameter poetry: silver age and late empire' *T.A.Ph.A.* 98: 77–150

DuQuesnay, I.M.Le M. (1984), 'Horace and Maecenas: The propaganda value of *Sermones* I', in *Poetry and politics in the age of Augustus* edd. T.Woodman & D.West (Cambridge) 19–58

Edwards, C. (1993), *The politics of immorality in ancient Rome* (Cambridge)

(forthcoming), 'Unspeakable professions: public performance and prostitution', in *Roman sexualities* edd. M. Skinner and J. Hallett

Ehrenberg, V. and Jones, A.H.M. (1976), *Documents illustrating the reigns of Augustus and Tiberius* (2nd ed., Oxford)

Elias, N. (1978), *The civilising process: I The history of manners* tr. E. Jephcott (Oxford)

Elliott, R.C. (1960), *The power of satire: magic, ritual, art* (Princeton)

Fiske, G.C. (1920), *Lucilius and Horace* (Madison; repr. Westport 1971)

Flintoff, T.E.S. (1990), 'Juvenal's fourth Satire' in *Papers of the Leeds*

International Latin Seminar Sixth Vol. edd. F. Cairns and M. Heath (Melksham) 121–37

Forbes, R.J. (1956), *Studies in ancient technology* IV (Leiden)

Fredericks, S.C. (1973), 'The function of the prologue (1–20) in the organisation of Juvenal's third Satire' *Phoenix* 27: 62–7

Fredericksmeyer, H.C. (1990), 'An observation on the programmatic satires of Juvenal, Horace and Persius' *Latomus* 49 (1990) 792–800

Fruelund Jensen B. (1986), 'Martyred and beleaguered virtue: Juvenals' portrait of Umbricius' *C. et M.* 37: 185–97

Gowers, E. (1993), *The loaded table. Representations of food in Roman literature* (Oxford)

Grant, M. (1967), *Gladiators* (Harmondsworth)

Gratwick, A.S. (1982), 'The satires of Ennius and Lucilius', in *The Cambridge history of classical literature II: Latin literature* edd. E.J. Kenney & W.V. Clausen (Cambridge) 156–71

Griffith, J.G. (1969), 'Juvenal, Statius, and the Flavian establishment' *G & R* 16: 134–50

(1970), 'The ending of Juvenal's first Satire and Lucilius, Book XXX' *Hermes* 98: 56–72

(1973), 'Caper exstat in ansa' *Greece & Rome* 20: 79–80

Hall, J. (1983), 'A black note in Juvenal: Satire V 52–55' *Proceedings of the African Classical Association* 17: 108–13

Hallett, J.P. (1989), 'Female homoeroticism and the denial of Roman reality in Latin literature' *Yale Journal of Criticism* 3: 209–27

Handford, S.A. (1947), *The Latin subjunctive*

Heitland, W.E. (1921), *Agricola* (Cambridge)

Helmbold, W.C. (1951), 'The structure of Juvenal I' *U.C.P.C.P.* 14: 47–60

Helmbold, W.C. and O'Neil, E.N. (1956), 'The structure of Juvenal IV' *A.J.Ph.* 77: 68–73

Henderson, J.G.W. (1989), '... when satire writes "woman"', in Braund (1989a) 89–125

Highet, G. (1954), *Juvenal the satirist* (London)

Hodgart, M. (1969), *Satire* (Verona)

Hopkins, K. (1983), *Death and renewal* (Cambridge)

Hudson, N. (1989), 'Food in Roman satire', in Braund (1989a) 69–87

Jones, F.M.A. (1990), 'The persona and dramatis personae in Juvenal Satire Four' *Eranos* 88: 47–59

Kenney, E.J. (1962), 'The first satire of Juvenal' *P.C.Ph.S.* 8:29–40

(1963), 'Juvenal: satirist or rhetorician?' *Latomus* 22:704–20

(1984), *The ploughman's lunch; Moretum* (Bristol)

Kernan, A. (1959), *The cankered muse: satire of the English Renaissance* (New Haven)

Kilpatrick, R.S. (1973), 'Juvenal's "patchwork" Satires: 4 and 7' *T.C.S.* 23: 229–41

(1986), *The poetry of friendship: Horace Epistles 1* (Edmonton)

Knoche, U. (1975), *Roman satire* tr. E.S. Ramage (Bloomington and London)

Konstan, D. (1993), 'Sexuality and power in Juvenal's second Satire' *L.C.M.* 18: 12–14

Krenkel, W.A. (1978), 'Männliche Prostitution in der Antike' *Das Altertum* 24: 49–55

LaFleur, R.A. (1974a), 'Catullus and Catulla in Juvenal' *Revue de Philologie* 100 71–4

(1974b), 'Artorius and Catulus in Juvenal 3' *Riv. Stud. Class.* 22 5–9

(1976), 'Umbricius and Juvenal Three' *Ziva Antika* 26: 383–431

(1979), '*Amicitia* and the unity of Juvenal's first book' *I.C.S.* 4: 158–77

Lattimore, R. (1962), *Themes in Greek and Latin epitaphs* (Urbana)

Levick, B. (1983), 'The *Senatus Consultum* from Larinum' *J.R.S.* 73: 97–115

Liebeschütz, J.H.W.G. (1979), *Continuity and change in Roman religion* (Oxford)

Lilja, S. (1983), *Homosexuality in Republican and Augustan Rome* (Helsinki)

Long, A.A. and Sedley, D.N. (1987), *The Hellenistic philosophers*, 2 vols. (Cambridge)

Mabey, R. (1972), *Food for free* (Glasgow)

MacMullen, R. (1967), *Enemies of the Roman order* (Cambridge, Mass.)

McGann, M.J. (1969), *Studies in Horace's first book of Epistles* (Brussels)

Martyn, J.R.C. (1970), 'A new approach to Juvenal's first Satire' *Antichthon* 4: 53–61

Millar, F. (1977), *The Emperor in the Roman world (31 BC–AD 337)* (London)

Mommsen, Th. (1882), 'Das Augustische Festverzeichniss von Cumae' *Hermes* 17: 631–3

Morford, M. (1977), 'Juvenal's fifth satire' *A.J.Ph.* 98: 219–45

Motto, A.L. and Clarke, J.R. (1965), 'Per iter tenebricosum. The mythos of Juvenal 3' *T.A.Ph.A.* 96: 267–76

Nadeau, Y. (1983), 'Juvenal traduced (Juvenal 2.149–159)' *L.C.M.* 8: 14–16

Nisbet, R.G.M. (1962), review of Clausen's 1959 Oxford Classical Text *J.R.S.* 52: 227–38 = (ed. S.J. Harrison) *Collected papers on Latin literature* (Oxford, 1995) 6–28

(1988), 'Notes on the text and interpretation of Juvenal' *B.I.C.S.* 51: 86–110 = *Collected papers* 227–71

Nutting, H.C. (1924), 'The indefinite first singular' *A.J.Ph.* 45: 377–9

Oost, S.I. (1958), 'The career of M. Antonius Pallas' *A.J.Ph.* 79: 113–39

Page, D. (1955), *Sappho and Alcaeus* (Oxford)

Parker, R. (1983), 'A note on Juvenal, Satire 1.17–18' *L.C.M.* 8: 123

Pearce, T.E.V. (1992), 'Juvenal 3.10–20' *Mnemosyne* 45: 380–3

Price, S.R.F. (1984), *Rituals and power. The Roman imperial cult in Asia Minor* (Cambridge)

Ramage, E.S. (1973), *Urbanitas: ancient sophistication and refinement* (Oklahoma)

(1989), 'Juvenal and the establishment: denigration of predecessor in the "Satires"' *ANRW* II 33.1: 640–707

Ramage, E.S. (1974), Sigsbee D.L. and Fredericks, S.C.. *Roman satirists and their satire* (New Jersey)

Raschke, W.J. (1987), '*Arma pro amico* – Lucilian satire at the crisis of the Roman Republic' *Hermes* 115: 299–318

Rawson, E. (1985), *Intellectual life in the late Roman Republic* (London)

Reckford, K.J. (1962), 'Studies in Persius' *Hermes* 90: 476–504

Relihan, J.C. (1993), *Ancient Menippean satire* (Baltimore and London)

Richlin, A. (1983), *The garden of Priapus* (New Haven and London; rev. ed. Oxford 1992)

(1984), 'Invective against women in Roman satire' *Arethusa* 17: 67–80

(1993), 'Not before homosexuality: the materiality of the *cinaedus* and the Roman law against love between men' *Journal of the History of Sexuality* 3: 523–73

Roby, H.J. (1882), *A grammar of the Latin language* (London)

Rooy, C.A. van (1965) *Studies in classical satire and related literary theory* (Leiden)

Rudd, N. (1966), *The Satires of Horace* (Cambridge)

(1976), *Lines of enquiry: studies in Latin poetry* (Cambridge)

Saller, R.P. (1982), *Personal patronage under the Early Empire* (Cambridge)

Scarborough, J. (1969), *Roman medicine* (London)

Schäublin, C. (1991), 'Juvenal 3,101f.' *Hermes* 119: 491–4

Scott, I.G. (1927), *The grand style in the Satires of Juvenal* (Northampton, Mass.)

Shero, L.R. (1923), 'The *cena* in Roman satire' *C.Ph.* 18: 126–43

Sherwin-White, A.N. (1967), *Racial prejudice in Imperial Rome* (London)

Smallwood, E.M. (1976), *The Jews under Roman rule* (Leiden)

Smith, W.S. (1989), 'Heroic models for the sordid present' *ANRW* II 33.1: 811–23

Snowden, F.M. (1970), *Blacks in antiquity* (Cambridge, Mass.)

Stegemann, W. (1913), *De Iuvenalis dispositione* (Weidae Thuringorum)

Sweet, D. (1979), 'Juvenal's *Satire* 4: poetic uses of indirection' *C.S.C.A.* 12: 283–303

Syme, R. (1939), *Roman revolution* (Oxford)

(1958), *Tacitus* (Oxford)

(1970), *Ten studies in Tacitus* (Oxford)

(1979), *Roman papers* vol. I ed. E. Badian (Oxford)

(1984), *Roman papers* vol. III ed. A.R. Birley (Oxford)

(1991), *Roman papers* vol. VII ed. A.R. Birley (Oxford)

Szemler, G.J. (1972), *The priests of the Roman Republic* (Brussels)

Tavris, C. (1982), *Anger, the misunderstood emotion* (New York)

Thompson, D'A.W. (1947), *A glossary of Greek fishes* (London)

Townend, G.B. (1973), 'The literary substrata to Juvenal's Satires' *J.R.S.* 63: 148–60

Toynbee, J.M.C. (1950), 'Some notes on artists in the Roman world' *Latomus* 9: 175–82

(1973), *Animals in Roman life and art* (London)

Tränkle, H. (1978), 'Zu zwei umstrittenen Stellen in der dritten Satire des Juvenals' *Z.P.E.* 28: 167–72

Vassileiou, A. (1984), 'Crispinus et les conseillers du prince (Juvénal, *Satires*, IV)' *Latomus* 43: 27–68

Wallace-Hadrill, A. (1982), 'Civilis Princeps: Between citizen and king' *J.R.S.* 72: 32–48

Walters, J. (forthcoming 1996), 'Soldiers and whores in a Pseudo-Quintilian declamation', in *Gender and ethnicity in the Roman world* edd. T.J. Cornell and K. Lomas. Accordia Research Centre Specialist Studies on Italy No. 6

White, K.D. (1970), *Roman farming* (London)

White, P. (1978), '*Amicitia* and the profession of poetry in early Imperial Rome' *J.R.S.* 68: 74–92

Wiedemann, T. (1992), *Emperors and gladiators* (London)

Wild, J.P. (1964), 'The textile term scutulatus' *C.Q.* 14: 263–6

Wilkins, J. and Hill, S. (1994), *Archestratus: the life of luxury* (Totnes)

Wilkinson, L.P. (1969), *The Georgics of Virgil* (Cambridge)

Wilson, H.L. (1900), 'The use of the simple for the compound verb in Juvenal', *T.A.Ph.A.* 31: 202–22

Winkler, M.M. (1983), *The persona in three Satires of Juvenal* (Hildesheim)

Wirszubski, Ch. (1950), *Libertas as a political idea at Rome during the late Republic and early Principate* (Cambridge)

Wiseman, T.P. (1970), 'The definition of "Eques Romanus"' *Historia* 19: 67–83

　(1971), *New men in the Roman senate 139 BC–AD14* (Oxford)

　(1974), *Cinna the poet* (Leicester)

　(1987), *Roman studies* (Trowbridge)

Witke, C. (1970), *Latin satire: the structure of persuasion* (Leiden)

Woodcock, E.C. (1959), *A new Latin syntax* (London)

Woodman, A.J. (1983), 'Juvenal 1 and Horace' *G. & R.* 30: 81–4

Yavetz, Z. (1958), 'The living conditions of the urban plebs' *Latomus* 17: 500–17

Zetzel, J.E.G. (1980), 'Horace's *Liber Sermonum*: The structure of ambiguity' *Arethusa* 13: 59–77

INDEX

For lists of stylistic and metrical features see the Introduction (pp. 24–30) and for an index of the proper names which appear in the text see the index to the *OCT*.

Lightning Source UK Ltd.
Milton Keynes UK
21 September 2009

143994UK00001B/1/A